VAUGHAN PUBLIC LIBRARIES
747
.78
Kro
2014
33288900357140
May. 02, 2014
WO
Kitchen and bath design presentation : d

D1072617

KITCHEN & BATH DESIGN PRESENTATION

KITCHEN AND BATH DESIGN PRESENTATION

Drawing, Plans, Digital Rendering

Second Edition

MARGARET KROHN, CKD, ASID, NCIDQ

DAVID NEWTON, CMKBD

Cover images: Design by Bryan Reiss, CMKBD
Co-designers: Susanna Caongor and Diane Murphy
Photo by John D Smoak III
Floor plan rendering provided by 20-20 Technologies
Cover design: Anne-Michele Abbot

This book is printed on acid-free paper. ♾

National Kitchen & Bath Association
687 Willow Grove Street
Hackettstown, NJ 07840
Phone: 800-THE-NKBA (800-843-6522)
Fax: 908-852-1695
Website: NKBA.org

Published by John Wiley & Sons, Inc., Hoboken, New Jersey.

Published simultaneously in Canada.

Library of Congress Cataloging-in-Publication Data

Krohn, Margaret.
Kitchen and bath design presentation : drawing, plans, digital rendering / Margaret Krohn, CKD, ASID, NCIDQ. – Second Edition.
pages cm
Includes index.
ISBN 978-1-118-56874-3 (cloth); 978-1-118-80646-3 (ebk.); 978-1-118-82237-1 (ebk.)
1. Kitchens–Design and construction. 2. Bathrooms–Design and construction. I. Title.
TH4816.3.K58K76 2014
747.7'8–dc23

2013026543

Printed in the United States of America

10 9 8 7 6 5 4 3 2 1

Sponsors

The National Kitchen & Bath Association recognizes, with gratitude, the following companies whose generous contributions supported the development of this second edition of *Kitchen & Bath Design Presentation* (formerly *Kitchen & Bath Drawing*).

GOLD SPONSORS

CHIEF ARCHITECT

DELTA FAUCET COMPANY

About the National Kitchen & Bath Association

The National Kitchen & Bath Association (NKBA) is the only nonprofit trade association dedicated exclusively to the kitchen and bath industry and is the leading source of information and education for professionals in the field. Fifty years after its inception, the NKBA has a membership of more than 55,000 and is the proud owner of the Kitchen & Bath Industry Show (KBIS).

The NKBA's mission is to enhance member success and excellence, promote professionalism and ethical business practices, and provide leadership and direction for the kitchen and bath industry worldwide.

The NKBA has pioneered innovative industry research, developed effective business management tools, and set groundbreaking design standards for safe, functional, and comfortable kitchens and baths.

Recognized as the kitchen and bath industry's leader in learning and professional development, the NKBA offers professionals of all levels of experience essential reference materials, conferences, virtual learning opportunities, marketing assistance, design competitions, consumer referrals, internships, and opportunities to serve in leadership positions.

The NKBA's internationally recognized certification program provides professionals the opportunity to demonstrate knowledge and excellence as Associate Kitchen & Bath Designer (AKBD), Certified Kitchen Designer (CKD), Certified Bath Designer (CBD), Certified Master Kitchen & Bath Designer (CMKBD), and Certified Kitchen & Bath Professional (CKBP).

For students entering the industry, the NKBA offers Accredited and Supported Programs, which provide NKBA-approved curriculum at more than 60 learning institutions throughout the United States and Canada.

For consumers, the NKBA showcases award-winning designs and provides information on remodeling, green design, safety, and more at NKBA.org. The NKBA Pro Search tool helps consumers locate kitchen and bath professionals in their area.

The NKBA offers membership in 11 different industry segments: dealers, designers, manufacturers and suppliers, multi branch retailers and home centers, decorative plumbing and hardware, manufacturer's representatives, builders and remodelers, installers, fabricators, cabinet shops, and distributors. For more information, visit NKBA.org.

Table of Contents

Preface

Successful kitchen and bath design projects involve the work of the designer along with other tradespeople and allied professionals. The NKBA project documents must be accurately completed to guide the installation and completion of all work to be done. The drawings will also help your client to visualize their newly proposed design space and to understand the design and function of the given space.

In this book you will learn about the standards for kitchen and bath drawings along with the NKBA forms that will assist you with your designs and project completion. There are standards in the design industry to ensure a clear understanding of the components found on each type of drawing. These drawings will be used by the contractors, plumbers, electricians, and others for the successful completion of your design project. Suppliers of products may also rely on your drawings for submitting bids and ordering products.

The successful kitchen and bath designer needs to produce professionally drafted drawings in accordance with the NKBA Graphics and Presentation Standards. These standards, found throughout this book, will be a reference for the designer for the completion of accurately drawn plans. Each drawing has a purpose along with its own specific information. Accuracy of the information and details on the drawings is imperative to ensure that installed items will fit properly in the space and are placed correctly in their designated location. Meeting a client's wants and needs while creating a functional, well-designed space for them is what kitchen and bath design is all about.

I would like to thank Johanna Baars, publication specialist at the NKBA for all of her work with the completion of this book. I would also like to thank Adrean Stephenson, AKBD, of Chief Architect Inc. for her assistance with the kitchen and bath drawings.

Acknowledgments

The NKBA gratefully acknowledges the peer reviewers of this book:

David Alderman, CMKBD
Corey Klassen, CKD
Judith Neary, CMKBD
David Newton, CMKBD
Hollie Ruocco, CMKBD
Mark White, CKD, CBD

NKBA Drawings and Documents

Kitchen and bath drawings are referred to as a *set* of drawings or plans. These drawings give a visual representation of how the space will look when completed as well as where items are to be installed. Each drawing has a purpose and presents information necessary for individuals involved with the project, including the installer, contractor, electrician, plumber, and others involved. Each page in the set of drawings is numbered and cross-referenced to the relevant drawing. There is an industry standard order of drawing placement within the set of plans.

An overview of each page found in a set of NKBA drawings and documents is described in this chapter. You will learn how to create the various drawings step-by-step as you read through this book. To help you focus on key components of this chapter, learning objectives are listed next.

Learning Objective 1: Identify drawings in a set of NKBA plans.

Learning Objective 2: Understand cut height and its relationship to the floor plan.

Learning Objective 3: Understand components found on the different types of drawings.

THE SET OF NKBA DRAWINGS

Each sheet in a set of drawings is identified with a title block placed at the bottom or right side of the page. Drawings are bound on the left side. The title block contains important information that identifies the type of drawing and project specifics (see Figure 1.1).

Together the drawings and documents communicate the entire scope of the project as well as all the pertinent details. We must have client approval on all drawings for the project to ensure there are no questions regarding the work that will be completed. It is important that the entire set of drawings be reviewed by everyone involved with the project. The typical set of NKBA project drawings consists of a title page, floor plan, construction plan, mechanical plan, and interior elevations. Detail drawings and cross-sectional drawings may be needed to show more specific details. A perspective drawing is often included to show a three-dimensional view of the space. Additional drawings may include a countertop plan, soffit

FIGURE 1.1 The title block on each sheet cross references the other drawings in the set of drawings.

plan, or reflected ceiling plan. Other documents also typically included are a schedule, specifications, and a design statement (see Figure 1.2).

Title Page

The title page is the cover page for a set of drawings. Information typically included on the title page is the client or building name, location, designer's name and design firm's name, a key to the symbols for materials, and an index of the drawings. It may also include an illustration (see Figure 1.3).

Floor Plan

The floor plan is the central reference point for all the other drawings in the set of documents. A floor plan is an overhead cutaway view of the room. It generally depicts the entire room and shows all major structural elements, such as walls, door swings, door openings, partitions, windows, and archways. It also shows cabinet, appliance, and fixture placement, dimensions, nomenclature, and other necessary notes. There are industry standards used for drafting a floor plan, so that other individuals involved in the project will be able to interpret the information on the drawings (see Figure 1.4).

The typical scale used for NKBA drawings is ½″ = 1′–0″ (1:20 metric). This scale allows the drafter to provide the required level of detail. The dimensions written on the plans are exact and are always used as the actual measurement when reading a plan. Never use a scale to measure dimensions on a floor plan. The plan could be distorted from duplication or a line could be off. Always use the dimensions written on the floor plan. Sometimes the drawings may not be perfectly to scale, in which case there may be a notation "NTS" ("not to scale") in the title block.

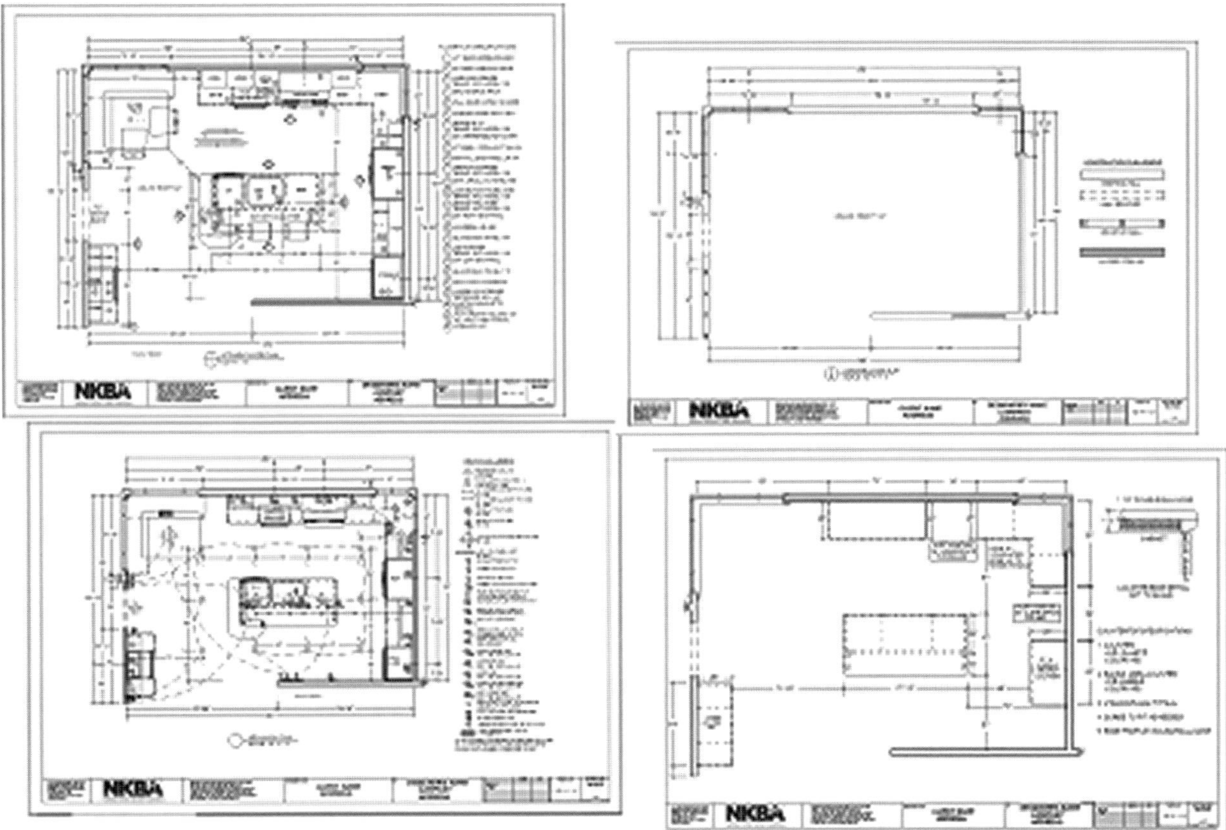

FIGURE 1.2 Drawings found in a typical set of NKBA drawings.

There are line types and symbols used on a floor plan and other drawings that are standard in the industry. Specifications are also placed on the floor plan to provide more specific information. These are explained in detail in chapter 4 (see Figure 1.5).

Construction Plan

A construction plan is another type of drawing found in the set of NKBA drawings. If walls or openings need to be altered from their original locations, a construction plan is required.

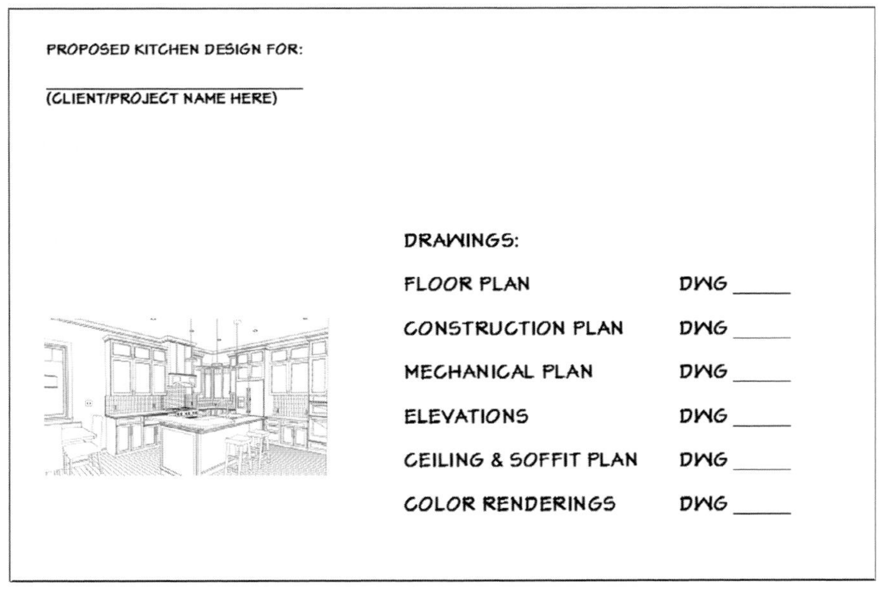

PROPOSED KITCHEN DESIGN FOR:

(CLIENT/PROJECT NAME HERE)

DRAWINGS:

FLOOR PLAN DWG _____

CONSTRUCTION PLAN DWG _____

MECHANICAL PLAN DWG _____

ELEVATIONS DWG _____

CEILING & SOFFIT PLAN DWG _____

COLOR RENDERINGS DWG _____

FIGURE 1.3 The title page is the cover page for the set of NKBA drawings. This page typically includes the client's name and an index of drawings.

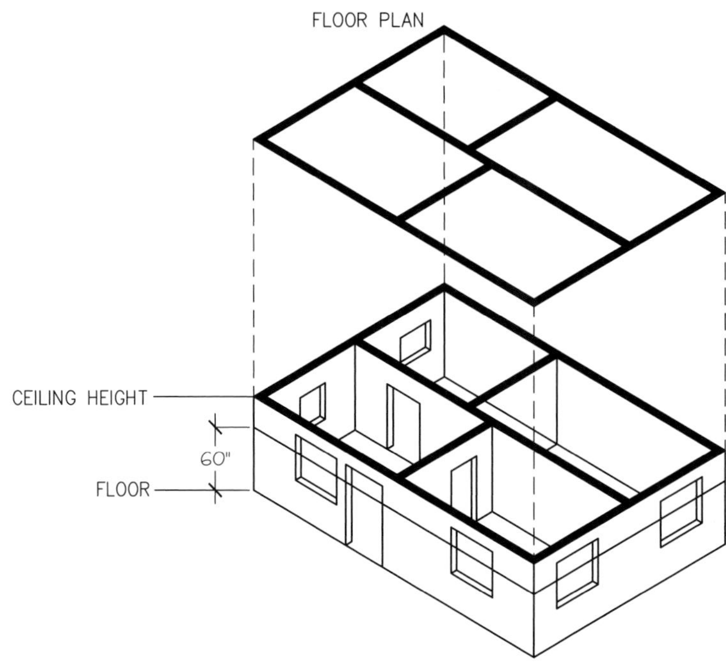

FIGURE 1.4 Cutting plane height (cut height) is at ceiling for NKBA drawings so all details may be captured in the design of the space.

This plan shows both the existing floor plan and the changes to be made to achieve the design. Changes include items such as removing and/or adding windows, doors, walls, plus more. Specific wall symbols are used to denote changes made to original floor plan of the space. More information can be found in chapter 6.

The construction plan includes only the walls, changes to the walls, dimensions, and a construction legend indicating what the symbols represent (see Figure 1.6).

FIGURE 1.5 NKBA floor plan with floor plan specifications on the right side.

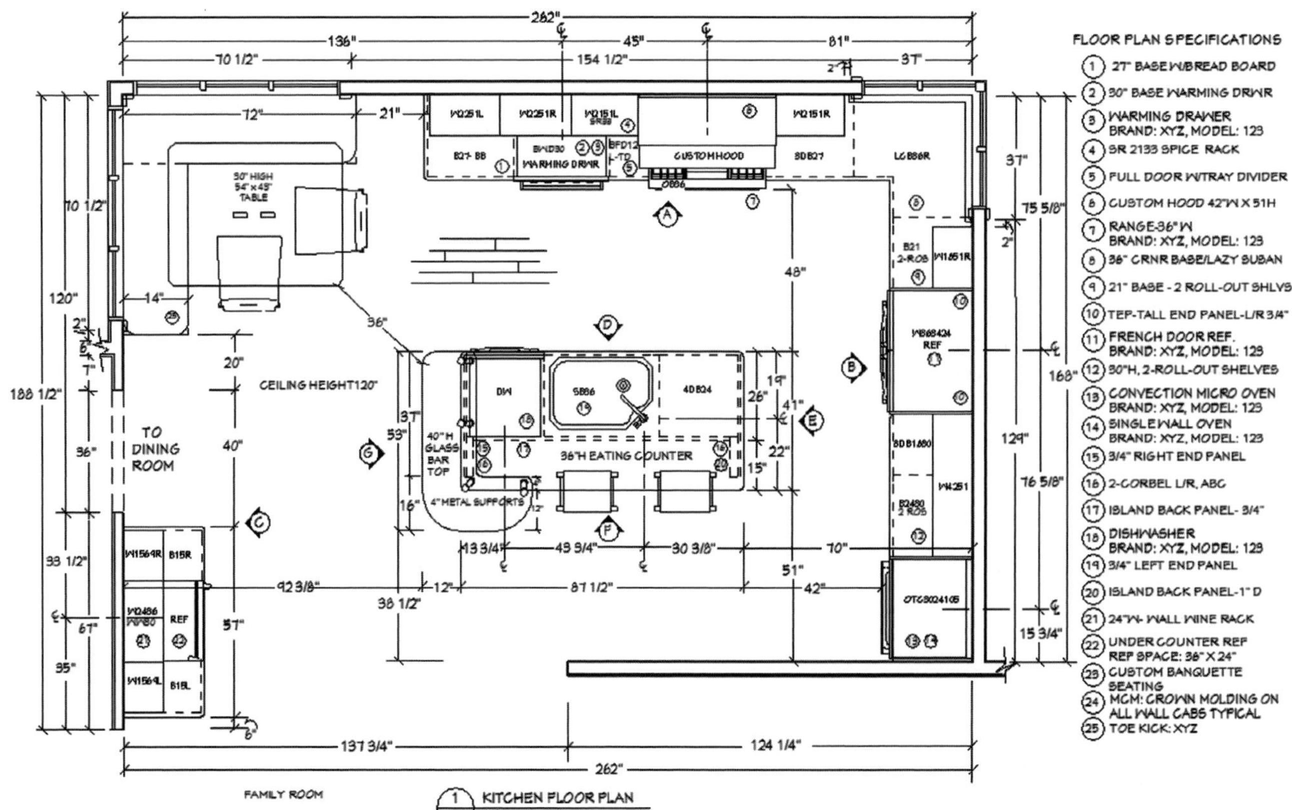

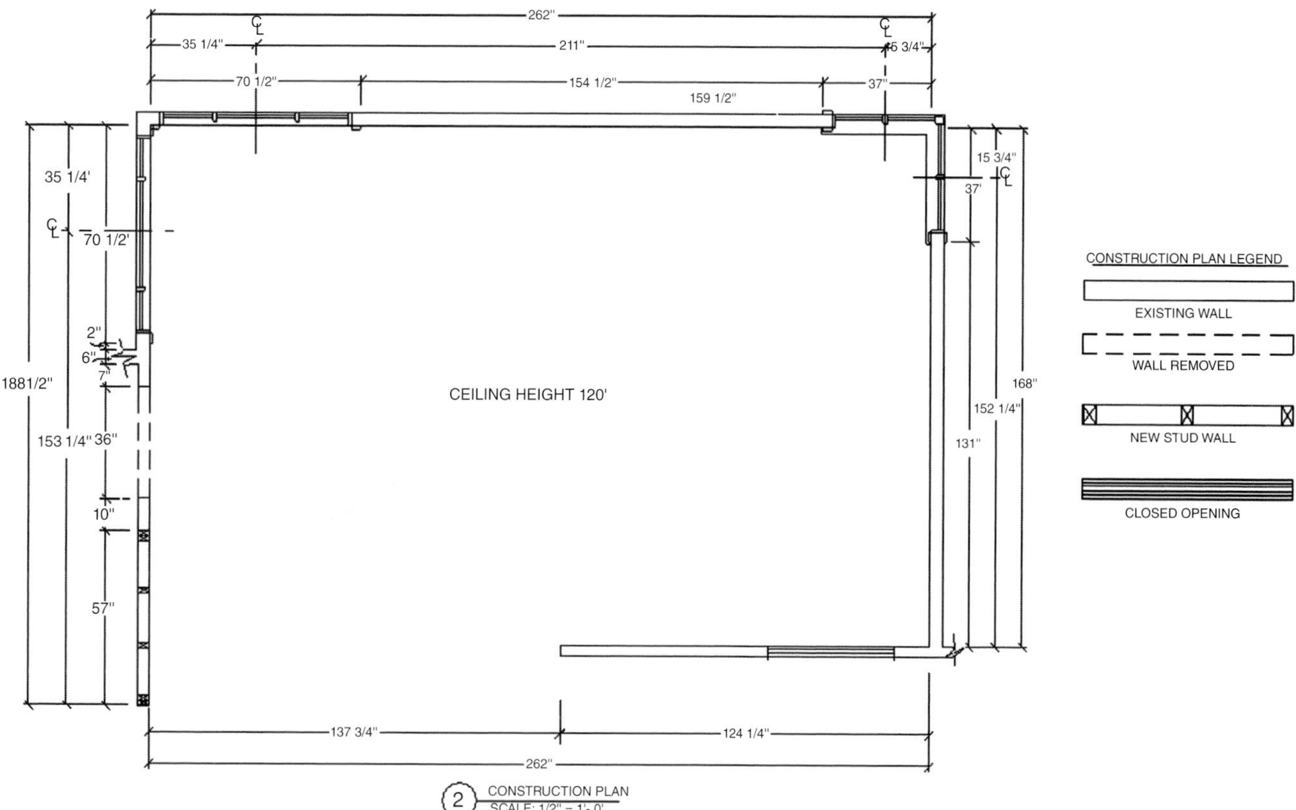

FIGURE 1.6 Construction plan indicating new walls and walls to be removed. Note construction legend on right side of drawing.

Mechanical Plan

Another drawing in the set of NKBA drawings is the mechanical plan. The mechanical plan indicates placement of the electrical system, lighting, plumbing, heating, ventilation, and air conditioning (HVAC). As with the other plans, standard symbols are used on the mechanical plan to denote each item found on the plan. (More information can be found in chapter 3.) The mechanical plan must have a legend that illustrates the symbols used on the plan along with descriptions, and it must cross reference all symbols on the floor plan. The mechanical plan contains a great deal of information. The cabinet nomenclature is omitted from the plan so that all information can be more easily read (see Figure 1.7).

It is important to understand mechanical plans because, as you create a design, you may need to determine whether there is any flexibility in the plumbing supply line, drain, or vent locations, for example. Most likely you will not illustrate the entire heating and air conditioning system, but you do need to identify where the vents are and should be aware of where the ducting is within the structure and how it will affect your design.

Interpretive Drawings

An interpretive drawing helps viewers visualize what the finished project will look like. Interpretive drawings are used as an explanatory means of understanding the floor plans. The most common interpretive drawings are interior elevations and perspectives.

Interior Elevation

The interior elevation (elevation) is a two-dimensional drawing of the interior wall as you are facing it. All walls with cabinets, the sides of an island, and any built-in items and architectural features need an elevation to show how they will look when installed. This drawing is to scale and includes the heights and widths of all items. Since this drawing is

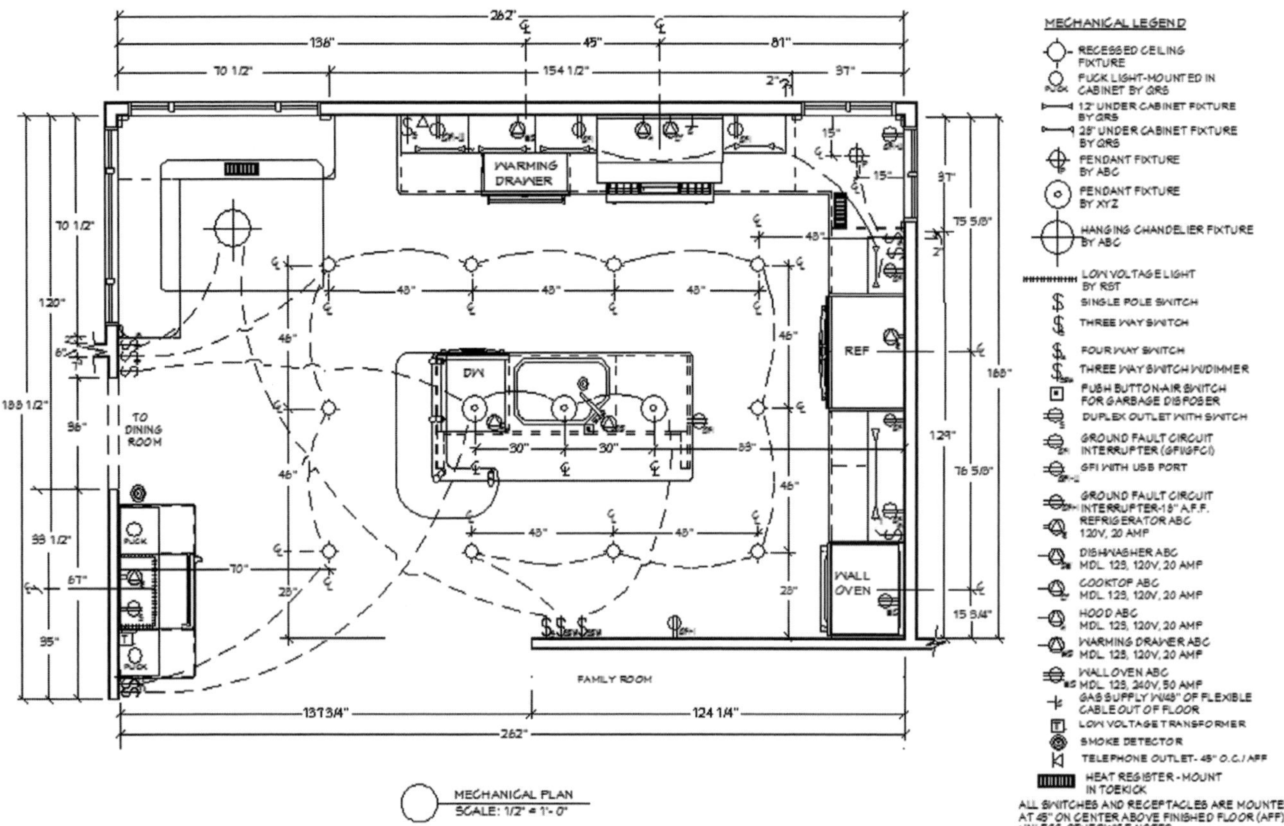

FIGURE 1.7 Mechanical plan showing plumbing, lighting, electrical, heating, and ventilation information. Note the mechanical legend on right side of the drawing.

two-dimensional, it is a flat surface and does not show the depths of items. The interior elevations are cross-referenced with the floor plan (see Figure 1.8.).

Perspective Drawings

The perspective drawing is a three-dimensional view that shows how the given space will look. The realistic appearance of a perspective makes it the ideal type of interpretive drawing because it most closely resembles what the human eye sees. Perspective drawings are not drawn to a *true* scale but to *perspective* scale. This means that items in the drawing appear larger as they are closer to the viewer. Since the perspective drawing is three-dimensional, you can see the depth of items so they look more realistic and in better proportion without distortion (see Figure 1.9).

Section Drawings and Detail Drawings

A section drawing (also referred to as a cross section) represents a vertical cut through the object to show the interior. A cross section can show the interior construction of an object, the relationships of floors in a building, or more detailed construction of items such as cabinetry, moldings, soffits, or backsplashes. To illustrate in more detail how these items are put together, an additional detail drawing may be necessary. The detail drawings show the relationship of parts and components for the specific object you are working with and are drawn at a larger scale. A typical section drawing is used to show how moldings may be stacked on a cabinet for a project (see Figure 1.10).

Additional drawings may need to be included, depending on the scope of work and how detailed and complex the counter and soffit may be. Designers should ensure that all aspects of their designs are clear so there will be no questions regarding the provided drawings.

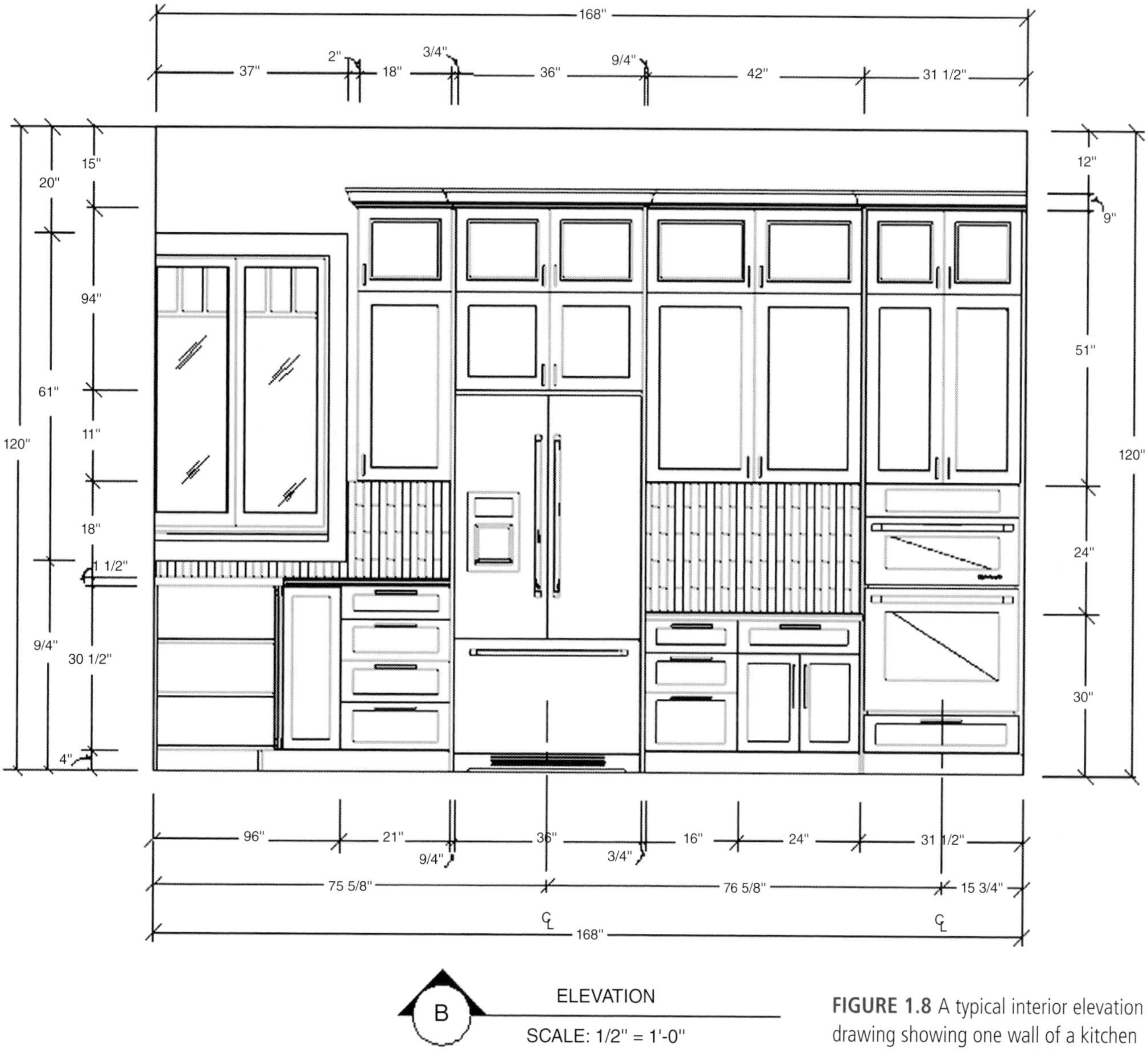

FIGURE 1.8 A typical interior elevation drawing showing one wall of a kitchen with the dimensions on all four sides. It is to scale in height and width but does not convey any depth.

FIGURE 1.9 A perspective drawing provides a three-dimensional view of the space, showing depth. This drawing closely resembles how the human eye sees a space.

Courtesy of Adrean Stephenson, AKBD, Chief Architect

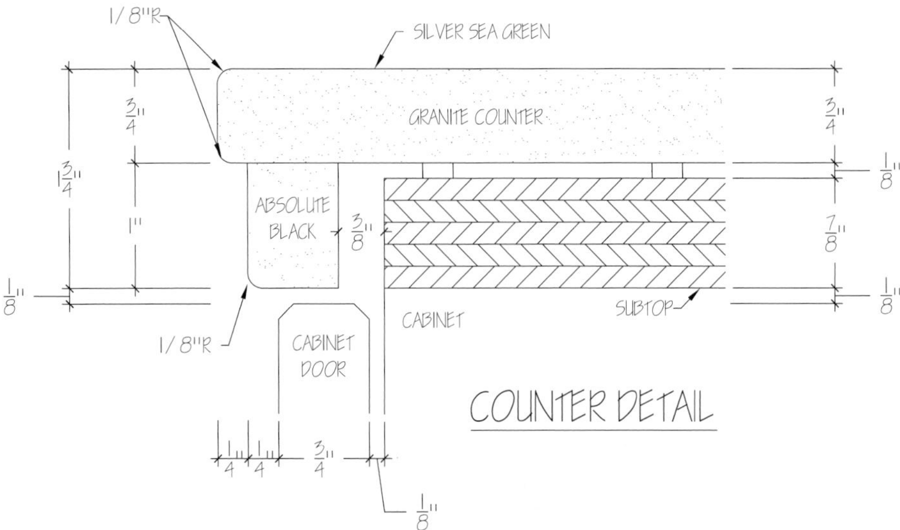

FIGURE 1.10 A section drawing showing a cutaway view of a countertop and how it relates to the cabinet. A detail drawing is an enlarged view of that section.
Courtesy of Leslie Cohen, CKD

Optional Plans

Countertop Plan

A separate countertop plan is helpful to illustrate the installation or fabrication to the allied tradesperson, particularly in complex projects, such as those that combine various counter materials or built-up edge treatments. A countertop plan shows only the walls of the space, the outline of the cabinets, fixtures and equipment, applicable notes, details, and dimensions. A detailed profile of the counter edge treatment is often provided at a larger scale to clearly illustrate the counter design and its overhang relative to the face of the cabinet or to indicate inset doors.

Soffit (Bulkhead) Plan

A drawing showing the space above the wall cabinets, called a soffit plan or bulkhead plan, is required when the soffit is a different depth than the wall or tall cabinet below it. It is also recommended when the soffit is to be installed prior to the wall or tall cabinets.

If the soffit is a complex design, cabinets may not need to be shown. An elevation of the soffit must be included on the soffit plan to further detail complex designs.

NKBA FORMS

In addition to the drawings for a design project, documentation must be provided for necessary project information. The NKBA has standardized forms that may be used for projects.

Schedule and Specifications

A *schedule* is a table that lists like items specified for the design project and may consist of a group of pages within the plans. The schedule lists important product specifics for the items specified for the home, such as cabinets, appliances, and so on. A reference number circled on the plan corresponds to a number on the schedule. A schedule can be considered a short form of specifications and is a quick way to find information at the job site.

Written documents accompanying the plans are called *specifications*, or *specs*. These are descriptions, in words, of the materials and products to be used and the quality expected. For example, appliances and plumbing fixtures are specified by brand and model number. Similarly, the grade of wood that is to be used for the flooring is spelled out.

The specifications can either be on the plans or in a separate document if they will complicate the drawing (see Figure 1.11). Specifications give more detailed expectations of product quality and quantity of materials to be used. A *takeoff* is the process of obtaining the correct information from the specifications or plans to calculate amounts of product needed for the given space. The specifications must be accurate with necessary information.

Design Statement

A design statement is a document created by designers stating how they met the client's wants and needs while justifying why they did what they did in the space. In the statement, designers summarize the design and product selections for clients. Often designers send a copy of the design statement home with clients after the design presentation to help them recall what was discussed during the presentation. A design statement is the designer's opportunity to explain and justify their design describing what was changed in the space, why it was changed, and how it was changed. In a one-page document of 250 to 500 words, the designer pulls together his or her thought process and the reasoning behind the design solution to the client's challenge.

A design statement should be concise and clearly outline the challenges the designer faced and overcame, such as budget, construction constraints, and client requests and lifestyle. Aesthetic choices should also be included to complete the presentation of the project. The key to a successful design statement is to keep it to the point and include how the client's wants and needs were met. Appendix A presents examples of design statements.

All individuals involved in the project must have a complete set of project plans and documents so they understand the scope of work and how items may affect their particular task. For example, the electrician must know if tile will be on wall, as that will affect the installation of outlets.

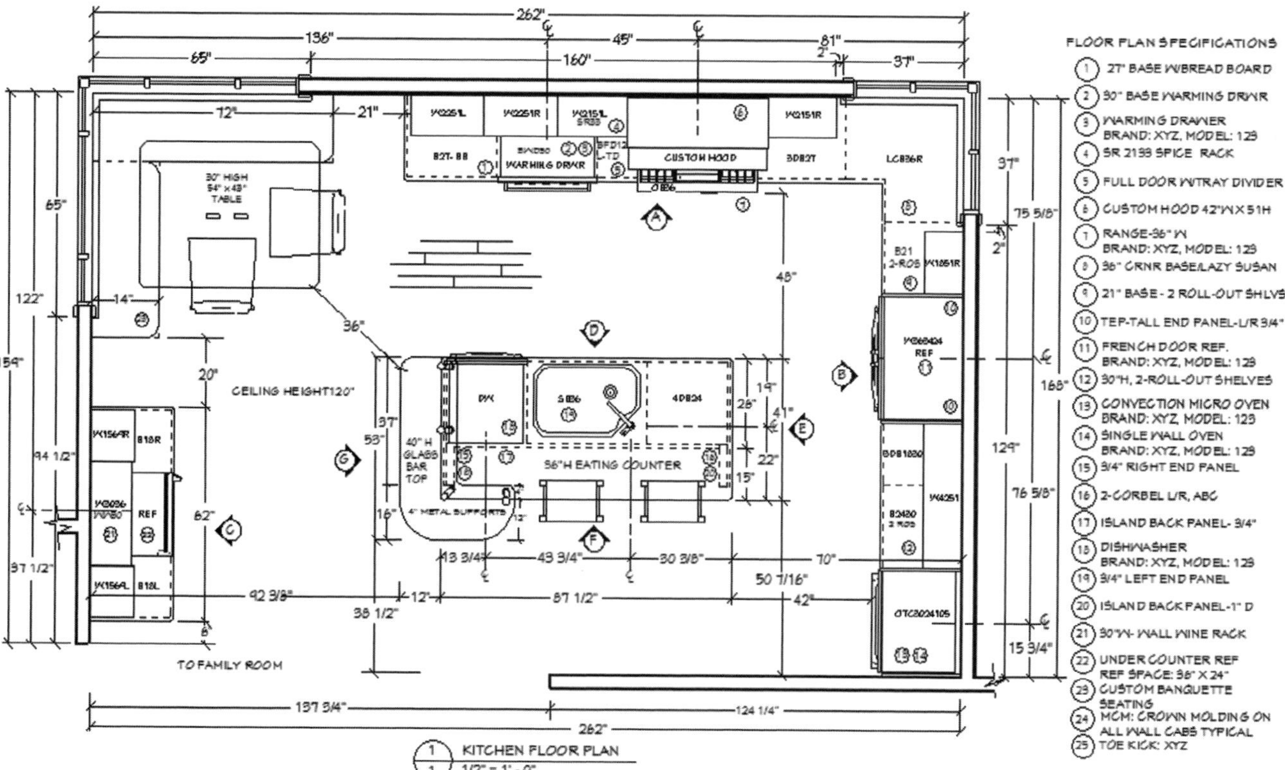

FIGURE 1.11 Floor plan specifications are included on the right-hand side of a floor plan and call out appliance brands and models as well as descriptions of nomenclature for clarification.

Additional Reference Drawings

There are other drawings you may need to reference for your project in order to obtain important information.

You may need to refer to the *architectural construction drawings* for information that could affect your kitchen or bath design. For example, with a remodel project, you need to know what is above or below the space you will be working on, as there could be factors that would affect your design. A designer also needs to know the spaces when working with new construction. Sometimes an idea will not be possible because of the impact it may have on other levels in the home.

Another type of plan you may need to review is a *site plan* or *plot plan*, which is an overhead view of the property around the building. You may want to verify that a new kitchen or bath addition will not come too close to property lines. Or you may want to know how the orientation of the building affects the kitchen or bathroom.

A drawing that shows how the building is affixed to the concrete walls below is called a *foundation plan*. In a remodeling project, you will need to find out if the walls surrounding the kitchen are load-bearing walls or nonstructural partitions. You may need a *structural framing plan* to illustrate just that. If your design calls for removing a wall, you need to understand how to make certain the structure remains secure and how it will remain secure.

Always make sure correct information is obtained from necessary reference drawings for your design project. Assumptions should never be made.

NKBA Drawings versus AIA Drawings

There are several major differences between architectural plans and kitchen and bathroom plans. For example, the NKBA standard drawings differ from the standard drawings of the American Institute of Architects (AIA). A few differences include scale and dimensioning. The scale for NKBA construction drawings is ½″, and the scale for architectural construction drawings is ¼″. The dimensioning is different as well. NKBA standards dimension to the finished inside wall. AIA standards dimension to the center of interior walls and to the outside of exterior walls. Later chapters cover additional details. As a designer, you need to be able to read a construction drawing and translate it into a drawing incorporating the NKBA standards.

Another difference is the height indicated in the drawings. Most architectural plans are drawn as if the space is cut at a height between 48″ and 60″ above the floor. However, if kitchen and bath plans were drawn based on this height, many cabinets and other important details above these heights would be left out. Therefore, kitchen and bathroom plans are drawn from the actual ceiling height so that all cabinets, counters, appliances, fixtures, and other details are shown.

As you learn more about measuring rooms and dimensioning plans in later chapters, you will see that it is the standard of the kitchen and bath industry to measure or dimension finished walls only. This standard has been established because of the critical fit of the products specified for the space. Centerlines for appliances and fixtures are also indicated for proper installation.

SUMMARY

Each drawing in a set of NKBA plans has a purpose and communicates important information for a design project. A title page is included so the reader will know which drawings are included in the set and where they are located. Each drawing has its own standardized symbols so it can be easily understood by all tradespeople and allied professionals.

Chapters 3 and 4 discuss industry standards for drafting. These industry standards help keep the information consistent from drawing to drawing.

As a designer, you need to be able to draft the necessary drawings in a set of plans and to understand the information on each drawing. The goal is to provide all necessary information so the project will be installed correctly. In addition to a visual representation of the space, the drawings provide information used for the ordering of all products specified for the space. Accuracy is critical in drawings.

REVIEW QUESTIONS

1. Which drawings must always be included in a set of NKBA plans? (See "The Set of NKBA Drawings" pages 1-2)
2. Explain why the mechanical plan doesn't show the cabinetry. (See "Mechanical Plan" page 5)
3. Why is a soffit (bulkhead) plan an optional drawing? (See "Soffit [Bulkhead] Plan" page 8)
4. What is the importance of the dimensions shown on an elevation? (See "Interior Elevation" page 5)
5. What information can the three-dimensional perspective show your client? (See "Perspective Drawings" page 6)

Measuring the Design Space

Kitchen and bath drawings provide much information for the successful design and installation of a space. It is very important to measure the design space accurately in order to draw the plans for a project correctly. Conduct a visual inspection of the space, discuss the wants and needs with the client, and make sure to measure and cross-reference all items. There are electronic tools available to measure a space, such as lasers, as well as applications that allow you to take pictures with smartphones and tablets and to place measurements directly on the digital image. This chapter focuses on the physical measurement and documentation of the space.

Learning Objective 1: Identify how to measure a space accurately.

Learning Objective 2: Identify differences in measuring a remodeled space and new construction.

STEPS TO ACCURATE MEASUREMENTS

Accurate measurements of the space must be taken in order to design the space correctly. As a kitchen and bath designer, you will need to go to the site to meet with your clients, complete a thorough visual inspection, discuss their wants and needs, and measure the space accurately. It is also important to note any factors that could affect either the remodel of a space or an installation, and to determine if there are any hidden structural items to take into account.

Designers need to be very thorough and pay close attention to all details throughout the entire design process. Before leaving to measure the job site, whether it is new construction or a remodel, think about the following:

- Have you confirmed the date and time to measure the job?
- Is the job site ready to be measured?
- Do you have directions, a GPS, or a map?
- Will you be measuring during the day or at night? An evening appointment to measure will not give you as good a view of the exterior walls that will be affected.
- Will the client, builder, contractor, or anyone else be at the job site during your visit?
- Do you need assistance from someone in your company?
- Do you have your cell phone with you?

Do you have a client survey or a list of questions to ask your client? The NKBA Client Survey Form is a must to complete with your client in the beginning phase of the design project.

By completing this Client Survey Form properly you will know the wants and needs of your clients as well as be able to design a space that will function well and be aesthetically pleasing for your client. You will need to find out how they live, what they like, what kind of storage they need, and much more. You will also find out what they do and do not like about their current kitchen, which can assist your new design of the space.

Tips for a Remodeling Job

- Call your clients one or two days prior to the job site visit to confirm the date and time, including how long the measuring process will take.
- Arrive no earlier than five minutes before the scheduled time or the client may not be ready for you.
- Park your vehicle where it will not block or impede the client's vehicles.
- Be considerate of the client's home, and remove your shoes or cover them before entering.
- Ask for permission before playing with or picking up small children or animals.
- Refrain from using the client's bathroom.
- Ask clients to move valuable items that might be in the way of measuring. Be mindful of the client's property and avoid any unnecessary handling of personal objects.
- Ask for permission to open all existing cabinets to look for hidden obstructions, pipes, and wires.
- Avoid any distractions and concentrate fully. Politely ask the client to refrain from conversation with you while you measure the space.
- Carefully and accurately measure and then remeasure all walls.
- Photograph existing walls for future reference during the design process.
- Take pictures beginning in one corner and go around the room clockwise. These panoramic pictures will help remind you what is adjacent to another item in the space. This method also helps ensure you do not miss an item since you have captured portions of walls and other items in space.
- Videotape the space if you can.
- If you find that existing mechanical or structural components are in questionable condition, it is acceptable to schedule another appointment to measure the job when you can bring/meet someone, such as a plumber, electrician, or contractor to assess the conditions and extent of work that may need to be done. Finish measuring at or before the time you told the client you would be completed.
- Schedule the next appointment, and discuss what the next steps are.

Tips for Measuring a New Construction Job Site

- Take into account job site conditions, weather conditions, and the task of measuring a new structure. You may need to wear a hard hat and boots and have a four-wheel-drive vehicle.
- Determine if the job site environment is safe.
- Are the floor plans and job folder available?
- Are the mechanical systems noted on the floor plans?

Make sure you have the following items with you for every measuring job. Even if you leave most of them in your car, they will be a lot closer than at your office should you need them.

Items to Bring to Every Measuring Job

- Client Survey Form to be filled in at client's house
- Twenty-five-foot metal tape measure with a 1″ blade
- Six- or eight-foot folding rule
- Framing square
- Level
- Pencils, pens of different colors, and grease pencils to mark on the floor the layout of the cabinets including nomenclature
- Calculator
- Masking tape
- Angled measuring tool to automatically calculate an angled wall
- Note pad or clipboard with graph paper

TABLE 2.1 Measuring Considerations

If You Choose to Measure...	You May Have the Advantage Because...	But You May Also Experience Disadvantages	Keep in Mind That...	Degree of Accuracy
Using the floor plans the client created	You can make major changes to the plan to better meet client needs.	The builder and client may make other changes after you order the cabinets and equipment.	All parties must agree to your suggestions before orders are processed. "Rough quote" only at this time.	LOW
After stud walls are in place	You can suggest major mechanical changes before the trades start their work.	Openings can still be relocated, but watch for concrete slabs that will affect the plan. Product can be ordered, but you must be very careful at this stage.	You must check size of wall coverings, floor materials, trim sizes, etc. Mark location of floor joists, studs, etc.	MEDIUM
After drywall is installed	The utilities are set, and most clients will not want to make costly changes at this point.	Clients may request changes but may not be willing to pay for them. Be sure to use change order forms.	You must check for additional wall coverings, floor material, trim sizes, etc.	HIGH
Before the remodeling project begins	You are responsible for the complete project so you will be aware of all changes.	If you are furnishing product only, watch for changes that you did not anticipate.	You will need to check the status of the project on a regular basis.	HIGH

- Flashlight
- Digital or video camera
- Hard hat and boots
- Small broom
- Small step ladder
- Business cards
- First aid kit
- A four-wheel-drive vehicle, if necessary (for new construction jobs)

When you measure can have a significant impact on the project as described in Table 2.1.

Measure the space in inches only, not feet and inches. NKBA plans are always drafted in inches (mm) rather than feet plus inches. Measuring in inches will help reduce the chance of errors when you later draft the plan. If measured in feet and inches, you will need to convert to inches and a mistake could happen during the conversion from feet to inches.

Always keep in mind that rooms aren't always square, walls are not always plumb, and floors are not always level. This applies to new construction as well as remodeling.

When preparing for a remodeling job, it's wise to follow a few simple steps to ensure concise and accurate planning.

MEASURING THE REMODELING JOB

When measuring an existing space, the designer needs to document all items within that given space along with adjacent items that relate to the space.

1. Visually inspect the space, and note all items within the space. Check for hidden ductwork, electrical items, and the like that you may not see initially.
2. Next sketch a proportionally correct room outline. Look at the big picture first and then focus on the details within the given space.
   - Some prefer to sketch the space on graph paper. This sketch does not need to be to scale but it should be in proportion at this point. With experience, you may use the squares on graph paper as an aid to figure out the placement of items in a ½″ scale on the sketch. Sometimes this method slows down designers who are trying to draft perfectly to scale. Remember that at this point, you only need a sketch of the space. Determine if you should use graph paper or plain paper for your sketch.

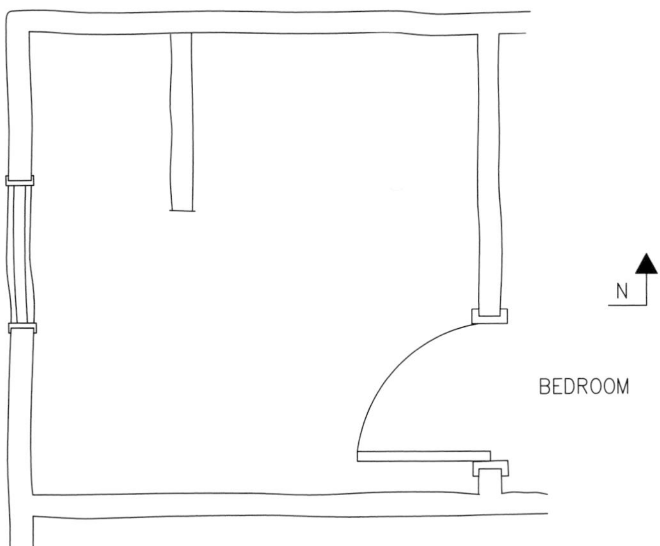

FIGURE 2.1 Sketch the space to be designed.
Courtesy of Erica Westeroth, CKD

- Choose one corner first and move clockwise around the space.
- Include the wall thicknesses.
- Locate all windows, doors, pass-throughs, and other openings. Note the door swings.
- Locate any other architectural feature in the room such as radiators or air ducts.
- Locate all water supply pipes , drainage pipes, vents, gas pipes, and electrical outlets.
- If possible, locate any load-bearing walls or headers. Sometimes a header can be hidden in a soffit/bulkhead. Rooms that are cantilevered often have a hidden header.
- Note the north/south orientation.
- Label adjacent rooms and include view information, such as facing a lake, woods, and the like (see Figure 2.1).

3. Measure the ceiling height in at least three locations. If the heights are not consistent, note the different heights. *Never* assume that a room is square or that walls are straight.

There are several techniques used for measuring the ceiling height:

- Use a pencil to lightly mark a midpoint on the wall (see Figure 2.2). Next, measure from the ceiling down to the mark and then from the mark to the floor. (Note: Use a 1″-wide tape measure; narrower tape measures can be flimsy and collapse easily.) For extra stability, some designers like to use the 1′ wooden tape that fold out. A good tape measure is well worth the investment.
- Another method for measuring the ceiling is from the ceiling down to the floor without marking the midpoint as in the previous method. Begin with the tape measure at the top of wall at ceiling. Push the tape down with your knee while holding it flat against the wall. Make sure the end of tape is at the ceiling and hasn't slipped down the wall (see Figure 2.3).

  A folding rule can be used in the middle of the room where there are no obstacles. An advantage of the folding rule is that it will stay vertical on its own.
- Another technique is to push the tape from the floor up to the ceiling. Repeat at several locations to determine levelness. Record the height in a circle at the center of the floor plan (see Figure 2.4).

You are now ready to measure all items you have located on your sketch of the space. Make sure to note necessary items on your sketch so that you have adequate information to draft the measured space at a later time.

4. When measuring, select one corner of the room to be your starting point. You will end at that location. Measure the walls in a clockwise manner. First measure the room's overall dimensions, and then go back and measure the smaller clearances and spaces in order to cross-reference all measurements. It is good to hold the tape measure at one corner and read all points along that line without moving the tape if possible. This method helps reduce the risk of inaccurate measurements from moving the tape measure.

FIGURE 2.2 Mark a midpoint on the wall.

FIGURE 2.3 Measure from the ceiling down.

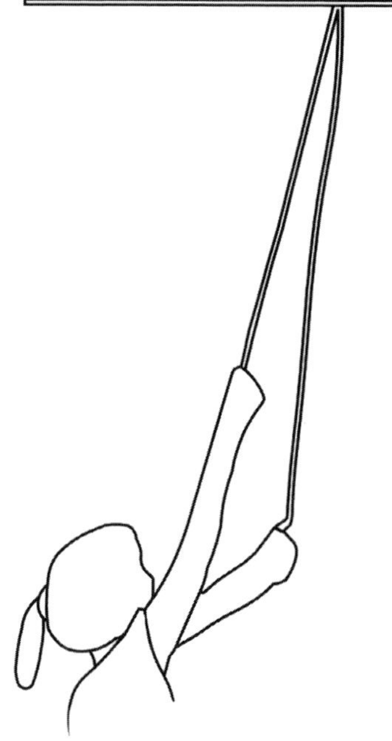

FIGURE 2.4 Measure from the floor up.

- If possible, clear a path approximately 36″ above the floor. If there is a window, measure at a point on the wall to catch those dimensions. You need to have the dimension from the wall to the outside of the window casing on both sides of the window.
- You can also lay the tape measure on the floor along the baseboards for accuracy and measure from one wall to the opposite wall. You will need to add in the thickness of the baseboard.
- If there are obstructions, place the tape on the wall. Make sure it is always level and taut. If the tape isn't pulled tight, it will sag and add extra length to that wall. If you have a carpenter's level, place it under your tape measure to make sure it is level.
- Measure the full length of the wall. Record the total dimension on your sketched drawing of the room. For recording this dimension on your sketch, a long dimension line can be drawn to the outside of this wall, parallel to the wall you have measured.
- Keep in mind that this is just a sketch with items sketched in proportion.

To check if the corner is square, use the following method: mark a point 36″ out from the corner on one wall and 48″ out from the corner on the adjacent wall, and measure the distance between the two points. If the distance is 60″, the corner is square. This formula is known as the Pythagorean theorem: $a^2 + b^2 = c^2$ (see Figure 2.5). Any other measurement indicates that the corner is out of square, and you should make a note on the plan. A framing square can also be used to determine the squareness of a room.

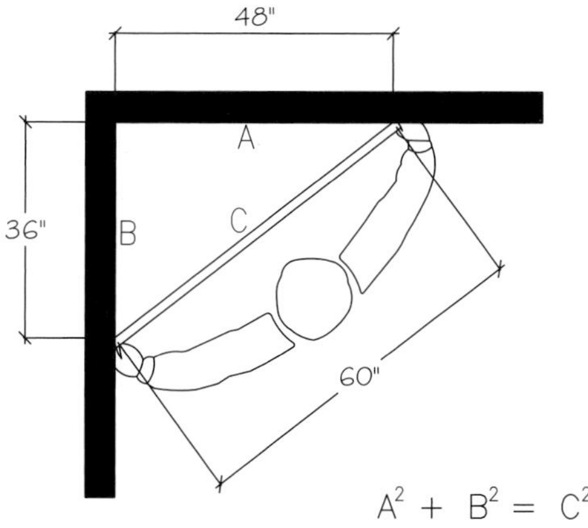

FIGURE 2.5 Use the Pythagorean theorem to check if the corner is square.

5. Next, measure the shorter distances of items on the wall. Begin measuring at your starting corner of the room.
   - Measure from your starting corner to the nearest opening or obstacle. This could be a door, window, pipe chase, architectural feature, and so on. You must be concerned with the usable wall space, and you will need to measure to the outside trim of doors and windows.
   - Record measurements on your floor plan sketch.
   - Next measure from outside edge to outside edge of door and window trim and record the dimensions. Make a note of the trim size.
   - Continue measuring items until you have reached the opposite corner of the first wall.
   - Make sure to measure all distances and note any changes in the wall such as a protrusion.
   - Verify you have the distance from the wall to window trim (casing), window trim to window trim, which is the (width of window plus trim/casing), and then window trim to wall. Verify all door measurements as you did for windows.
6. Confirm the accuracy of your measurements by comparing the sum of all individual dimensions to the total overall wall measurement.
   - Use your calculator to add the measurements and confirm the accuracy of the measurements taken of that first wall.
   - The shorter dimensions should add up to the overall wall dimension.
7. Continue measuring the length of each remaining wall, going clockwise around the room.
   - Place all dimensions on your room sketch.
8. Next measure the heights of windows, doors, radiators, soffits/bulkheads, and any other objects not yet accounted for in the given space.
   - Use the NKBA Client Survey Form dimension page, which has diagrams for measuring windows, existing appliances, radiators, and more.
   - Include heights for windows from floor to ceiling; include sills, door height, ventilation, air conditioning units, and any other measurement not previously noted.
   - Make sure to take measurements of existing appliances if they are to be used in the new design (see Figure 2.6).

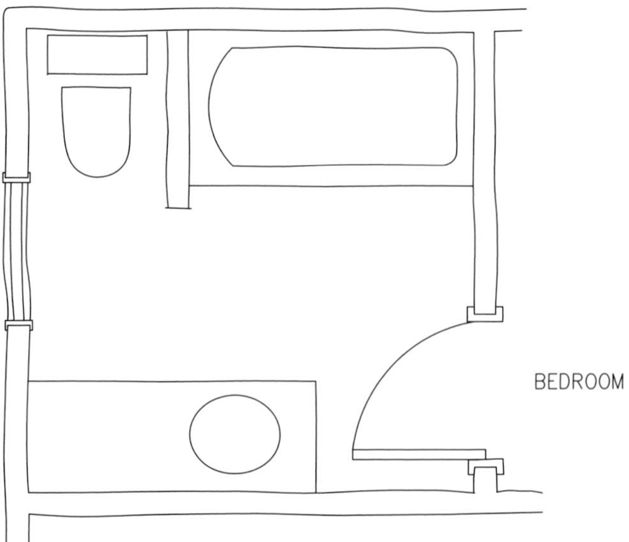

FIGURE 2.6 Your sketch now includes doors, windows, and other obstacles.
Courtesy of Erica Westeroth, CKD

9. Locate the center points of all plumbing, venting, electrical, and lighting items.
   - Beginning at your starting corner of the wall, measure from that corner to the center of outlets, switches, fixtures, appliances, lighting, venting, and plumbing. Measure to the center points of items on ceiling as well. (Note: Double-check to make sure that you have included all center points of each item so you can later complete your NKBA drawings.)
   - On your sketched floor plan, record these center point locations.
   - Use architectural symbols to denote type of item (see Figure 2.7). These symbols can be found in chapter 3.

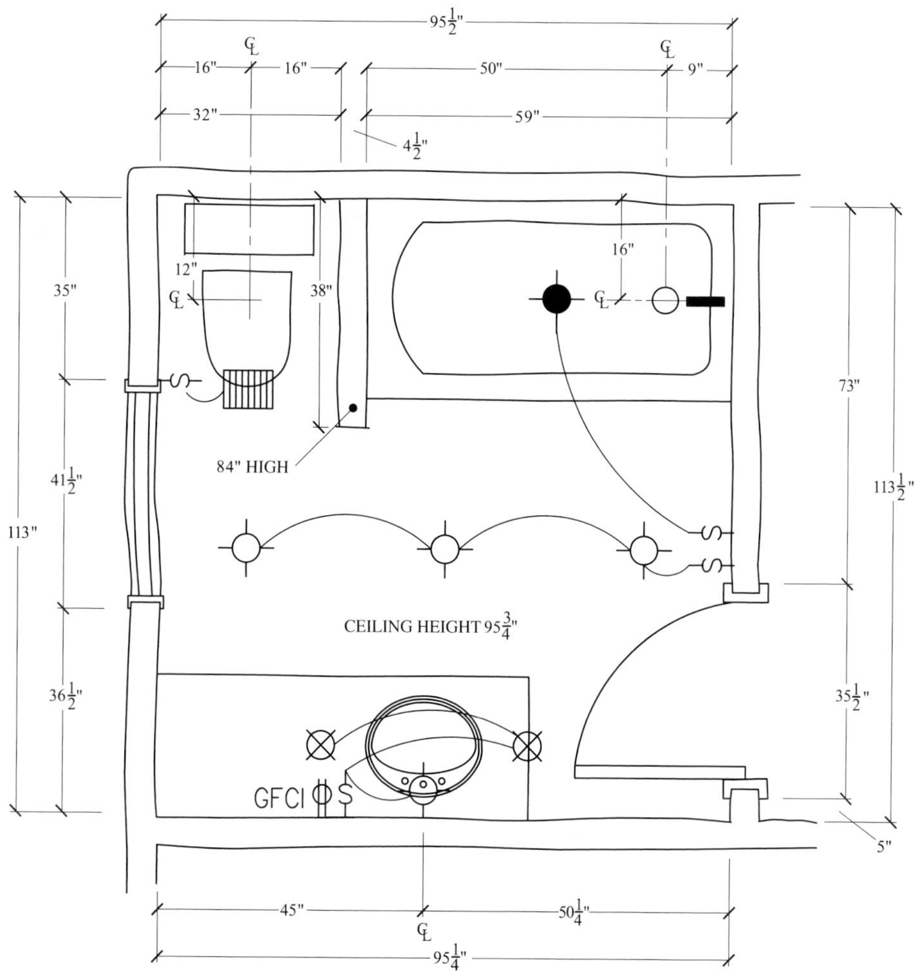

FIGURE 2.7 Indicate plumbing, electrical, and lighting on your sketch. *Courtesy of Erica Westeroth, CKD*

10. Many designers prefer to draft a "before" or "existing" floor plan:
- Measure all cabinets, fixtures, and appliances.
- Sketch an elevation of the walls to ensure that everything is dimensioned accurately and nothing is overlooked.

11. Make your final inspection.
- Visually inspect the area to make sure all items have been measured.
- Measure any freestanding furniture pieces or other architectural features.
- Check the electrical service panel conditions.
- Check any areas that may be affected during the remodeling project, such as the basement or attic.
- Confirm access to all spaces as needed for remodel project.

12. Take photos of the existing space for reference during the design process. Videos are also helpful.
- Photos help document what the space looked like prior to demolition.
- The photos can also be added to your company's portfolio to show "before" and "after" images.
- Always make sure you have your client's permission to use any photos from their projects in design contests or publications.

MEASURING NEW CONSTRUCTION

Measuring for a new construction project is a little different from measuring for a remodel project. With new construction, you need to verify that items were installed in accordance with the construction drawings provided by the architect. These items include windows, doors, plumbing, electrical, and other mechanicals that should be verified during the framing stage. Sometimes things change from the original drawing. Measuring on site is called *field measuring*. Any discrepancies with the plans and measurements should be discussed with the builder or homeowner.

1. When measuring a new construction project, the dimensions are typically made from stud wall to stud wall.
2. Architectural elements such as doors and windows must be located/measured from the stud wall to the rough opening. Make sure you take into account the thickness of products placed on the floors, walls, and ceiling.
3. Verify where the doors and windows lead, their size, direction of opening, and trim size.
4. Note on the Client Survey Form the type and thickness of the material to be used for finishing the walls, ceilings, and floors.
5. After you have measured the space, adjust the rough dimensions by subtracting finish material and finish depths for each wall surface so that the plan reflects finished wall dimensions.
6. The thickness of the gypsum board must be accounted for in your dimensions.
7. Be sure to confirm what finished materials are to be used before placing any product orders. The finished dimensions can make a big difference in product specifications. For example, adding 1/16″ flooring product with a 3/8″-thick flooring product alters the finished floor-to-ceiling dimensions, which in turn affects the heights of tall cabinets and soffits.

ANGLES AND CURVES

Angles

Even though an electronic tape measure automatically measures angled walls, as a designer, you should know how to measure all types of walls. The most accurate approach is to first lay out a right triangle on the floor in the corner. Measure at least two of its sides, and apply the appropriate trigonometric formula. Determine the angle to be found. Then identify the opposite, adjacent, and hypotenuse sides of the triangle. (The opposite side is the one directly opposite the angle. The hypotenuse is the longest side of the triangle, and the remaining leg is the adjacent side.) Use one of the next trigonometric formulas to determine the angle.

- Sine (SIN) equals the opposite side divided by the hypotenuse.
- Cosine (COS) equals the adjacent side divided by the hypotenuse.
- Tangent (TAN) equals the opposite side divided by the adjacent side.

In our example, the opposite side and the hypotenuse are known; therefore, the sine formula is used. The answer is a decimal number, which should be rounded to the nearest ten thousandth. Then use the Table of Trigonometric Functions (Table 2.2) to find the correct angle. To use the table, look under the appropriate column (SIN, COS, or TAN) and find the closest decimal number. Then find the corresponding angle, which is shown at the far left of that row (see Figure 2.8).

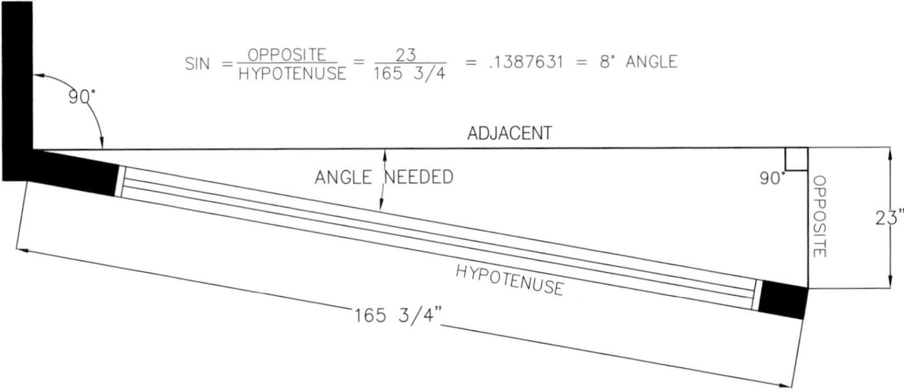

FIGURE 2.8 Finding an angle.

TABLE 2.2 Table of Trigonomometric Functions

Degrees	Radian Measure	Sin	Cos	Tan		Degrees	Radian Measure	Sin	Cos	Tan
0	0.00000	0.00000	1.00000	0.00000		46	0.80285	0.71934	0.69466	1.03553
1	0.01745	0.01745	0.99985	0.01746		47	0.82030	0.73135	0.68200	1.07237
2	0.03491	0.03490	0.99939	0.03492		48	0.83776	0.74314	0.66913	1.11061
3	0.05236	0.05234	0.99863	0.05241		49	0.85521	0.75471	0.65606	1.15037
4	0.06981	0.06976	0.99756	0.06993		50	0.87266	0.76604	0.64279	1.19175
5	0.08727	0.08716	0.99619	0.08749		51	0.89012	0.77715	0.62932	1.23490
6	0.10472	0.10453	0.99452	0.10510		52	0.90757	0.78801	0.61566	1.27994
7	0.12217	0.12187	0.99255	0.12278		53	0.92502	0.79864	0.60182	1.32704
8	0.13963	0.13917	0.99027	0.14054		54	0.94248	0.80902	0.58779	1.37638
9	0.15708	0.15643	0.98769	0.15838		55	0.95993	0.81915	0.57358	1.42815
10	0.17453	0.17365	0.98481	0.17633		56	0.97738	0.82904	0.55919	1.48256
11	0.19199	0.19081	0.98163	0.19438		57	0.99484	0.83867	0.54464	1.53986
12	0.20944	0.20791	0.97815	0.21256		58	1.01229	0.84805	0.52992	1.60033
13	0.22689	0.22495	0.97437	0.23087		59	1.02974	0.85717	0.51504	1.66428
14	0.24435	0.24192	0.97030	0.24933		60	1.04720	0.86603	0.50000	1.73205
15	0.26180	0.25882	0.96593	0.26795		61	1.06465	0.87462	0.48481	1.80405
16	0.27925	0.27564	0.96126	0.28675		62	1.08210	0.88295	0.46947	1.88073
17	0.29671	0.29237	0.95630	0.30573		63	1.09956	0.89101	0.45399	1.96261
18	0.31416	0.30902	0.95106	0.32492		64	1.11701	0.89879	0.43837	2.05030
19	0.33161	0.32557	0.94552	0.34433		65	1.13446	0.90631	0.42262	2.14451
20	0.34907	0.34202	0.93969	0.36397		66	1.15192	0.91355	0.40674	2.24604
21	0.36652	0.35837	0.93358	0.38386		67	1.16937	0.92050	0.39073	2.35585
22	0.38397	0.37461	0.92718	0.40403		68	1.18682	0.92718	0.37461	2.47509
23	0.40143	0.39073	0.92050	0.42447		69	1.20428	0.93358	0.35837	2.60509
24	0.41888	0.40674	0.91355	0.44523		70	1.22173	0.93969	0.34202	2.74748
25	0.43633	0.42262	0.90631	0.46631		71	1.23918	0.94552	0.32557	2.90421
26	0.45379	0.43837	0.89879	0.48773		72	1.25664	0.95106	0.30902	3.07768
27	0.47124	0.45399	0.89101	0.50953		73	1.27409	0.95630	0.29237	3.27085
28	0.48869	0.46947	0.88295	0.53171		74	1.29154	0.96126	0.27564	3.48741
29	0.50615	0.48481	0.87462	0.55431		75	1.30900	0.96593	0.25882	3.73205
30	0.52360	0.50000	0.86603	0.57735		76	1.32645	0.97030	0.24192	4.01078
31	0.54105	0.51504	0.85717	0.60086		77	1.34390	0.97437	0.22495	4.33148
32	0.55851	0.52992	0.84805	0.62487		78	1.36136	0.97815	0.20791	4.70463
33	0.57596	0.54464	0.83867	0.64941		79	1.37881	0.98163	0.19081	5.14455
34	0.59341	0.55919	0.82904	0.67451		80	1.39626	0.98481	0.17365	5.67128
35	0.61087	0.57358	0.81915	0.70021		81	1.41372	0.98769	0.15643	6.31375
36	0.62832	0.58779	0.80902	0.72654		82	1.43117	0.99027	0.13917	7.11537
37	0.64577	0.60182	0.79864	0.75355		83	1.44862	0.99255	0.12187	8.14435
38	0.66323	0.61566	0.78801	0.78129		84	1.46608	0.99452	0.10453	9.51436
39	0.68068	0.62932	0.77715	0.80978		85	1.48353	0.99619	0.08716	11.43005
40	0.69813	0.64279	0.76604	0.83910		86	1.50098	0.99756	0.06976	14.30067
41	0.71558	0.65606	0.75471	0.86929		87	1.51844	0.99863	0.05234	19.08114
42	0.73304	0.66913	0.74314	0.90040		88	1.53589	0.99939	0.03490	28.63625
43	0.75049	0.68200	0.73135	0.93252		89	1.55334	0.99985	0.01745	57.28996
44	0.76794	0.69466	0.71934	0.96569		90	1.57080	1.00000	0.00000	
45	0.78540	0.70711	0.70711	1.00000						

Curves

Measuring a curved wall requires finding the radius of the curve. Using a yardstick as your straight line, first locate a straight line that terminates at any two points along the curve. This line is referred to as a *chord*. Find the rise by determining the exact center of the chord and measuring the perpendicular length from this point to the wall. For kitchen and bathroom planning purposes, a 36″ chord dimension is recommended because a 36″ cabinet is the widest unit you should place against a curved wall (see Figure 2.9).

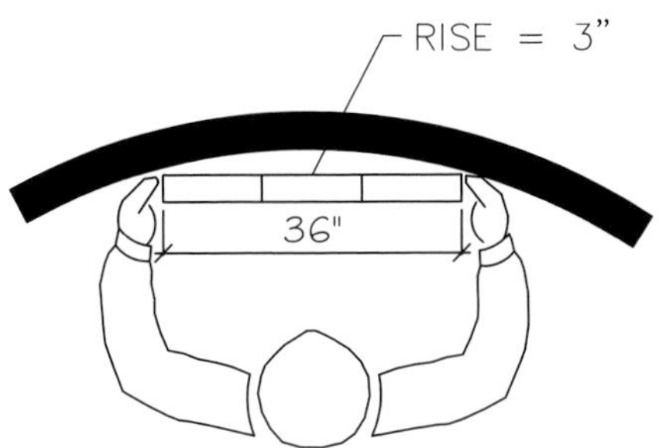

FIGURE 2.9 Measuring a curved wall.

Use the following formulas to determine the radius:

First find the diameter: ((Chord/2)^2 + Rise^2)/Rise = Diameter

Then find the radius: Diameter/2 = Radius

For example, if you were to use a yardstick (36″) as a chord and found the rise to be 3″, the formula would be calculated as follows:

$$\frac{\left(\frac{1}{2}(36)\right)^2+3^2}{3} \rightarrow \frac{18^2+3^2}{3} \rightarrow \frac{324+9}{3} \rightarrow \frac{333}{3} \rightarrow 111 \text{ is the diameter}$$

$$\frac{111}{2} \rightarrow 55\frac{1}{2} \text{ is the radius}$$

Now that the radius is established, you can determine the length of the curve (the *arc*) with this formula:

$A = \pi \times r \times <$

where

$A =$ length of the arc (curve) 180
$\pi =$ pi, which is 3.14
$r =$ radius
$< =$ angle
$\times =$ multiply

TIPS FROM THE PROS

The kitchen and bathroom designer needs to thoroughly understand a set of drawings before beginning the takeoff. Seasoned experts in the kitchen and bath industry share the following hints.

- Never plan a room that will have furniture in it without first knowing the size of the furniture and where it will be placed.
- When you are doing a hardware takeoff, be methodical. For example, when you are doing a takeoff for cabinet and entry doors, start by counting the number of doors in the entire plan or refer to the door schedule. Make sure you end up with that number of doors and corresponding hardware when you finish your takeoff. Consider dividing the doors by

groups: cabinets, key lock, passage, and privacy. Then count the hardware by areas, and total to check quantity. Missing items during the takeoff is very costly in terms of reordering, delays, and frustration. Check and double check!

- If you add any items that are not on the schedule, consider whether they will change the plans. For example, if you decide to add a barbecue in an island, you have changed the mechanical plans. You may need to add electrical and/or gas supply, along with ductwork for ventilation. Any changes in framing, electrical, plumbing or construction that products require must be clearly communicated to the builder or architect so that the appropriate notes can be incorporated into the plans.

SUMMARY

Measuring the kitchen or bath space accurately is critical to the success of the design project. The floor plan and other drawings must be drawn to scale based on accurate measurements taken of the space. The products need to fit in the given spaces correctly, and their mechanicals, such as electrical and plumbing, must be properly placed. Construction and project installation scheduling may hinge on the completion of other related tasks. For instance, the cabinetry must fit in the space properly so the electrician and plumber can install the appliances or fixtures in the correct locations. Items that are not placed correctly can delay work necessary for completion and set back other scheduled install dates. Such delays will require the rescheduling of tradespeople, which can be costly and will likely delay project completion. The steps for measuring in this chapter should assist you in measuring a space correctly. Be organized and professional by making sure you have all necessary items with you when you measure at the job site.

REVIEW QUESTIONS

1. Why is it important to complete the NKBA Client Survey Form at the measuring of a client's space? (See under "Steps to Accurate Measurements" pages 13–14.)
2. Why must we measure the space only in inches (mm) rather than feet plus inches? (See under "Steps to Accurate Measurements" page 15.)
3. Why is it important to take photos of the measured site? (See under "Steps to Accurate Measurements" page 14.)
4. What surface of the wall is typically measured for new construction? (See under "Measuring New Construction" page 20.)
5. What is the formula used to measure a corner to see if it is square? (See under "Measuring the Remodeling Job" Figure 2.6 page 17.)

The Tools & Techniques of Hand Drafting

To successfully complete a hand-drafted drawing, the draftsperson needs the correct hand-drafting tools. It is important to learn the skill of hand drafting even with the use of computers for drafting. Hand drafting helps provide a greater understanding of the whole process of designing a space. Using the correct drafting techniques helps produce a professionally drafted drawing. Training in hand drafting also has the additional benefit of providing a sound understanding of angles. With all the different configurations of houses and the spaces within, understanding angles can help you with the calculations necessary for good design.

Learning Objective 1: Identify drafting tools and how to use them.

Learning Objective 2: Identify good drafting techniques.

DRAFTING TOOLS AND TECHNIQUES

Several tools are used in architectural hand drafting, and each has its own function to help the draftsperson create the final drawing. We will go through each tool and the recommended way to use it.

Drafting Tables

There are several different styles and models of drafting boards available for hand drafting. Most designers have a dedicated workplace for their hand drafting as well as for their CAD (computer-aided drafting). It is important to have a drafting surface that is comfortable to work with and has adjacent space for all of your drafting tools. Two types of drafting tables most commonly used are the drafting table with a base and the portable drafting table. Each table must have a straightedge to work with.

Drafting Table with Base

The drafting table must fit the individual's needs. There are several styles and models to choose from. Prices vary according to size and the materials it is made from. Most tables either have four legs or a pedestal base. Some drafting tables have an adjustable top that can be set to the preferred angle for the individual drafting. Other models are designed with a top that can be raised or lowered to allow either standing or sitting, which is good

FIGURE 3.1 Stationary drafting tables come in a variety of sizes.
Courtesy of Alvin & Co., Inc.

for preventing fatigue while drafting. There are also models of drafting tables that fold up, and some have casters so they can be moved. Other models have lighting incorporated as well.

Make sure the table size will fit the largest vellum you will be working with. A wood top should be covered with a smooth surface so you won't get indentations in the wood surface from drafting. Most people prefer a replaceable vinyl cover. (The material commonly used is Vyco/Borco.) The drafting table is an investment. Do your research before purchasing so it best meets your needs and provides a good work environment (see Figure 3.1).

Portable Drafting Tables

Portable drafting tables are designed to sit on another surface, such as a conventional table. They come in various sizes and materials, most commonly wood or plastic. Portable tables are convenient because you can take them to different locations. They also are useful when space is limited.

The NKBA offers a portable drafting table made of a lightweight plastic. It comes with a parallel bar that can be locked and accommodates the standard NKBA 11″ × 17″ vellum. There is also a protractor on the parallel bar (see Figure 3.2 and Figure 3.3).

Parallel Bar

The parallel bar is the long, straight tool on a drafting table used to draw horizontal lines and as a base for drawing a vertical line with a triangle. The parallel bar may be fastened to the

FIGURE 3.2 NKBA portable drafting table and vellum.

drafting table or may be removable. Attached parallel bars use a wire and pulley system where the bar slides on the wire. These wires can be adjusted and must be kept tight so the parallel bar remains straight on the table. The removable parallel bar typically has a lock to hold the bar in place so it won't move when you are drafting a line. The parallel bar is preferred over the T-square by most designers since you don't need to hold it in place while drawing a line (see Figure 3.4).

FIGURE 3.3 Portable drafting board with parallel bar.
Courtesy of Alvin & Co., Inc.

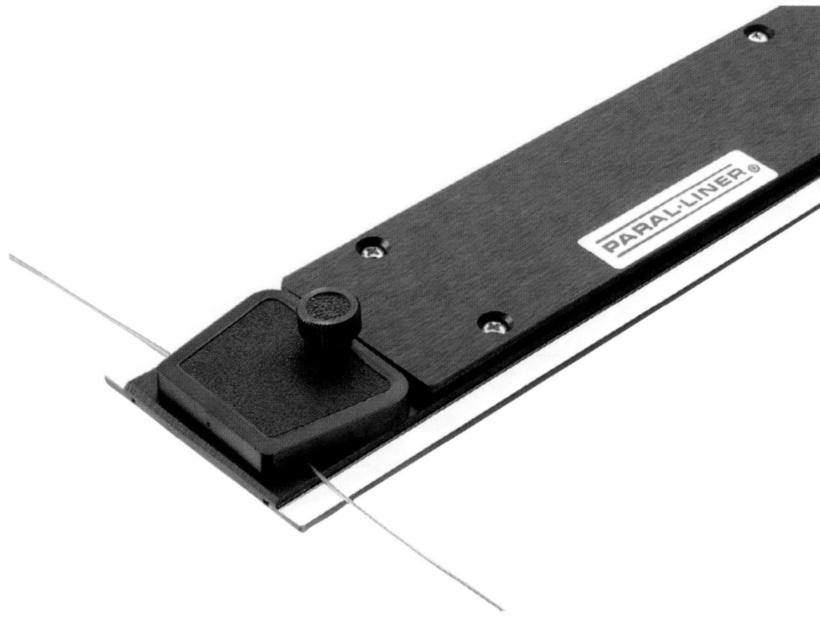

FIGURE 3.4 Parallel bar using wire and pulley system.

T-square

A T-square is a less expensive tool that can be used as a straightedge if you don't have a parallel bar. The T-square can be placed on the left or right side of the drafting table, depending on whether you are right- or left-handed. It must be held in place so that it won't slip while you are drafting a line. T-squares come in different lengths to fit various table sizes (see Figure 3.5).

Drafting Machine

A drafting machine is a device that is attached to the drafting table. It is more expensive than a parallel bar system but it has several tools built in. There are vertical and horizontal blades that have the imperial scale and metric scale along with a built-in angular scale. Drafting tables may be equipped with either a parallel bar drafting system or a drafting machine. (see Figure 3.6).

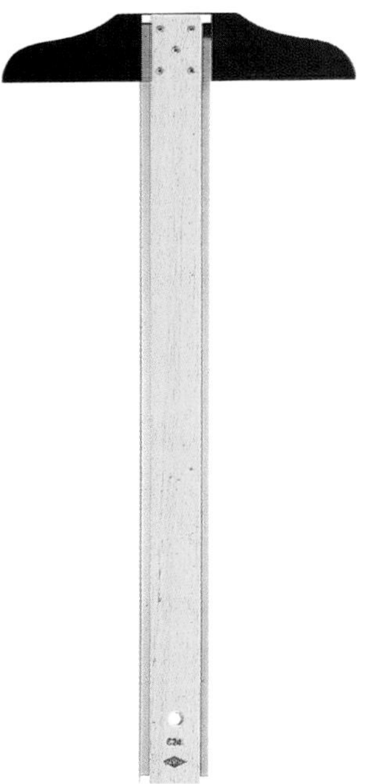

FIGURE 3.5 The T-square. Hold it firmly in place against the table edge.

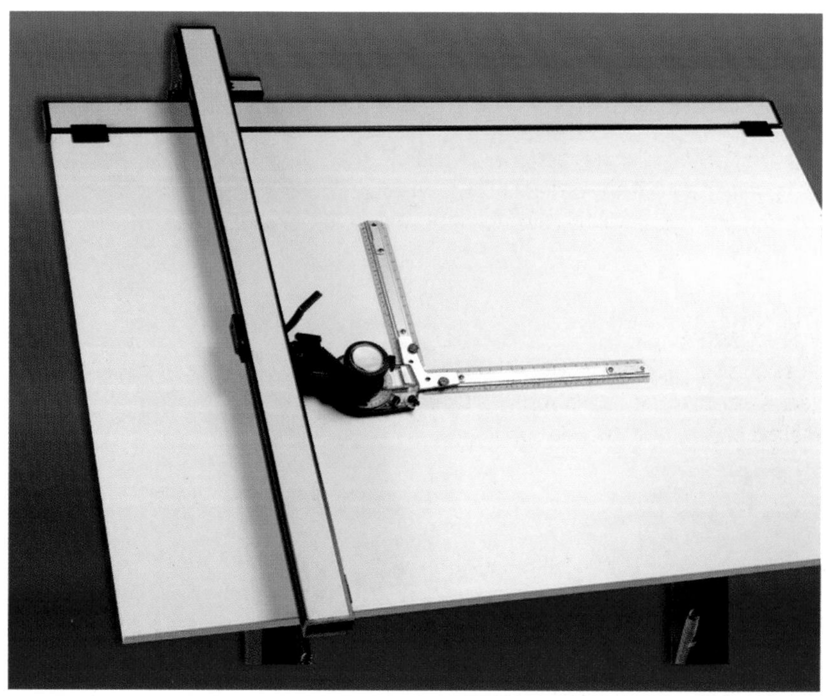

FIGURE 3.6 Drafting machine fastened to the drafting board. Can be left- or right-handed.

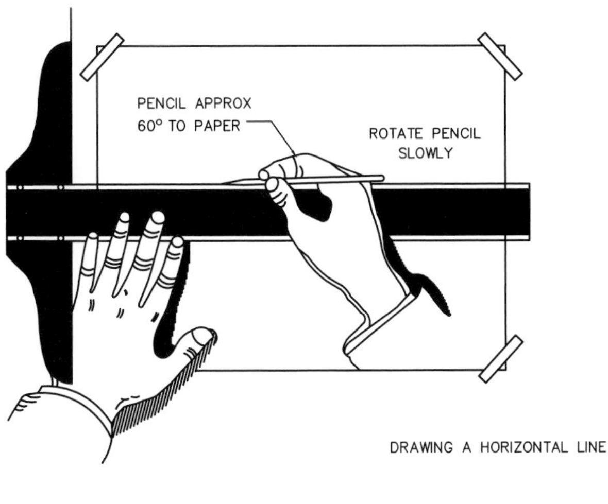

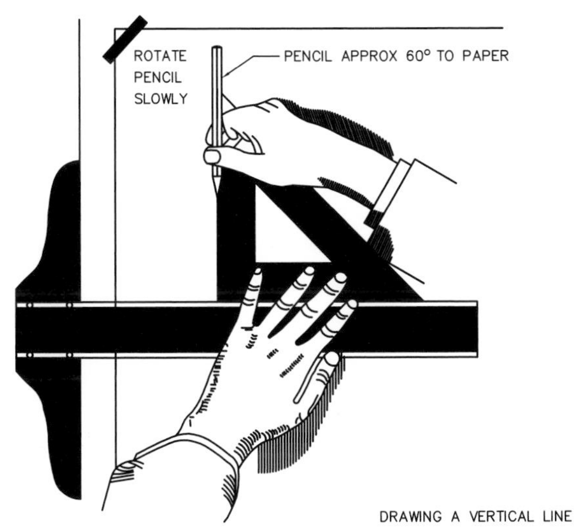

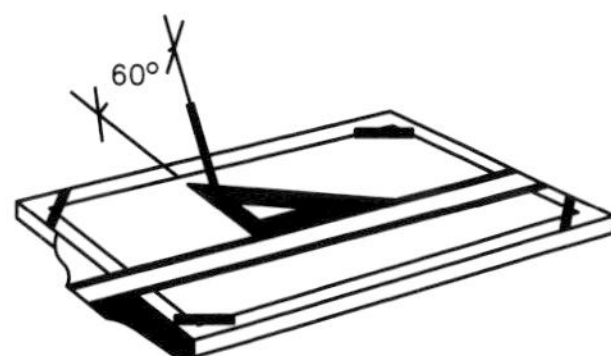

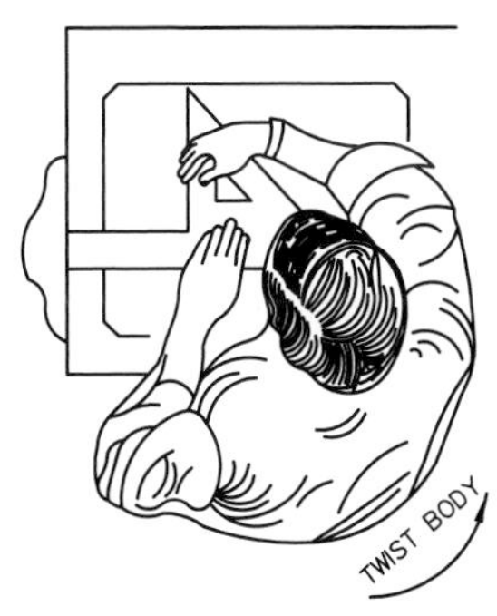

FIGURE 3.7 Drawing horizontal and vertical lines.

Technique for Drawing Horizontal Lines

Whether you use a parallel bar, T-square, or drafting machine to draw your horizontal lines, make sure the straightedge is accurate and straight. Horizontal lines are drawn either from left to right or right to left. It depends on whether you are right- or left-handed (see Figure 3.7). The technique will be covered in the lead holder section.

DRAWING MEDIA

In the design industry, several types of paper are used for the various drawings and stages of a project. Final drawings are a result of planning and putting ideas onto paper, ideas that become the basis for a designed space.

Tracing Paper

Tracing paper is a less expensive, semitransparent paper used for preliminary designs, sketching items, and when designing the space. It is available in white and yellow (bumwad). Tracing paper has several names, such as trash or trace paper. Tracing paper is available in rolls of various widths and in tablet form. Designers use this least expensive paper to brainstorm new ideas, create bubble diagrams, and work out the design in the space. Since it is more transparent than vellum, you can place one piece over another to trace the items you like from one design and then add the new items and changes to the drawing. Most often you do not erase on tracing paper; but rather place a new sheet on top and discard what isn't needed. Tracing paper also works well to figure out items first before drafting on the vellum. For example, you can use tracing paper to figure out floor plan placement to ensure everything fits properly, work with your electrical and lighting layouts, and design the given space.

Vellum

Vellum is used for the final drawings. It is a semi-opaque, high-quality paper that can be used with lead or ink. Vellum is "toothed" (rough) on the drawing side and is available plain or with a preprinted title block on each sheet. The NKBA offers vellum with the title block preprinted or purchase to its members that you may use for your final drawings. In chapter 5 you will learn techniques for drafting final plans on the vellum.

Drafting Film

Drafting film is another type of paper used in design. These sheets of polyester film and plastic work well for ink and plastic lead work. One popular brand of film used is Mylar®. Vellum is most often used in kitchen and bath design.

Standard Paper Sizes

The standard size of vellum used for NKBA drawings is 11″ × 17″ (297 × 432 mm). You may need to use a larger sheet, depending on the size of space.

Table 3.1 shows the standard sizes of paper used in the design industry based on specifications from the American National Standards Institute (ANSI). You may work with plans of different sizes in accordance with the size of the project and what will fit on the vellum. CAD programs also use printers and plotters that are set up in accordance with these standards.

DRAFTING PENCILS AND OTHER TOOLS

Several types of lead pencils and holders are used for architectural drafting. The leads range from hard (9H) to soft (6B). The different pencils each have different types of lead.

Wood-Cased Pencils

Wood-cased pencils have been around for many years but are not used as much in today's design work. The lead is encased inside the wood exterior and is typically sharpened with a draftsman's pencil sharpener to sharpen the wooden exterior. The lead then needs to be sharpened using sandpaper or a lead pointer. Some prefer to use an electric or battery operated sharpener. Sharpening manually sharpens the point exactly how the drafter prefers. Each lead pencil is marked with the particular hardness of lead within.

TABLE 3.1 Standard Paper Sizes

Type	Architectural Size (Inches)	Type	Metric Size (mm)
A	8 ½ × 11	A4	210 × 297
B	11 × 17	A3	297 × 240
C	17 × 22	A2	420 × 594
D	24 × 36	A1	594 × 841
E	36 × 48	A0	841 × 1189

Standard Lead Holder (Traditional)

The standard lead holder is sized for the 2 mm lead. There are different 2 mm leads, ranging from 9H (extremely hard) to 6B (extremely soft). The leads typically are sharpened with a lead pointer. There are recommended sharpened tips for each lead hardness. The harder leads will have more of a sharpened point whereas the softer leads will have more of a conical point. For example, the 4H lead should be sharpened to a point, but not so sharp that it could tear your vellum. The H or 2H should be sharpened to a more conical point. If you have made your lead too sharp, simply scribble a little on a piece of paper to take off the sharp point. Always rotate your lead holder slowly while drawing your line to achieve a consistent line weight (thickness). Also, when you rotate your lead while drawing the line, it will not have a flat side. This will produce a drafted line of equal thickness from end to end. To refill your lead holder, insert the lead in the bottom of the lead holder by pushing down on the top of the holder.

Tip

Have a lead holder for each type of lead. This helps to eliminate a mess from changing the leads, because when you change the lead your fingers will get black from the graphite.

Technique for Drawing Lines

When drawing a line, hold the lead holder at an angle between 40 and 60 degrees and slowly rotate the holder away from you as you draw the line. The lead holder can be held between the thumb and pointer finger while resting on your third finger. Roll the lead holder away from you with your thumb. For horizontal lines, pull the lead holder along the parallel bar or straight edge while rolling it slowly away from you. Rotating the lead holder will produce a line of consistent line weight (thickness).

Fine-Line (Micro) Mechanical Pencil

The micro (fine-line) mechanical pencil has different sizes of lead as well as different leads for each size. Again, these range from 9H (extremely hard) to 6B (extremely soft). These leads do not require sharpening. The pencil sizes used for design include 0.3 mm, 0.5 mm, 0.7 mm, and 0.9 mm. The size of the lead will determine the line width. The pencil can be rotated while drawing the line to achieve good line weight. The lead is inserted in the bottom of the pencil. Several pieces of lead can be placed in the lead holder. Push the top of the pencil down to push the lead through as needed (see Figure 3.8).

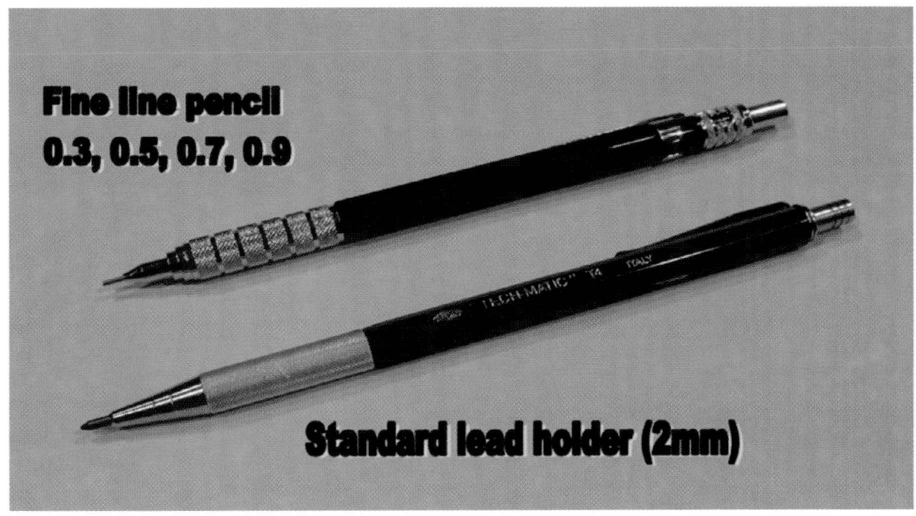

FIGURE 3.8 Standard lead holder and micro-lead holder.

LEADS

The leads used for architectural drafting produce different line thicknesses, known as line weight. Line weight is affected by the paper used (vellum), pressure applied while drawing the line, and the lead used. Leads range from 9H (extremely hard) to 9B (extremely soft) (see Figure 3.9). The softer leads in the B range are more suited for sketching, as they are very soft and will smudge. A harder lead will produce a thin line, whereas the soft lead will produce a thicker, darker line.

Each designer needs to determine which lead is appropriate for his or her own drafting. The tooth or roughness of the vellum will affect the lead. A harder lead is needed if the vellum is rough. The typical leads used for drafting are the H and 2H for most line work and 3H and 4H for the lighter line and for more accuracy. Each individual applies pressure differently while drafting, which affects the line produced, as does the brand of lead used. There are recommended leads to be used depending on the type of line desired.

Lead Pointer

The lead pointer is the sharpener used for sharpening the lead used in standard lead holders (see Figure 3.10). Arrows on the top of the lead pointer are for measuring depths for the particular lead so you will know how far the lead must be out to sharpen effectively. This barrel-shaped sharpener has a hole on top that the lead holder is placed into. Often you need to turn the lead holder slightly so it drops far enough into the sharpener. Next, rotate the lead holder clockwise while applying slight pressure toward the outside edge. You will hear a grinding sound, indicating that the lead is inserted properly and is being sharpened. Once the lead is sharpened properly it can be dipped in the white filter on the top of the sharpener. This will remove any extra graphite remaining from sharpening.

For softer leads the point should be more conical. Harder leads have more of a sharp point. Remember that a lead that is too pointed can tear the vellum. A wood-cased pencil is a bit harder to sharpen. One of the best sharpeners to use for these pencils is a battery or electric sharpener. The hand sharpeners take longer to make the lead pointed and can cause fatigue of the hand or wrist.

Drafting Tape: Rolls or Drafting Dots

Use drafting tape to adhere your paper to the drafting table. This tape is less sticky than masking tape or Scotch™ tape so it does not tear your vellum when removed. You can purchase drafting tape in drafting dots or tape rolls. The dots come in a dispenser and have

LEAD WEIGHTS FOR PENCILS

9H	
8H	Hard Leads Range
7H	Use for light layout line and
6H	for lines requiring more
5H	accuracy-detail work.
4H	
3H	
2H	Medium Leads Range
H	Use for architectural line work,
F	lettering, and general work.
HB	
B	
2B	
3B	Soft Leads Range
4B	Used mainly for sketching.
5B	Too soft for drafting.
6B	

FIGURE 3.9 Range of lead hardness.

FIGURE 3.10 Lead pointer used to sharpen lead.

a clean circular edge. Tape rolls are less expensive than the dots. When you tear off a piece from a roll, typically the edge is ragged. When removing either drafting tape or dots, you must be careful not to tear off the corner of the vellum.

Erasers

Erasers are designed to work on the specific media we use in the field of design. These erasers come in block or stick form. Some are plastic or vinyl formulated to work on vellum or film. The stick form, often called a click eraser, has a hollow tube that can be refilled with a new eraser and works well. Another type of eraser is the electric eraser, which is available in plug-in or battery-operated cordless models. If you hold the powered eraser in one place for too long on drafting paper, you can burn a hole through your vellum. The Pink Pearl® eraser is another smudge-free eraser used for most surfaces.

When drafting, sometimes it is hard to erase lead on the vellum. In chapter 5 we will cover techniques for using light layout lines before we darken so we can erase the lines easily.

Eraser Shield

An eraser shield is a small, thin piece of metal with different sizes and shapes of openings used for erasing lines on a drawing. This tool allows you to precisely erase a part of one line without accidentally erasing a line in the near vicinity. This shield saves wasted time from having to redraw a line that was not to be erased. It is a good habit to use this tool when you erase on your drawings.

Drafting Brush

Drafting (dusting) brushes have wooden handles and long, soft bristles typically made of horsehair. They are available in several sizes. Use this brush to brush away eraser shavings or

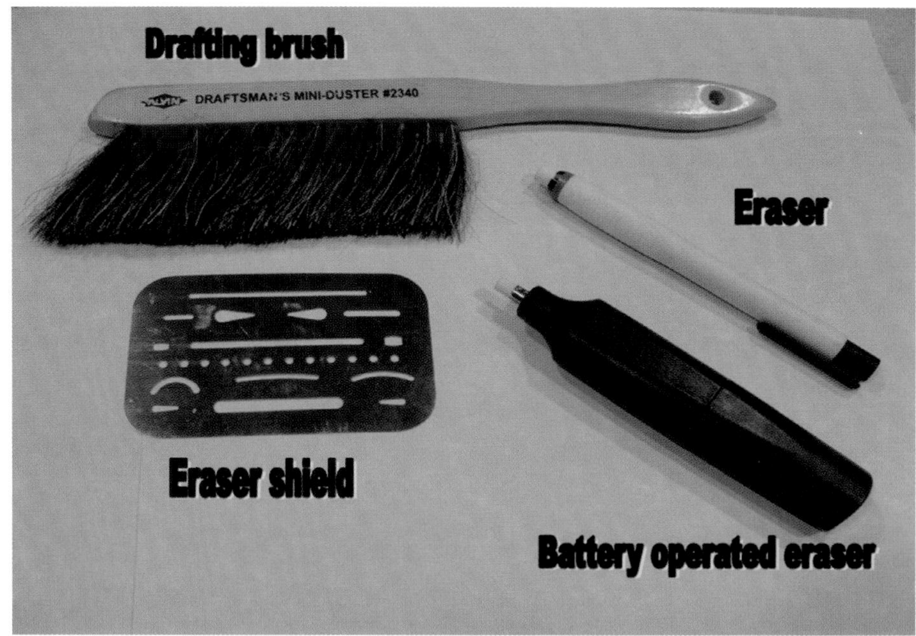

FIGURE 3.11 Two of many available erasers, eraser shield, and drafting brush. The eraser shield allows for precision erasing. Always use the drafting brush to brush off eraser crumbs and graphite.

any lead particles from the drawing without smearing the lines. Do not use your hand to brush off any particles; doing so can smudge the drawing, and oils from your hands can get on the vellum (see Figure 3.11).

Triangle

Triangles are used to draw vertical and angled lines. They are made out of transparent plastic and come in clear or various colors. The contrasting color is easy to see when drafting on vellum. The most commonly used triangles are 45-degree and 30/60-degree ones (see Figure 3.12). These triangles come in several sizes. Commonly used sizes range between 8 and 10″ (203 mm and 254 mm). A 4″ (101 mm) 45-degree triangle is great for detail work. Some triangles have a beveled edge that helps prevent the ink from seeping under the

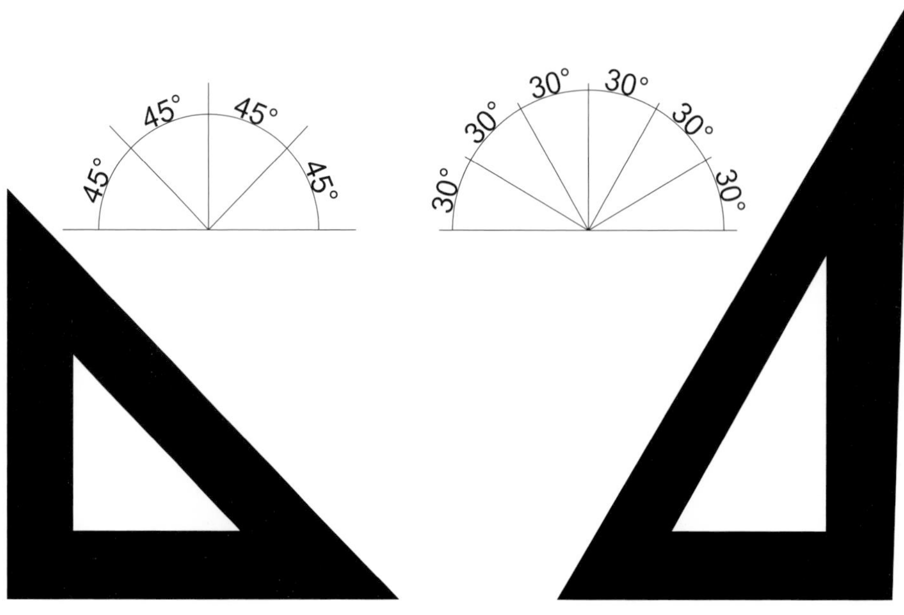

FIGURE 3.12 45-degree and 30/60-degree triangles. Note the angle on the triangles.

triangle and smearing. The triangle sits on the parallel bar or T-square. The following are techniques used to draw angled lines properly without the triangle tipping or moving out of place.

TECHNIQUE FOR DRAWING VERTICAL LINES

To draw a vertical line, first place the triangle on the upper edge of the parallel bar (see Figure 3.13). Place your hand on the triangle to hold it. Next, draw the vertical line in the direction away from the parallel bar. This helps to keep the triangle anchored against the parallel bar. Place the pencil at the base of the triangle at the parallel bar, and draw a line by pulling the pencil upward and away from you. Hold your lead holder at an angle between 40 and 60 degrees, and slowly roll the pencil away from you while pulling upward to draw a consistent line in thickness (line weight). Be aware of the end of triangle when completing the line, as often the line extends past the triangle's end. To continue drawing the vertical line, simply lift the parallel bar slightly and move it and the triangle upward on the drawing paper.

To draw an angled line, draw in the direction toward the parallel bar. This direction helps keep the triangle in place so it will not tip to the side while it is anchored against the horizontal surface. Begin by placing the triangle on the upper edge of the parallel bar. Place your free hand on the triangle to hold it. With your lead holder near the top edge of the triangle's angled side, pull the lead holder down toward the parallel bar while holding it at a 30-degree angle and rotating slowly away from you to achieve consistent line weight. This method does take a bit to get used to, but it saves time because it prevents the triangle from moving. Therefore, you will not have to erase lines and draw them over.

Triangles can be flipped from one side to another while placed on the parallel bar or T-square to achieve the desired angled line and direction of angle. The NKBA triangle shown in Figure 3.14 includes templates for kitchen and bath fixtures.

Adjustable Triangle

The adjustable triangle is another useful drafting tool (see Figure 3.15). It can be adjusted to degrees of angles ranging from 0 to 45 degrees. These triangles also have beveled edges so inking may be done without the ink seeping under the triangle.

Store all triangles properly to prevent chipping.

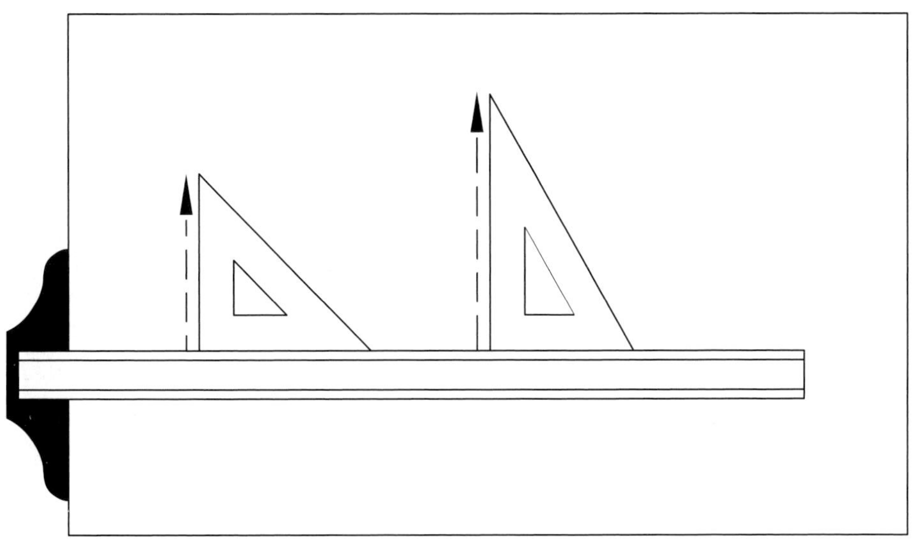

FIGURE 3.13 Draw vertical lines from the bottom up so the triangle doesn't tip. For angled lines, draw line from top and draw toward the parallel bar.

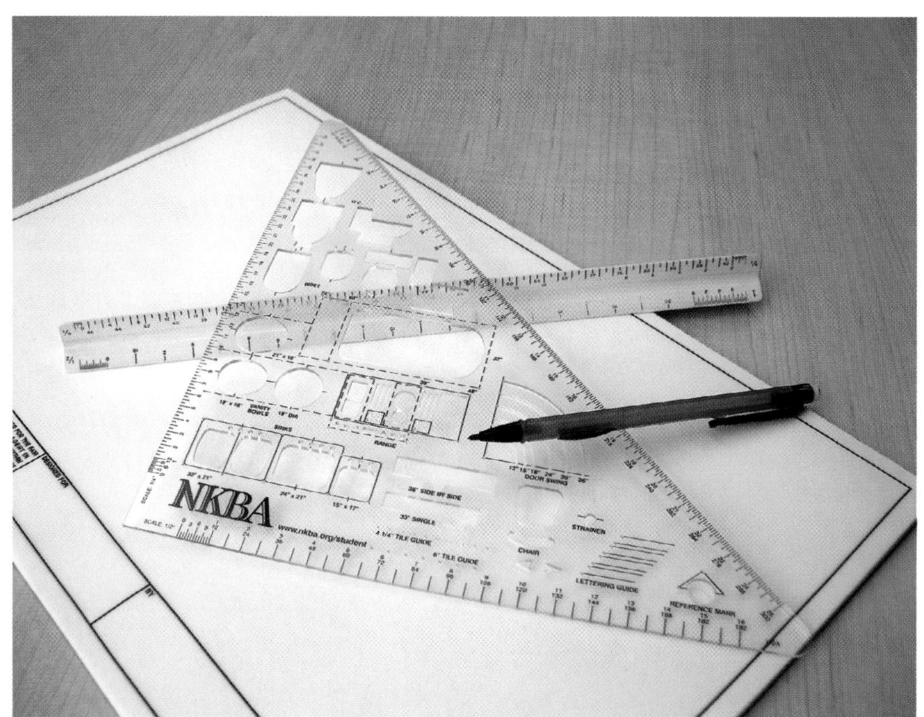

FIGURE 3.14 NKBA triangle with template. This 45-degree triangle has convenient units of measurements on sides.

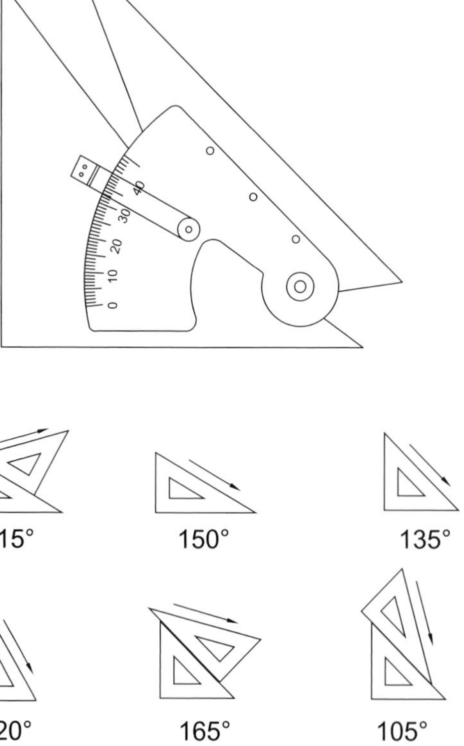

FIGURE 3.15 Adjustable triangles allow you to draw different angles.

Protractor

A protractor is another tool we can use for drawing and measuring angles (see Figure 3.16). Protractors are available in either plastic or metal and come in half-rounds that measures angles 0 to 180 degrees and full circles that measure 360 degrees. The degrees for each angle are listed on the semicircular edge. These degree marks can be read from left to right or right to left, depending on the type of angle you are working with. In kitchen and bath design, we often need to draw an angle we can't achieve with the triangle. The protractor can assist us in drafting the correct angle.

To measure an angle using the protractor, align the horizontal line of the angle with the protractor. Place the crosshair in the center of the horizontal edge of the protractor on the line where the angled line converges with the horizontal line on your plan. Next, determine what number the angled line intersects on the curved edge of the protractor to determine the degree of the angle. The same rule applies for using the top or bottom row of numbers on the protractor. Use the appropriate row of numbers on the protractor's edge to determine the degree of the angle.

Scale

In kitchen and bath design, drawings are drafted in a measureable scale. A scale is used to measure and also to draw objects so they will fit on a certain size of paper accurately, in proportion to the scale specified. In the design industry, standard sizes of scales are used for specific drawings. If a drawing is "to scale," the items are proportionately accurate so items and distances can be dimensioned and measured accurately in the scale used. A drawing that is not to scale is not accurate; correct dimensions cannot be determined from that drawing. Drawings not to scale can give a visual representation of what the item or space will look like. Most drawings that we draft in kitchen and bath design are drawn to scale.

The scale used for NKBA drawings is ½″ =1′– 0″ (1:20) this means that on a drawing, a line half an inch long is equal to 1′– 0″ (1′). American Institute of Architects (AIA) standards for construction drawings are drawn at a scale of ¼″ = 1′– 0″. Designers must be able to interpret drawings in another scale and draft it in accordance with the NKBA Graphic Standards.

Architects Scale

The architect's scale measures items in units of feet and inches. The typical architects scale used by designers is triangular shaped and has eleven different scales on the sides. On each side of the architects scale there are two scales printed. Each scale is half the amount of the other on that same side. For example, the ½″ and 1″ scale are on the same side. The ⅛″ and ¼″ scales are on the same side. One side of the scale is read from left to right while the other reads right to left. It is very important to determine which row of numbers to read for the particular scale you are working with. The "0" mark helps determine if you need to read the

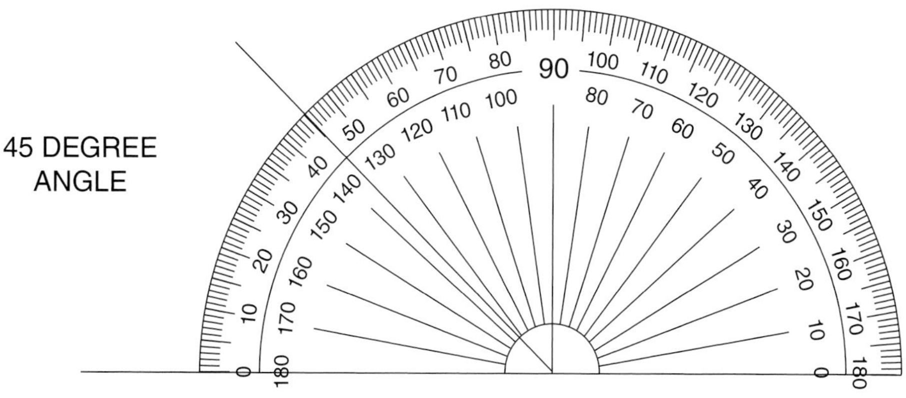

FIGURE 3.16 A protractor can be used for drawing an angle or measuring an angle. Note: As mentioned, the NKBA drafting table has a protractor built into the parallel bar.

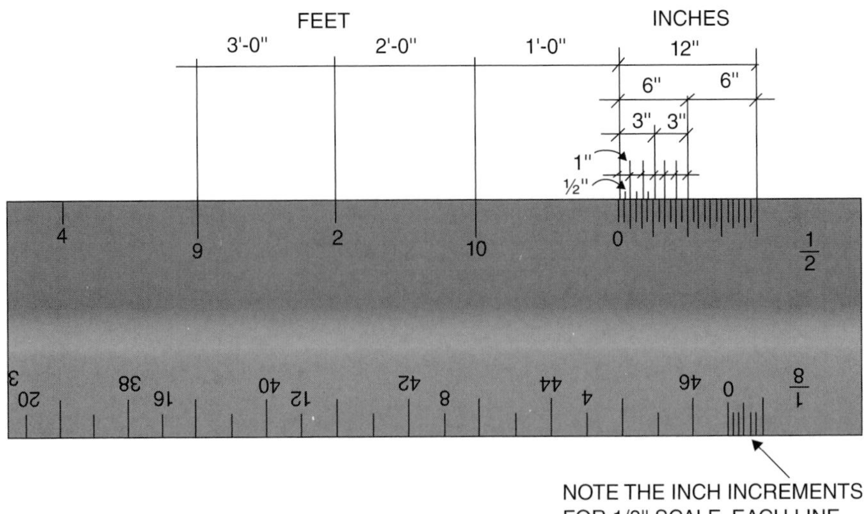

FIGURE 3.17 Comparison of 1/2″ and 1″ scale.

upper row or the bottom row of numbers on the particular side for the given scale. There are also 6″ flat scales with beveled edges available as a smaller the portable scale (see figures 3.17 and 3.18).

Metric Scale

The metric scale measures System International (SI), or metric units. Millimeters (mm) are the most commonly used measurement for architectural drawings.

Common units include the meter, which at 39⅓″ is slightly more than 1 yard. The centimeter is 0.39″. You can reduce or enlarge the metric scale by moving the decimal point. To convert inches to millimeters, divide inches by 25.4. To convert inches to centimeters, divide inches by 2.54.

Like the architect's scale, the metric scale also has six edges. We work with 1:20 for the ½″ scale (see Figures 3.19 and 3.20.).

Templates

Templates are pieces of plastic with shapes cut out to use for floor plans or elevations. Many templates are available, with shapes for kitchen items, bath items, door swings, geometric shapes, furniture, and many more. Manufacturers also have templates for their products, such as cabinetry, plumbing, appliances, and furniture, among others. Templates come in different scales (see Figure 3.21).

Since the NKBA plans are drafted in ½″ scale, make sure to use a template with that scale. Many templates used in residential design are ¼″ scale. The smaller-scale template can be

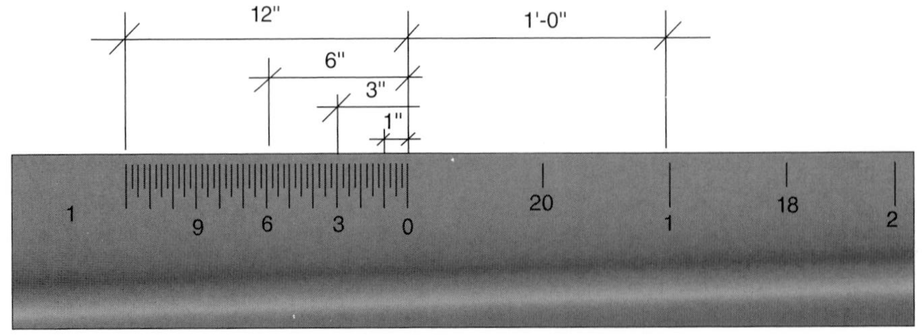

FIGURE 3.18 Reading the scale.

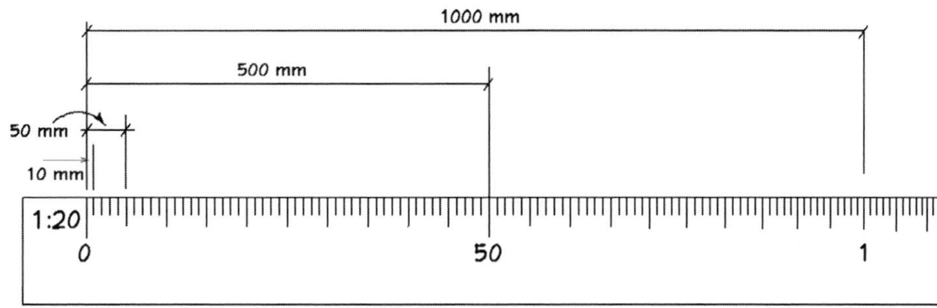

HALF SCALE = 1:20 (CLOSE TO 1/2" SCALE)

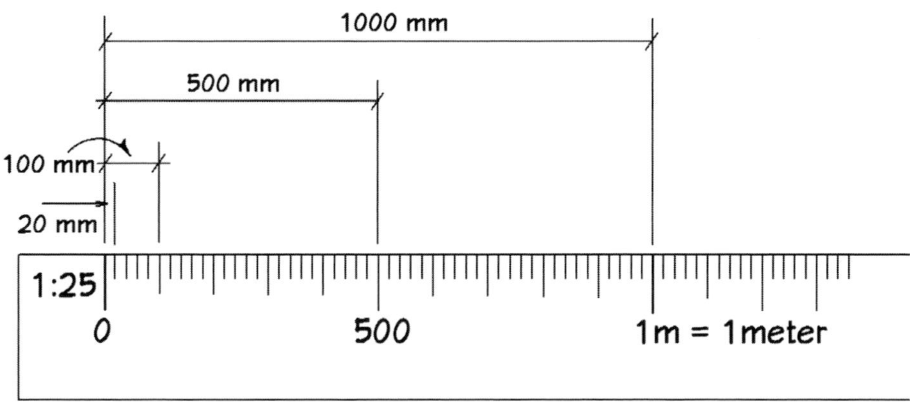

ONE TWENTY FIFTH SCALE = 1:25

FIGURE 3.19 Metric scale increments.

photocopied and enlarged to the ½″ scale and used as an underlay. The underlay is placed under your sheet of vellum and the shape is traced. The NKBA triangle/template has very useful cutouts to use for floor plans and elevations. It also has door swings and lettering guides. Figure 3.14 shows the NKBA template.

Compass

A compass is used to draw circles and arcs. Several styles of compasses are available (see Figure 3.22). One end of a compass has an adjustable needle point while the other end has a lead point. The drafting compass is designed to hold a piece of lead, not a whole pencil, which is a great feature. The wheel in the center or on the side can be adjusted. There are attachments for drawing larger circles and for holding pencils and pens, if desired. To keep the circle radius consistent, you must sharpen the pencil lead in a beveled fashion with the beveled edge facing out. To do so, rub the bevel side of the lead back and forth along sandpaper. The bevel point should be between 1⁄64″ and 1⁄32″ shorter than the needle point.

To draw a circle using a compass, adjust the compass to size of the circle desired. The radius will be half of the diameter. A 1″ radius will produce a 2″ circle. The diameter is the distance

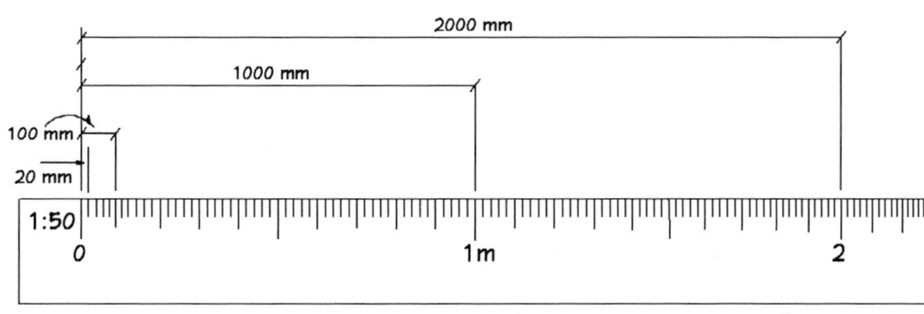

ONE FIFTIETH SCALE = 1:50 (CLOSE TO 1/4" SCALE)

FIGURE 3.20 Metric scale.

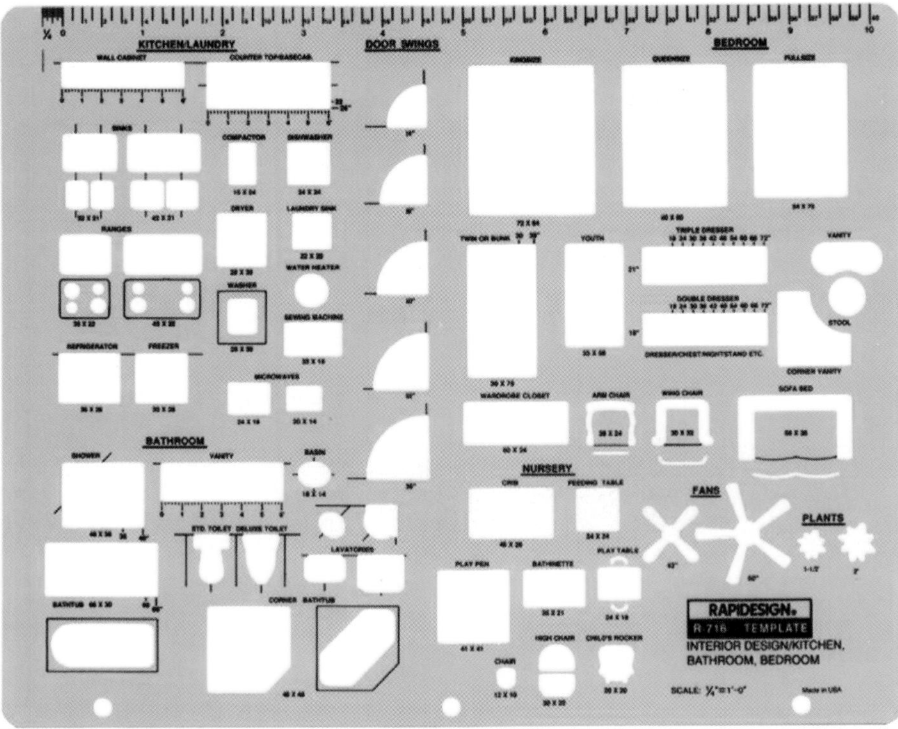

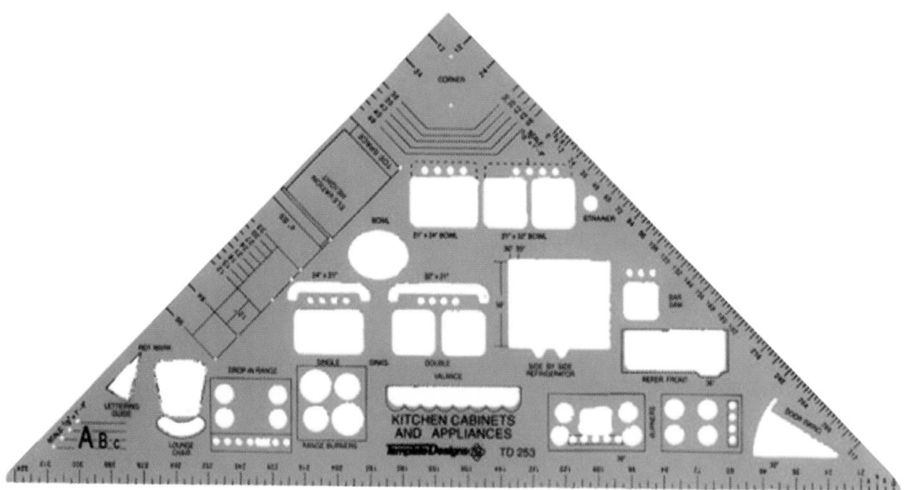

FIGURE 3.21 Examples of templates.
Courtesy of Alvin & Co., Inc.

from one side of the circle to the other. Place the needle in location for the circle to be drawn, hold the compass perpendicular to the paper, and swing the lead without applying too much pressure, which can create a hole in the paper. Place a small piece of tape under the needle pointer to help prevent a hole or a tear from occurring at that location.

Dividers

Dividers are used to transfer distances of items without needing the actual dimensions. A divider looks like a compass but has two points and no lead. To use, place the divider at the end points of the line or space you want to transfer the distance from. Next, hold the divider in that position and move it to where you would like the line or distance placed. To double the distance, "walk" the divider once while holding onto the top of the divider which will add the distance on that measurement.

Irregular Curves: "French Curves"

Templates for irregular curves, or French curves, come in many sizes and styles and are made of plastic. The curves are available in clear and different colors, which allow for contrast

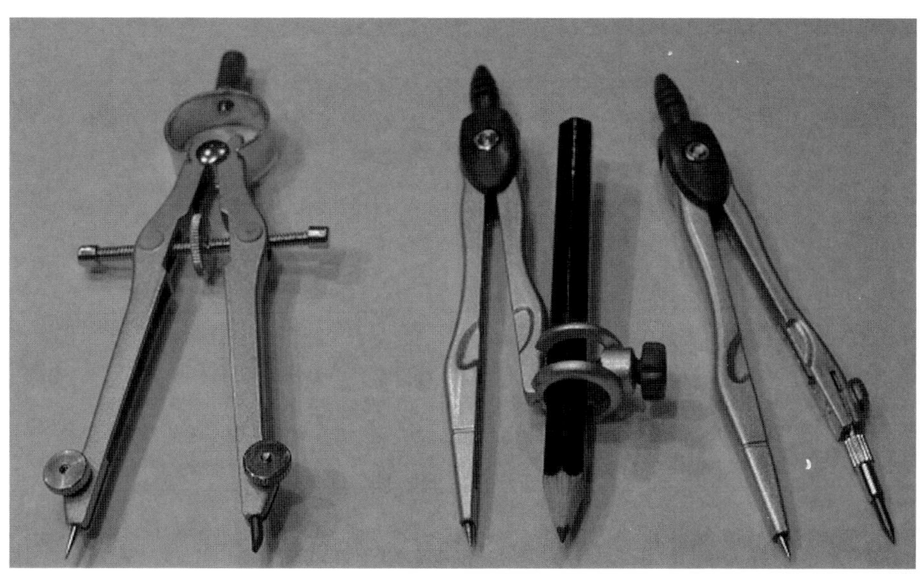

FIGURE 3.22 The drafting compass is used to draw circles and arcs. The divider is used to transfer distances between items without needing the exact dimensions.

against the drawing surface so you can see the line better when drawing. The irregular curve is used to draw arcs of varying sizes on a drawing. It is best to have several irregular curves of different lengths.

To use the irregular curve on a drawing, select the side of the curve that gives you the arc you are looking for. When you need to continue drawing the line longer, move the curve and select one of the curved sides so you can continue drawing your line in a continuous manner (see Figure 3.23).

Flexible Curve

A flexible curve is a piece of rubber with a flat bottom that can be shaped to form any curve. Some flexible curves have a scale on them for measuring. The flexible curve will assist you in hard-lining any curved line that cannot be drawn using a compass, irregular curve, or template.

FIGURE 3.23 French curves come in different sizes and configurations.

Press-on or Stick-on Lettering

Plan enhancement sheets of press-on lettering, symbols, people, and accessories are available to place on drawings. Label makers are another inexpensive way to label items on your drawing. Labels come in clear, black, or white (see Figure 3.24).

Pens and Lettering Guides

Technical Pens

Technical pens are used for inking a drawing. There are two types, are renewable and nonrenewable.

Renewable pens are designed so that you can refill the ink when it runs out. These pens require more maintenance to keep clean and in good condition than nonrenewable pens do. Shaking the pen will create a rattling noise so you will know it isn't clogged. Do not overfill renewable pens, and clean them after each use. Some pens are available with a snap-on cartridge ink refill. These come in different sizes with the range of 000 to 4 recommended for drafting. The 000 size produces thinner lines, and 4 produces thicker lines.

Nonrenewable pens are similar to felt-tip pens. These pens are less expensive than renewable ones, are not refillable, and are discarded when empty. The sizes of these pens are 01, 03, 05, and 07. The largest is 07.

Inking Considerations

- Hold the pen perpendicular to the drafting board to ensure good ink flow.
- Use a triangle with a lip or beveled edge to prevent ink from seeping under it and smearing. You can tape coins to the back of triangle to raise it.
- Always lift the tools, and don't drag on the ink.

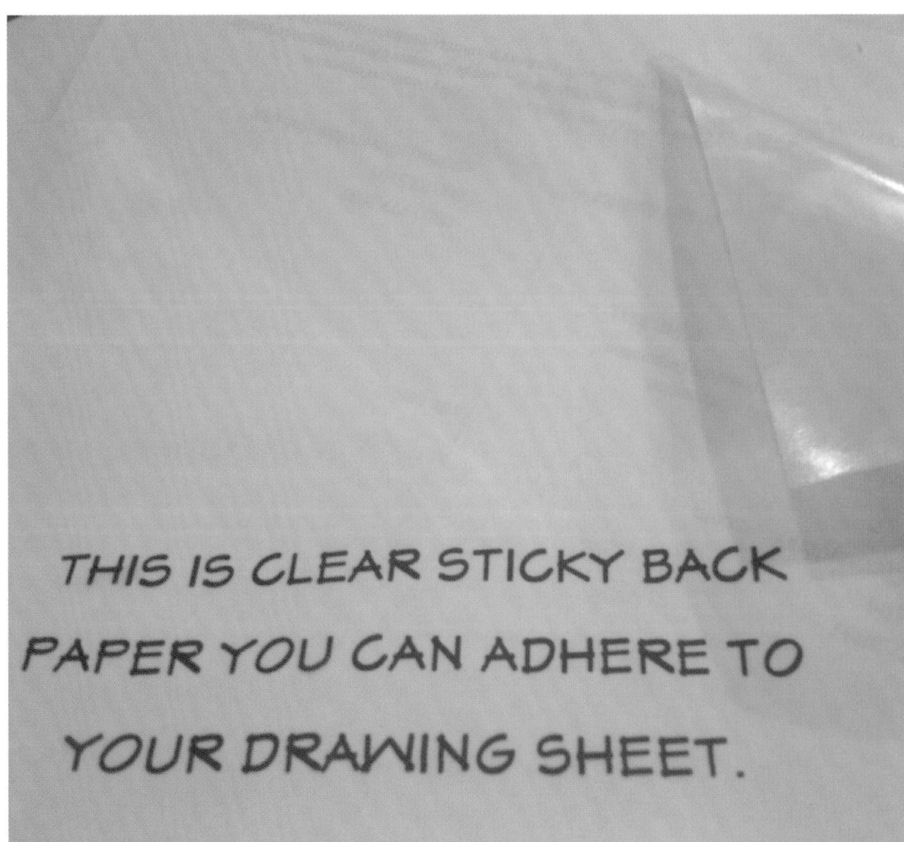

FIGURE 3.24 Sticky-back paper can be used to label your drawings in a quick manner. Simply type or photocopy item on the sheet and adhere to your vellum.

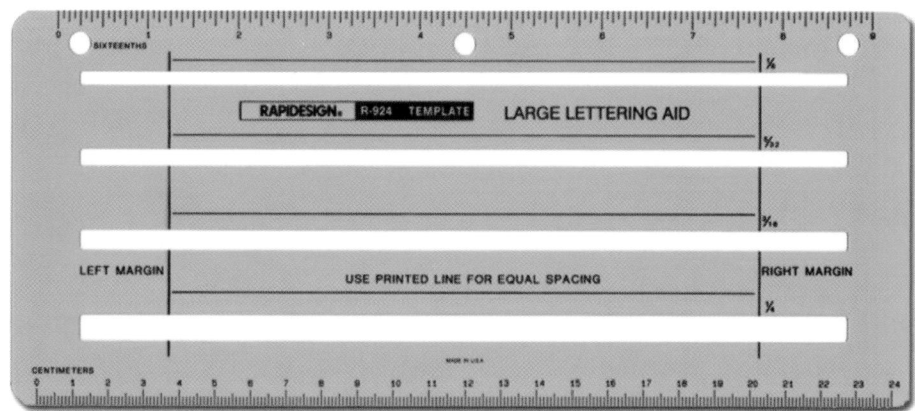

FIGURE 3.25 Simple lettering guide assists with drawing horizontal lines for architectural lettering.
Courtesy of Alvin & Co., Inc.

- Keep the pens moving at the same speed. Stopping or slowing can cause the ink to pool.
- When inking a drawing, start at the top. Draw all horizontal lines beginning on the left side and working to the right. Next draw all vertical lines. Allow the lines to dry properly.
- Always clean renewable pens well and maintain properly

Lettering Guides

Lettering guides are used to draw light guidelines for architectural lettering. The lines are drawn lightly and are used as a guide for the height of letters. Two main types of lettering guides are used in the industry: the lettering aid and the Ames Lettering Guide.

The lettering aid is a simple lettering guide that allows you to quickly draw guidelines for lettering one line of text (see Figure 3.25). Standard heights of letters range from $\frac{1}{8}$ to $\frac{1}{4}$″.

The Ames Lettering Guide shown in Figure 3.26 is the most commonly used guide in design. It enables you to draw guidelines for multiple rows of text. You can select the height and spacing for the desired lettering. The guide allows one to architecturally letter drawings at various heights with spacing that is standard in the industry.

The Ames Lettering Guide is based on the units of 32nds. You can set the center dial to the number that enables you to achieve a specific height. For example, if we want $\frac{1}{8}$″-high letters, turn the center dial so that the number 4 lines up with the tick mark at the bottom of the circle. This means that $\frac{4}{32}$ can be reduced to $\frac{1}{8}$″. Your letters will be $\frac{1}{8}$″ high, with a spacing of $\frac{1}{16}$. If you set the dial to 8, you will have $\frac{1}{4}$″-high letters since $\frac{8}{32}$ can be reduced to $\frac{1}{4}$. Note the various rows of holes on the dial. Each can be used to create different spacing with the letter heights.

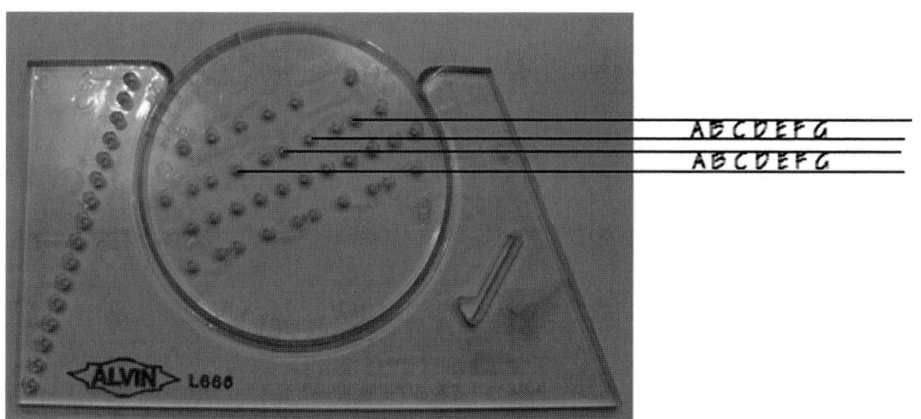

FIGURE 3.26 Ames Lettering Guide.

How to use the Ames Lettering Guide

Begin by drawing letters ⅛″ high with 1⁄16″ spacing between:

1. Have your drafting table set up and ready to draft.
2. Turn the center circle piece of your Ames Lettering Guide so that the number 4 lines up with the tick mark at the bottom of the circle.
3. Place your lettering guide on the top edge of your parallel bar. Position lettering guide so it is at the left side of parallel bar.
4. A sharp lead—a 4H or 0.3 works well. Insert your lead in the top hole found in the third row of holes from top.
5. Slide the lettering guide across the paper against the parallel bar to draw your light guideline. Keep your lettering guide in that position on the parallel bar.
6. Next, skip a hole and place your lead in third hole in same row. Slide your lettering guide going in the opposite direction against the parallel bar to draw the next guideline. Maintain the position of the lettering guide.
7. Place your lead in the next hole down in the same row which is the fourth hole. Slide the lettering guide to the opposite side to draw the guideline. Maintain the position of the lettering guide.
8. Skip a hole and place your lead in the sixth hole in same row. Slide the guide back to the opposite side to draw the guideline. Note: you now have ⅛″ guidelines with a 1⁄16″ spacing.
9. Keep drawing lines back and forth to form guidelines that you will use for lettering.
10. When you reach the last hole, place hole number 0 on the last line drawn and repeat steps 3 through 8.
11. If you want ¼″-high letters, place the lead in every fourth hole in row 3.

Architectural Lettering

Architectural lettering (lettering) is a technique used for writing notes on a drawing. The style of architectural lettering is consistent in height and will remain legible if the drawings are reduced in scale (see Figure 3.27). Lettering makes a drawing look professional. Sloppy or bad lettering can take away from the drawing. As a designer, it is good to use architectural lettering for all other writing you do besides your drawings.

In architectural lettering, the letters are all caps and the style can vary slightly. The vertical lines remain completely vertical while the horizontals are typically slanted upward. Some individuals vary the slanted lines by using a thicker line for them.

Use a quick hand motion to draw the vertical lines. If you draw the lines slowly, your hand can get shaky and produce a line that is not vertical. The more you practice, the better your letter strokes will be. Some people use a triangle to draw the vertical lines. To do so, they draw the vertical lines first, then the horizontal ones. It is good to train your hand to draw without the use of a triangle.

FIGURE 3.27 Architectural lettering styles.

LETTERING ON KITCHEN & BATH PLANS
SHOULD BE PERCEIVED AS
HAVING EQUAL VISUAL SPACING

VISUAL SPACING

MECHANICAL SPACING

LETTERING ON KITCHEN & BATH PLANS
SHOULD NOT HAVE ACTUAL
MECHANICAL SPACING

FIGURE 3.28 Spacing for lettering is visual; it is not exactly between the letters but is perceived to be.

The spacing of architectural lettering is more visual than mechanical. This means that the spacing differs depending on the letter width. For instance, an *I* would be closer to the adjacent letters than a *P* (see Figure 3.28.). Use lettering guides to establish consistent heights of letters throughout the drawings. Your lines can go slightly past the guidelines, but they should not be shorter.

Standard heights of lettering are used on drawings. Just as with the line weights, there is a hierarchy of lettering (see Figure 3.29). Again, the standardized lettering height creates a consistent, professional-looking drawing. Four sizes of lettering are used. Typically the most general information is lettered with the largest size of ½″ and the most detailed information is at a shorter height of ⅛″.

- ½″ height: Title block lettering
- ¼″ height: Titles of legends, specifications, and drawings
- ⅛″ to 3⁄16″ height: Nomenclature, specifications, notes
- ⅛″ height: Notes on drawing details

Drawing Enhancements

Color enhances a drawing. Hints of color can be added for contrast. (see Figure 3.30). The use of colored markers and pencils is an art form all its own (see Figures 3.31 and 3.32). Hinting at the color of cabinets and fixtures makes a presentation come to life without being distracting. There are a wide variety of colored markers and pencils from which to choose.

1/2" = TITLE BLOCK

1/4" = TITLE OF LEGEND/SPECIFICATIONS

1/8 TO 3/16" = NOMENCLATURE, SPECIFICATIONS, NOTES

1/8" = NOTES ON DRAWING DETAILS

FIGURE 3.29 Architectural lettering heights used.

When selecting colored pencils, look for soft, heavily pigmented leads, which give even tones and make blending easy. Using markers designed for use with a specific medium will ensure good results.

The type of paper used for marker and pencil renderings greatly affects the finished appearance. Markers can be used on almost any type of drafting or art paper. Watercolor markers are designed to work well on vellum and other papers. Pencils are also recommended for use with vellum. When reproducing colored drawings in black and white, first make a copy using scrap paper because colors may appear muddy or parts of the drawing may be obscured.

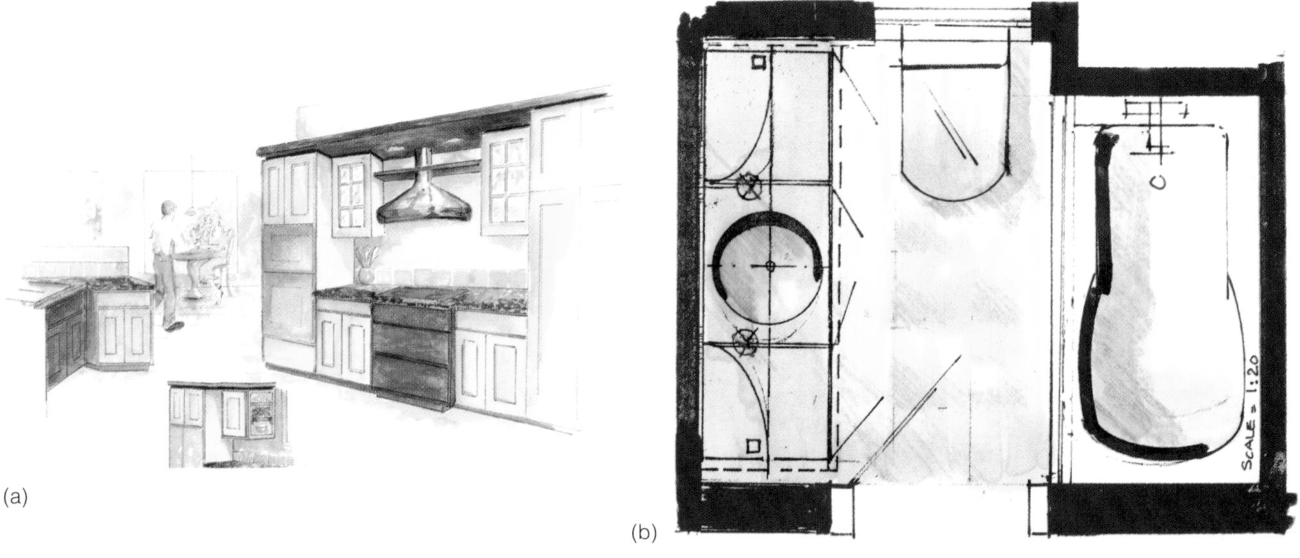

FIGURE 3.30 Use of color on plans, elevations, and perspectives.
A courtesy of Trudy Summerill; B and C courtesy of Ines Hanl

FIGURE 3.31 An example of a drawing enhanced with color and shading effects.
Courtesy of St. Charles of New York

FIGURE 3.32 An example of a drawing enhanced with colored markers. Note the shading.
Courtesy of Richard Landon, CMKBD

FIGURE 3.33 Tabletop portfolio. Portfolios come in various sizes and shapes.
Courtesy of Alvin & Co., Inc.

PORTFOLIOS

Throughout your design career, you will present your projects to clients, potential employers, home show attendees, or others. You need to decide which presentation style suits you, depending on where you will be presenting and the best way to show off the project.

Some smaller portfolios stand to resemble a tabletop easel for convenient viewing. You may also consider a notebook-style presentation that can be given to the client once the project is installed. You can insert contact information for your company and the selected manufacturers' products so the client has one source to go to when questions arise after the project is complete (see Figure 3.33).

One way to present a project is to create a portfolio that allows you to put the drawings into acetate or plastic sleeves and flip through them like a book. An 18″ × 24″ portfolio is a popular size. It is easy to carry and small enough to show the client at a table or desk. Drawings are placed in the sleeves so they face the person across from you. This allows room for labels or notes in addition to the 11″ × 17″ drawings. An 11″ × 17″ portfolio has sleeves that fit only the drawings. If you get a portfolio with a binder, you can change out the drawings while they are still in the sleeves if necessary (see Figure 3.34).

You may prefer to show the project mounted on matte board or foam core board and displayed on an easel (see Figure 3.35). Each drawing is mounted onto an individual board using a spray adhesive on the back of the drawing. The board usually is cut to the same size as the drawing. Some designers add a matte around it as a frame or cut off the title block, leaving just the drawing and adding a colored border with marker or tape. If time allows or the presentation warrants it, add materials samples, appliance photographs, and other items on the board to complete the presentation. The board is referred to as a presentation board, sample board, or concept board.

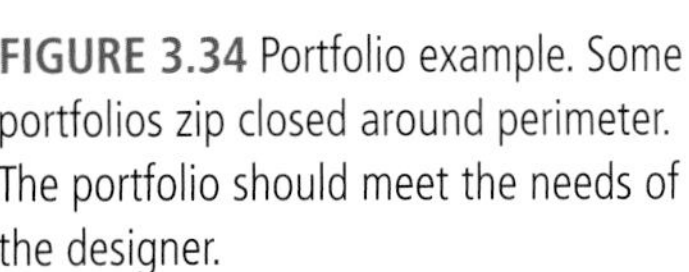

FIGURE 3.34 Portfolio example. Some portfolios zip closed around perimeter. The portfolio should meet the needs of the designer.
Courtesy of Alvin & Co., Inc.

FIGURE 3.35 Mounted and/or matted projects are a standard way to present projects to a client.

Some designers simply place a piece of black fabric on the table and place product samples on there for the client to view. Many times designers don't have the time to put a board together.

Digital boards are also used. A presentation board can be put together using a computer to place pictures on the electronic board of products and colors used in the design.

Notebook Presentations

Consider what you will do with your project drawings after completing each job. Perhaps make an album of before-and-after photographs, placing them next to reduced drawings of the new designs. This becomes a great portfolio to show prospective clients who visit your showroom and is easily transported to home shows. Keep in mind that you should be collecting your projects in a portfolio for future job interviews.

Another technique used for presenting drawings is to create a PowerPoint presentation. This works well when conducting a presentation to more than one individual.

Storage

After you have completed the drawings, you need a way to store them safely. (see Figure 3.36). The type of presentation you choose may be the best way to store the project. For example, a shelf of notebooks, one for each client, can be very handy. Some companies prefer to store all their projects in a cabinet with shallow drawers designed to accommodate large drawings. Cabinets made of cardboard may have drawers that pull out individually so they can be taken to a presentation. Many designers still prefer to roll large drawings and store them in tubes. This method can be convenient if you need to mail drawings, but rolled drawings make presentations more difficult because the drawings do not lay flat and need to be weighted on the ends while you show each one.

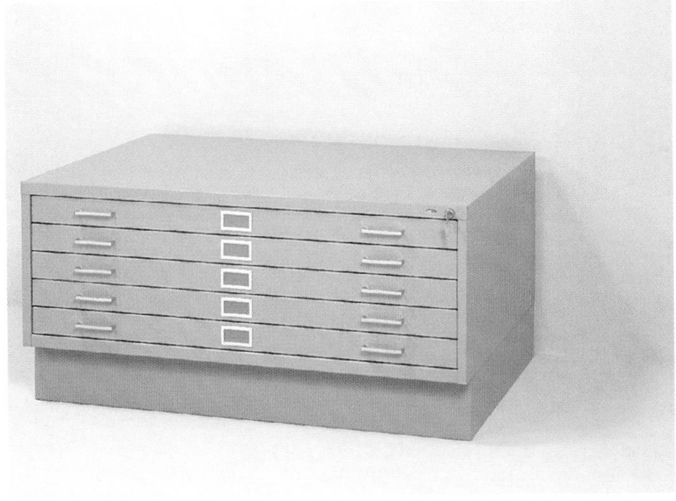

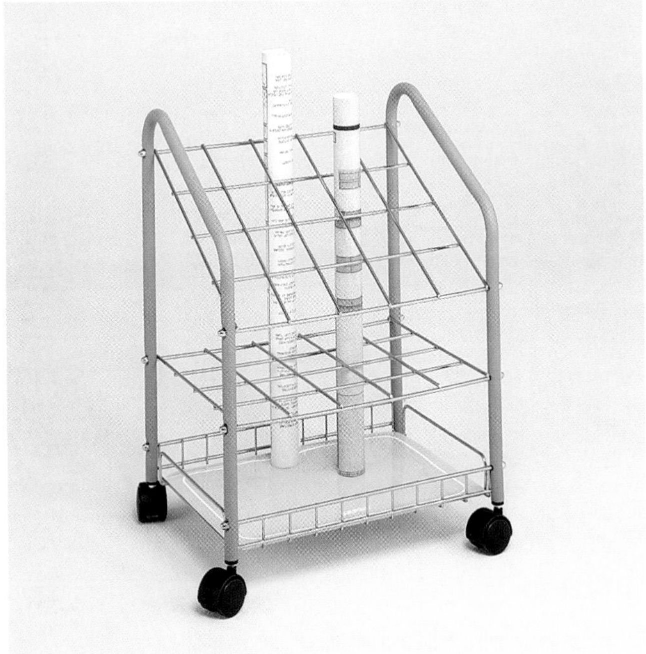

FIGURE 3.36 Examples of storage for drawings.
Courtesy of NKBA

ADDITIONAL TECHNIQUES TO DRAW ANGLED LINES AND UNDERSTAND ANGLES

There are several techniques we use to draw angled lines and also to understand angles better within a space. As designers, we often need to find the center point of a line that does not have a dimension or need to create a proportioned division of that given line. The techniques presented next will assist you with those unique situations.

Drawing Parallel Lines

When the floor plan contains an odd-angled wall you may want to repeat the line of the angle elsewhere within the space. The first step is to draw this by placing any side of your triangle along the given angled line. Move the straightedge in position along the bottom edge of your triangle.

For the second step, while holding the straightedge in place, slide the triangle into the new desired position, being sure to keep the bottom edge against the straightedge. Draw your line (refer to Figure 3.37).

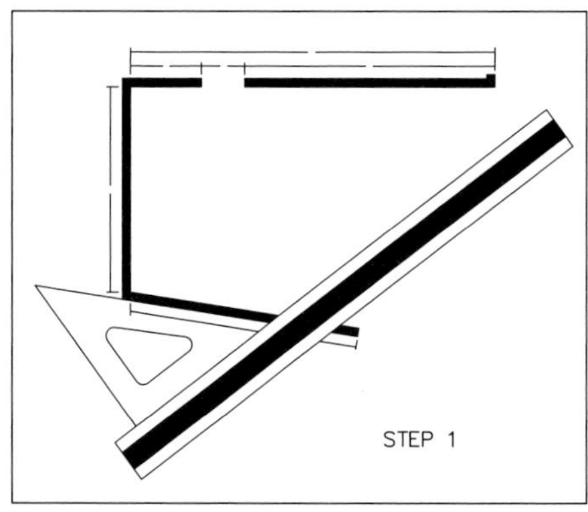

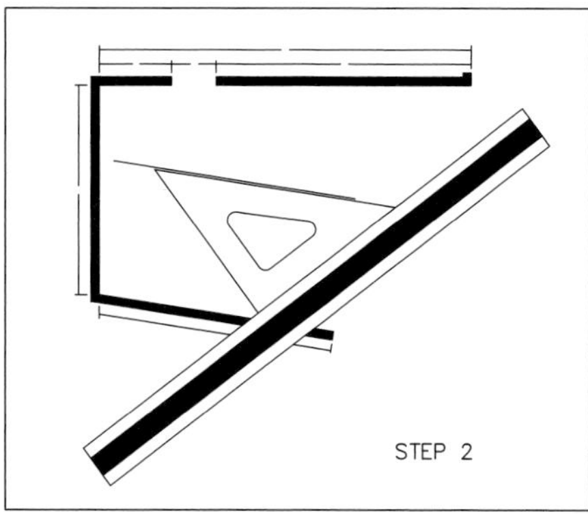

FIGURE 3.37 Constructing parallel lines.

Drawing Perpendicular Lines

Now that you've constructed the parallel line, you'll probably need to draw a perpendicular line through it. Step 1: place your straightedge in position with the 45-degree triangle (short side) aligned with the line. Step 2: hold the straightedge in place and slide the triangle until it is at the desired place of intersection. Draw a line through the point (refer to Figure 3.38).

Bisecting a Line

To produce symmetrical design drawings, you need to know how to bisect a line. Bisecting a line involves finding the center point of that line. For instance, given a length of wall on which you need to center a sink cabinet, you will first need to bisect the wall line in order to determine its midpoint.

One option is to bisect a line with a compass. Set the compass larger than half the length of the line and draw an arc from each end of the line so that the two arcs intersect each other. Draw a line where these intersect. The line that passes through the intersecting points of the arcs bisects the original line.

Another option is to use a straightedge and triangle to bisect a line. Hold the straightedge parallel to the line, and draw an equal angle from each end with your triangle toward the center of the line. Then draw a vertical line through the intersection and bisect the original line (see Figure 3.39).

Dividing a Line into Equal Parts

Kitchen drawings often involve decorative tile patterns that need to be illustrated in both floor plan and elevation views. A common illustration might include a 3″ × 3″ tile accent stripe between two rows of 12″ × 12″ tiles. After you draw the 12″ tile, you can find the 3″

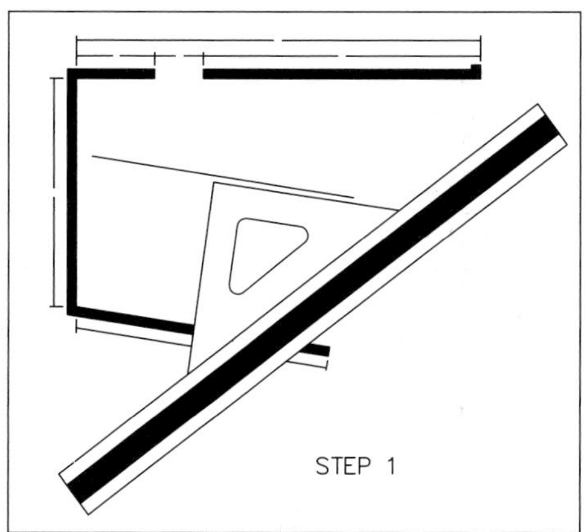

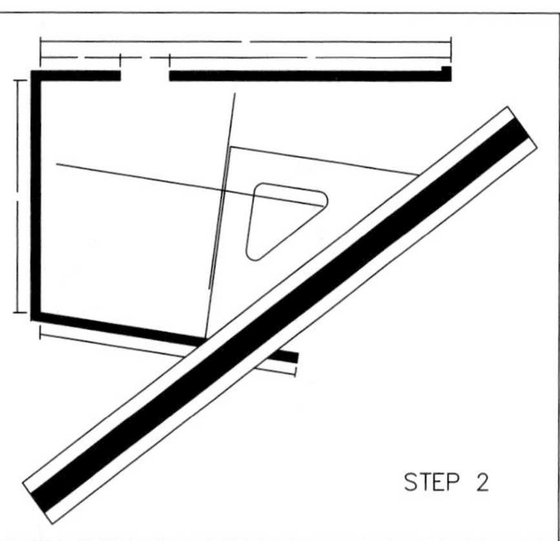

FIGURE 3.38 Constructing perpendicular lines.

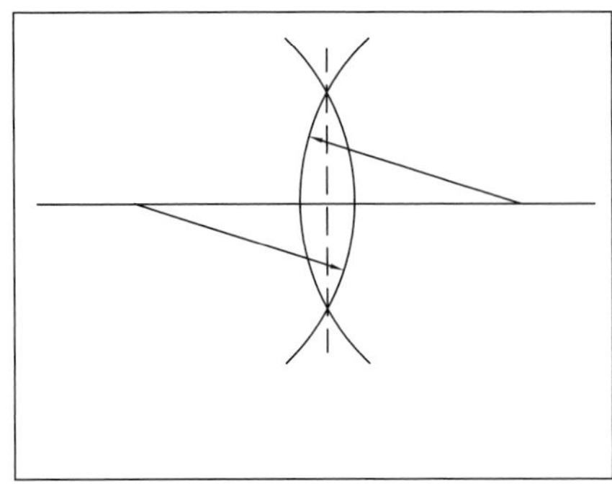

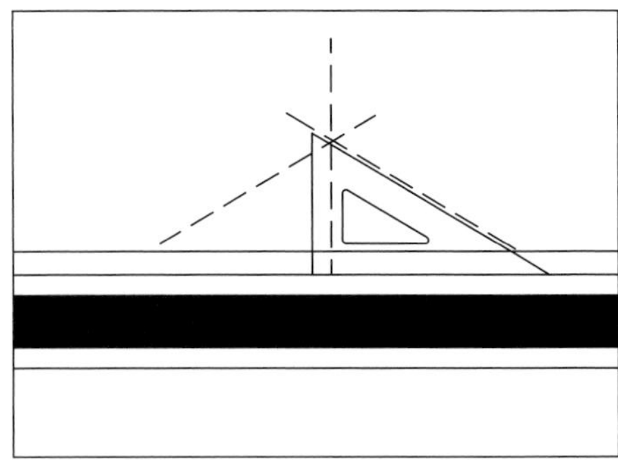

FIGURE 3.39 Bisecting a line.

OPTION 1

OPTION 2

tile lines by dividing the 12″ length into four equal parts. Here is an easy method for dividing a line equally using an architect's scale:

1. Draw a line at any angle from one end of the line to be divided. This line does not have to be the same length as the line to be divided; rather, it should be of a length that can be easily divided by the required number of equal parts on the scale being used (see Figure 3.40).
2. Mark the angled line into equal divisions using your scale. Draw a line from the last mark to the opposite end of the line to be divided. Parallel to that last line drawn, draw lines through the remaining marks and through the line to be divided.

Dividing a Space into Equal Sections

Use a similar method when the space to be divided is between two parallel lines (see Figure 3.41). Find the beginning and end of the number of sections required on your scale. Pivot the scale until it spans the space equally and mark the intermediate points. Draw parallel lines through the points.

You can use this method to draw windows or glass door cabinetry with mullions or to locate light fixtures evenly in a given space.

Definition of Angles

An angle is formed by the meeting of two lines. How the two lines meet defines the type of angle. The three types of angles are acute, right, and obtuse. An acute angle is one that is less than 90 degrees. An angle equal to 90 degrees or with two perpendicular legs is a right angle. Any angle more than 90 degrees is called an obtuse angle (see Figure 3.42).

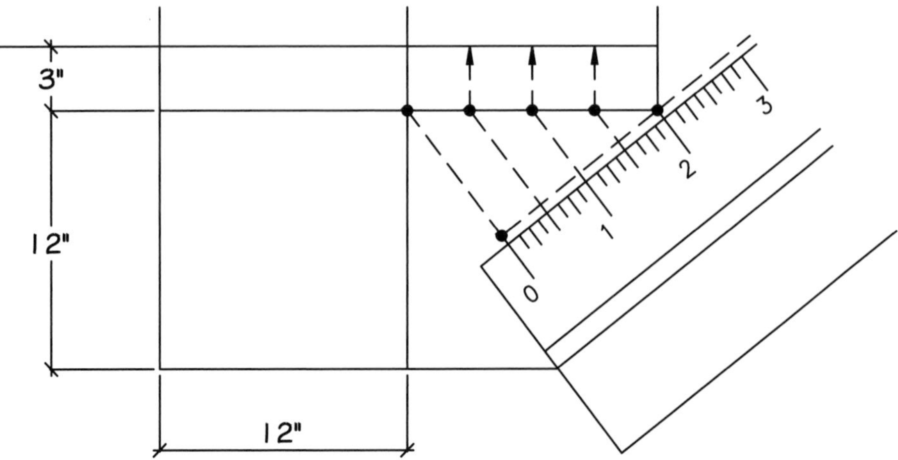

FIGURE 3.40 Dividing a line into equal parts.

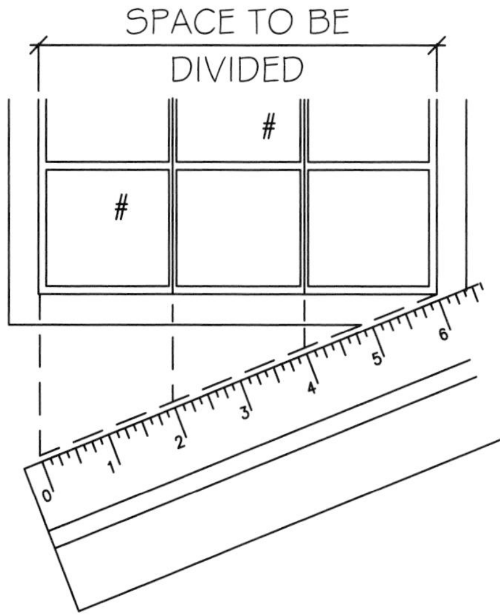

FIGURE 3.41 Dividing a space into equal parts.

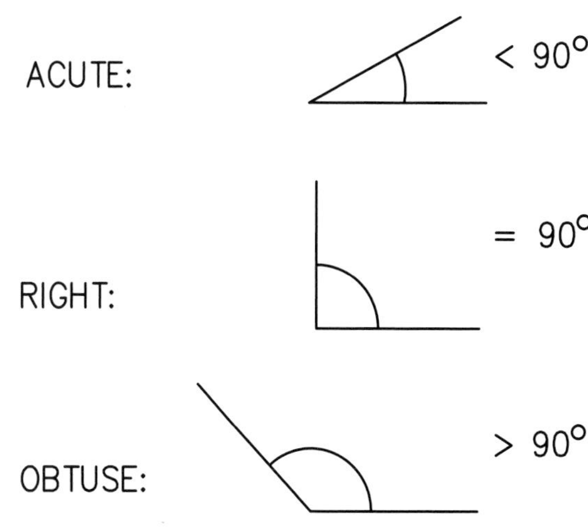

FIGURE 3.42 It is important for a designer to know the types of angles.

Definition of Triangles

Angles are also used to define the types of triangles they create. An acute triangle has three angles each less than 90 degrees. The right triangle has one angle equal to 90 degrees, and the obtuse triangle has one angle more than 90 degrees (see Figure 3.43).

The right triangle is the most common angle in angular design situations. To determine the dimensions of cabinetry to be installed on an angle, identify the triangles it forms and their side dimensions. List the known geometric factors: one angle is 90 degrees, one leg of the triangle is equal to the cabinet depth, and the other two angles are determined by your choice for placement.

The interior angles will add up to 180 degrees. Therefore, if you are placing a cabinet at a 45-degree angle, the remaining angle will also be 45 degrees. If you are placing a cabinet at a 30-degree angle, the remaining angle will be 60 degrees (see Figure 3.44).

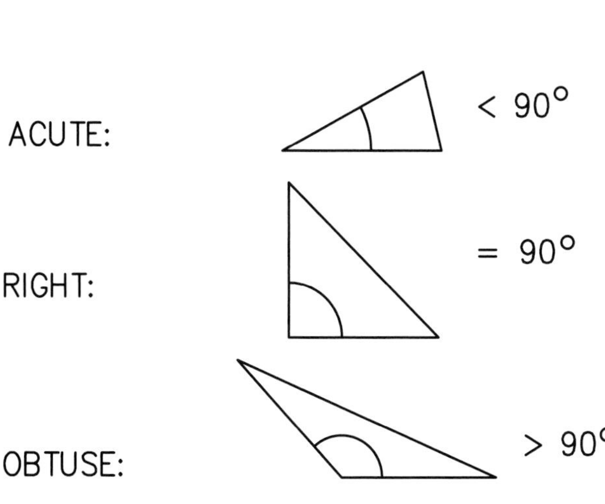

FIGURE 3.43 Triangles have same names as angles.

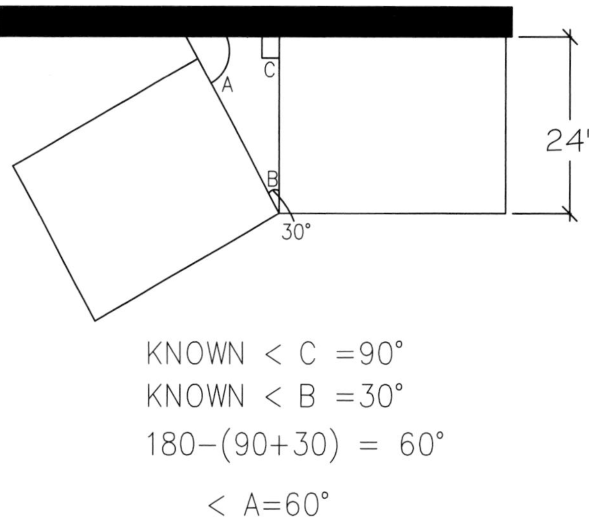

FIGURE 3.44 Identifying the dimensions of cabinetry to be installed on an angle.

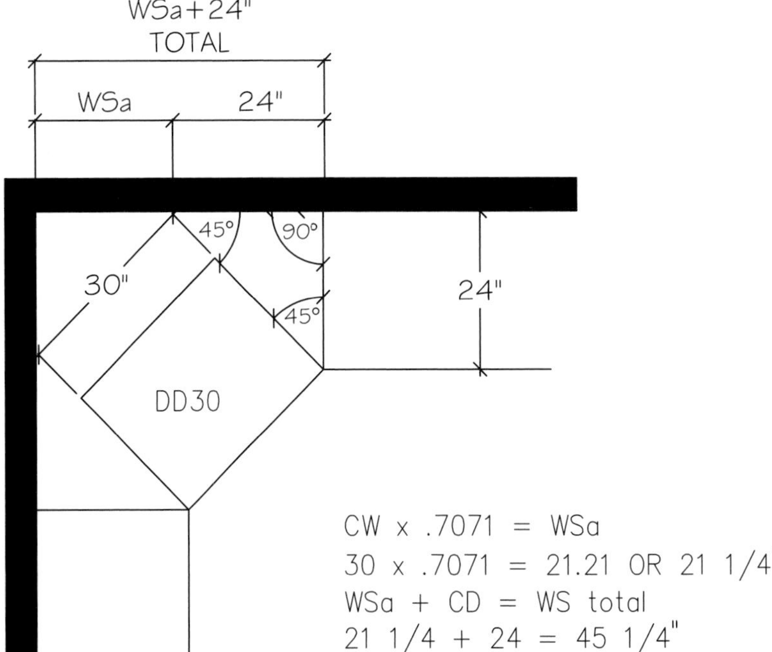

FIGURE 3.45 Determine the wall space required for a given angled cabinet installation.

To compute the wall space required to place a 30″-wide desk drawer at a 45-degree angle in the corner, use these formulas (see Figure 3.45):

CW × .7071 = WSa
where:
CW = Cabinet width
.7071 = Formula constant
WSa = Wall space "a"

WSa + CD = TW
where:
CD = Cabinet depth
TW = Total wall space

Constructing an Angle Equal to a Given Angle

In new construction, your drawing information will often have to be taken from an architect's blueprint. To transfer an odd angle from a blueprint to your own drawing, follow these steps (see Figure 3.46):

1. Draw an arc of any radius from the intersection of the angle on the blueprint.
2. Next draw an arc with the same radius on your drawing.
3. Return to the blueprint. Use your compass to determine the distance from intersection "x" to intersection "y." Draw an arc from intersection "y" through intersection "x."
4. Repeat this process on your own working drawing. Draw the arc through the previous arc you just drew.
5. The point of intersection of the two arcs will also intersect the angle's second leg.

Constructing Curved Lines with Arcs

Drawing custom countertop plans requires constructing various curved lines. Figure 3.47 shows the two options.

Option 1

1. When the arc is tangent to a right angle, draw an arc with the given radius from the right angle intersection through the two legs.

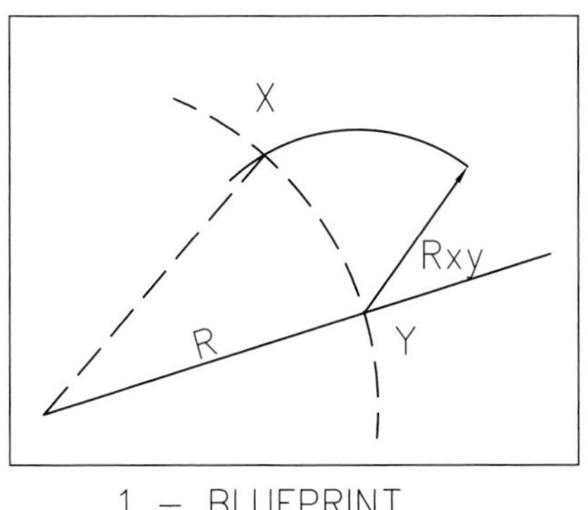

1 – BLUEPRINT

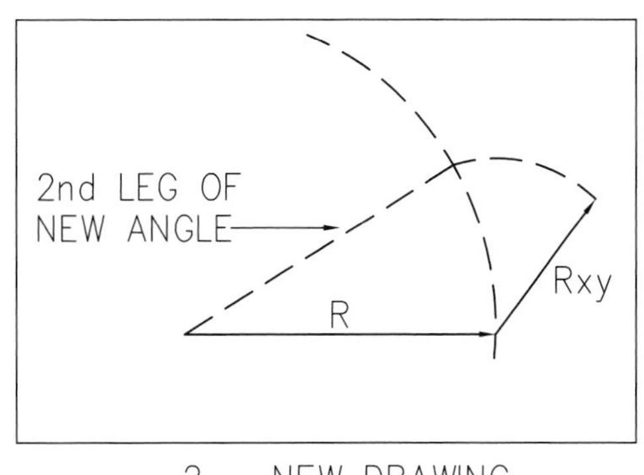

2 – NEW DRAWING

FIGURE 3.46 Constructing equal angles in plan view.

2. Where the arc intersects the legs, draw another arc inside the right angle from each point so they intersect.
3. From their point of intersection, draw another arc which will be tangent to the right-angle legs.

Option 2

1. When the arc is tangent to two lines that are not perpendicular, the arc radius must be an equal distance from each line.
2. Determine the radius center by constructing parallel lines an equal distance from each line. Extend these lines until they cross. The point of intersection is the radius location.

Constructing an Ellipse

You will need to construct an ellipse whenever you draw a perspective that has a circular element in it. Cooktop burners and vanity sinks are good examples of when you might need to draw an ellipse. There are two ways to construct ellipses.

Option 1

1. Determine where the widest point (major axis) will fall and then where the thinnest point (minor axis) will fall.

OPTION 1

STEP 1 STEP 2 STEP 3

OPTION 2

STEP 1 STEP 2 STEP 3

FIGURE 3.47 Constructing curved lines with arcs.

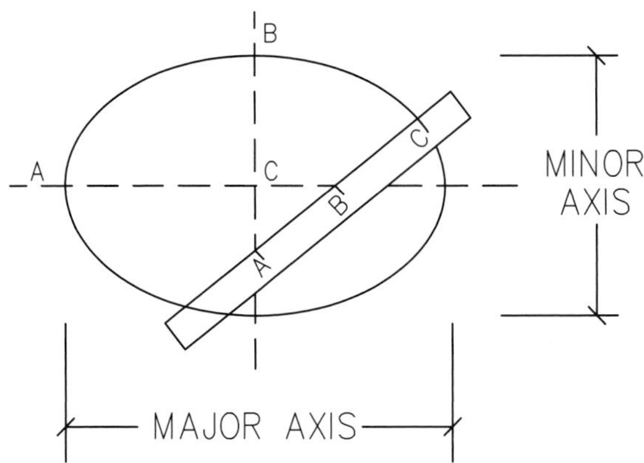

FIGURE 3.48 One technique to construct an ellipse in plan view.

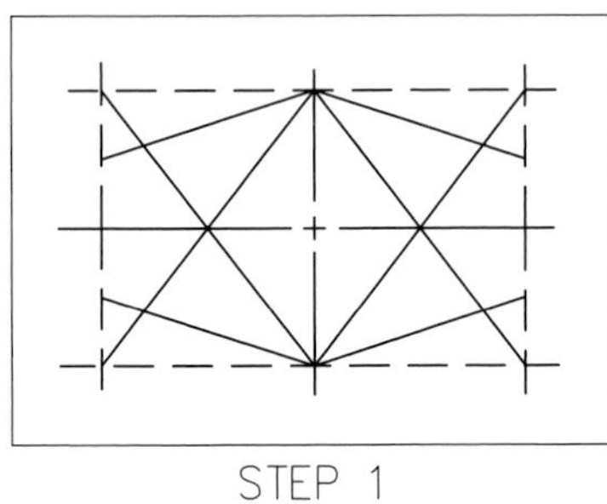

STEP 2

FIGURE 3.49 Another technique to construct ellipse in plan view.

2. On an edge of a sheet of paper, mark three points, A, B, and C, so that AC equals half the major axis and BC equals half the minor axis.
3. Slide point A up and down along the minor axis while pivoting from the same point and keeping point B on the major axis.
4. Mark several points at C through the process in step 3 and draw a smooth curve connecting these points (see Figure 3.48).

Option 2

An alternative is to sketch a rectangle that will contain the ellipse.

1. Locate the major (widest point) and minor axis (thinnest point). Refer to step one.
2. Divide the rectangle by bisecting the line segments as illustrated in the section titled "Bisecting a Line."
3. Sketch the ellipse to align with the designated points (see Figure 3.49).

SUMMARY

Hand drafting is an important skill for designers to have. Knowing how to hand draft will also help with drafting on the computer and understanding the design process. Learning the proper techniques for hand drafting will assist you in drafting professional-looking, well-drafted drawings. Some drawings will have more details, and proper drafting is important to show the design intent. Kitchen and bath drawings communicate information to all individuals involved in the design project. It is important that the drawings are legible and completed in accordance with NKBA standards. Architectural lettering plays an important role in the drawings. The designer must also understand the basics of angles to better assist with the planning of angled walls and other elements of the design.

REVIEW QUESTIONS

1. What size paper are NKBA drawings typically drafted on? (See "Standard Paper Sizes"page 30)
2. How do leads differ in hardness? (See "Leads"page 32)
3. What directions do you draw a vertical line and an angled line? (See "Technique for Drawing Vertical Lines"page 35)
4. List two key points regarding architectural lettering (lettering). (See "Architectural Lettering"pages 44–45)
5. Describe two techniques for bisecting a line. (See "Bisecting a Line"page 51)

Drafting Conventions: Line Types, Symbols, and Techniques

Each drawing in a set of NKBA plans gives information necessary to install all components in the given space. Just as we use specific tools for hand drafting, each line on a drawing represents a particular feature. Standardized line types have been developed for the industry and are known as the Alphabet of Lines. Standardized symbols and lines on a drawing assist communication between all parties involved. Individuals involved may include designers, architects, contractors, vendors, and more. Each company may have its own protocol for the set of drafting standards to be used that may vary slightly from those of another company. As you will learn shortly, there may be several acceptable symbols for a particular item.

There are hand-drafting techniques used to produce professionally drafted drawings as well. The lines produced will be affected by the "tooth" (roughness) of the vellum and how much pressure the draftsperson applies. There are lead recommendations for each line type, and these recommendations can vary slightly with each individual draftsperson and his or her drafting style. The draftsperson must draft with the various recommended leads to determine which one produces a suitable result.

Learning Objective 1: Demonstrate understanding of line types known as the Alphabet of Lines.

Learning Objective 2: Demonstrate understanding of line weight and good technique.

Learning Objective 3: Understand industry-standardized symbols used on drawings.

LINES AND TECHNIQUE

In the design industry, there are standardized line types and correct techniques to be used for producing professionally hand drafted drawings. In this chapter we will study what constitutes good drafting technique for each line type.

Line Quality

Line quality refers to how good the lines on a drawing look. When drafting, we want to achieve good line quality and have a professionally drafted drawing. All lines must be consistent and accurate. All corners need to be crisp with no gaps or extended lines. There are drafting techniques we can use to achieve professionally drafted drawings.

Line Weight

Line weight refers to the thickness of the line. Each line has a level of importance on a drawing. This importance is often referred to as the *line hierarchy*. For example, a wall line should be thicker than a door swing line. The following are techniques to produce a well-drafted set of drawings.

- Think thick and thin for the lines. The line should be proper thickness in accordance with its importance on a drawing.
- Good line weight can be achieved by rotating your lead holder away from you slowly with your thumb while pulling the lead holder at an angle across the vellum against the parallel bar or T-square.
- If you do not rotate your pencil the lead can become flat which creates a line that is not uniform in thickness. The goal is to have a line of uniform thickness from end to end.
- The lines should be dark with the correct thickness from end to end.
- All corners must be closed with no lines overlapping.
- Always use the eraser shield to erase any extra lines or double lines on the drawing. It helps prevent you from accidentally erasing an adjacent line and wasting time redrawing the line.
- Use your drafting brush to remove any eraser crumbs. Do not use your hand to brush them off, as this can smear the lead on your drawing. A drafting brush will help keep your drawing clean with no dark lead smudges.

Line Types

Lines on a drawing have their own special meaning and purpose. Standardized line types were developed for use in the industry. These line types are referred to as the Alphabet of Lines. Each line type should exhibit a certain thickness on a finished drawing, known as line weight. The thickness relates to the importance of the line on a drawing. The typical leads used are H, 2H, 4H (2 mm), and/or 0.03 mm, 0.05 mm, 0.07 mm, and 0.09 mm. Line weight on a drawing varies from a thin line to a thicker line. The line types typically used on NKBA drawings are illustrated in Figure 4.1.

FIGURE 4.1 Line types used on floor plan.

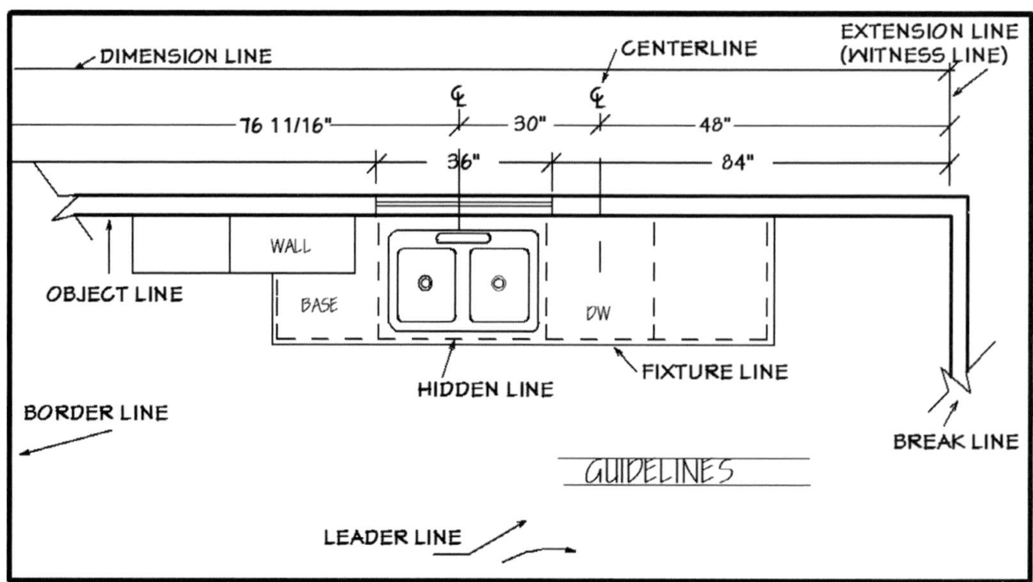

Visible Object Lines

Visible object lines, shown on Figure 4.2, define the main outline of objects. On a floor plan, items include walls, cabinets, counter, flooring, furniture, some appliances, and any other item not covered or hidden in any way. The lines for visible objects will vary in weight and thickness in accordance with the object's importance on a drawing. Walls typically are drawn as thicker visible object lines. Lines for cabinets, fixtures, and other items are drawn with a medium thin yet dark line. Wall lines are thicker than door lines. The door line isn't lighter but may look lighter since it is a thinner line. No matter how thick or thin a line is, it needs to be dark enough to be visible when the drawing is reproduced.

Typically a 0.9 mm lead is used to produce the thick line, 0.5 mm lead is used for a medium line, and 0.3 mm lead is used for the thinnest line. For the standard 2 mm lead holder, the H lead produces a thicker line and 4H produces a thinner line. These are general guidelines. With the standard leads, the lead necessary to produce a particular line thickness will vary with the user, tooth of the vellum (roughness), and the pressure applied while drawing. Most draftspeople use a range from H to 4H. Many prefer to use a 2H for drafting the object lines with a 2 mm standard lead holder (see Figure 4.1).

Fixture Lines

Fixture line is a term often used for the lines that form the shapes of kitchen, laundry, and bathroom fixtures and appliances. A fixture line is thinner than a wall line.

Hidden Object Lines (Hidden Lines)

Hidden object lines (hidden lines) show edges and surfaces that are not visible but are hidden below a visible surface. Lines for the base cabinets are drawn as hidden object lines since they are below the counter surface. We typically do not indicate the toekick or shelving, as doing so would make a drawing too busy. The hidden line for the base cabinets on a floor plan ends where the front of the wall cabinet line begins. Objects in an island, such as cabinets and appliances that are below the counter surface, must be indicated with a hidden object line as well. A half wall supporting a counter such as an eating bar would also need to be dashed as it is under the counter surface.

Hidden lines are drawn with short dashes ⅛″ (3 mm) long. The spacing between dashes is 1/32″ (1 mm). The adjoining hidden lines must touch each other at corners and also touch the solid line if it intersects. To ensure a clear definition of lines and corners, there should be no gaps. These lines should be a medium line weight.

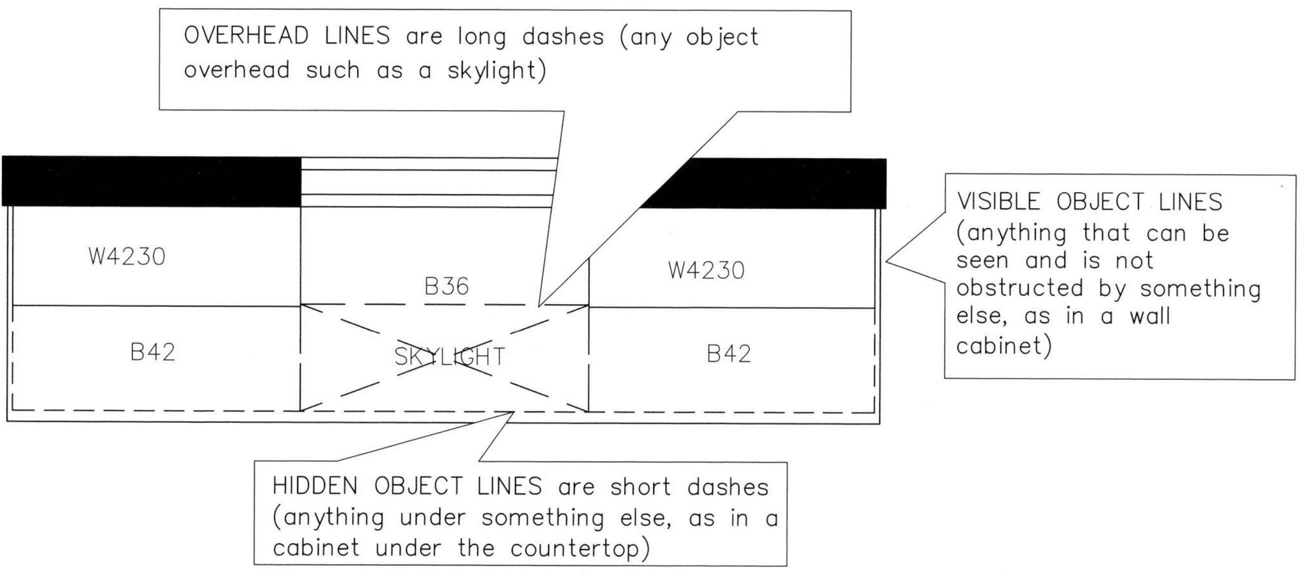

FIGURE 4.2 Visible and hidden object lines and overhead lines indicate the items on a drawing.

Overhead Lines

Overhead lines represent objects above the floor plan cutting plane line at the ceiling plane. These include items such as skylights, soffits, extensive moldings, and the like. Overhead lines are thin, dark, longer dashed lines ¼″ to ⅜″ in length (see Figure 4.2).

Dimension Lines

Dimension lines are used to show all of the necessary dimensions and clearances on a drawing. Dimension lines run parallel to object lines and show distances with a size dimension. On an NKBA drawing, dimension lines have the numerical dimension in the line itself. All dimensions for NKBA drawings are indicated in inches (mm) and fractions of an inch (mm). The dimensions are placed in the line and are positioned so all can be read from the bottom of the drawing. This method is referred to as "read from the bottom". Another acceptable method for dimensioning has the horizontal dimensions read from the bottom of plan and the vertical dimensions read from the right side of the plan. This method is referred to as "read from the right." Both methods are used in the kitchen and bath industry. In AIA standard drawings, dimensions are placed above the line. Dimension lines on NKBA drawings are spaced at a minimum of 3⁄16″ (5 mm) apart, with ½″ (12 mm) spacing most commonly used. Chapter 5 discusses dimensioning techniques.

The dimension line itself is drawn as a thin dark line. It is thinner than the object lines so there is no confusion between the two. The dimension line ends at the intersection point of the extension line (witness line) by ⅛″ (3 mm). Leads used are the 2 mm, 2H, or 4H, 0.25 mm or 0.3/0.5 mm. Again, for NKBA standard drawings the dimension must be placed *in* the dimension line and for AIA standard drawings the dimension is placed *above* the dimension line (see Figure 4.1).

Extension Lines (Witness Lines)

Extension lines extend out from the visible object line of the walls or objects and are used to terminate the dimension lines. Extension lines are thin, solid dark lines. The extension line must not touch the wall or object and should have a 1⁄16″ (1.6 mm) to ⅛″ (3 mm) gap from wall or object line. In the industry, a 45-degree slash is used to terminate dimension lines. Dimension lines can extend ⅛″ (3 mm) past extension lines or end at extension lines. For horizontal dimensions, the slash goes from bottom left to upper right. For vertical dimensions, the slashes go from upper left to bottom right (see Figure 4.1).

Centerlines

The *centerline* is used when dimensioning to locate the center points of appliances and fixtures on NKBA drawings. This helps ensure proper installation of plumbing and electrical items. The centerline is also used to place the center points of new windows on the construction plan. Center lines are drawn with alternating long and short dashes. The long dashes are between ¾″ to 1″ (19 mm to 25 mm) long. The short dashes are ⅛″ (3 mm) long. The space between dashes is 1⁄16″ (1.6 mm). The centerline is labeled CL. Always make sure to start and end a center line with the long dash. Chapter 5 presents more details regarding dimensioning. In NKBA standard drawings, windows and doors are not centerlined as they are in AIA construction drawings (see Figure 4.1).

Cutting Plane Lines

Cutting plane lines on a drawing show where a cut or slice has been made to create a section view. The cutting plane line is a thick, dark line with arrows on the ends to show the direction where the section was taken on the drawing. The line is either a series of dashes of equal length or a series of long and short dashes. If the symbol has two arrows, it refers to a section drawing. If it has only one arrow, it refers to a detail drawing.

Section Lines

Section lines on a drawing indicate a surface that has been cut or sliced in a section view. Section lines are thin lines drawn parallel to each other at a 45-degree angle and spaced evenly at 1⁄16″ (1.6 mm) apart to 1⁄8″ (3 mm) apart. Section lines are also referred to as hatching. A section view/drawing is often used to show the interior components of an item, such as a cabinet; it can also show how something is constructed.

Break Lines

Long *break lines* are most commonly used to indicate where a part of the drawing was removed or not drawn in its entirety. The break line is often used on a wall to indicate that the wall continues on. Break lines can be used for many different items on a floor plan, section, or other drawings. Short break lines have the same purpose as long break lines. They show where an item on a drawing would continue on (see Figure 4.1).

Leader Lines

Leader lines are very useful for placing text or a dimension in a limited space on a drawing and for adding specific notes pertaining to the drawing. The leader line can be a straight line or curved. There are several acceptable types of leader lines used on a drawing.

Leader lines typically have an arrow at one end and a note for the drawing at the other end. Several types of leader lines are acceptable. The leader is a thin dark line (see Figure 4.1).

Construction Lines/Layout Lines

Construction lines or *layout lines* are very light lines that are used to assist the draftsperson with drawing and placing object lines. These lines are drawn lightly and are easily erased if necessary.

Guidelines

Guidelines are light lines used for architectural lettering on a drawing. These lines are drawn lightly and are not meant to be erased. A lettering guide or Ames lettering guide is most often used to draw these guidelines. The guidelines will regulate the height of letters so they are consistent on a drawing.

Borderline

The *borderline* is the heaviest line found on a drawing. This is the line drawn around the perimeter of the vellum. It should be located ½″ in from the edge of the vellum. Title block vellums have the borderline preprinted. If you do not have preprinted vellum, you may draw the borderline and titleblock on every drawing sheet All drawings should have a borderline and titleblock. Figure 4.3 summarizes line types found on drawings.

Tips for a Professionally Drafted Drawing

Follow these tips for good drafting techniques that will result in professional-looking drawings.

- Close all gaps at corners. Drawing should have crisp corners.
- Erase any extra lines or double lines using an eraser shield.
- Rotate your lead holder slowly while drawing the line to achieve consistent line weight (thickness).
- Use appropriate line weights for line importance on a drawing.
- Lift the parallel bar when moving it so it does not smudge lines.
- Always use a drafting brush and never your hand to remove eraser crumbs.
- To prevent lines from smudging, place a piece of tracing paper over the completed part of drawing when drafting an adjacent area so your hand does not rest on the drawing itself.

STANDARD SYMBOLS FOR DRAWINGS

In the industry of design and architecture, standardized symbols are used to represent various elements found in drawings. These standardized symbols are understood by all trades and other individuals involved with the project. In the kitchen and bath industry, we use

LINE TYPES

VISIBLE OBJECT LINE
FIXTURE LINE
HIDDEN LINE (HIDDEN OBJECT LINE)
OVERHEAD LINE
DIMENSION LINE — DIMENSION — 45 DEGREE SLASH(TICK) — 22"
EXTENSION (WITNESS) LINE — EXTENSION
CENTERLINE — ℄
CUTTING PLANE LINE
SECTION LINE (CROSSHATCH)
LONG BREAK LINE
LEADER LINES
CONSTRUCTION LINES/LAYOUT LINES
GUIDELINES — GUIDELINES FOR LETTERING

FIGURE 4.3 Line types found on drawings.

standardized symbols from the AIA on our floor plans and other related drawings. In this book, we also look at some other acceptable symbols.

Drawing standards are necessary for universal communication within the design industry. Each drawing in the set of NKBA plans has a great amount of important information needed for the design project. The symbols on a drawing represent items such as walls, appliances, fixtures, lighting, electrical components, flooring, and the like. Each different drawing within the set of plans has its own purpose and symbols to represent items specific to that drawing. For example, the mechanical plan shows all of the electrical components on that drawing. If the electrical components were placed on the floor plan, it would be far too busy and could be confusing to interpret. On a construction plan, we show the symbols for walls to be removed and existing or new walls to be constructed. Construction plan symbols would be too much information to fit on a floor plan. There are symbols specifically used for floor plans, elevations, mechanical plans, construction plans, and other drawings.

Wall Symbols

Two techniques are used to draw the walls on an NKBA floor plan. The walls typically are just two thicker lines representing the sides of wall and are not filled in, or they can be pochéd solid and filled in with lead or black ink (see Figure 4.4.). However, because filling in the opening by hand is very time-consuming, open walls are used most often.

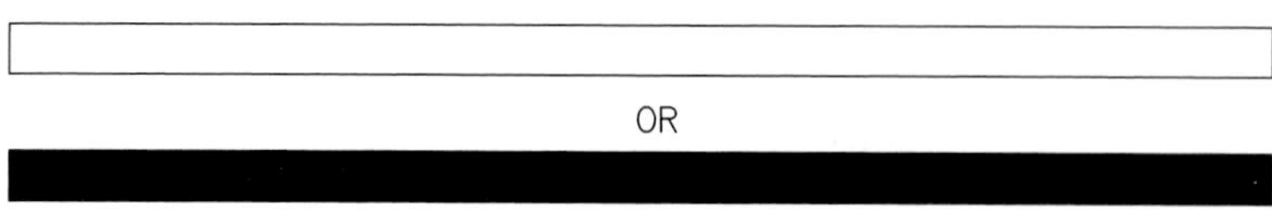

FIGURE 4.4 Acceptable walls used for floor plan. Walls are open or pochéd solid. These symbols are used for floor plans and construction plans.

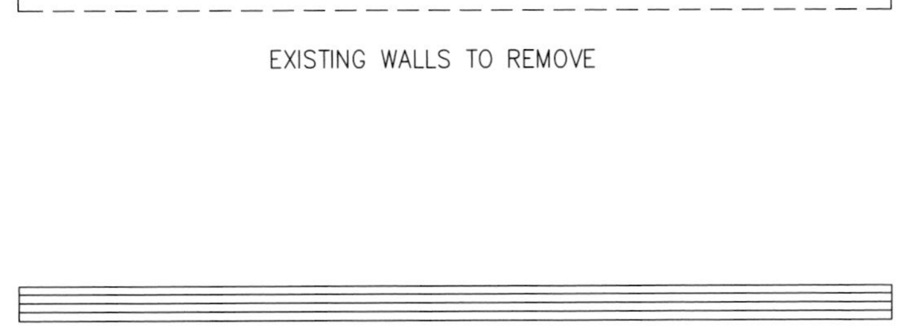

FIGURE 4.5 Wall symbol for existing walls to be removed. This symbol is typically shown on a construction plan.

FIGURE 4.6 Wall symbol for existing openings to be enclosed. This symbol is typically shown on a construction plan.

The term *poché* (po-shay) means to draw a repetitive pattern to represent the material texture of a particular item. For example, when a wall is pochéd, it is drawn with the appropriate symbol such as the solid black wall.

If there is a half-wall, a note must be placed by the wall stating the height of the half-wall. If this half-wall is under a surface such as a counter, the wall would be drawn with a hidden line.

Walls are drawn to scale in the thickness that represents how they are constructed. Typical existing interior walls are drawn at 4½″ (114 mm) thick. Exterior walls are drawn 6″ (152 mm) thick. The scale for NKBA drawings is ½″ = 1′-0″ (1:20 metric).

The following walls symbols are typically used for construction plans. Construction plans show any changes made to the existing walls. Newly constructed walls should indicate the type of material used in construction (see Figures 4.5 to 4.9).

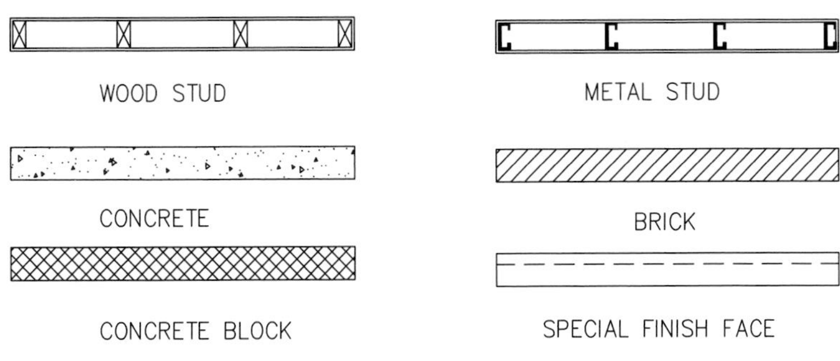

FIGURE 4.7 New walls to be constructed. Newly constructed walls should indicate the type of material used in construction.

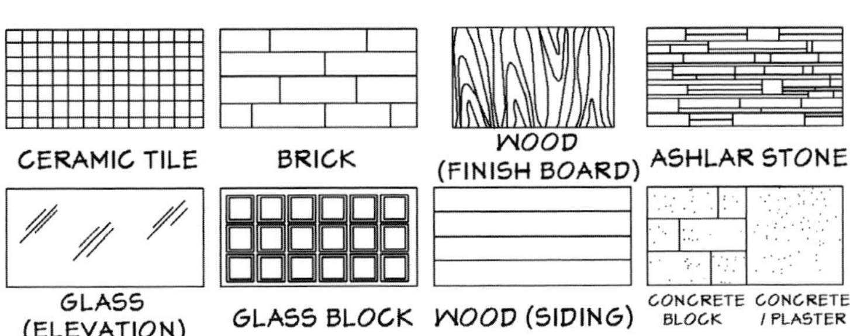

FIGURE 4.8 Material poché for horizontal surfaces and elevation views includes items on drawings such as flooring and counter materials.

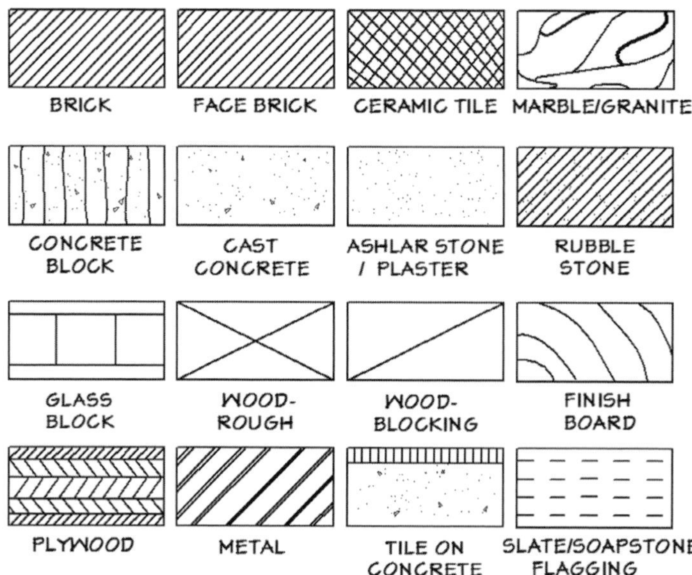

FIGURE 4.9 Material poché for section view.

Door Symbols

Each door type has its own symbol that is standard in the industry. The floor plan symbols represent what the door looks like on the floor plan and also how it opens into the given space. The door thickness, swing, and casing should be indicated on the floor plan. The door is drawn to scale and is the same length as the opening. It is standard in the industry to draw the swing on the floor plan with a 90-degree opening. The door may be drawn at a 45-degree opening if there is an adjacent door. When placing the door on a floor plan, it should open into the room and open against the wall.

The lines for the door symbol and door swing need to touch the walls at the door opening. There should not be a gap. The door swing can be drawn using a ½″ (12 mm) template (see Figure 4.10). If a template is not available, you may use a circle template to draw the arc of the door swing.

FIGURE 4.10 Using a template to draw a door symbol on a floor plan.

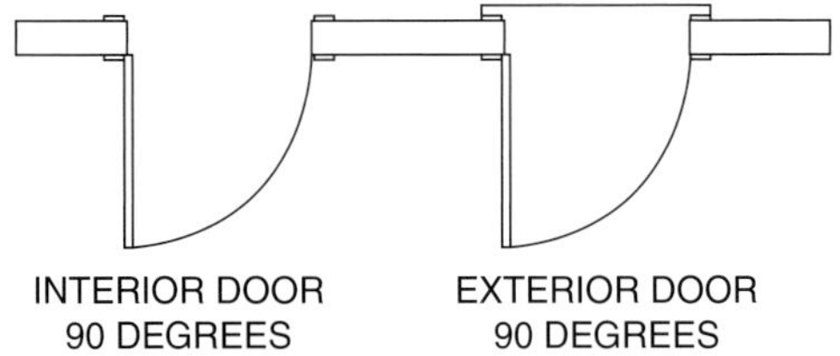

FIGURE 4.11 Door symbols for interior and exterior doors. Note the threshold line for the exterior door 90-degree opening.

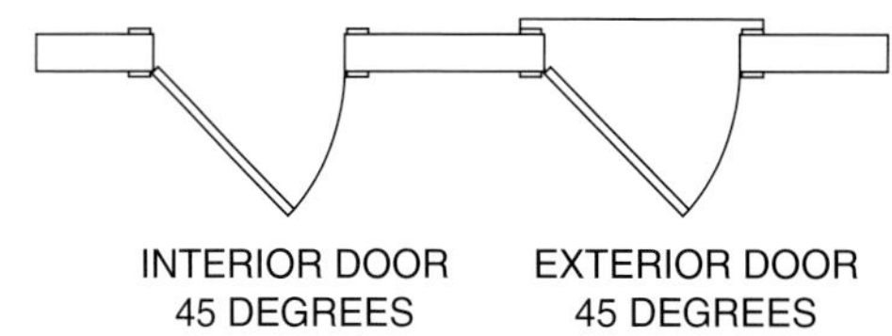

FIGURE 4.12 Door symbol for door opening 45 degrees on plan. This symbol may be used if two doors are in close proximity to each other.

A door schedule is only required with new doors. The door schedule is a table that lists all specifics for doors in regards to size, quantity, manufacturer, and other important information. New doors are indicated by a letter in a circle placed inside each door opening on the floor plan and cross-referenced in the door schedule. If there is only one new door, the schedule information can be indicated directly on the floor plan in note form. Figures 4.11, 4.12, and 4.13 show typical door symbols used on kitchen and bathroom drawings.

Window Symbols

Each type of window is represented by its own symbol. On a floor plan, the type of window must be indicated as well as the casing. Sills typically are not shown unless a particular interior treatment is to be used. An elevation shows how the window will look in two dimension on the wall.

For a casement window, it is optional to indicate the direction of the glass swing. The glass swing is indicated with a dashed line. Glass block is shown as a series of squares or rectangles with a listing in the specifications. Skylights are shown using long overhead lines and are labeled inside the symbol. Pertinent information must be referenced at the side. Figure 4.14 shows typical window symbols you will find on a floor plan. Glass block is shown as well.

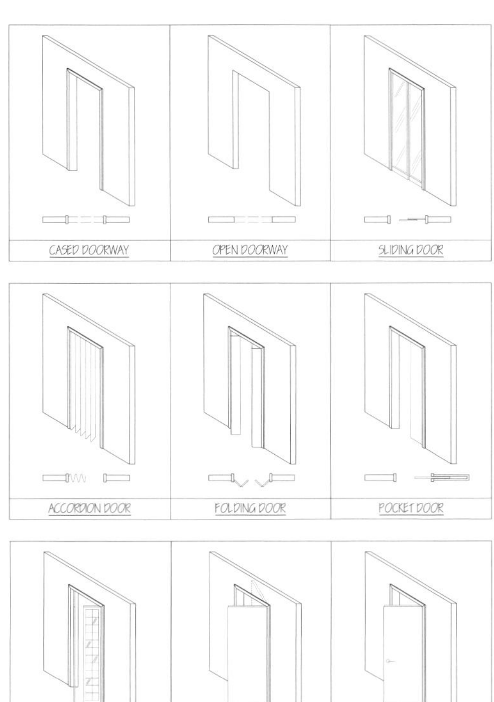

FIGURE 4.13 Door symbols typically used on kitchen and bath drawings.

INTERIOR BARN DOOR

DUTCH DOOR

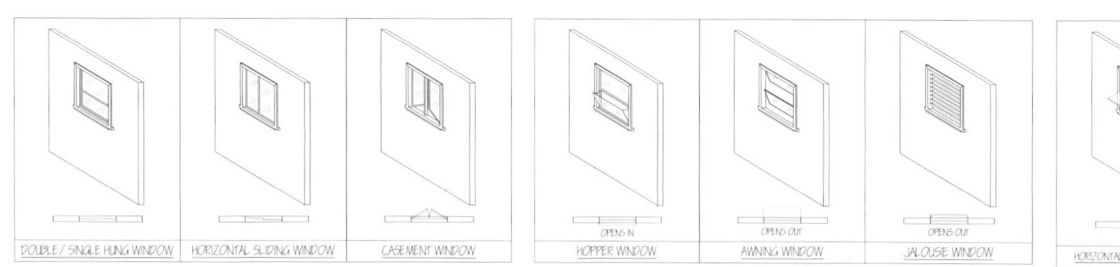

FIGURE 4.14 Floor plan symbols for windows and glass block.

Stair and Ramp Symbols

Stair symbols represent the various types of stairs found in residential construction. A directional arrow placed on the stair symbol indicates the direction of the stairs. The direction either "UP" or "DOWN" is also written by the arrow. The direction would be from the given floor to the direction the stairs go. A break line often is used to indicate that the stairs continue to another floor. Most draftspeople draw all treads on the plan. Indicate the direction of the slope with an arrow leading from the main floor area to the secondary area and the word "UP" or label "DOWN" if the direction of stairs goes down from the referenced floor (see Figure 4.15).

Elevator Symbols

Elevators and hydraulic lifts are indicated with an "x" inside the outline of the item. The "x" is used to indicate that the unit runs through the entire space beyond the floor and/or ceiling. Include the appropriate door symbol to show the elevator opening (see Figure 4.16).

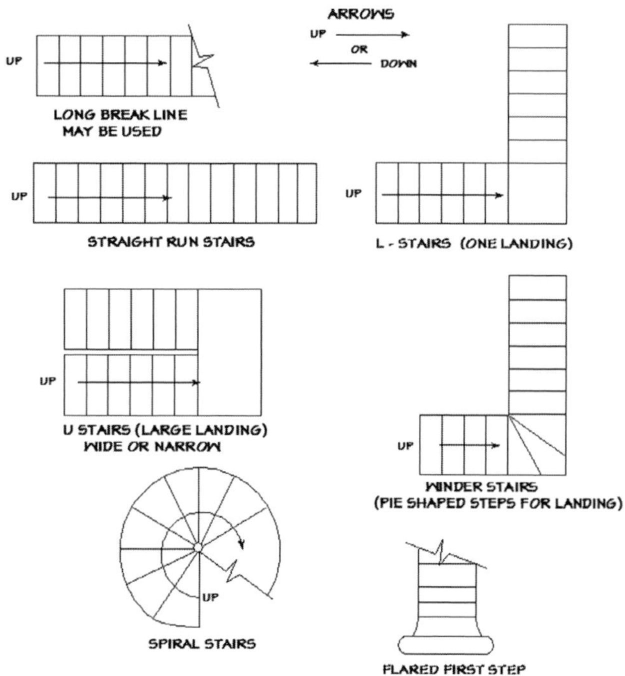

FIGURE 4.15 Stair and ramp symbols used on floor plans.

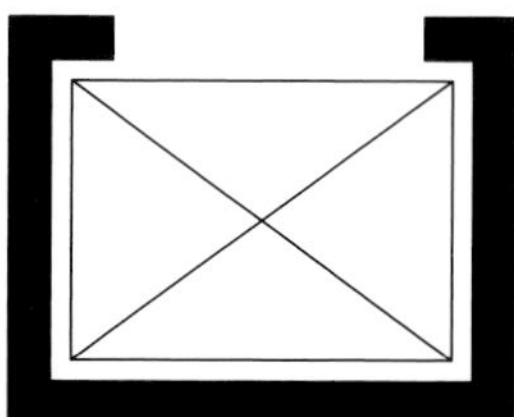

ADD APPROPRIATE DOOR SYMBOL TO ELEVATORS AND LIFTS

FIGURE 4.16 Elevator symbol. The symbol is similar to a shower symbol but does not show a drain, as a shower would.

Kitchen Appliance and Kitchen Fixture Symbols

There are standardized symbols for kitchen appliances and fixtures. The floor plan symbols are drawn as representations of how the item looks in plan view. Some manufacturers have templates with appliances and fixtures on them. You also can duplicate images of the appliances by using shapes found on a geometric template. Figure 4.17 shows typical kitchen appliance symbols and fixtures found on the floor plan.

Appliances must be labeled on a drawing for identification. Typically, a circled number is placed on or by the appliance. This circled number is also placed in the specifications on the right side of the drawing with a description of the item. The number on the plan and information in the specifications must cross-reference one another. Some designers prefer to include a label with the name of appliance on the floor plan next to the item. Make sure there is enough room for the description so the drawing doesn't become too cluttered. Chapter 5 presents additional information regarding the specifications.

Indicating the appliance door swings on the floor plan with a dashed line is optional. This technique shows the appliance door clearances within the space on the floor plan. The NKBA Kitchen & Bathroom Planning Guidelines show recommendations for appliance door clearances to create a functional workspace.

Bathroom Fixture Symbols

Bathroom spaces also have standardized symbols used for floor plans (see Figure 4.18). These include lavatories, showers, fittings, grab bars (see Figure 4.19), accessories, and more. The symbols are identified by a circled number and cross-referenced in the specifications on the right side of floor plan drawing or may be labeled on floor plan if there is enough space for the lettering.

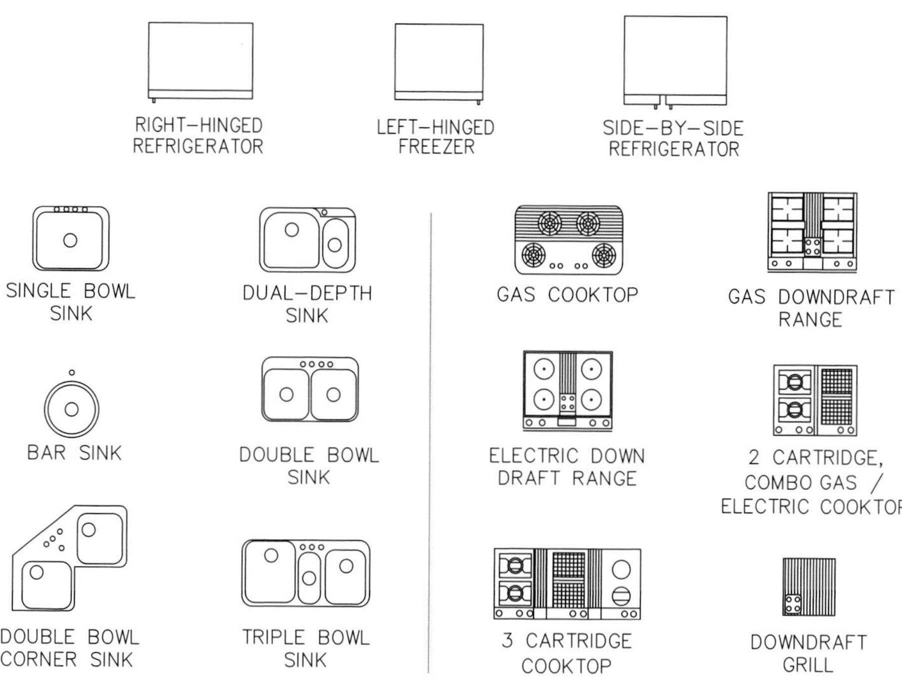

FIGURE 4.17 Typical appliance symbols.

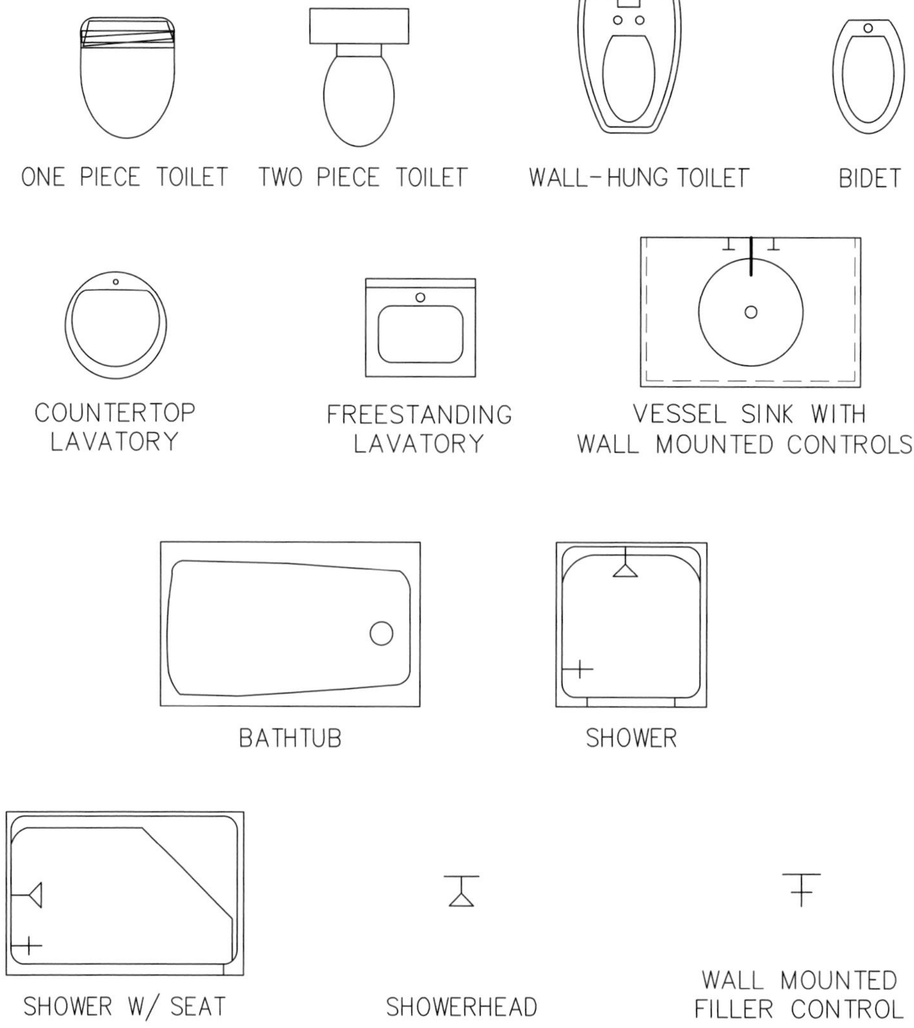

FIGURE 4.18 Typical symbols for bathroom fixtures.

Flooring Symbols

Flooring symbols for the material used may be indicated on the floor plan (see Figure 4.20). The acceptable technique is to draw a partial example of the flooring. Note that the entire space does not need to be drawn with the symbol. Rather, fade out the symbol at the edge to end drawing the flooring symbol. Indicate the description in the specifications on the right side of drawing. If there is not enough room on the drawing to provide a good indication of the material to be used, it is best to leave the material symbol off of the drawing to prevent any confusion. Figure 4.21 shows typical floor plan material symbols.

Mechanical Symbols

Kitchen and bathroom mechanical plans have specific standardized symbols used to indicate the lighting, electrical, plumbing, heating, and ventilation. It is very important to use these symbols accurately because professional tradespeople must be able to interpret your drawing and install items in exact specified locations. Every symbol on the floor plan

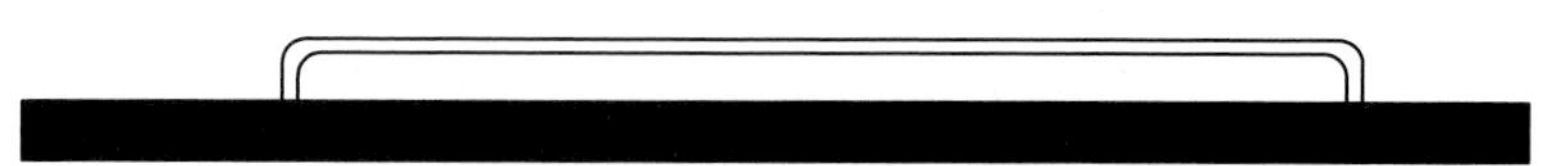

FIGURE 4.19 Symbol for handrail, grab bar, or towel bar. Draw the thickness of the bar to correspond to the thickness of the object.

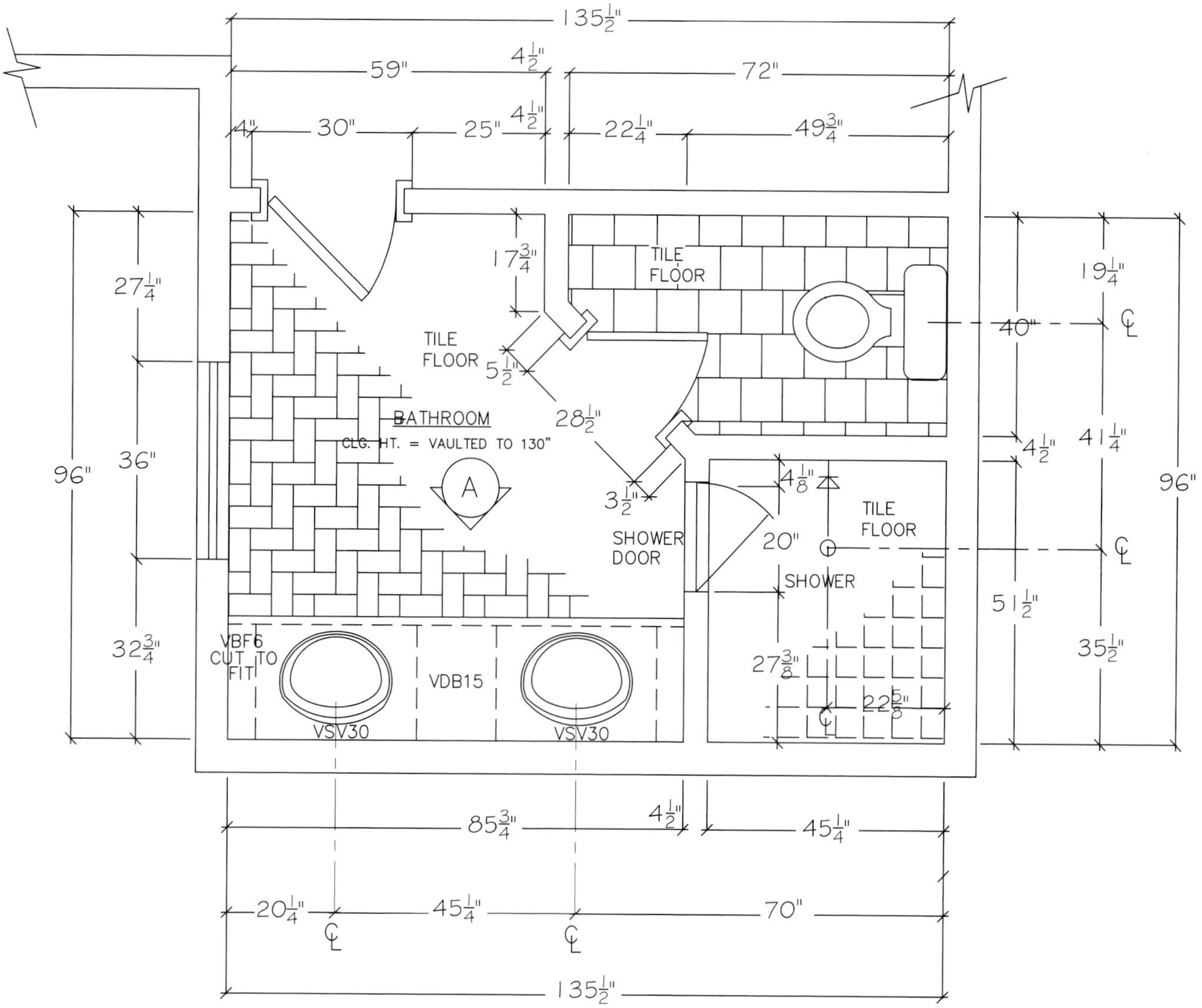

FIGURE 4.20 Examples of symbols for finished floor materials. (Courtesy of Simone Feldman, CKD, CBD)

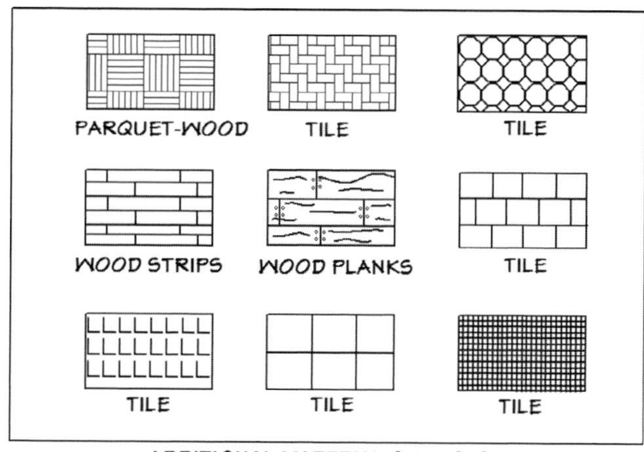

FIGURE 4.21 Floor plan material symbols.

SYMBOL	APPEARANCE	NOTES	SYMBOL	APPEARANCE	NOTES
S	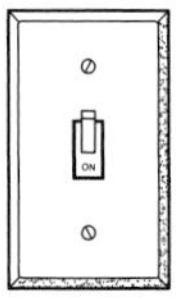	SINGLE POLE SWITCH ACTIVATES ONE OR MORE LIGHTS OR FIXTURES FROM ONE LOCATION.	S_D		DOOR SWITCH ACTIVATES LIGHTS OR FIXTURES BEHIND DOOR WHEN DOOR IS OPENED. USED FOR PANTRY OR CLOSET.
S_3		3-WAY SWITCH ACTIVATES ONE OR MORE LIGHTS OR FIXTURES FROM TWO LOCATIONS. REQUIRED FOR ROOMS WITH TWO ENTRANCES.	S_P		SWITCH W/ PILOT LIGHT PILOT LIGHT IS LIT WHEN SWITCH IS IN THE ON POSITION. USED FOR BASEMENT, ATTIC AND GARAGE LIGHTS.
S_4		4-WAY SWITCH USED WITH TWO 3-WAY SWITCHES TO ACTIVATE ONE OR MORE LIGHTS OR FIXTURES FROM THREE LOCATIONS.	(S)	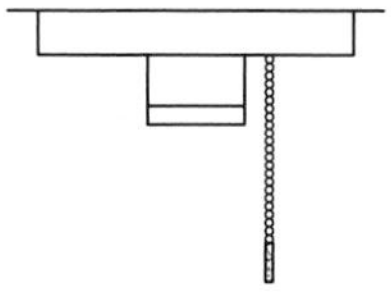 SIDE VIEW	CEILING PULL SWITCH PORCELAIN LIGHT FIXTURE WITH PULL CHAIN TO ACTIVATE LIGHT. IDEAL FOR ATTICS, CRAWL SPACES, ETC.
SSS		THREE SWITCHES AT ONE LOCATION. THREE SINGLE POLE SWITCHES IN A THREE GANG BOX ILLUSTRATED.	S_2	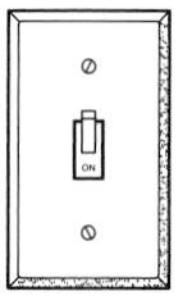	DOUBLE POLE SWITCH SELDOM USED IN THE HOME. NORMALLY USED FOR 240-VOLT APPLIANCES THAT ARE SWITCHED. CAN BE CONFUSED WITH A 4-WAY SWITCH, BUT IS MARKED ON AND OFF.
S_{DM}		DIMMER SWITCH USED TO CONTROL THE INTENSITY OF ONE OR MORE LIGHTS FROM ONE LOCATION. ROTATES FROM OFF TO FULL ON. OTHER TYPES OF DIMMER SWITCHES WILL USE THIS SAME SYMBOL.	S_K	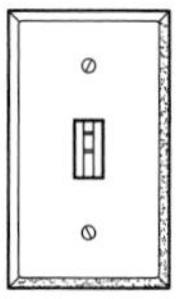	KEY SWITCH SELDOM USED IN THE HOME. A KEY MUST BE USED TO ACTIVATE THE SWITCH. OFTEN USED IN PUBLIC SPACES SUCH AS PUBLIC RESTROOMS.
S_{3DM}		THREE-WAY DIMMER SWITCH SAME AS ABOVE BUT USED TO CONTROL LIGHTS FROM TWO LOCATIONS. ONLY ONE OF THE THREE-WAY SWITCHES CAN BE THE DIMMER SWITCH.	T *	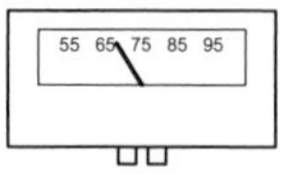 55 65 75 85 95	ELECTRIC THERMOSTAT WALL MOUNTED UNIT TO CONTROL ROOM OR HOME TEMPERATURE. * INDICATE TYPE: C - COOLING H - HEATING C/H - COOLING/HEATING
S S S	LIGHT FAN HEAT	THREE SWITCHES STACKED AT ONE LOCATION. TYPICALLY USED FOR BATHROOM VENTILATION UNITS.	(H)	40 30 20 10 OFF 50 60 70	HUMIDISTAT CAN BE PRE-SET TO TURN BATHROOM FAN ON AUTOMATICALLY WHEN THE HUMIDITY REACHES A SET LEVEL.

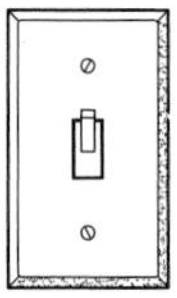

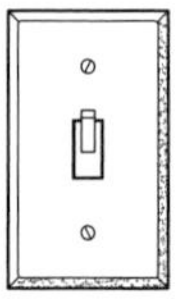

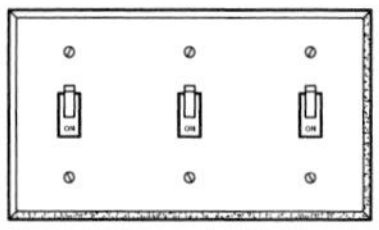

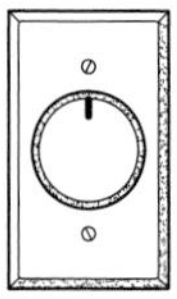

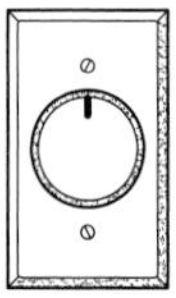

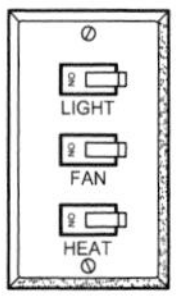

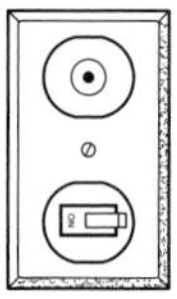

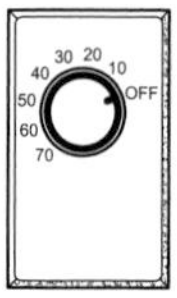

FIGURE 4.22 Switch symbols.

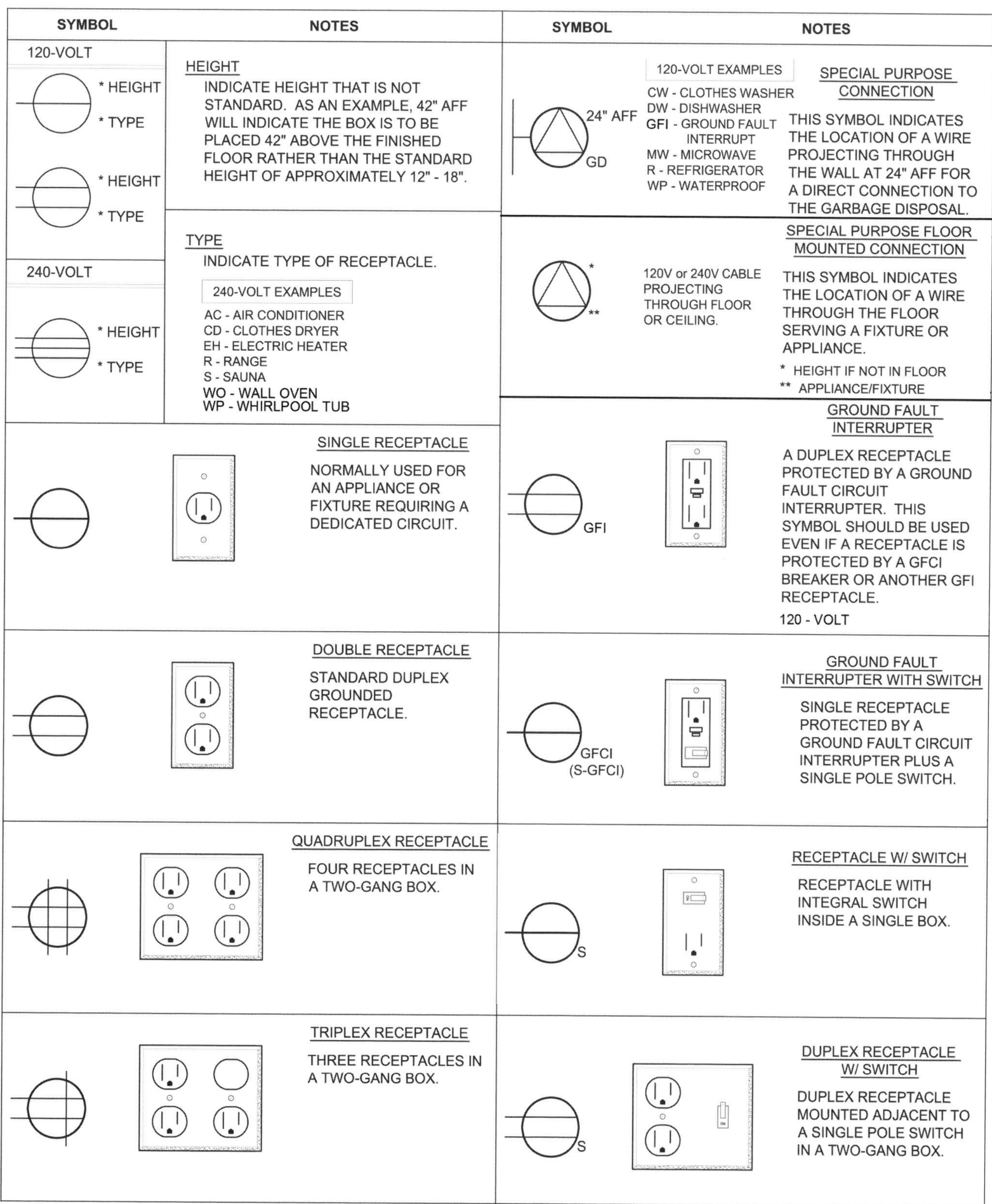

FIGURE 4.23 Receptacle symbols.

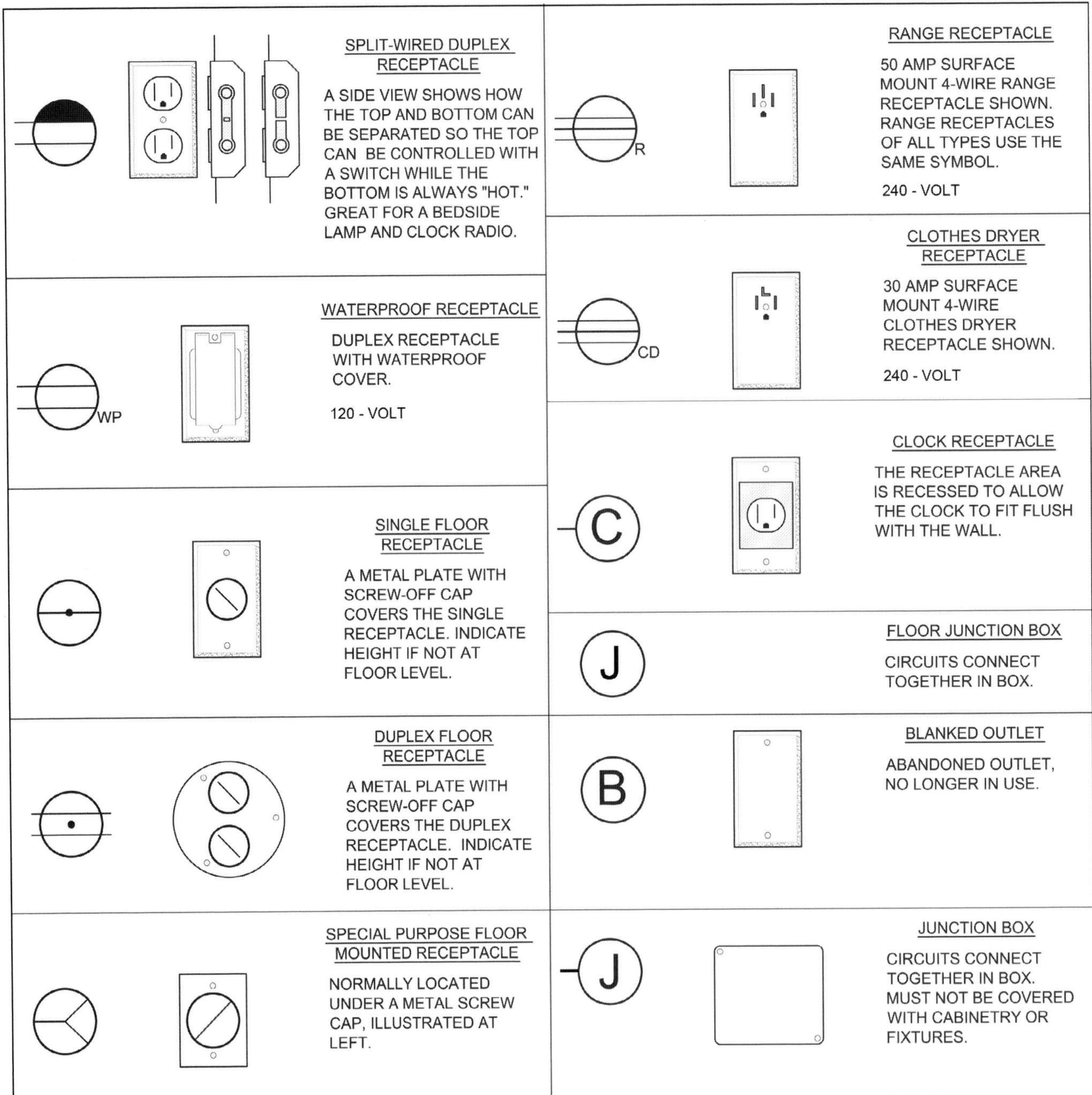

FIGURE 4.23 Receptacle symbols (continued).

must be cross-referenced with the symbols in the mechanical legend. Although the list of symbols is extensive, sometimes a symbol does not exist for a new specific item, especially with ever-changing technology. Most symbols found in Figures 4.22 to 4.27 are consistent with the AIA's *Architectural Graphic Standards Manual*. However, some symbols are unique to the NKBA to keep up with changes to the products that kitchen and bath designers must specify. Occasionally you may encounter a product and may not be sure of the correct symbol. If a resource fails to provide you with the correct symbol, you

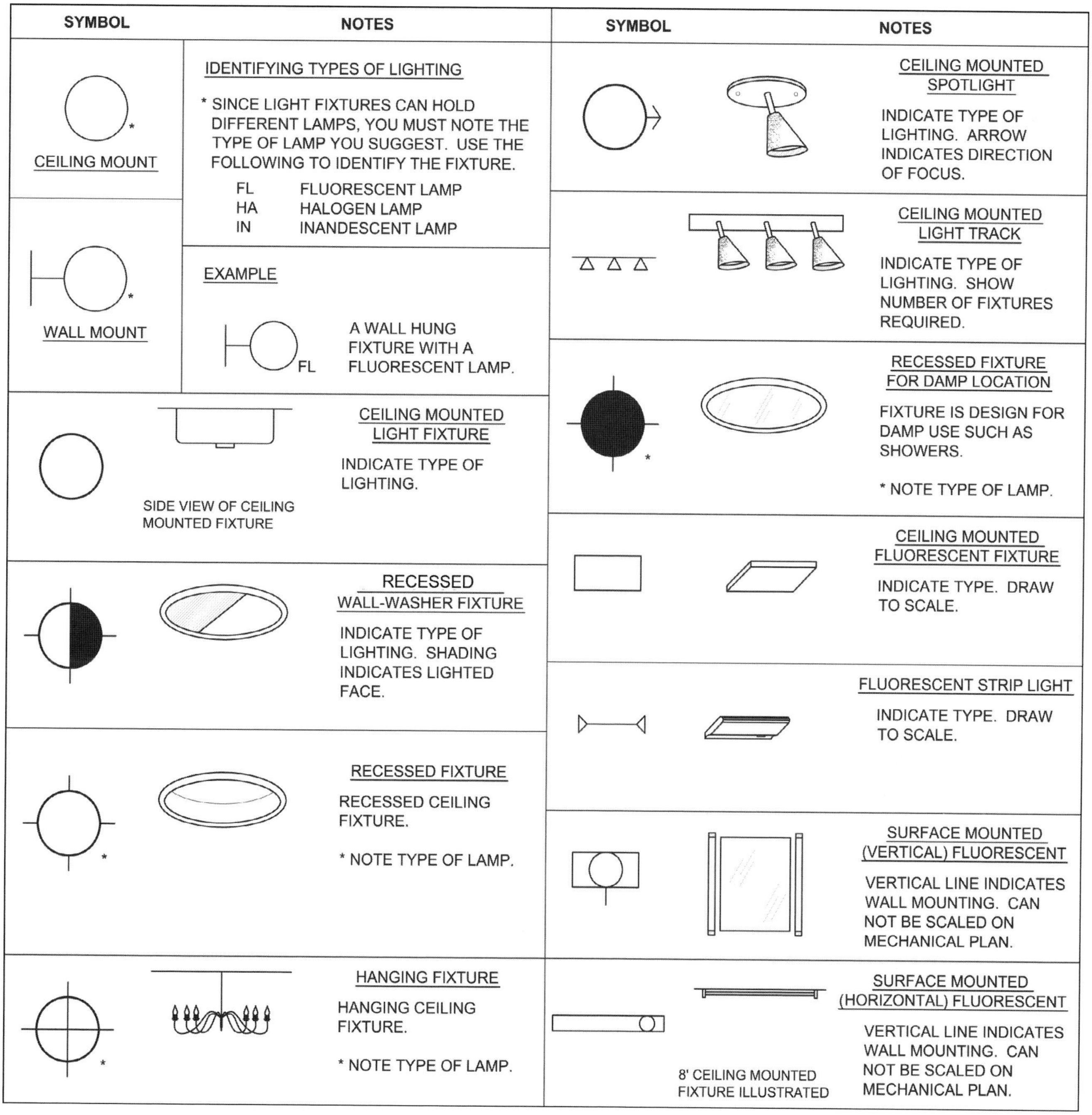

SYMBOL	NOTES
* CEILING MOUNT	IDENTIFYING TYPES OF LIGHTING * SINCE LIGHT FIXTURES CAN HOLD DIFFERENT LAMPS, YOU MUST NOTE THE TYPE OF LAMP YOU SUGGEST. USE THE FOLLOWING TO IDENTIFY THE FIXTURE. FL FLUORESCENT LAMP HA HALOGEN LAMP IN INANDESCENT LAMP
* WALL MOUNT	EXAMPLE FL A WALL HUNG FIXTURE WITH A FLUORESCENT LAMP.
SIDE VIEW OF CEILING MOUNTED FIXTURE	CEILING MOUNTED LIGHT FIXTURE INDICATE TYPE OF LIGHTING.
	RECESSED WALL-WASHER FIXTURE INDICATE TYPE OF LIGHTING. SHADING INDICATES LIGHTED FACE.
*	RECESSED FIXTURE RECESSED CEILING FIXTURE. * NOTE TYPE OF LAMP.
*	HANGING FIXTURE HANGING CEILING FIXTURE. * NOTE TYPE OF LAMP.

SYMBOL	NOTES
	CEILING MOUNTED SPOTLIGHT INDICATE TYPE OF LIGHTING. ARROW INDICATES DIRECTION OF FOCUS.
	CEILING MOUNTED LIGHT TRACK INDICATE TYPE OF LIGHTING. SHOW NUMBER OF FIXTURES REQUIRED.
*	RECESSED FIXTURE FOR DAMP LOCATION FIXTURE IS DESIGN FOR DAMP USE SUCH AS SHOWERS. * NOTE TYPE OF LAMP.
	CEILING MOUNTED FLUORESCENT FIXTURE INDICATE TYPE. DRAW TO SCALE.
	FLUORESCENT STRIP LIGHT INDICATE TYPE. DRAW TO SCALE.
	SURFACE MOUNTED (VERTICAL) FLUORESCENT VERTICAL LINE INDICATES WALL MOUNTING. CAN NOT BE SCALED ON MECHANICAL PLAN.
8' CEILING MOUNTED FIXTURE ILLUSTRATED	SURFACE MOUNTED (HORIZONTAL) FLUORESCENT VERTICAL LINE INDICATES WALL MOUNTING. CAN NOT BE SCALED ON MECHANICAL PLAN.

FIGURE 4.24 Lighting symbols.

may need to create your own. When creating a symbol, you must describe it in the mechanical plan legend. Do not take this as permission to develop your own set of mechanical symbols.

Keep in mind that there are several acceptable industry symbols for some items. Company protocol may dictate which one to use. The following pages include mechanical symbols seen on most kitchen and bath drawings. Next to each symbol is a description and picture of the item.

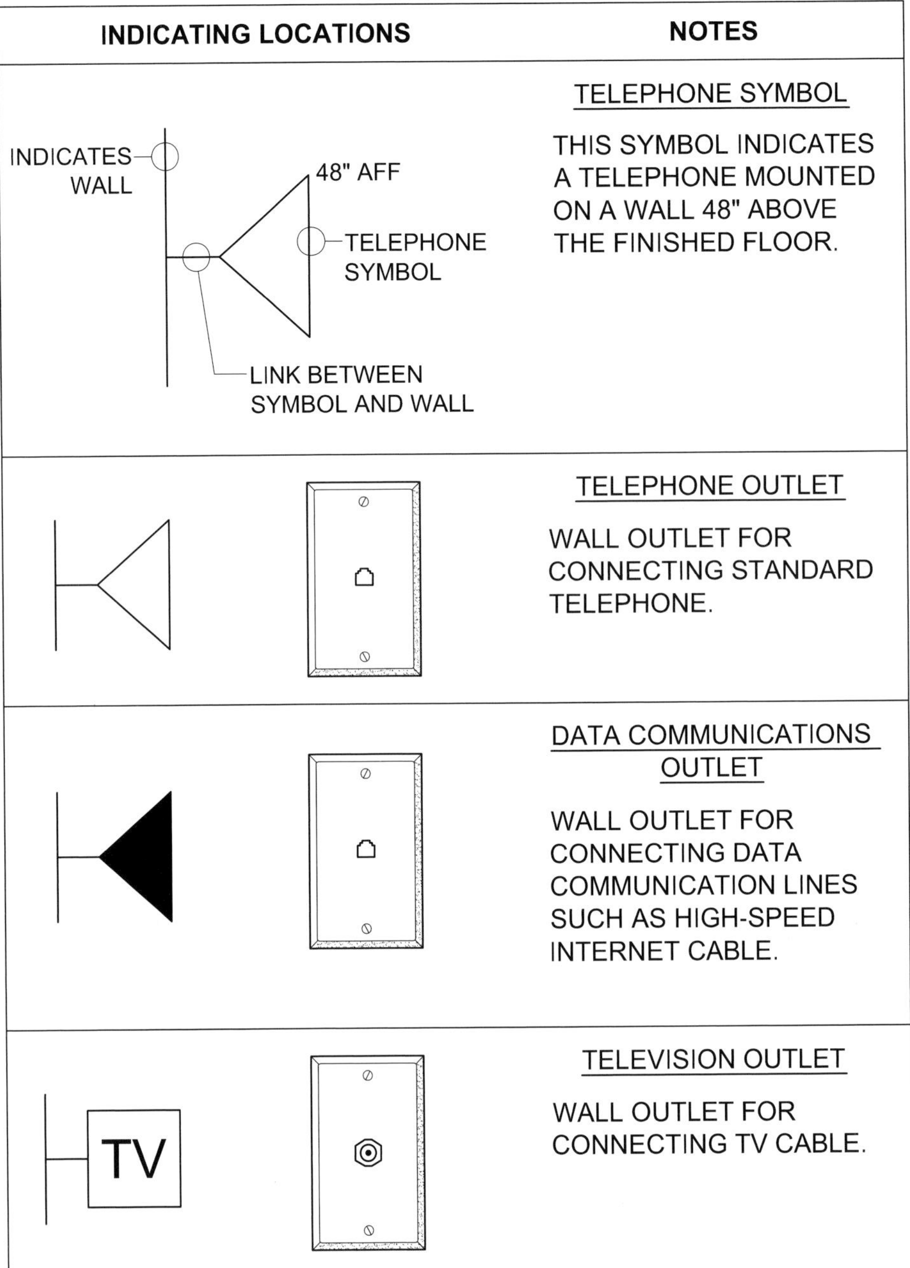

FIGURE 4.25 Communication symbols.

Graphic Symbols

Symbols are placed on the floor plan to indicate that an elevation drawing and/or a section drawing is available (see Figure 4.28). These symbols link drawings together. The title symbol is used for the title of a drawing. This will indicate the number assigned to the drawing.

For the elevation symbol a circle with an arrow is used. The arrow points to the wall for which the elevation was drawn and where the viewer would look. The elevation is a two-dimensional drawing and shows exactly what is placed on that wall.

The detail symbol locates the area or component that is drawn to a larger scale to show how the item is constructed. The number of the drawing and the number of the sheet where the drawing can be found are placed in the circle.

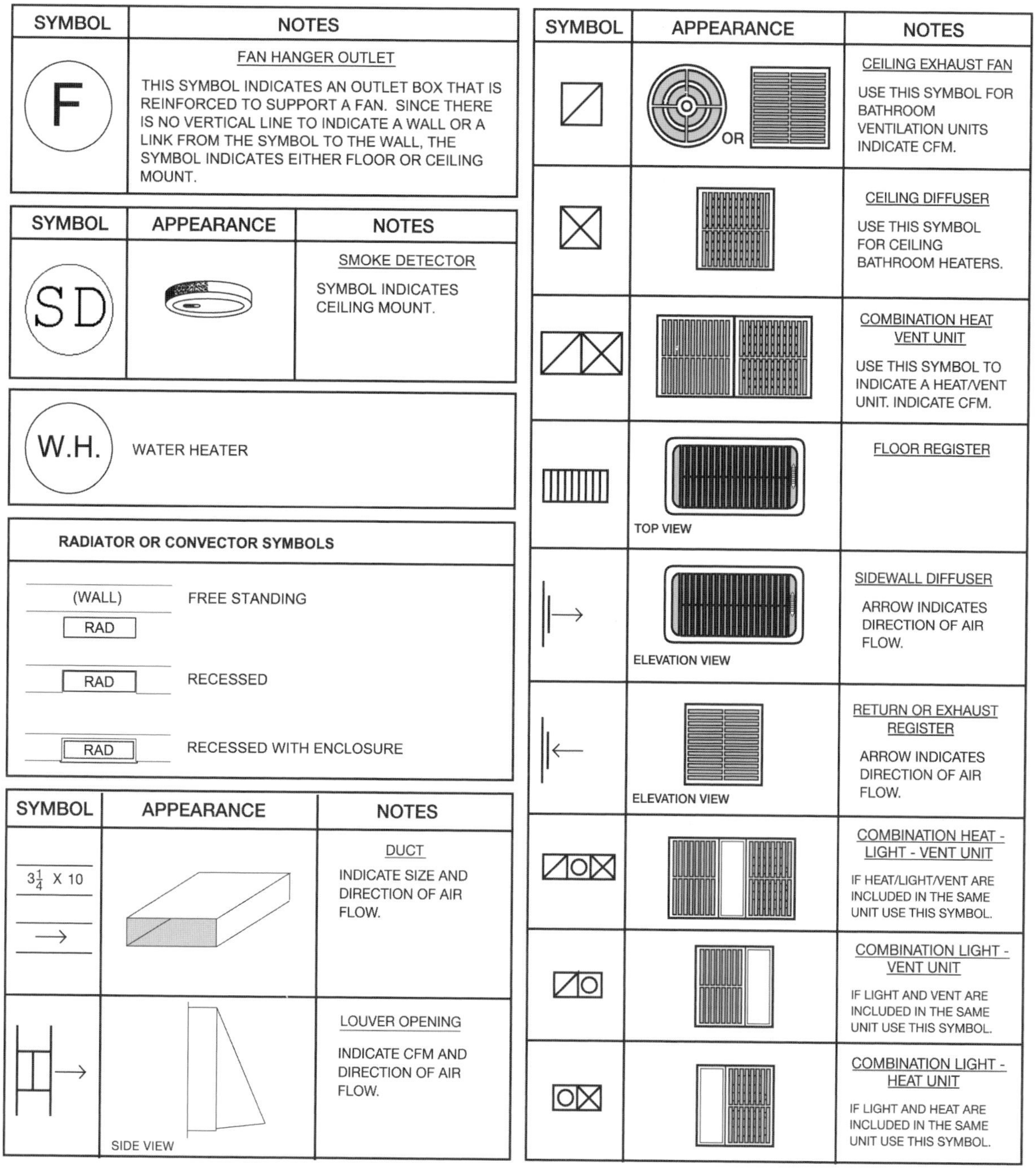

SYMBOL
NOTES
F
FAN HANGER OUTLET
THIS SYMBOL INDICATES AN OUTLET BOX THAT IS REINFORCED TO SUPPORT A FAN. SINCE THERE IS NO VERTICAL LINE TO INDICATE A WALL OR A LINK FROM THE SYMBOL TO THE WALL, THE SYMBOL INDICATES EITHER FLOOR OR CEILING MOUNT.
SYMBOL
APPEARANCE
NOTES
SD
SMOKE DETECTOR
SYMBOL INDICATES CEILING MOUNT.
W.H.
WATER HEATER
RADIATOR OR CONVECTOR SYMBOLS
(WALL)
RAD
FREE STANDING
RAD
RECESSED
RAD
RECESSED WITH ENCLOSURE
SYMBOL
APPEARANCE
NOTES
3¼ X 10
DUCT
INDICATE SIZE AND DIRECTION OF AIR FLOW.
LOUVER OPENING
INDICATE CFM AND DIRECTION OF AIR FLOW.
SIDE VIEW
SYMBOL
APPEARANCE
NOTES
OR
CEILING EXHAUST FAN
USE THIS SYMBOL FOR BATHROOM VENTILATION UNITS INDICATE CFM.
CEILING DIFFUSER
USE THIS SYMBOL FOR CEILING BATHROOM HEATERS.
COMBINATION HEAT VENT UNIT
USE THIS SYMBOL TO INDICATE A HEAT/VENT UNIT. INDICATE CFM.
TOP VIEW
FLOOR REGISTER
ELEVATION VIEW
SIDEWALL DIFFUSER
ARROW INDICATES DIRECTION OF AIR FLOW.
ELEVATION VIEW
RETURN OR EXHAUST REGISTER
ARROW INDICATES DIRECTION OF AIR FLOW.
COMBINATION HEAT - LIGHT - VENT UNIT
IF HEAT/LIGHT/VENT ARE INCLUDED IN THE SAME UNIT USE THIS SYMBOL.
COMBINATION LIGHT - VENT UNIT
IF LIGHT AND VENT ARE INCLUDED IN THE SAME UNIT USE THIS SYMBOL.
COMBINATION LIGHT - HEAT UNIT
IF LIGHT AND HEAT ARE INCLUDED IN THE SAME UNIT USE THIS SYMBOL.

FIGURE 4.26 Miscellaneous symbols.

ADDITIONAL MECHANICAL SYMBOLS
SWITCH WITH TIMER
SWITCH FOR LOW VOLTAGE SWITCHING SYSTEM
PUSH BUTTON AIR SWITCH
GFI-U
GFI WITH USB PORT
ST
STEAM
WP
WHIRLPOOL
LOW VOLTAGE TRANSFORMER
P1
PENDANT FIXTURE
P2
PENDANT FIXTURE
HANGING CEILING FIXTURE
LOW VOLTAGE TASK LIGHT
WALL HUNG FIXTURE
WALL SCONCE
HEAT LAMP
PUCK
PUCK LIGHT
NEW LED PENDANT
NEW LED PENDANT
NEW LED ROPE LIGHTING
G
GAS SUPPLY
SMOKE DETECTOR
S
SPEAKER

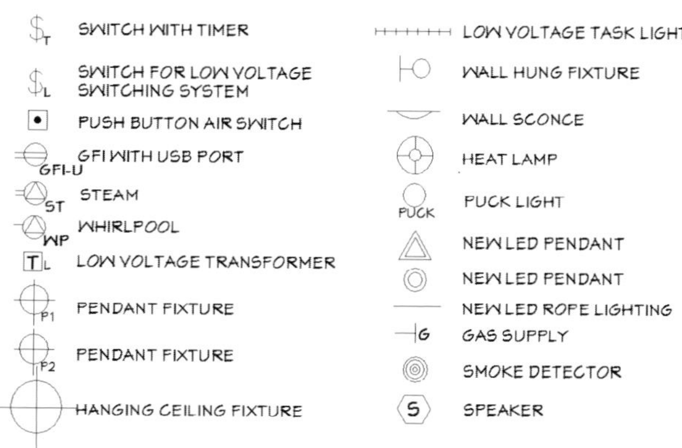

FIGURE 4.27 Additional mechanical symbols.

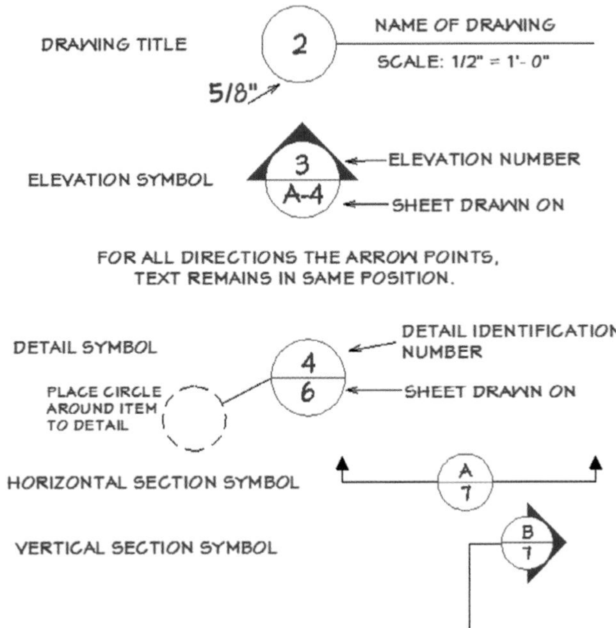

FIGURE 4.28 Title, elevation, and section symbols.

For the section symbol, a circle is used with a long line that cuts through the area where the section is. The number above the line in the circle indicates the number of the drawing. The number below the line indicates the page it is found on. The section can be located on the floor plan or an elevation depending on where the cut was made. Note the symbol for a horizontal cut and a vertical cut.

SUMMARY

Using standardized symbols for all drawings in a set of plans helps with communication among all trades, allied professionals, and clients. The AIA has standard symbols typically used in the industry. There are some variations of certain symbols that are also acceptable in the design industry.

Line quality on a hand-drafted drawing is important. Line weight helps the viewer to better understand the details of the space. A hierarchy of lines exists, along with recommended line weights. The leads designers use can vary depending on which lead better meets their needs for producing the desired line thickness.

The types of lines are standardized and must be used in their proper locations on the drawings. The centerline is very important for kitchen and bath design. It denotes the center points of appliances and fixtures necessary for proper installation.

REVIEW QUESTIONS

1. Explain what line quality on a drawing means. (See "Line Quality" page 57.)
2. Explain what line weight on a drawing means. (See "Line Weight" page 58.)
3. What does the hidden line represent on a floor plan? (See "Hidden Lines" page 59.)
4. Why do we have standardized symbols on drawing? (See "Standard Symbols for Drawings" pages 61–62.)
5. What does an elevation symbol represent? (See "Graphic Symbols" page 74.)

The NKBA Floor Plan

Drafting and Dimensioning the Plan

The floor plan conveys much information for everyone involved in a project, whether it is new construction or remodeling of an existing space. Floor plans are standardized for several reasons. The floor plan must create a clear understanding of the scope of the project for everyone involved in the job. Incorporating standardized line types and symbols helps to limit the chance of error caused by misinterpretation of information on the floor plan. The dimensioning on drawings also ensures proper placement and installation of components in the space.

There are some differences between the NKBA standards for drawings and the American Institute of Architects (AIA) standards for drawings. With the NKBA standards, the walls are dimensioned to the finished interior walls. The AIA standards have dimensions to the centers of the interior walls and to the outside of exterior walls. The units of measure for NKBA are in inches whereas for AIA standards it is feet and inches. Throughout this chapter we look at some of the differences. Designers must know how to interpret the AIA standards on a drawing and be able to draft the drawings in accordance with the NKBA standards.

It takes thoughtful planning before a floor plan of the space can be developed. The process, called *programming,* helps the designer gather important information needed to develop the space and design a layout. Programming is very efficient and helps you have a solid understanding of the client's wants and needs along with providing a good direction for the development of the floor plan.

> *Learning Objective 1: Draft a floor plan in accordance with NKBA standards.*
>
> *Learning Objective 2: Dimension a floor plan in accordance with NKBA standards.*
>
> *Learning Objective 3: Identify elements that must be included on floor plan.*

PROGRAMMING

Before we get to the point of drafting our floor plan, there is much planning before a floor plan of the space can be developed. This process, called *programming*, helps to gather the important information in order to develop the space and design a layout. When you are initially working with a new or remodeled space and trying to figure out how to lay out that space, programming is an efficient way to help you have a good direction for the project. During the programming stage, the designer develops the direction for the design and may come up with some good solutions for the design project.

Programming is a necessary, time-saving step in kitchen and bath design and is done before you start drafting a floor plan. Programming includes collecting, analyzing, sketching, and listing information that is needed to complete the design. At this point, you have the "footprint" or dimensions of the space you will be working with for a design. Programming is often used for planning an entire floor plan for a home.

We use the NKBA Client Survey Form to make a list of the requirements for appliances, cabinet accessories, colors, materials, and the like. This form helps you to focus on your client's wants and needs.

Once you have obtained information using your client survey and have determined the client's requests and space constraints, you can then begin to figure out a workable solution on tracing paper before you start drafting the plan on vellum. You need to know your design direction first or there will be a great deal of editing of the floor plan.

The next step is to determine the adjacencies of the areas. You need to determine who uses the space and which activities will be conducted in the kitchen. The client may have some strong ideas about where they would like things placed. Perhaps they have a particular window where they would like to have seating or they want to include a computer workspace in the kitchen.

Bubble Diagrams

Drawing a bubble diagram helps us determine the adjacencies of a space.

- The bubble diagram consists of circles drawn to represent the work centers or areas and placement of the work triangle. The work triangle consists of the cooking surface, sink, and refrigerator.
- The bubble diagram is not to scale (see Figure 5.1).

To begin the bubble diagram, we figure out the work areas in the space and use bubbles with the name of the area or center written in the bubble. In kitchen design we need bubbles to represent the three areas of the work triangle: sink, refrigerator, and cooking surface. You can also have a bubble to represent the breakfast nook, island, pantry, and the like. The

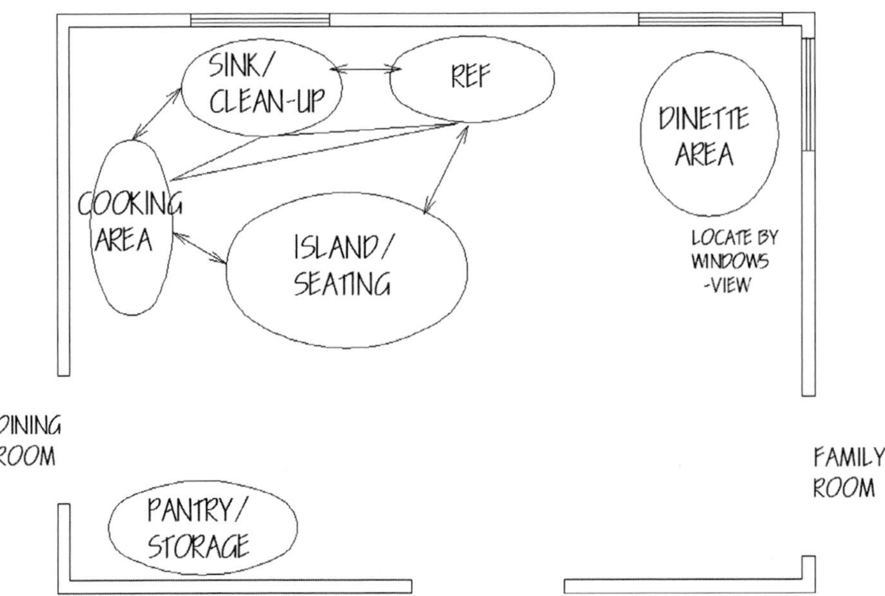

FIGURE 5.1 The "bubbles" show the relationships of areas in the kitchen.

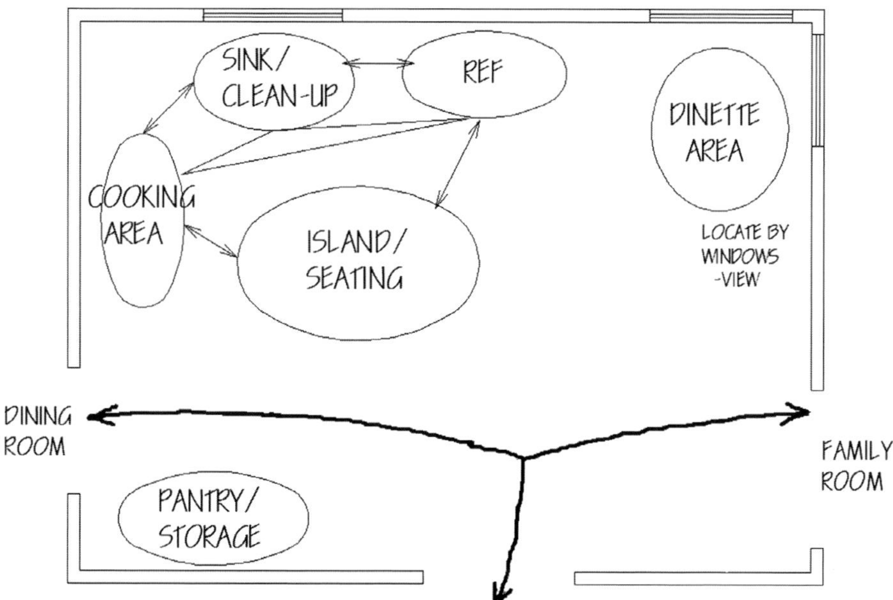

FIGURE 5.2 Traffic flow is indicated with a dark line.

bubble diagram shows the relationships of items in the space. By placing bubbles of our intended main areas in the given space, we can further develop those areas into a rough layout that can then be developed into the floor plan. For bathroom design, you will need bubbles to represent the sink area, toilet, shower, and or tub area. Traffic flow can be indicated with a dark line as shown in Figure 5.2.

The bubble diagram can be fine-tuned for a second draft. The second draft expands on the bubbles (areas) and develops a rough placement of the elements in the drawing such as cabinetry, appliances, and the like (see Figure 5.3).

Developing the space bubbles into the rough placement for the elements in the design will save you time (see Figure 5.4). This rough draft can then be developed into a layout or floor plan of the space in accordance with the NKBA Kitchen & Bathroom Planning Guidelines.

Once you have completed the programming step, you are ready to draft your floor plan.

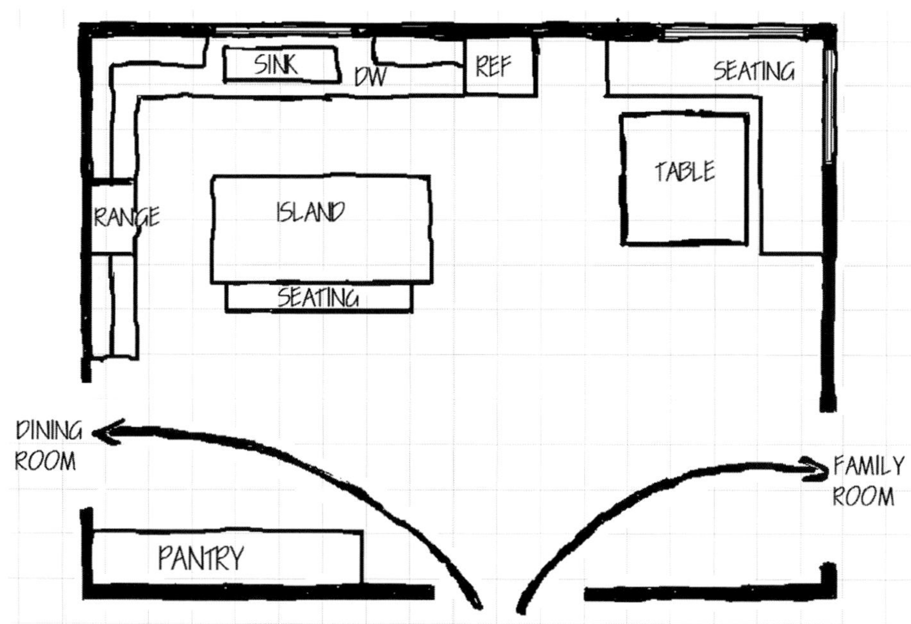

FIGURE 5.3 The second draft fine-tunes the bubble diagram.

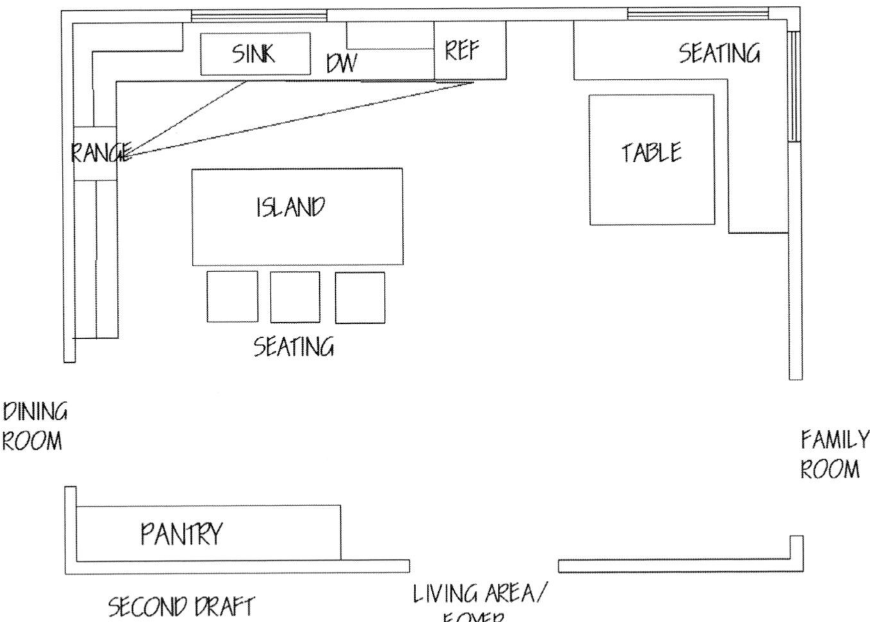

FIGURE 5.4 Illustrates a kitchen bubble diagram that has been developed into a rough placement of the items. This will be further developed into a floor plan.

FLOOR PLAN CONSIDERATIONS

At a minimum, NKBA floor plans must show these details:

- Overall length of wall areas to receive cabinets, countertops, fixtures, or any equipment occupying floor and/or wall space.
- Each wall opening (windows, arches, and doors), major appliances, and fixed structures (chimneys, protrusions, and partitions) individually dimensioned from the outside casing.
- Casing on doors and windows. The casing size must be noted in the specification list on right side of the floor plan drawing.
- Fixtures that will remain in place (include items such as radiators).
- Ceiling heights and room name.
- Additional notes for any deviation from standard height, width and depth (cabinets, countertops, etc.).
- All cabinet nomenclature and floor plan specifications.
- The exact height, width, and depth for areas to be left open in order to receive equipment, cabinets, appliances, and fixtures at a future date.
- Suggestion of flooring materials.
- All pertinent symbols for floor plan, including elevation symbols and drawing title.

Cut Line Height

The cut line height in a space determines how the floor plan elements will look. Items on a floor plan are drawn below this cut line height. The floor plan is an orthographic drawing viewed from the top, and it shows the walls, doors, windows, fixtures, cabinetry, appliances, built-ins, stairs, fireplaces, and other items in that given space. There are differences between the NKBA standards and the AIA standards on a drawing.

For NKBA kitchen and bath drawings, we need to show many details on a drawing. Cabinetry, moldings, and other design features must be indicated. The cut line height for the floor plan is at ceiling height. This results in the wall cabinets drawn as a solid line on the floor plan since all are below this cut line height. More details for cabinetry can be shown on the drawing. The base cabinet line is dashed since it is under the counter surface.

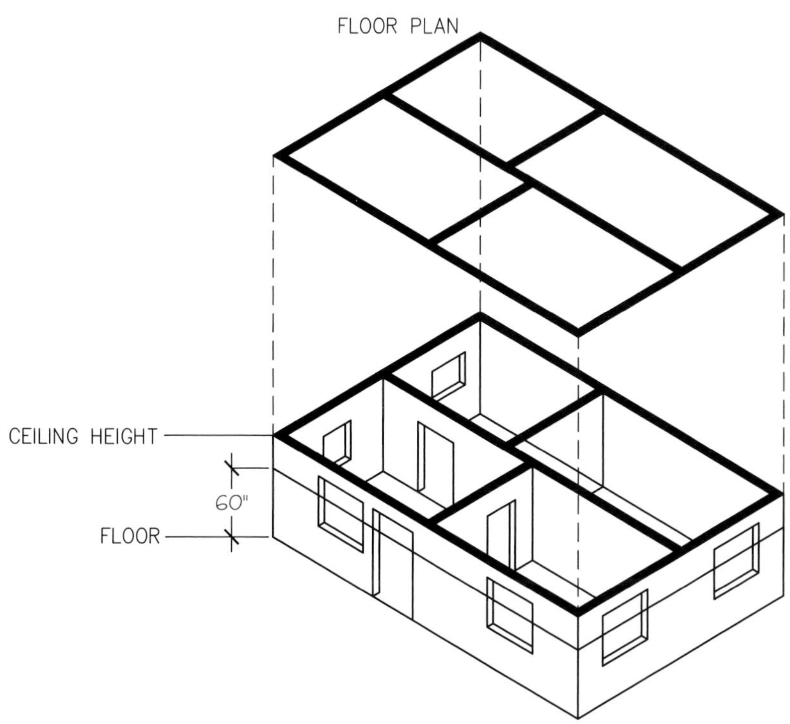

FIGURE 5.5 NKBA standard cut plane height for the floor plan is at ceiling height. AIA standards have cut plane height between 48″ and 60″ off the floor.

For drawings in accordance with the AIA standards, the cut height is placed between 48″ and 60″ This results in the wall cabinets drawn as a dashed line on a floor plan since the wall cabinets are above this cut line height (see Figure 5.5).

NKBA Floor Plan Basics

- The scale used for NKBA floor plans is ½″ = 1′-0″ (1:20).
- Wall cabinets, tall cabinets, appliances, and furniture are drawn with a solid line.
- Base cabinets are drawn with a dashed line (- - - - -) since they are under the counter surface. Any item placed under another surface is drawn with a dashed line.
- The dashed line for the base cabinets stops where it meets the wall cabinets.
- The counter is drawn with a solid line indicating the appropriate overhang.
- Soffits/bulkheads and skylights are drawn with a long dashed line.
  - If the soffit/bulkhead is a different depth than the wall or tall cabinet below, a separate soffit/bulkhead plan or reflected ceiling plan is required.
- The room name and ceiling height must be noted on the plan.
- Specifications must be placed on the right-hand side of floor plan. If there is not enough room, it is acceptable to place them on a second sheet of vellum.
- All cabinets must be labeled with nomenclature and referenced with specifications as necessary.
- For the specifications, a circled reference number must be placed on or by the item and also in the specifications with the description or notes as needed.
  - A list of basic nomenclature can be found in appendix B.
  - Floor plan specification information can be found in the "Dimensioning the Floor Plan" section of this chapter.
- The floor plan must show all major structural elements, such as walls, door swings, door openings, partitions, windows, archways, equipment, and any architectural feature.
- The floor plan must depict the entire room when possible.
- Adjacent rooms or areas must be indicated with a note.
- When the entire room cannot be depicted, you must show the area where the cabinetry and appliances are permanently installed.
- Any wall continuing on past the given space must terminate with a break line to indicate the wall is continuous.

- Elevation symbols must be included on the floor plan for all walls needing interior elevation. Islands also need interior elevations.
- The floor plan must be dimensioned in accordance with the NKBA Graphics and Presentation Standards.

Drafting a Floor Plan

Before you can begin to draft the floor plan, you need to make sure you have your drafting table set up with your drafting tools readily available.

1. Set the drafting table at a proper angle for the individual drafter. Ten to fifteen degrees works well for most designers. It is best to have a dedicated area for your drafting.
2. Align and adhere your paper to the drafting board using drafting tape or drafting dots. The borderline on a preprinted sheet of vellum can be used to align, or simply align the edge of the sheet of vellum.

   Place the drafting tape diagonally across the four corners of paper. Place the tape so that you can peel it off when the drawing is finished without tearing the corner of the vellum. If you are using drafting dots, place a dot at the four corners so it covers the corner of the paper and attaches to the table. The tape for both must be placed correctly so it is easily pulled off of the vellum/paper.

   Align the paper with the parallel bar or straightedge (see Figure 5.6).

   Note: If you are tracing another drawing, you must adhere that drawing to the drafting surface separate from the vellum placed over it.

3. Determine the placement of the floor plan on the drawing sheet.
   - Place the floor plan specifications on the right side of drawing. If there is not enough room, they may be placed at the bottom, although the right side is preferred. Leave 2½″ to 3″ of space for the floor plan specifications.
   - Allow space for the dimension lines on all sides of the room. Dimensions are placed at a minimum of 3⁄16″ or ½″ apart. Typically there are three lines of dimensions. Keep evenly spaced on all sides of the walls in the room.
   - Depending on the configuration of the space, you may need more room at the top, bottom, or sides if there is a projection of the walls or some other architectural feature.
   - Allow room for the title of your drawing at the bottom of the drawing sheet below the floor plan.

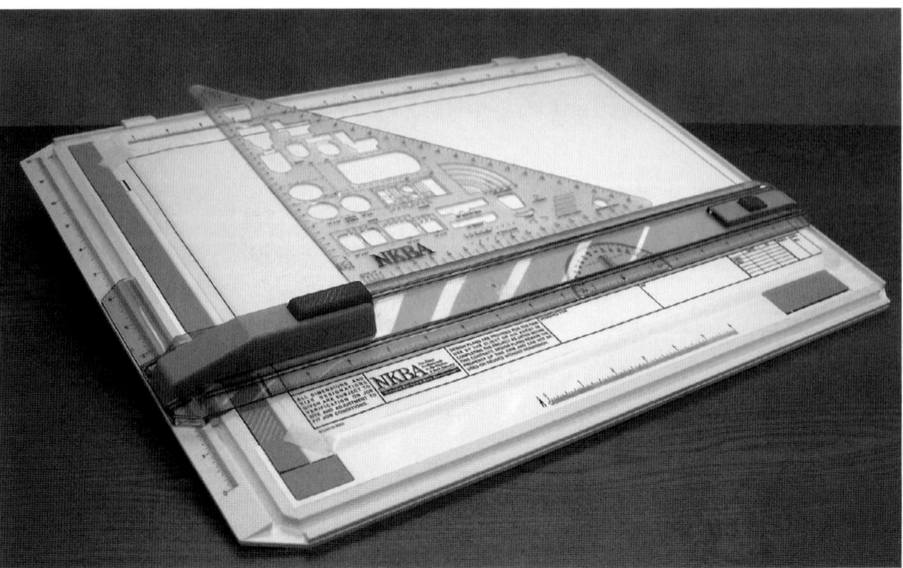

FIGURE 5.6 Align the sheet of vellum using your parallel bar or straightedge and one of the horizontal border lines. *Courtesy of NKBA*

Tip

Use a piece of tracing paper to roughly lay out the perimeter of the space. Calculate the space needed for dimensions, title, and floor plan specifications to help figure placement of your floor plan on the drawing sheet. This technique helps prevent unwanted lines on a sheet of vellum that are often hard to erase.

4. The walls can now be lightly penciled in. Lightly draw the perimeter of the walls for the space.
   - Draw the interior wall line of the room first.
   - Next draw your second line for the wall thickness the correct distance away from the first line.
   - Interior walls are drawn at 4½″ (114 mm). This includes the stud plus gypsum board on both sides.
   - Exterior walls are drawn at 6″ (165 mm).
   - Drawing the walls lightly at this point allows you to erase and adjust the lines as needed. It is much harder to erase a darker line on a sheet of vellum (see Figure 5.7).
   - Drawing light walls initially will also help you catch any mistakes that may have been made by incorrect measuring or drawing a line at the wrong length.
   - Verify that the walls are correct length at this point. Double check your measurements.
   - For NKBA drawings, wall dimensions are from finished inside wall to finished inside wall.
5. Locate all doors and windows along the walls (see Figure 5.8).

FIGURE 5.7 Lightly penciled-in walls. Verify the length of all walls drawn at this point.

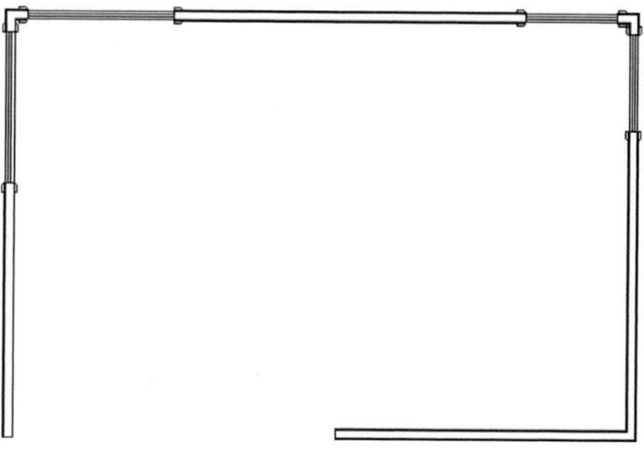

FIGURE 5.8 Locate the doors and windows on walls.

- Locate doors and windows from at least two different points to ensure accuracy.
- Draw the door and window casings on the plan. Show the dimension from outside casing to outside casing. In kitchen and bath design, we need to have the exact usable wall space. The actual opening is smaller without the casing.
- Write the size of casing in your specifications on the right side of the drawing.

6. Verify all wall lengths and placement of openings.
   - Make necessary changes as needed.
   - The lines are light at this point, so they are easily changed.
   - Again, the measurements are from inside wall to inside wall.
7. Darken the wall lines.
   - Now that wall, window, and door placement have been verified, you can darken the walls.
   - The line weight can now be introduced.
8. Draw in window and door symbols, and then darken your lines.
   - Wall lines should be thicker than the window or door symbol lines. Adhere to the hierarchy of lines on a drawing.
9. Next, draw in the cabinets, equipment, fixtures, furniture, and clearances around these items.

   At this point you will have gone through the process of designing the space and have met the NKBA Kitchen & Bathroom Planning Guidelines.

   - It is best to draw in these items lightly at first and then darken the lines when you have accurate details (see Figure 5.9).

Tips

- Avoid smearing the pencil lead. Lift your parallel slide or straightedge when moving it. Never drag it across your drawing. Doing so will smudge your lines.
- Erase carefully so that you don't tear the paper. Be very careful with electric or battery powered erasers; they can burn a hole right through your vellum.
- Always use your drafting brush, not your hand, to remove eraser shavings and graphite.

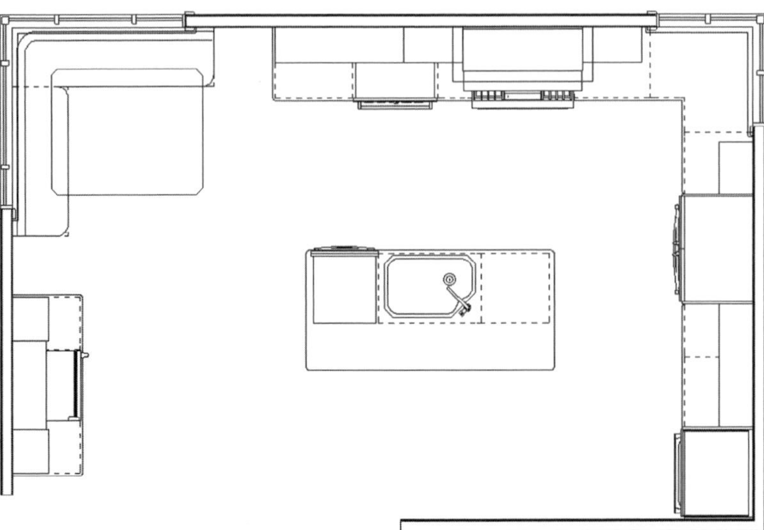

FIGURE 5.9 Draw in the cabinets, equipment, fixtures, and furniture lightly and then darken your lines.

10. Next, darken all the solid object lines. Solid objects include items such as the cabinets, appliances, fixtures, and countertops.
- Draw the base cabinet lines with a hidden line since the base cabinet is hidden under the surface of the counter. Any item below another surface is hidden and therefore dashed.
- To help keep the dashes consistent on a drawing, many designers use a straightedge with divided markers, such as the ones found on the NKBA template.

11. The next step is to dimension your drawing (see Figure 5.10).
- NKBA dimensions differ slightly from AIA standards. More details about dimensioning are found in the section titled "Dimensioning the Floor Plan." Follow the standard NKBA dimensioning technique.
- The dimension lines drawn will depend on the items along that given wall.
- Line 1 is closest to the wall and shows all usable wall space.
- Line 2 is in the center of three lines. It shows all center points of appliances and fixtures.
- Line 3 is the outermost line and shows the overall length of wall.
- All walls and interior clearances must be dimensioned.
- Peninsulas and islands must be dimensioned.
- The number of dimension lines for each side will vary with what items are on that wall. If there are no openings or appliances, you may have just one dimension line for the overall wall.
- Every wall must have at least an overall dimension.
- Dimension lines around walls should be evenly spaced, if possible.

FIGURE 5.10 Dimensioned floor plan.

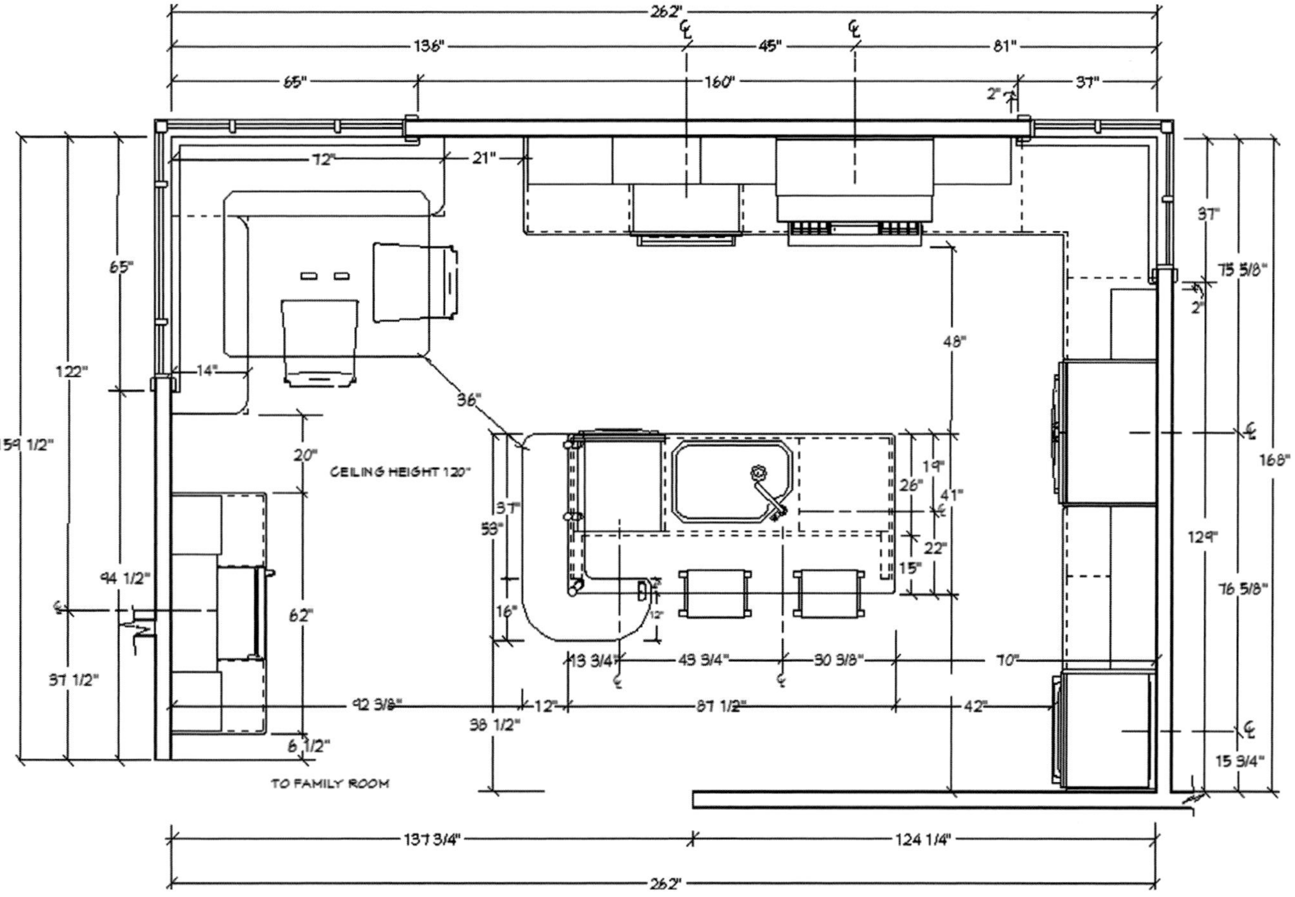

12. Draw additional pieces not yet included on the floor plan and all details of items such as cabinetry, appliances, and so on.
    - Add details to the items.
    - Draw additional pieces not included yet, such as chairs, accessories, flooring, and others.
13. Label all items in accordance with the NKBA Graphics and Presentation Standards. Include cabinets, appliances, equipment, and nomenclature designations.
    - Letter nomenclature and center the nomenclature on cabinets.
    - Use your lettering guide for consistency. Make all letters ⅛″ high.
    - Cabinets should be designated and identified by manufacturer's nomenclature. (See appendix B for cabinet nomenclature.)
    - Designate cabinet system trim and finish items outside their area with a leader line clarifying exactly where the trim piece is located (see Figure 5.11). Use the nomenclature from the specific cabinet manufacturer.

Some Nomenclature Basics

Keep in mind that cabinet nomenclature can vary among the different lines although there are basics in common (see Figure 5.12).

- W ___ ___. W represents a wall cabinet. Width is listed first, then height. Assume 12″-deep standard. If depth differs, you must note it on the plan and/or the specs (example: W2436).
- B ____. B represents base. List the width of the cabinet. Assumed depth is 24″ (standard) and assumed height is 34½″. If depth differs, you must note the depth on the plan and/or the specs (example: B18).
- T ___ ___. T represents tall cabinet. List the width first, then the height. Depth often is listed at the end, or it can be noted in the specifications.
    - Some cabinet lines also refer to a tall cabinet as U, for utility cabinet.
- L or R indicates the hinged side as you face the cabinet.
- Refer to appendix B for more standard nomenclature.
- Letter any necessary notes on the floor plan for clarification.
- Make sure your room is labeled and your ceiling height is noted.
- Add the title below the drawing.
- Include additional notes for any deviations from standard height, width, and depth of cabinets, countertops, and the like.

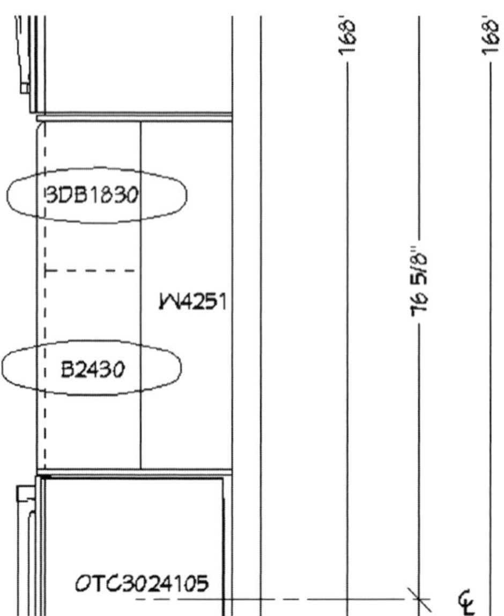

FIGURE 5.11 Center nomenclature on cabinets.

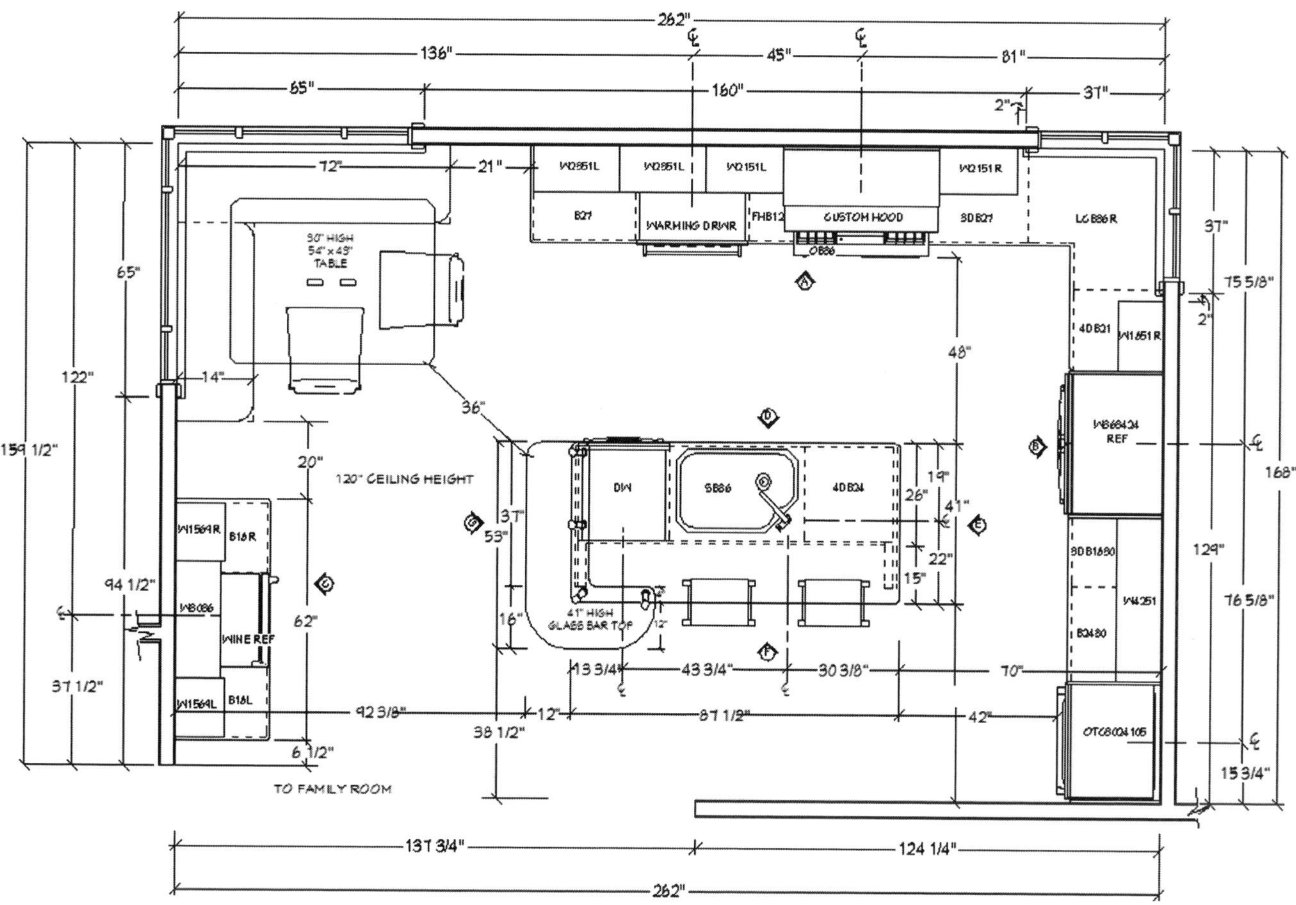

FIGURE 5.12 Add interior details, nomenclature, labeling, and notes to complete the floor plan.

Note: Once you have determined which walls require an interior elevation, place the elevation symbol with referenced information in the correct position on the floor plan.

14. Last, complete the floor plan specifications.
    - The floor plan specifications can provide further explanation of a particular item and can be used if there is not enough space for the label on the plan.
    - Often you need to explain the nomenclature letters and describe what the letters represent.
    - Identify any deviation from standard height, width, and depth of cabinets, countertops, and the like in the floor plan specifications.
    - Identify items by a circled reference number that corresponds to the information found in the specifications (see Figure 5.13).
    - Nomenclature should be centered on the cabinet. Place the circled reference number below the nomenclature in a consistent manner (see Figure 5.14).
    - Note any crown molding and toekick.
    - Note appliances, including manufacturer and model numbers.
    - List the exact opening in height, width, and depth for areas to be left open to receive equipment, cabinets, appliances and fixtures at a future date (see Figure 5.15).
    - Some design firms prefer to call out all cabinet nomenclature in the floor plan specification listing.
    - Equally acceptable is the use of a circled reference number to designate each cabinet on the floor plan, and elevations with the cabinet code listed within the individual unit width on the elevations or in a separate cross-reference list on the elevations.

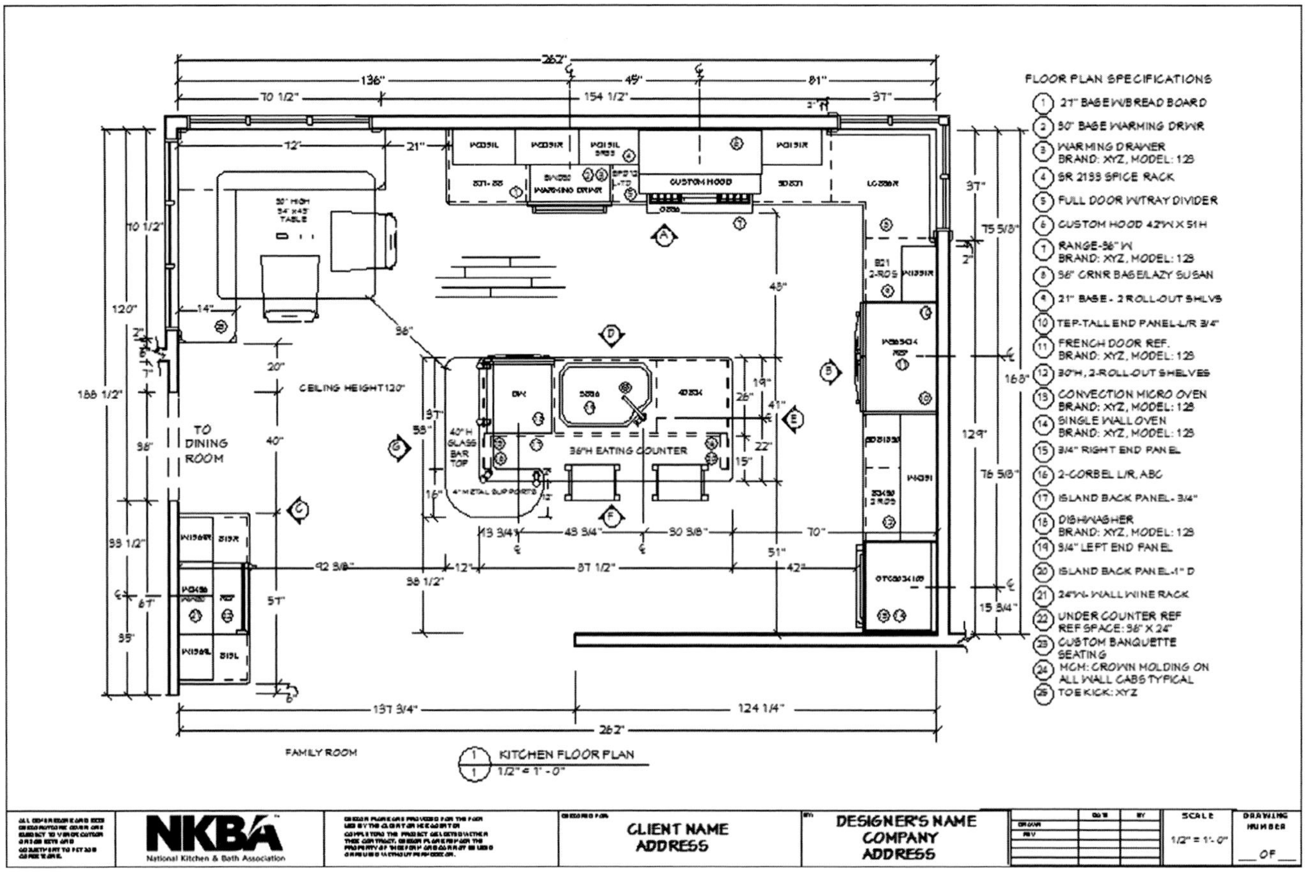

FIGURE 5.13 Add the specifications on floor plan.

- Regardless of the cabinet designation system selected, additional information for supplementary fixtures, appliances, equipment, accessories, and special provisions pertaining to the cabinets must be indicated within the cabinet or equipment area by a reference number in a circle. Then list this additional information in the specifications on the floor plan drawing or a separate sheet of paper.
- Show special-order materials or custom design features, angled cabinets, unusual tops, molding, trim details, and the like in a section view, a plan view in a scale larger than ½″ = 1′-0″), or an elevation view. Refer to appendix A for sample plans.

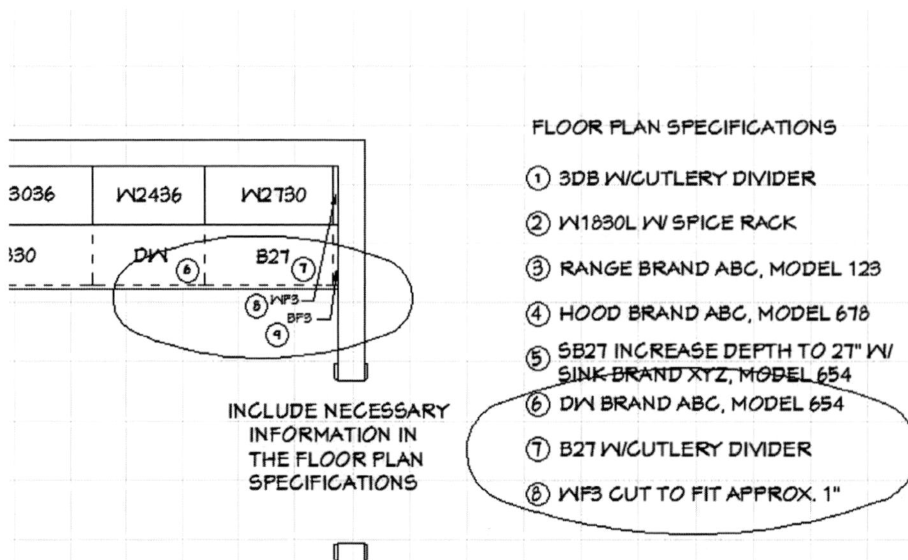

FIGURE 5.14 Nomenclature centered on cabinets. A circled number references the item on the floor plan and in floor plan specifications. Use a leader line with arrow for labeling items in tight places.

4DB21
W1851R
75 5/8"
12
36" x 69" REF SPACE
INDICATE EXACT
SPACE LEFT
OPENFOR
FUTURE REF
W363424
REF
12
168"
168"
3DB1830

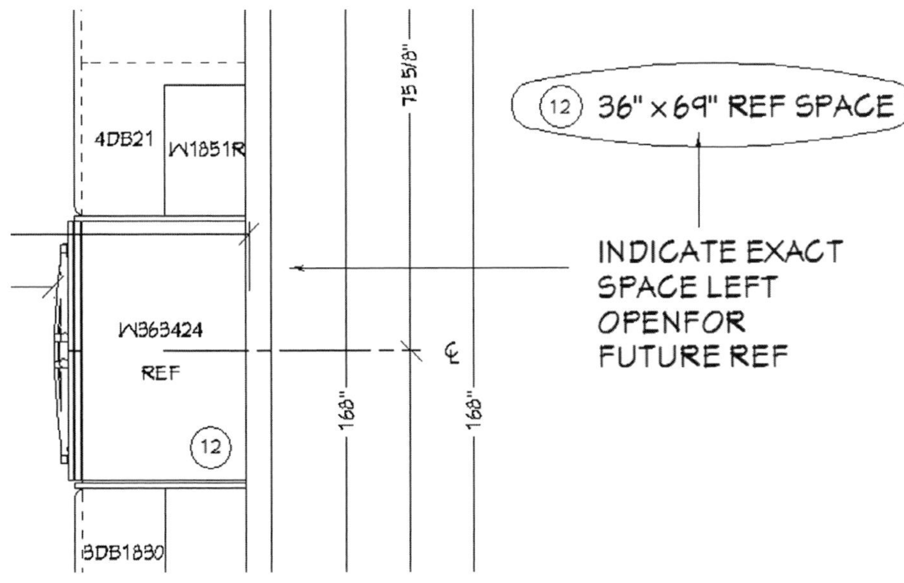

FIGURE 5.15 Floor plan specifications with descriptions. Note appliance space that is left open for future appliance installation. Nomenclature is centered on cabinet with a circled number placed below.

15. Complete the title block.

- Identify your company, client information, job identification, scale, drawing number, your name as designer as well as the draftsperson's name. Include additional information as needed (see Figure 5.16).

FIGURE 5.16 Complete the title block on the drawing.

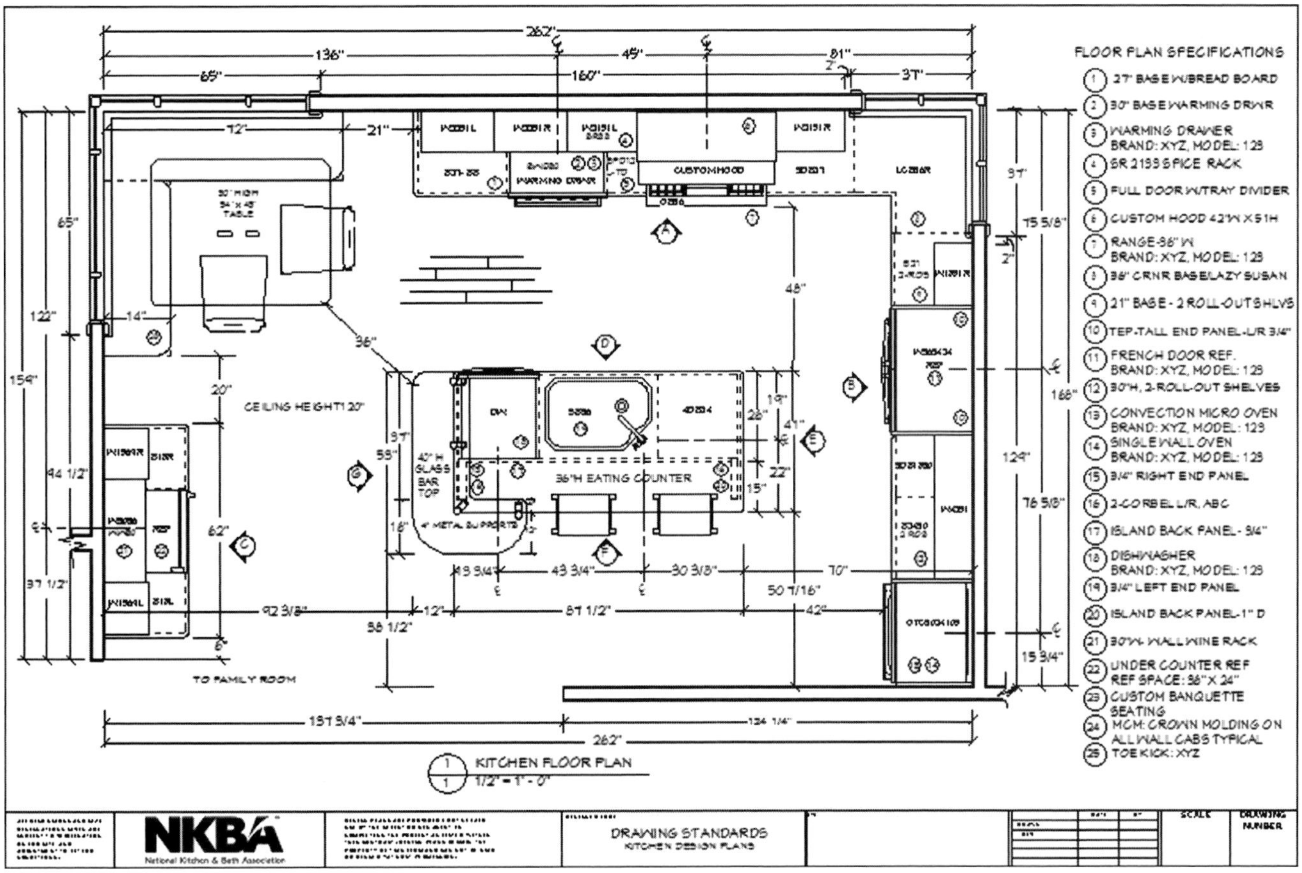

FLOOR PLAN SPECIFICATIONS
1 27" BASE W/BREAD BOARD
2 30" BASE WARMING DRWR
3 WARMING DRAWER BRAND: XYZ, MODEL: 123
4 6R 2133 SPICE RACK
5 FULL DOOR W/TRAY DIVIDER
6 CUSTOM HOOD 42"W X 51H
7 RANGE-36" W BRAND: XYZ, MODEL: 123
8 36" CRNR BASE/LAZY SUSAN
9 21" BASE - 2 ROLL-OUT SHLVS
10 TEP-TALL END PANEL-L/R 3/4"
11 FRENCH DOOR REF. BRAND: XYZ, MODEL: 123
12 30"H, 2-ROLL-OUT SHELVES
13 CONVECTION MICRO OVEN BRAND: XYZ, MODEL: 123
14 SINGLE WALL OVEN BRAND: XYZ, MODEL: 123
15 3/4" RIGHT END PANEL
16 2-CORBEL L/R, ABC
17 ISLAND BACK PANEL - 3/4"
18 DISHWASHER BRAND: XYZ, MODEL: 123
19 3/4" LEFT END PANEL
20 ISLAND BACK PANEL-1" D
21 30"W WALL WINE RACK
22 UNDER COUNTER REF REF SPACE: 36" X 24"
23 CUSTOM BANQUETTE SEATING
24 MCM: CROWN MOLDING ON ALL WALL CABS TYPICAL
25 TOE KICK: XYZ
CUSTOM HOOD
CEILING HEIGHT 120"
36"H EATING COUNTER
42"H GLASS BAR TOP
TO FAMILY ROOM
262"
136"
65"
160"
45"
81"
37"
KITCHEN FLOOR PLAN
1/2" = 1'-0"
NKBA
National Kitchen & Bath Association
DRAWING STANDARDS
KITCHEN DESIGN PLANS
SCALE
DRAWING NUMBER

DIMENSIONING THE FLOOR PLAN

Dimensions on a floor plan are critical for the correct installation of all components in the kitchen or bath space. Mechanicals such as plumbing, gas, and electrical must be installed in the correct location for the appliances and fixtures and are impacted by the placement of the cabinetry. Accurate dimensioning on the floor plan will assist in a successful project installation.

There are a few differences between the NKBA and the AIA standards for dimensioning (see Figure 5.17). For dimensioning in accordance with the NKBA standards, we are concerned with the usable wall space. Every inch and fraction of an inch is very important. The dimensions are taken from inside wall to inside wall so the designer knows exactly how much space there is to work with. The drawing also must have the appliances and fixtures centerlined for correct placement. Dimensions always go to the outside edge of the casing around windows and doors for accurate usable wall space.

NKBA dimensioning standards:
- Indicate all dimensions with inches only.
- Dimension to the surface of the interior wall.
- Dimension to the outside of the casing on doors and windows.
- Centerline all appliances and fixtures.

AIA dimensioning standards:
- Indicate dimensions with feet and inches.
- Dimension to the center of interior walls and to outside of exterior walls.
- Dimension to the centers of doors and windows.

These dimensions must be shown on every floor plan as minimum requirements:

- Overall length of wall areas to receive cabinets, countertops, fixtures, or any equipment occupying floor and/or wall space. This dimension should always be the outside line.
- Each wall opening (windows, arches, and doors), major appliances, and fixed structures (chimneys, protrusions, and partitions) must be individually dimensioned.
- Trim size must be noted in the specification list. Dimensions are shown from outside trim.
- Fixtures remaining in place, such as radiators, must be outlined on the floor plan. These critical dimensions should be on the first dimension line.
- Ceiling height must appear on the floor plan.
- Additional notes must be included for any deviation from standard height, width, and depth of countertops and cabinets.
- The exact opening must be given in height, width, and depth for areas to be left open to receive equipment, cabinets, appliances, and fixtures at a future date.

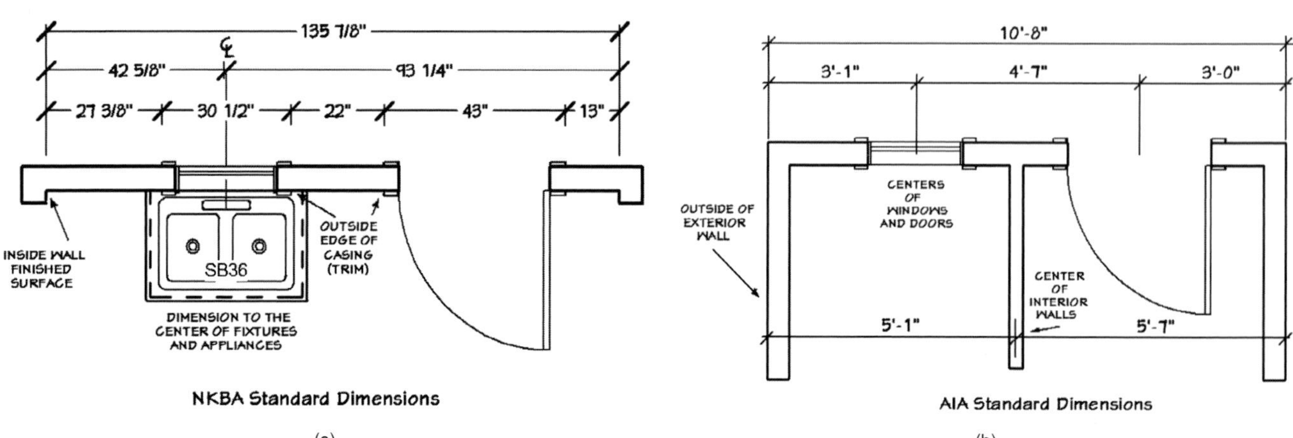

FIGURE 5.17 Dimensioning differences with NKBA standards and AIA standards.

- Items such as island and peninsula cabinets must be shown with the overall dimensions given from countertop edge to opposite wall so they are anchored with accurate dimensions, or fixed object across such as cabinet or counter edge. The clearance must be indicated from countertop edge to countertop edge. If there is an appliance handle projection, the clearance dimension must go to that object. In accordance with the NKBA Kitchen & Bathroom Planning Guidelines, the work aisle in the space should be 42″ (1067 mm) from counter edge to counter edge.
- Feet and inches must always be written with a dash between the feet and inches. For example ½″ scale: 1′-0″. This clarifies that the units are feet and inches and reduces the chance of an error made when reading the dimensions.

Dimensioning basics:

- Dimension all walls of the space.
- Use inches for all dimensions.
- Place dimensions outside the wall. Dimensions for islands and interior clearances may be placed on the interior of the plan.
- Space dimension lines no closer than 3⁄16″ (5 mm) from a wall or other dimension line. Preferred distance is ½″ (13 mm).
- Never allow the extension line (witness line) to touch a wall line. Leave 1⁄16″ (2 mm) gap.
- Use a 45-degree slash to terminate the dimension line.
- Two techniques are used to letter numbers on dimension lines:
  a. Horizontal and vertical dimension lines can be lettered parallel to the title block at the bottom of the vellum, and the numbers break the dimension line near its midpoint. This is referred to as "read from the bottom" (see Figure 5.18).
  b. Vertical dimension lines can be lettered so all vertical dimensions are read from the right side of drawing with the horizontal dimensions read from the bottom of plan. This is referred to as "read from the right." The number breaks the dimension line at its midpoint (see Figure 5.19).

Technique for dimensioning the floor plan:

1. To begin, choose one wall to start your dimensioning.
2. Draw your extension lines (witness lines) from the inside wall corners.
   - Leave 1⁄16″ (2 mm) gap so the extension line does not touch the wall line.
   - The extension line (witness lines) can extend 1⁄16″ to ⅛″ (2 to 3 mm) past the last dimension line.

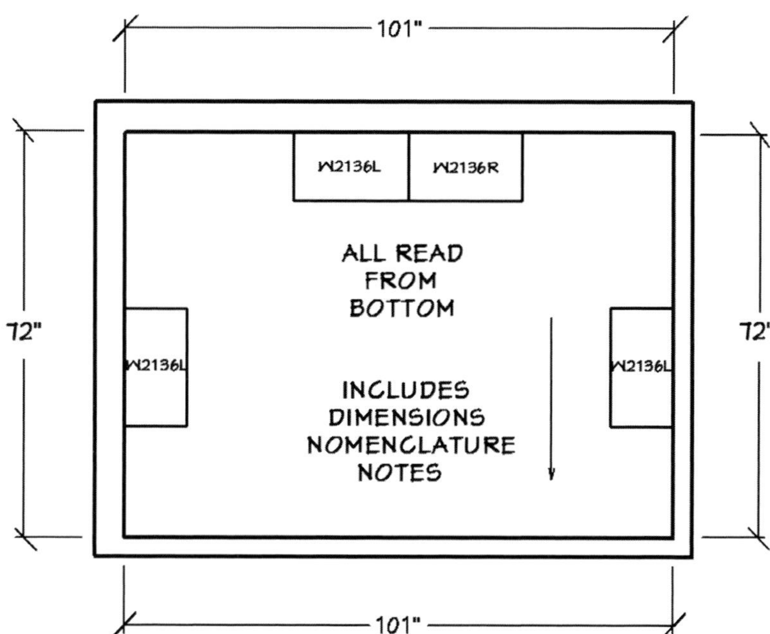

FIGURE 5.18 Dimensions all parallel to title block at bottom of vellum. Numbers read from bottom of plan.

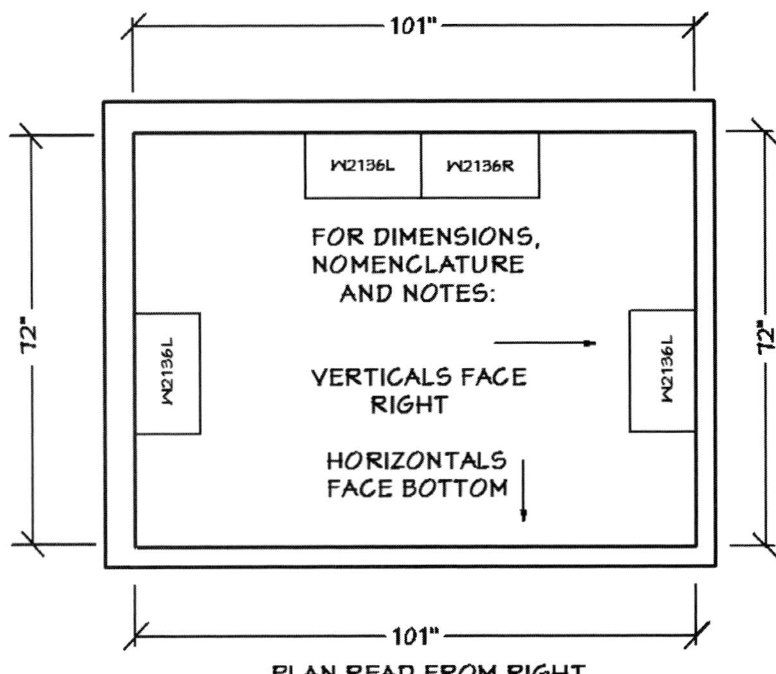

FIGURE 5.19 Acceptable method is to have horizontal dimensions read from bottom of plan and vertical dimensions read from right side of plan.

3. Draw the first dimension line. This line is closest to the wall and is referred to as line 1 (see Figure 5.20).
   - The first dimension line indicates usable wall space. Items to dimension include from inside wall surface, wall openings, outside casing of windows and doors, fixed structures, chimneys, radiators, protrusions, and partitions. A wall perpendicular to that dimensioned wall should be noted as well.
   - Window and door casing sizes must be noted in the floor plan specifications.
   - Draw a line across from extension line to extension line, parallel to the wall. The line can terminate at the extension line. It is acceptable for the dimension line to extend past the extension line ⅛″ (3 mm) on both ends of the line.
   - Place this line no less than 3⁄16″ (5 mm) from wall. The preferred distance is ½″ (13 mm). Space the lines the same distance apart on all walls for consistency.
   - Place short vertical lines on the dimension line to indicate those items to be dimensioned on this first line. Again, these include from inside wall, wall openings, outside casings of windows and doors (trim), fixed structures, chimneys, radiators, protrusions, partitions, and perpendicular walls. Walls perpendicular to the dimensioned walls need to be indicated.
   - The first dimension line must clear any projection that may be on the given wall. The line may need to be placed farther out from the wall itself.
   - Place a 45-degree slash at the point where the extension (witness) line intersects. An arrow or dot is sometimes used, but the 45-degree slash is the industry standard.
   - The number goes "in" the dimension line. The number should be in the open space on the dimension line.

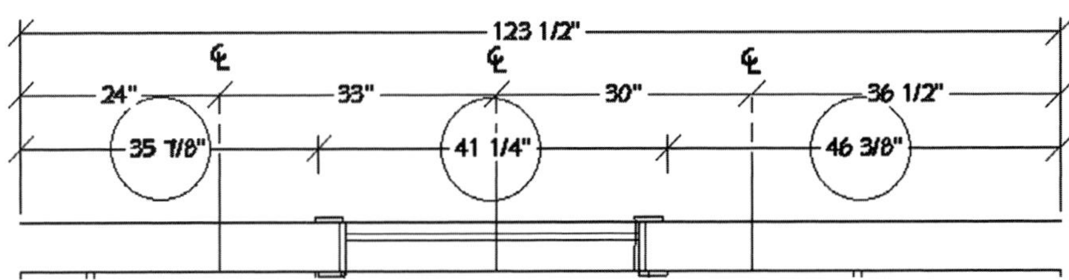

FIGURE 5.20 First dimension line is closest to the wall. This indicates usable wall space. Dimension from interior wall to casings, openings, and any change in wall surface.

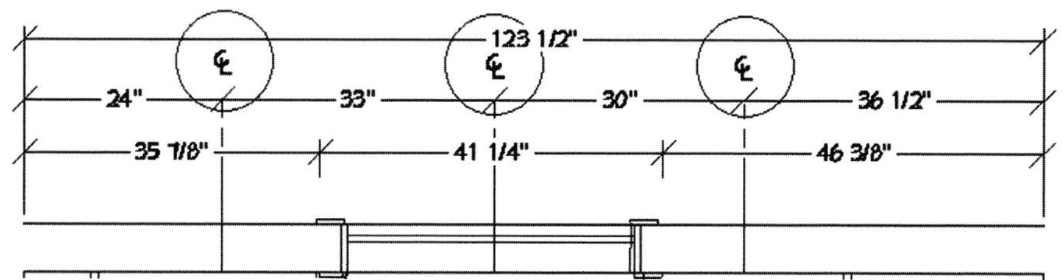

FIGURE 5.21 The second dimension line indicates the center points of all appliances and fixtures.

- For horizontal dimensions, the slash goes from bottom left to upper right (/).
- For vertical dimensions, the slash goes from upper left to bottom right (\)

  Note: If the particular wall you are dimensioning does not have any openings, such as windows or doors, and there is no change in the wall, you will not need the first dimension line.

4. Draw the second dimension line, also referred to as line 2 or the center line.
   - This dimension line indicates all center points of appliances and fixtures placed along that wall.
   - Draw the second dimension line a minimum of 3⁄16″ (5 mm) from the first dimension line. The preferred distance is ½″ (13 mm).
   - Draw your line in accordance with length as for first dimension line.
   - Locate the center points of all appliances and fixtures on the dimension line with the centerline symbol. Centerline is a series of long and short dashes (see Figure 5.21).
   - Place a 45-degree slash at the point where the centerline meets the dimension line. Place a CL at the top of that center line.

   Note: You must provide centerline dimensions for equipment in two directions when possible to indicate the exact location of the equipment for plumbing and wiring purposes. This is especially true for appliances or fixtures placed in a corner or in an island or peninsula. For a bathroom, the shower drain must be centerlined from two points to make sure it is placed properly.
5. Draw the third dimension line (the overall dimension line). It is referred to as line 3 (see Figure 5.22).
   - The third overall dimension line is the line farthest away from the given wall.
   - This line is the overall length of the wall from inside wall to inside wall.
   - Draw this wall the same length spaced apart the same distance as for the first and second dimension lines.
6. Repeat steps 1 through 5 for each wall in the room perimeter.
   - The number of dimension lines for a particular wall depends on what is along that wall. If there are no openings, appliances, or fixtures along that wall, only one line may be necessary. A wall can have one, two, or three dimension lines. Dimension lines should be evenly spaced for all the walls.
7. Dimension the interior of the floor plan.
   - It is best to set up "strings" for your interior dimensions. This means that adjacent dimensions can all be put on one dimension line "string".
   - Dimension items such as peninsula cabinets and islands.
   - Note the clearances of work aisles, traffic paths, and other clearances.

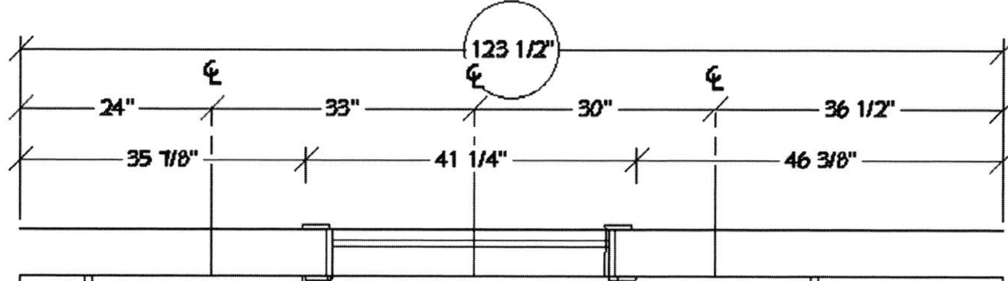

FIGURE 5.22 The third dimension line is the overall dimension of the wall.

- Show the dimension from the countertop edge to the opposite wall. Identify the exact location of the structure by dimensions that position or anchor it from two directions. The preferred placement of the dimension is from a return wall or face of cabinets.
- If there is an appliance or fixture in the island or peninsula, it must be centerlined from two directions so the mechanicals can be installed in correct location.
- Place the overall dimensions, centerlines, and other necessary dimensions close to the island or peninsula within the floor plan. Strings can be set up that include the clearances around island.

  Note: Finished interior dimensions are used on all project documents to denote available space for cabinetry and/or other types of equipment. If you are responsible for specifying the exact method of wall construction, finish, and/or partition placement, include partitions in accordance with the AIA Standards on the construction plan as well as the finished interior dimensions.

General notes about dimensioning centerlines on kitchen and bathroom plans:

- Items requiring a centerline include: appliances, sinks, tubs/showers, toilets, bidets, fan units, light fixtures, heating and air conditioning ducts, and radiators.
- Pull centerline dimensions from return walls or from the front of cabinets/equipment opposite the mechanical element.
- On the floor plan indicate the centerlines of mechanicals and fixtures by the symbol (CL) followed by a long-short-long broken line that extends into the floor area.
- When there are a total of three dimension lines, the center line is typically the second line (center).Keep in mind that a wall may have only one dimension line for the overall dimension. It may have only two lines, or it may have all three. It depends what is placed along the particular wall (see Figure 5.23).
- Regardless of the cabinet designation system selected, you must indicate additional information for supplementary fixtures, appliances, equipment, accessories, and special provisions pertaining to the cabinets within the cabinet or equipment area by a reference number in a circle. List this additional information in the specifications on the floor plan drawing or on a separate sheet of paper.
- Show special-order materials or custom design features, angled cabinets, unusual tops, molding, trim details, and the like in a section view (or cut view), a plan view in a scale larger than ½″ = 1′-0″), elevation view, or as a detail drawing. Refer to appendix A for sample plans.

FIGURE 5.23 Dimension lines on various walls.

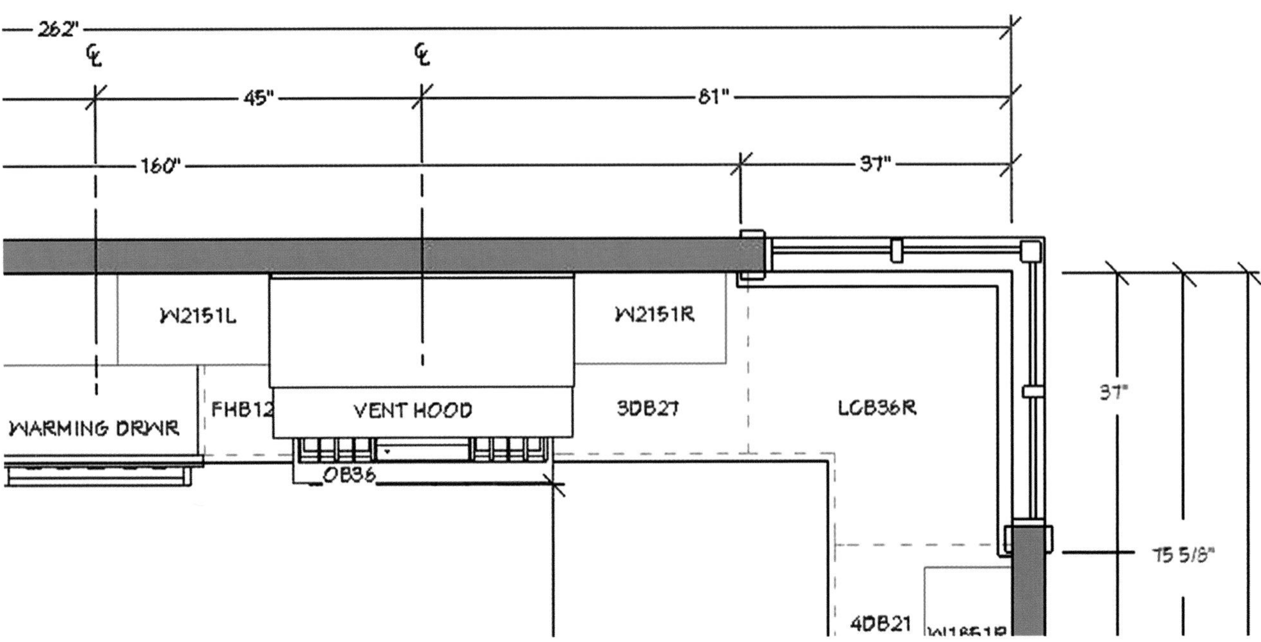

SUMMARY

As designers, we must be able to interpret drawings completed with AIA standards and draft drawings completed in accordance with NKBA standards. Knowing every fraction of an inch of space we have to design within makes for a successful project completion. Using the correct techniques for drafting the space is important.

By determining the placement of the elements on your sheet of vellum initially and using light layout lines, you will be more efficient and not waste time reworking the drawing later. The goal is to produce an accurate, professional-looking drawing. Dimensioning a drawing accurately is critical for the design project. All specified items must fit into the designed space properly. The installation of the cabinetry, appliances, electrical, and the like is influenced by the timing of other work completed. Proper placement of items is key to a smooth installation job and for the design intent of the space. Programming will help you develop a well-planned floor plan of the space in an efficient manner.

REVIEW QUESTIONS

1. How does the cut line height correspond to the floor plan? (See "Cut Line Height" pages 80–81)
2. Why do the dimensions stop at the casings of the window for NKBA floor plans? (See "Dimensioning the Floor Plan" page 90)
3. How should nomenclature be placed on a cabinet? (See "Drafting a Floor Plan—Step 13" page XX)
4. When would a drawing only need two dimension lines for the particular wall? (See "Dimensioning a Floor Plan—Step 4" page 83).
5. What are the two acceptable techniques for dimensioning the floor plan? (See "Dimensioning Basics"—Figures 5.18–5.19" pages 91–92)

NKBA Drawings in a Set of Plans

Now we look at the various drawings found in a set of NKBA kitchen plans and bath plans. The NKBA drawings in a given set supply the necessary information needed for the project. Attention to detail is critical for completing the plans so that no item is overlooked. This chapter presents the drawings to be completed along with instructions for completion and what needs to be included. Each drawing has a purpose in supplying the correct information for the project, although some drawings are optional. For a simple soffit/bulkhead, for example, a drawing may not be necessary. For more complex designs, drawings are necessary to convey the design and for installation.

Learning Objective 1: Learn which drawings must be included in a set of NKBA drawings and which are considered optional.

Learning Objective 2: Know what information must be placed on each drawing.

Learning Objective 3: Understand all components placed on each drawing.

FLOOR PLAN

The floor plan conveys much information for everyone involved in a project, whether it is new construction or remodeling of an existing space. Floor plans are standardized for several reasons. The floor plan must create a clear understanding of the scope of the project for everyone involved in the job. Incorporating standardized line types and symbols helps limit the chance of error caused by misinterpretation of information on the plan. The dimensioning on drawings also ensures proper placement and installation of components in the space. Chapter 5 presents details on floor plans and dimensioning them.

DRAFTING THE CONSTRUCTION PLAN

Any change made to the original structure of the kitchen or bath requires a construction plan. If walls or openings are altered from their original locations or other structural changes or additions are planned, a construction plan is required. The purpose of the construction plan is to show the relationship of the existing space with that of the new design.

A construction plan shows both the existing conditions of the structure or the architect's plan along with the changes required to the structure in order to accomplish your design. Note

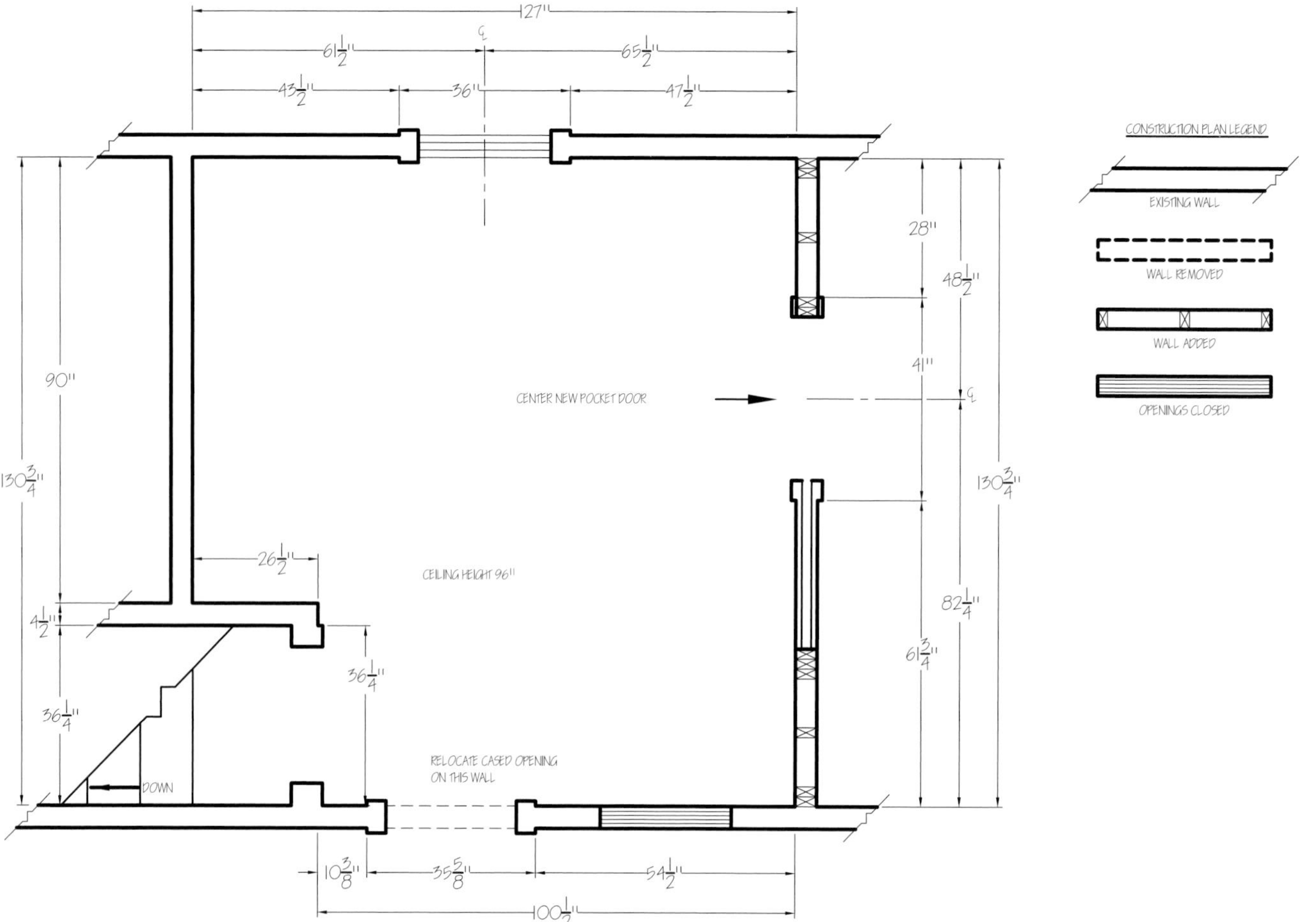

FIGURE 6.1 Walls found on the construction plan. Any change to existing walls needs to be indicated on the construction plan.

that *any* changes to the structure must be approved by the builder or licensed remodeler before you proceed with the project.

The construction plan indicates all changes made to the existing walls, windows, doors, or other structural item in that space. This drawing is separate from the floor plan. The two drawings must be cross-referenced so users can see the exact changes to be made to the original space.

As with other plans, standardized symbols are used on a construction plan to indicate the existing walls or changes made. These symbols are placed on the construction plan at the location of the change to the existing structure and in the construction plan legend. The construction plan symbols are listed next (see Figure 6.1.).

- EXISTING WALL: existing walls that will not be changed.
- WALL REMOVED: any existing wall including portions of wall to be removed.
- WALL ADDED: any new wall added to existing structure. This can include closing off an opening such as an existing window, existing door or any other type of structural opening.
- WALL CLOSED OFF: this includes closing off openings such as windows or doors.

DRAWING THE CONSTRUCTION PLAN

1. Draw walls exactly like the floor plan of the given space (footprint). Common practice is to trace the floor plan so you have exact wall locations.
2. Do not show cabinetry or fixtures on the construction plan.
3. Show existing walls and all changes to be made to the existing walls. This includes changes to structure, windows, doors, and walls and walls removed, walls added, and openings closed.

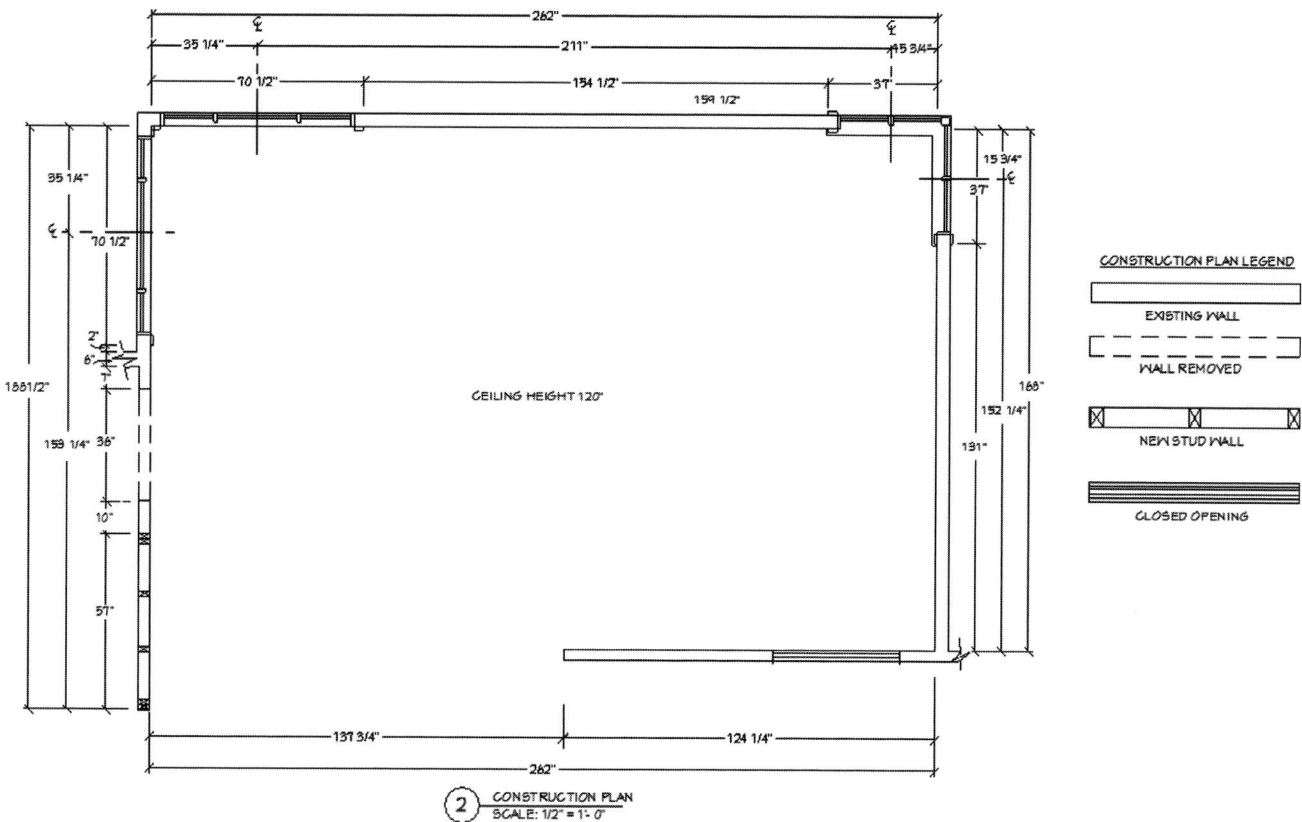

FIGURE 6.2 Construction plan.

4. Dimension all walls.
- All dimensions are in inches (mm) only.
- All dimensions are from the interior finished surfaces.
- Locate new windows and doors from the outside casing on each side of the window or door (also called trim to trim).
- Dimension to center points of new windows or doors that have been added or relocated in the space.
- No dimension is necessary for walls that are closed off.
- Interior wall thickness is 4½″ (114 mm) finished. Exterior wall thickness is 6″ (165 mm) finished.
- Verify and confirm all wall thickness for every individual project.

5. For half-walls, indicate height with a note by the wall. Use a leader line if necessary. Half-walls are used for counters, room dividers, and so on. The plan must include a note indicating height of half-walls.

6. Note ceiling height on drawing.

7. Place notes on plan as needed.

8. Include a construction plan legend for wall symbols and descriptions.

9. Note new windows and doors by the manufacturer brand and model numbers.
- A separate window and/or door schedule can be used (see Figure 6.2).

DRAFTING THE MECHANICAL PLAN

The mechanical plan is another drawing found in the set of NKBA drawings. This plan communicates to the allied trades the exact locations and specifications of all plumbing, electrical, heating, ventilation, fixtures, and equipment, and how they relate to the cabinetry. The mechanicals must be placed in the correct location for appliances and fixtures, which will be affected by the placement of the cabinetry as well. All items must be installed in accordance with the drawings.

The NKBA standard mechanical plan includes the electrical, lighting, plumbing, heating, air conditioning, and ventilation systems (HVAC). The American Institute of Architects (AIA) standard plans have separate electrical, lighting, and other plans. For kitchen and bath design, they are all on one plan for reference. As a designer, you help to ensure that outlets and switches are placed correctly in accordance with local building codes and are aesthetically pleasing with the design. Placement of mechanicals in a tiled backsplash area is especially important.

There are several acceptable symbols for items in the design industry. Each company may prefer to use certain symbols. All symbols must be placed on the floor plan and cross-referenced with a description in the mechanical legend.

Steps in the Mechanical Plan

1. Draw the mechanical plan to the same configuration as the floor plan. Do not include nomenclature and specifications on the plan. Including nomenclature on the cabinetry would make the plan too busy. Do draw the outline of walls, cabinets, and fixtures on the plan.
2. Label appliances on the plan so they are clearly defined.
3. Place all mechanicals in correct locations using correct symbols in compliance with local building codes. This includes outlets, switches, lighting, and the like.
4. Place switches on the plan. When placing the switches, think of all the tasks that will be completed along with how the overall kitchen or bathroom space will function.
   - The symbol for a switch is an S. The "S" is typically 3⁄16 to 1⁄4" (5–6 mm) long, placed perpendicular to wall (see Figure 6.3).
   - Place switches on the latch side of a door.
   - Place switches at both entrances into the room. Clients should not have to backtrack to turn a light on or off.
   - There are several switch symbols. Chapter 3 presents all the symbols. Some commonly used switches are listed next.
     - S is a single switch. This means one switch and the light source. It could be one light or several lights.
     - S3 is a three-way switch. This means there are two switches plus the light source.
     - S4 is a four-way switch. The four-way switch is tied in with the three-way switch so there are three switches plus light source.
     - SDM indicates a dimmer on that switch so the lights can be dimmed.

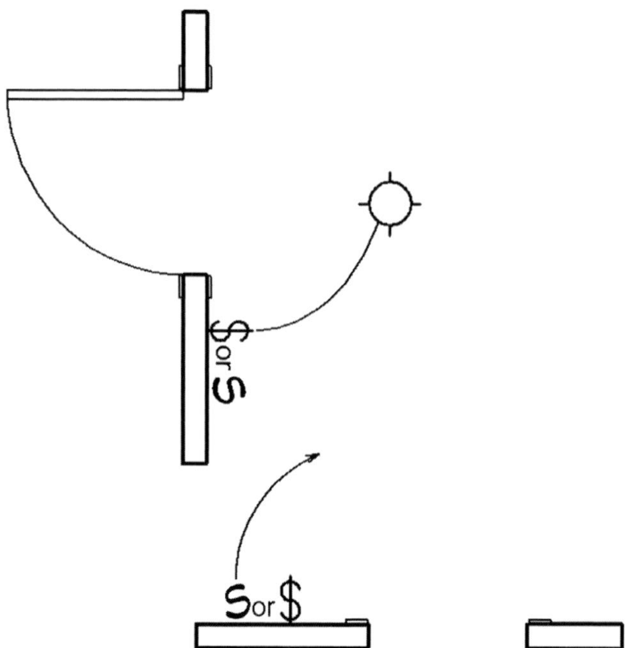

FIGURE 6.3 Switches in electrical plan.

- Place a switch by the sink for a task light over the sink area. Remember that a peninsula or island will need task lighting above also.
- Items that need their own switches include undercabinet lighting, toe-kick lighting, cove lighting, lights in cabinets, and the garbage disposal, among others.
- Think of "layering" the lighting. Different areas can have their own switch so lights are turned on/off at different times for desired lighting. For instance, because clients may want to have only the toe-kick lighting on, it should have its own switch.
- A switched outlet is an outlet with a switch by it.
- Switches are placed at 42 to 48″ (1067 to 1220 mm) A.F.F. (above finished floor). The typical measure is 44″ O.C. from finished floor.

Tip

When designing, it helps to visualize all tasks completed in the space. How will you enter the room, turn on the light, and then turn off the light when exiting the space? How will you turn on and off other lighting? What other tasks will be completed in the addition to cooking?

5. Place outlets on the plan. Like other symbols, receptacle symbols, referred to as outlets, have special purposes (see Figure 6.4).

- Use a GFCI (GFI; ground-fault circuit interrupter) per code for all outlets placed along the counter in a kitchen. Check local codes.
- Place outlets along the kitchen counter no more than 4′-0″ apart. This does not apply to the peninsula if it is greater in length than 24″ (610 mm).
- Islands or peninsulas must have one outlet.
- Each small separate section of a wall along kitchen counter must have an outlet.
- Outlets are 120 volt or 240 volt.
- 120-volt outlets are standard convenience outlets. Appliances such as the dishwasher, refrigerator, and range hood use 120v. The circuit must be wired properly so that lights don't dim when an appliance goes on or there is a surge in power usage.
- Use 240 volts (220v) for any appliance that generates heat: cooktop or range, dryer, sauna, and room air conditioner.
- Place dedicated outlets for all appliances behind the appliances at the correct height.
- Check the appliance specifications for correct placement of outlets.
- Mark special-purpose outlets on the plan with a circle with a triangle within. These are for appliances and must have the letters of the appliance written in the lower right-hand corner.
- Remember to consider small counter appliances in the kitchen and the bathroom area. These will need outlets.
- Use GFI outlets in the bathroom. There must be at least one outlet by the vanity on the side wall or partition within three feet of each basin or the inside or face of a cabinet 12″ below the counter. Do not use face-up outlets on a vanity top; listed countertop-mounted outlets are fine. Check local codes.
- Use 3⁄16 to ¼″ circles on the floor plan for outlets. (Typically 3⁄16″ is preferred.) Draw outlets with a smaller circle than used for a light symbol. The size of circle indicating the light is ¼″ to 5⁄16″. The size difference must be evident on the mechanical plan. A geometric template is useful to draw the symbols. The lines on symbol must touch the wall.
- Use a circle with two lines for the duplex outlet. The lines represent how many plug-ins there are. A single outlet is a circle with one line; it has one plug-in. A floor outlet will not have lines. Again, the lines on the outlet must touch the wall.
- Use three lines for a 240v outlet (220v). This outlet is designed for appliances that generate heat and is grounded.

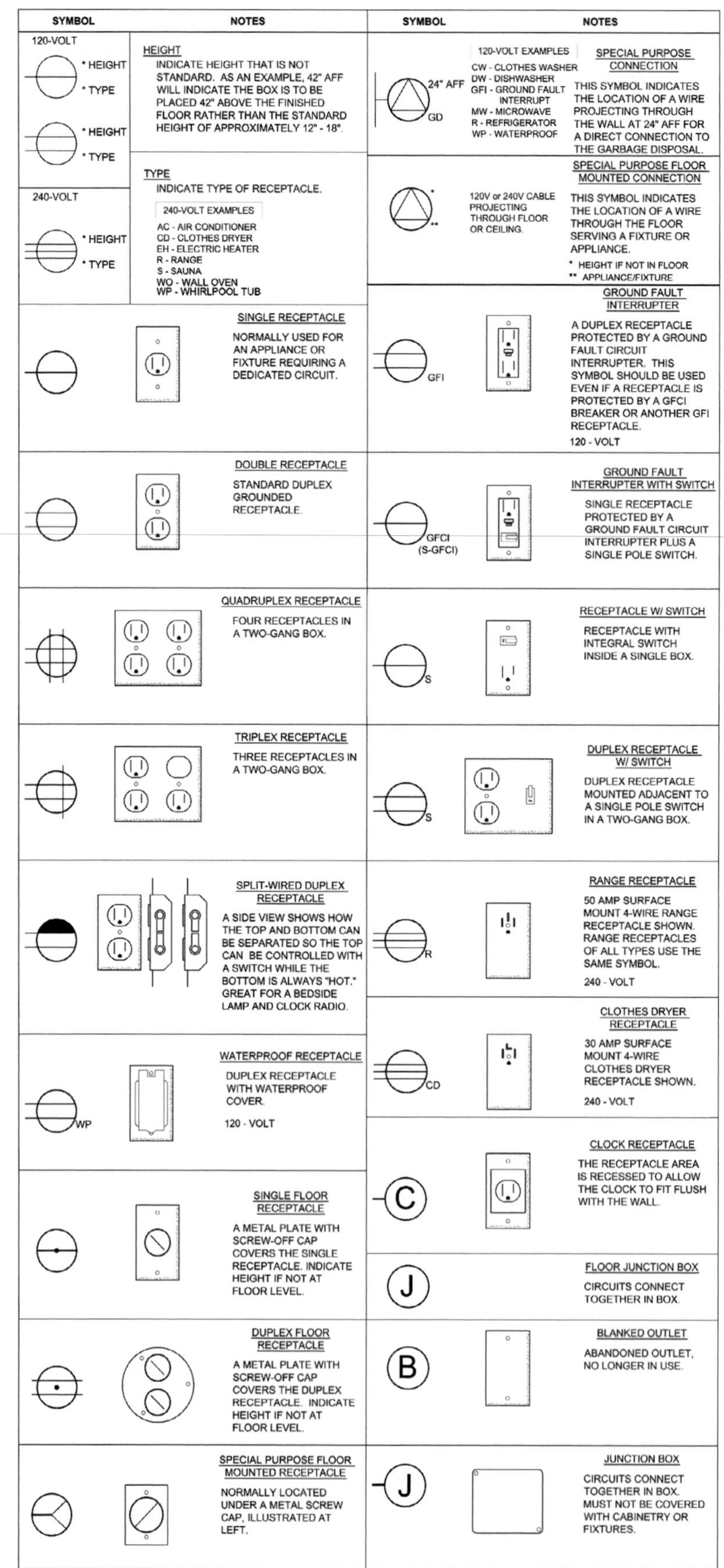

FIGURE 6.4 Outlet symbols commonly used for kitchen and bath design

- Draw a split-wired outlet as a circle with half colored in black. This outlet is cold on top and hot at the bottom. A switch operates the top outlet. Split-wired outlets are useful for plugging in lights that a switch will turn on. A switch can be hooked to the split-wired outlets, but it cannot be hooked in with any additional light.
- If an appliance is to be hard-wired, place a note in the mechanical specs. Always refer to the appliance specifications to verify whether the appliance needs to be hard-wired or not. Failing to allow for hard-wiring can be a costly mistake.

6. Include lights on the plan. Lights on the mechanical plan have their own symbols and placement recommendations. Designers must provide for three main areas of light:

a. General lighting: overall lighting of the space

b. Task lighting: light provided over task areas, such as the sink, island, and peninsula, and under cabinets

c. Ambient (or mood) lighting: specialized with each design

The beam spread and type of light must be considered. The goal of good lighting is to not create any shadows or scallops of light on the cabinetry. Also, do not place too many recessed lights close together in one area. The light placement should look balanced on the ceiling and in the given space.

- Most recessed lights typically are placed 36″ to 48″ apart. It depends on the lamp.
- Draw circles for lighting on the plan at the size of ¼″ or 5⁄16″. Preferred is 5⁄16″ (8 mm). See chapter 3 for all lighting types and symbols.

7. Include switch lines in the plan. On the drawing, the switch line represents what switch turns on which particular light (see Figure 6.5).

- The switch line starts at a switch, goes to the light sources, and ends at the opposite switch.
- If only one switch turns on a light, the switch line goes from the switch to the light and ends there.
- A switch line should not go back to same switch. It should touch each light and then end at other switch.
- The NKBA standards use a solid line for a switch line. The AIA standards use a dashed line for a switch line.
- Draw the switch line as a line with an arc, never as a straight line. Use a French curve to draw the curves lines.

8. Show where the gas line will be for any gas appliance. Also indicate the register placement and any other heating system.

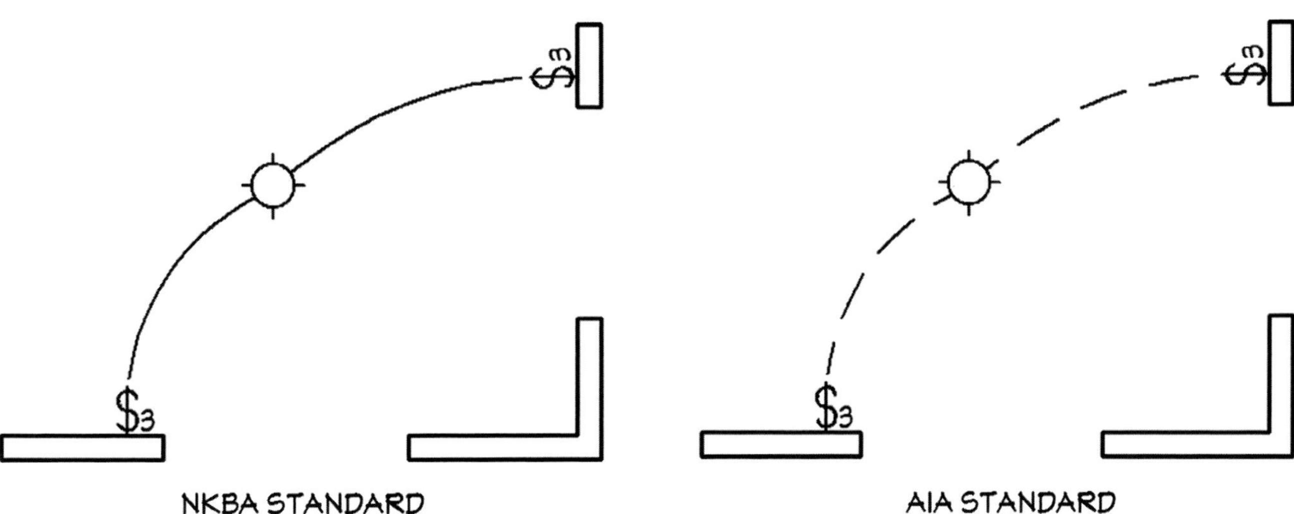

FIGURE 6.5 Proper placement of switch lines.

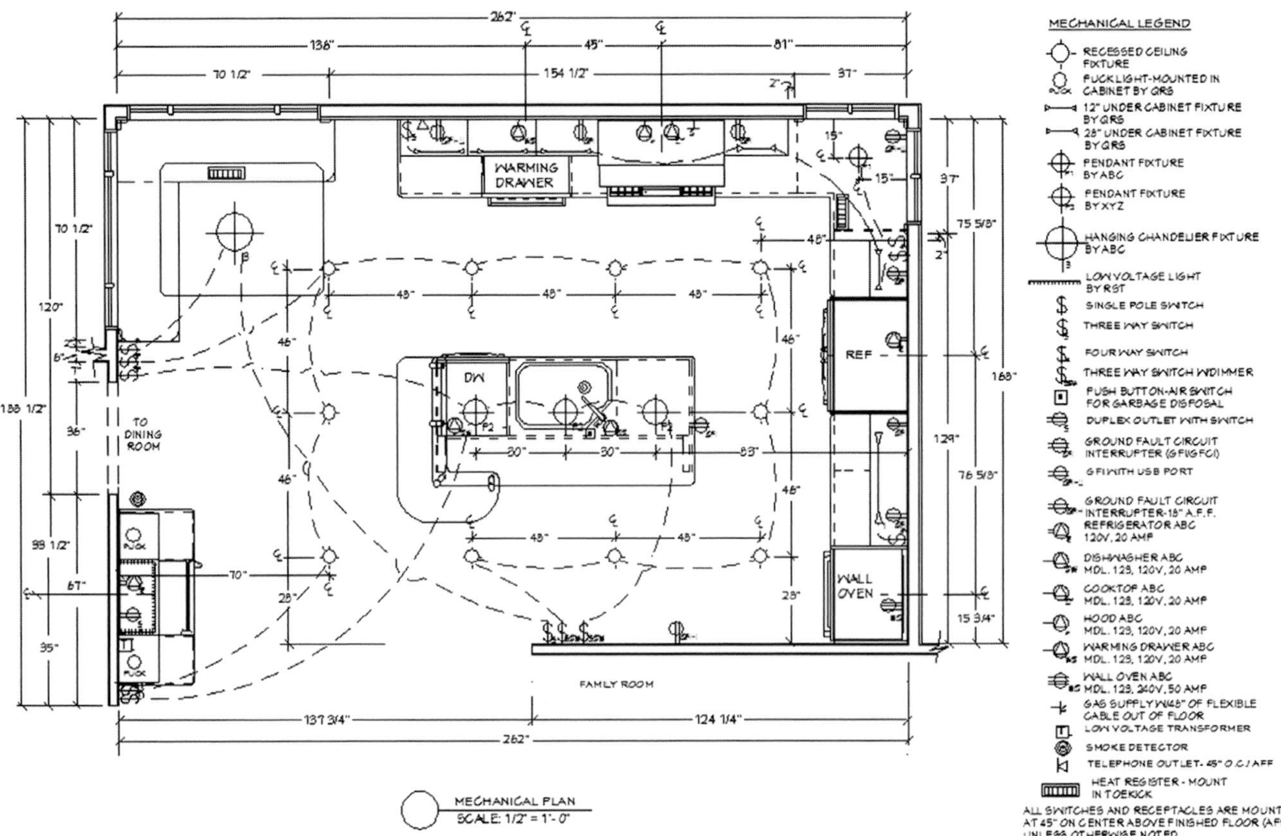

FIGURE 6.6 Mechanical plan shows the placement of electrical, heating, and ventilation.

9. If any minor wall or door construction changes are a part of the plan, detail them on the mechanical plan or on a separate plan.
10. Include a legend for all mechanical plans. Place the legend on the right-hand side of the drawing, or at the bottom if there is no room on the right-hand side. Cross-reference every symbol on the floor plan and place all symbols in the mechanical legend.
11. Show all dimensions.
    - List all overall room dimensions.
    - Give centerline dimensions for all equipment in two directions when possible—especially for items that are installed in a corner, peninsula, or island.
    - Dimension centerlines from the wall for accurate placement. It is acceptable to dimension to a fixed object facing item such as a cabinet.
    - Centerline ceiling-mounted fixtures from the walls for accurate placement.
    - Centerline these items: all appliances, sinks, tub controls, tub drain, shower controls, shower drain, toilets, bidets, fan units, towel warmers, light fixtures, heating and air conditioning ducts, radiators.
    - Use the centerline symbol for all items that are centerlined (see Figure 6.6).

Reflected Ceiling Plan

Some designers and companies prefer to put the lighting on a reflected ceiling plan (RCP). The RCP is a separate drawing that shows all fixtures on a ceiling, such as lights, speakers, fans, and vents (see Figure 6.7). The plan is called *reflected* because the items

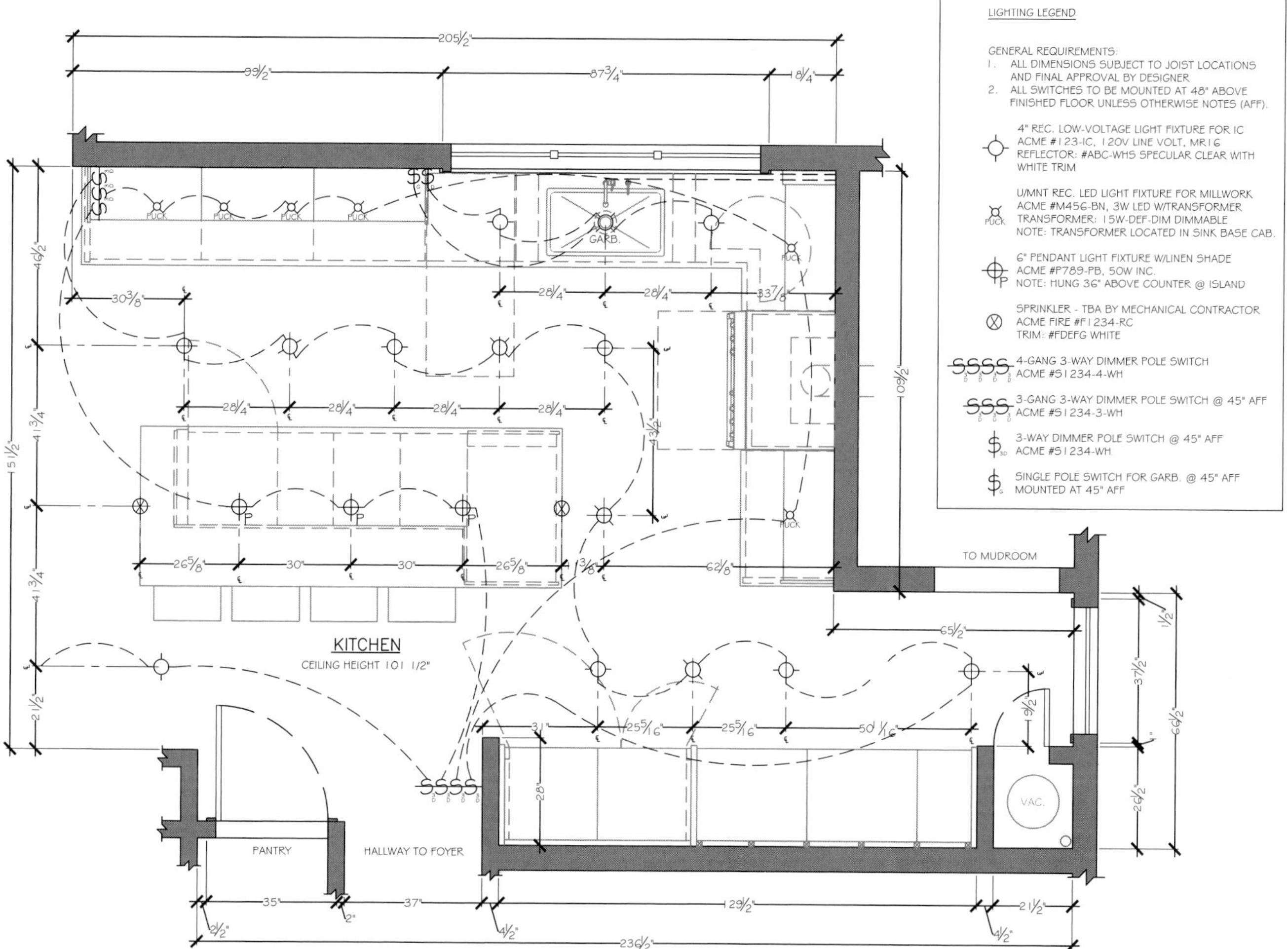

FIGURE 6.7 Reflected ceiling plan for kitchen.
Courtesy of Corey Klassen, CKD

on the RCP are shown as if a mirror were on the floor, below the ceiling, reflecting the image.

- Show overall room dimensions on the RCP.
- Draw the diameter fixtures to scale.
- Indicate heights of switches. Place switch lines on the plan.
- Center-lined all ceiling-mounted fixtures from the wall or closest fixed object.

Drawing a Countertop Plan

A separate countertop plan is not required with your presentation to the client since the floor plan indicates the outline of the countertop. However, a countertop plan may be helpful to illustrate the installation or fabrication to allied tradespeople, particularly in complex projects, such as those that combine various counter materials or built-up edge treatments (see Figure 6.8). Often countertop plans are sent to a company for a bid.

Drawing the Countertop Plan

- On a countertop plan, include only the walls of the space and outline of cabinets, fixtures, and equipment.
- Place all applicable notes, details, and dimensions on this plan for clarification.

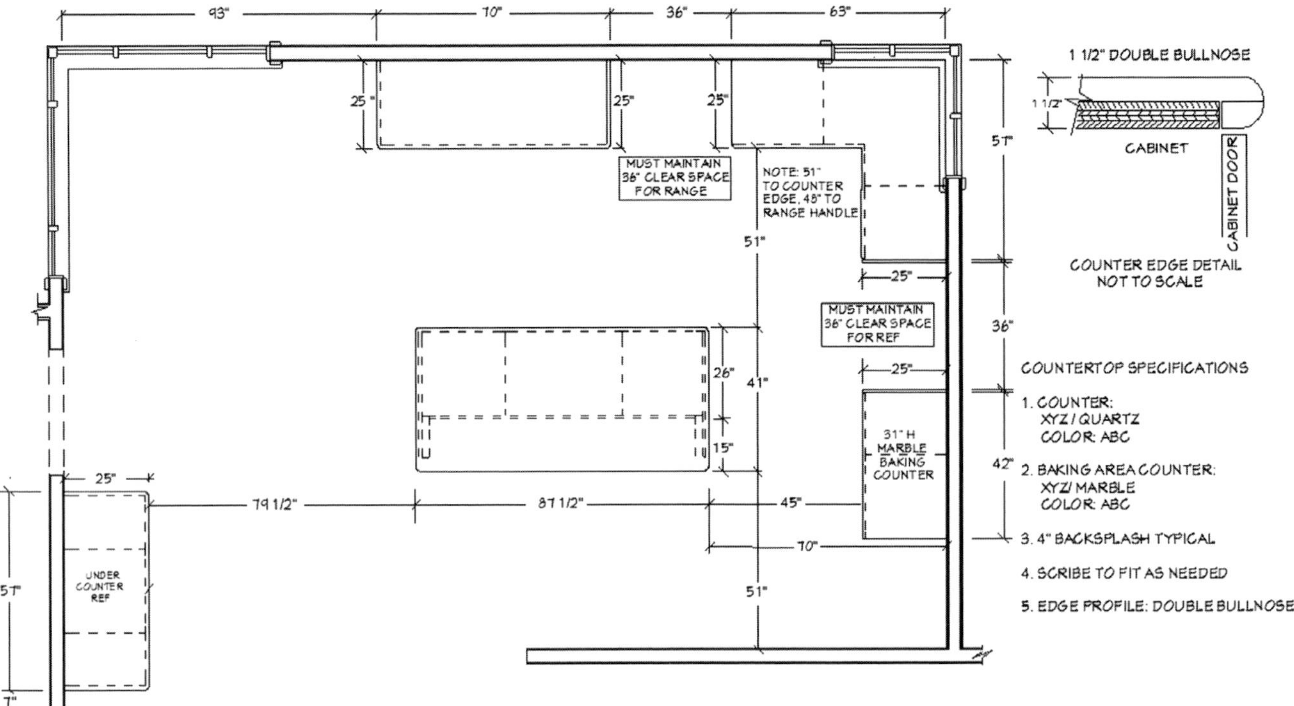

FIGURE 6.8 This countertop plan shows counter placement and notes specific to the project. Typically a detail drawing shows edge treatment.

- Dimension this drawing. There may be up to three dimension lines for each counter section.
  - Dimension line 1 shows the center of any cutouts, such as those for sinks and cooktops.
  - Dimension line 2 indicates the overall counter length.
  - Dimension line 3 indicates the overall available wall length.
- Use notes on the drawing to explain cutouts, corner treatments, edge treatments, depth changes, and other important details specific to the counter installation.
- Draw a detail of the counter edge profile to clarify the counter design and overhang relative to the face of the cabinets.
- The standard depth of kitchen counters is 25″. The standard depth of bathroom counters is 22″.
- Counter depth can be affected by an inset, lipped, or full overlay door and must be noted on drawing.

Drawing an Interior Elevation

The interior elevation is another drawing found in the set of NKBA plans. An interior elevation is an orthographic drawing of a wall—a two-dimensional view, looking flat at the wall and showing no depth. The purpose of the interior elevation is to show the height of all items on the particular wall and the widths of each item.

You must draw an interior elevation for each wall with cabinetry. You also must draw the sides of an island to show how the island will look installed. Any built-in item needs an elevation. The bathroom will need elevations to show the details on each wall and to locate where items will be installed. These elevations are important so there is no question as to how the space will look after installation.

1. Draw the interior elevation.
   - The interior elevation is ½″ = 1′-0″ scale (1:20)
   - Place an elevation symbol on the floor plan to cross-reference the elevation it corresponds to. (See chapter 3 for symbols used.) Use a circle with an arrow to number the elevation and page number the drawing is found on.
   - Start in one corner of the room and draw walls for elevations in a clockwise direction.
   - For the given wall, the elevation should line up exactly as the floor plan is drawn, but project on the wall in a two-dimensional view showing no depth. Draw each cabinet, filler, space, and the like on that specific wall.
   - Add details to the cabinets, appliances, and other items on that wall.
   - Show line weights on drawings.
   - There are several acceptable methods for drawing cabinets that are perpendicular to the elevation wall. One way is to use a heavier object line for the cabinet perpendicular to elevation wall. Another method is to draw a large X on the side of that wall cabinet and on the base cabinet to signify that the cabinets continue in the opposite direction. The cabinet still takes up space on your elevation wall but is drawn with an X on it.
2. Dimension the elevations.
   - Divide the drawing in half from top to bottom and from left side to right side.
   - Dimension items on the top half of the drawing to the top of the drawing.
   - Dimension items on the bottom half of the drawing to the bottom of the drawing.
   - For vertical dimensions, dimension items closer to the left side on that side. Items on the right half should go to that side. If standard heights are indicated on one side, they do not need to be repeated on the other side. Make sure to include all vertical heights of all items in the space.
   - Dimension all sides of the elevation.
3. Dimension the horizontal elements on the top and bottom of elevation.
   - Dimension all lines for bottom half and then all lines for top half.
   - Use dimension line 1 to indicate the width of all items including any spaces.
   - Use dimension line 2 to indicate the centerlines of all appliances and fixtures. Bring the centerlines for appliances on the bottom half of the wall down to the lower dimension lines. Appliances in upper half go to dimensions at top.
   - Use dimension line 3 to show the overall dimensions.
4. Dimension all of the vertical elements on either the right side or the left side of the wall.
   - You must account for all vertical measurements. These include the toe-kick, base cabinet, counter thickness, backsplash, space between upper and lower cabinets, wall cabinets, crown molding, soffit or bulkhead if present, and space to ceiling above. You also must account for the height of appliances, windows, doors, and all other details.
   - You may decide on which side to place the vertical dimensions.
5. Label your elevation symbol on the floor plan.
   - Use an identification letter on each elevation you complete. Then place the elevation symbol on the floor plan to correspond with the correct elevation view on the specified page.
6. Place the title on the plan with the scale. (See examples of elevations in Figures 6.9 and 6.10.)

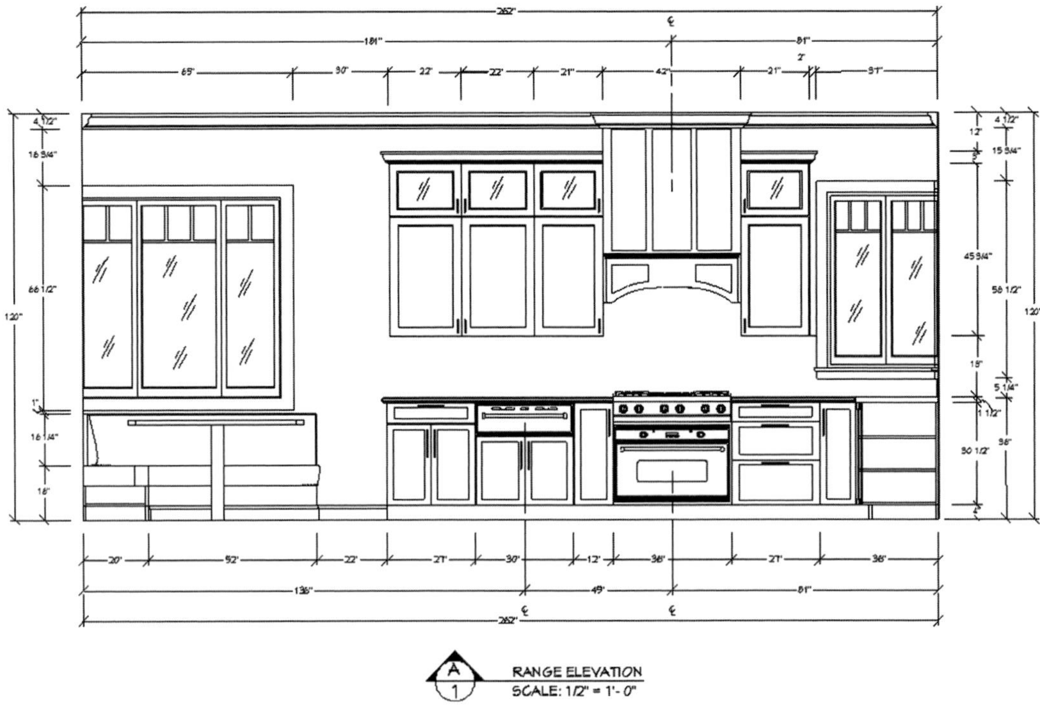

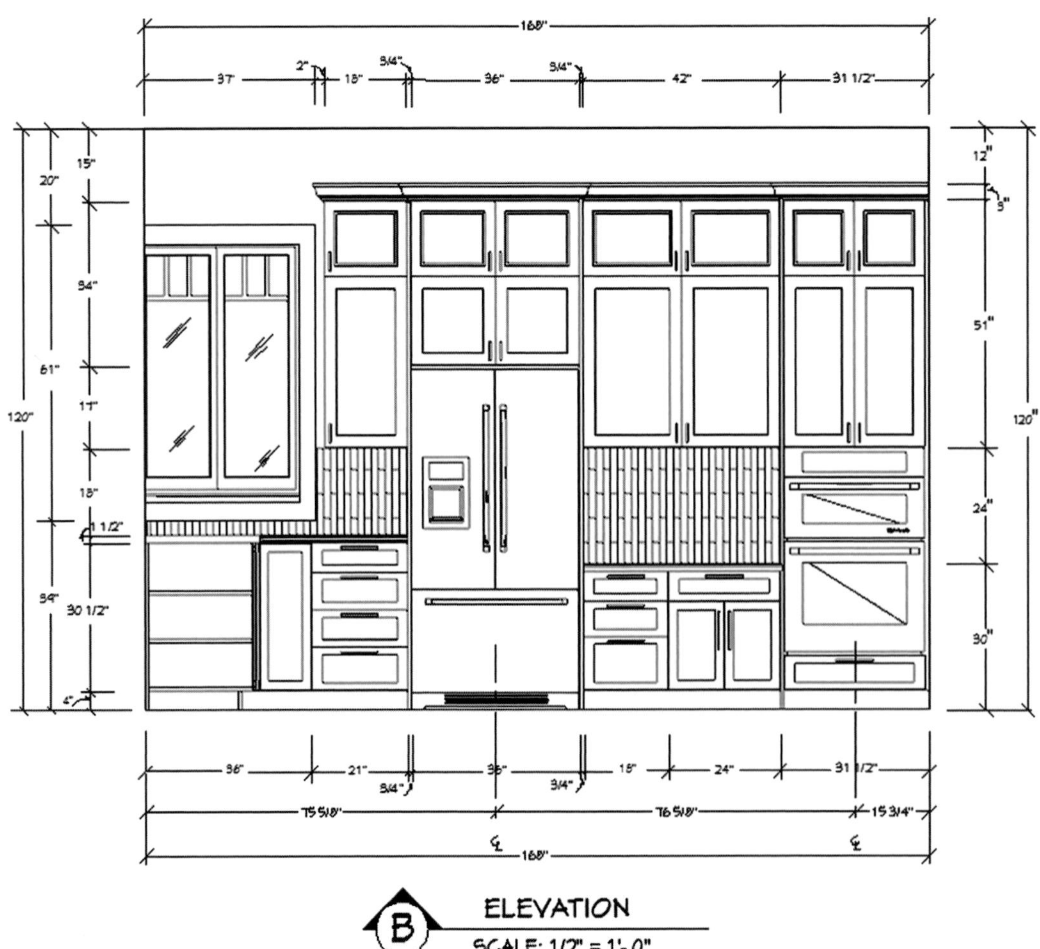

FIGURE 6.9 Kitchen interior elevation *(Continued)*

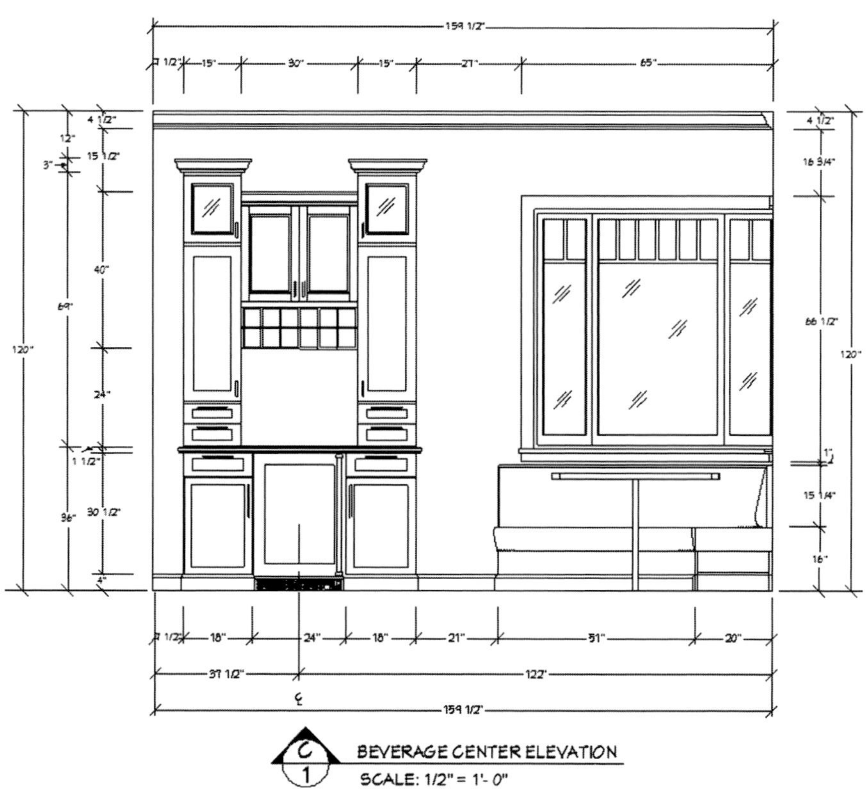

FIGURE 6.9 Kitchen interior elevation.

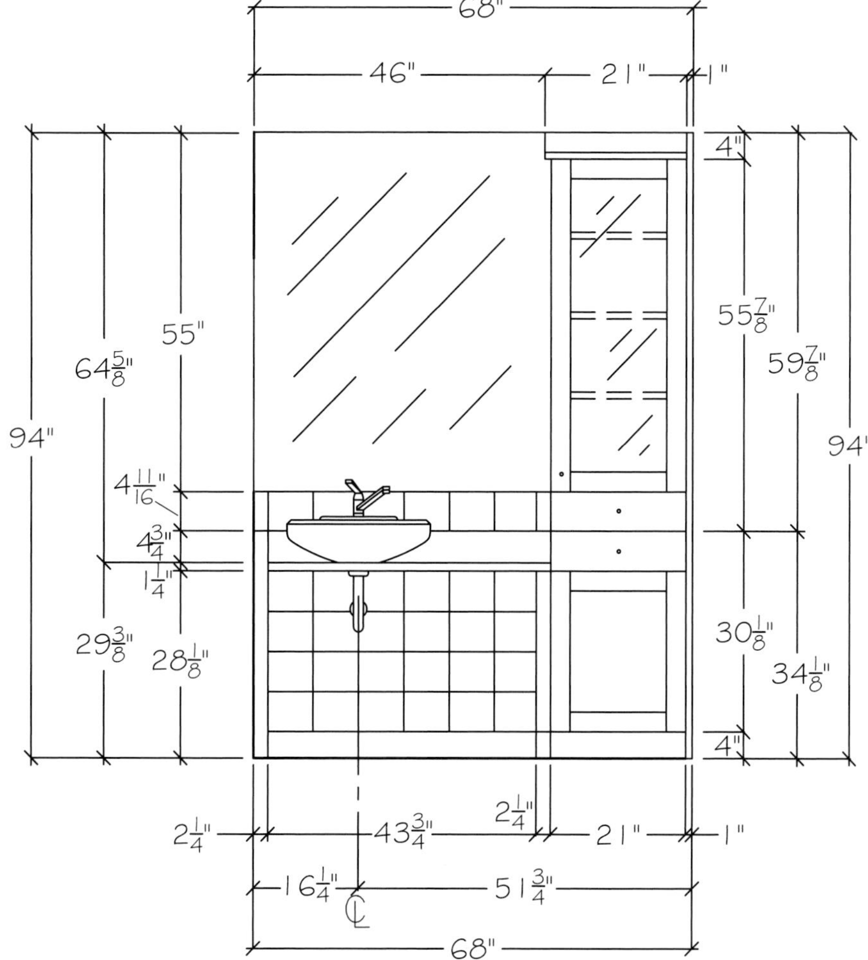

FIGURE 6.10 Bathroom elevation.
Courtesy of Sharon Armstrong

Section Drawings and Detail Drawings

You may need to show section or detail drawings on a drawing. Section and detail drawings clearly show the relationship of complex details and how an item is constructed. They are commonly used for showing edges of counters, stacked moldings, and many other details.

Section Drawing

A section drawing (cross-section) represents the vertical plane cut through an object. It is used to show the vertical relationship of the materials used.

The cutting plane line on the floor plan indicates where the section drawing was taken from. These drawings are drawn in ½″ scale. These drawings are useful to show how items are put together (see Figure 6.11).

Detail Drawing

A detail drawing is an enlargement of a specific area of the structure or components. Details show larger views of the area. The scale of a detail drawing is typically ½″ = 1′-0″ (1:20) to 3″ = 1′-0″. Most often the larger scale is used to show the more complex details (see Figure 6.12).

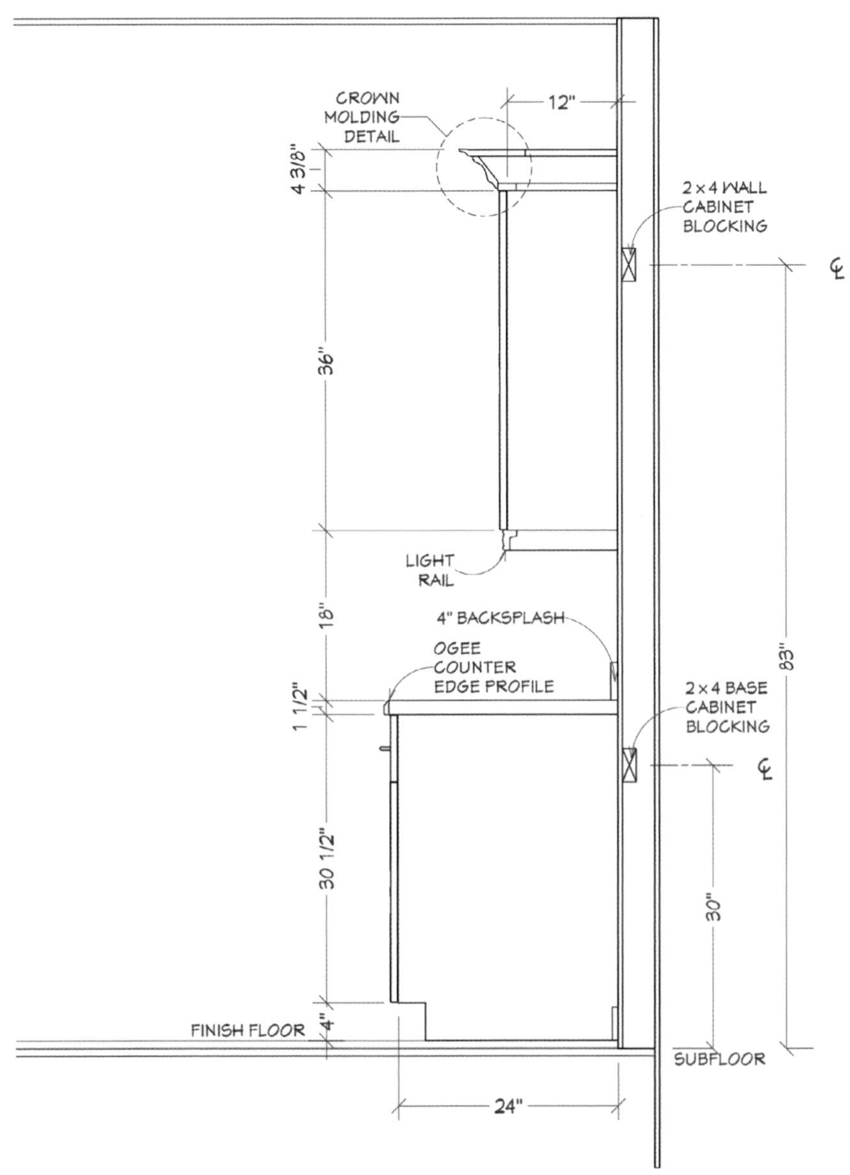

FIGURE 6.11 Section drawing of cabinet wall.

Courtesy of Adrean Stephenson, AKBD, Chief Architect

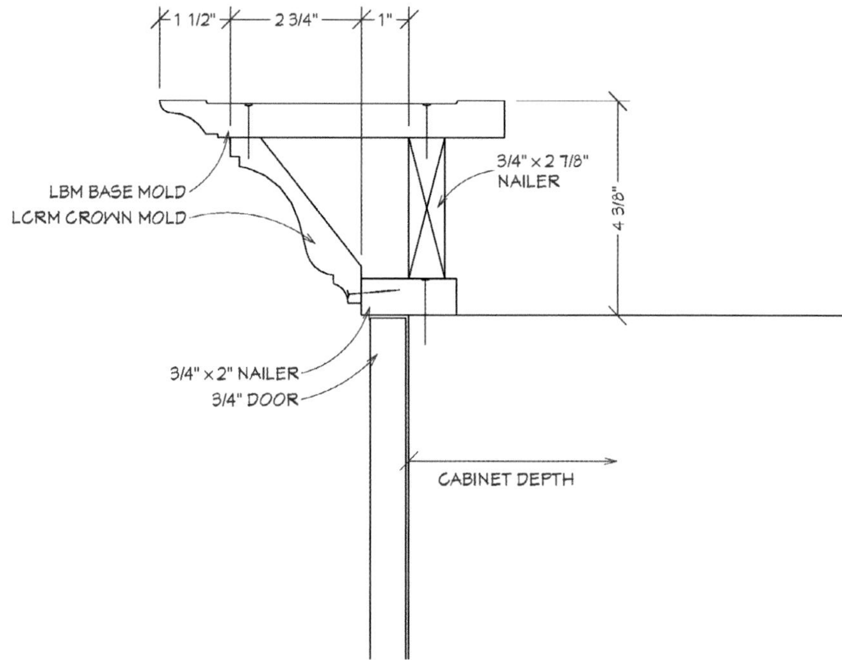

FIGURE 6.12 Detail drawing of molding installation.

Courtesy of Adrean Stephenson, AKBD, Chief Architect

Soffit Plan (Bulkhead)

The soffit plan (bulkhead) is not a required drawing but may be helpful in conveying your design to the client. A separate soffit (bulkhead) plan is required if the depth is different from the depth of the wall cabinets.

- The soffit (bulkhead) plan includes only the walls of the space, outline of cabinets, fixtures and equipment. If the design is complex, you may want to leave out the cabinets and show the wall only.
  - Show the thickness of the cabinet door or notation of inset doors, if they are used.
  - Compare the soffit (bulkhead) and cabinet dimensions in order to ensure consistent reveals.
- Use the overhead line type to indicate the soffits (bulkhead).
- For clarification, place all applicable notes, details, and dimensions on this soffit (bulkhead) plan.
- Dimension this drawing, showing the width and depth of the soffit (bulkhead).
  - Provide a cross-section drawing to show how the components fit together. You can place this drawing on the same sheet of vellum as the soffit (bulkhead) drawing (see Figure 6.13).

INTERPRETIVE DRAWINGS

Perspective or isometric drawings can give three-dimensional views of the space and are used often in design. These views show depth and give a visual representation of the relationship of all objects in the design. Although these drawings are not required, they are useful to show to clients.

Paraline Drawings

Paraline drawings (also known as pictorial drawings) provide a visual representation of the space or object showing depth. In these drawings, all lines are parallel and are skewed along two axes. This allows viewers to see three sides of the object. Sometimes an item may look a bit distorted since the parallel lines do not converge to a vanishing point, as they do in perspective drawings.

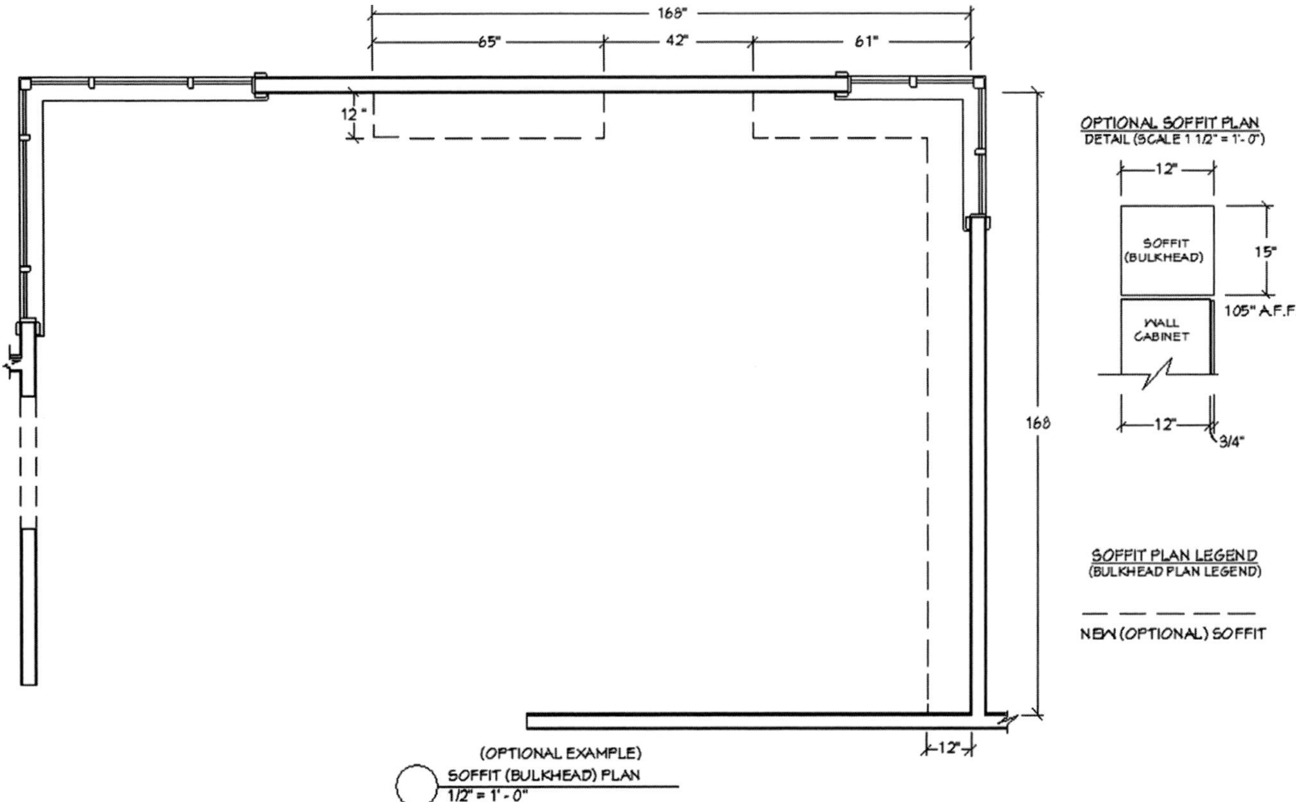

FIGURE 6.13 The soffit (bulkhead) plan shows details of soffit (bulkhead) The overhead lines, long dashes, denote the soffit/bulkhead.

There are two categories of paraline drawings: axonometric drawings, which include isometric, diametric, and trimetric drawings, and oblique drawings. The most commonly used paraline drawing is the isometric drawing, which has all angles drawn at 30 degrees. The angles are measureable and drawn to scale. This drawing gives a good representation of the object or space, showing true shape and size. Vertical lines always remain vertical. A circle will look like an ellipse. An isometric drawing is a quick way to draw an island, cabinet, or room. Typically an isometric object is typically drawn at a scale of 1" = 1'- 0". An isometric of a room is typically drawn at a scale of ½" = 1'-0" (1:20) (see Figure 6.14).

Perspective Drawings

A perspective drawing is a visual representation of the space in a three-dimensional view. With a perspective drawing, all lines are either vertical or angled to their respective vanishing points placed on the drawing. This process allows a room to look more in proportion and not

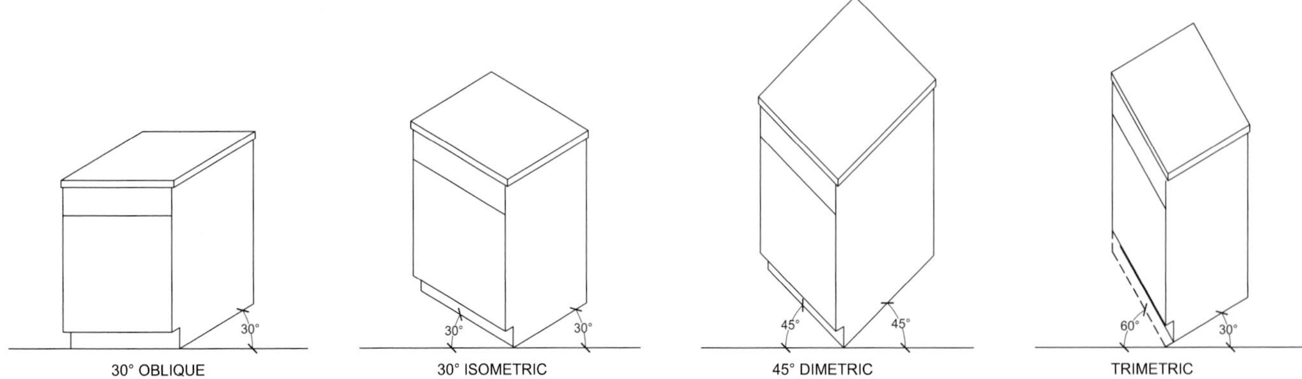

FIGURE 6.14 Different angles for drawings. An isometric drawing is used most commonly. All angles are drawn at 30 degrees and to scale.

distorted. The angled lines in a perspective drawing are still parallel to one another and are drawn in a perspective scale (which means that the objects get larger as they get closer to the viewer). Some spaces may need more than one perspective drawn to capture the designed space. Perspective drawings truly help all involved visualize the installed space with the details, products. and materials used.

There are three categories of perspective drawings: one-point perspective, two-point perspective, and three-point perspective (see Figures 6.15, 6.16, 6.17, 6.18). One-point and two-point perspectives are used most often in kitchen and bath design.

A one-point perspective has one vanishing point along one wall. All lines converge to that one vanishing point. With the two-point perspective, there are two vanishing points, one on either side of the space. All lines in the drawing converge at the appropriate vanishing point.

To draw a perspective in kitchen and bath design, it is best to construct a perspective grid so items are placed more in proportion. The drawing itself is in a perspective scale, but the back corner of the perspective grid is drawn as a true-height wall to scale. You need this for a reference point. The perspective scale means that the items in the drawing get larger as they get closer to the viewer. You can purchase grids for one-point and two-point perspective drawings. The grids, which are placed under the sheet of vellum, assist you in placing details on the perspective drawing.

Bird's-Eye View

A bird's-eye view (or top-down perspective) is a view looking down into the space from a point above, typically at the ceiling (see Figure 6.19). This view shows the overall spatial relationship of items in the given space.

Enhancing the Drawing

The lines of a perspective drawing define its limits, but you can add realism with shading, highlights, color, people, and accessories. Shading adds interest to floor plans and elevations. However, be careful not to enhance drawings so much that you distract viewers from important information.

FIGURE 6.15 One-point perspective drawing.
Courtesy of Peter Ross Salerno, CKMBD

FIGURE 6.16 Perspective created using computer.
Courtesy of AutoKitchen

FIGURE 6.17 Two-point perspective.
Courtesy of Barbara-Herr Marietta, Pennsylvania

FIGURE 6.18 Perspective created using computer software.
Courtesy of Chief Architect

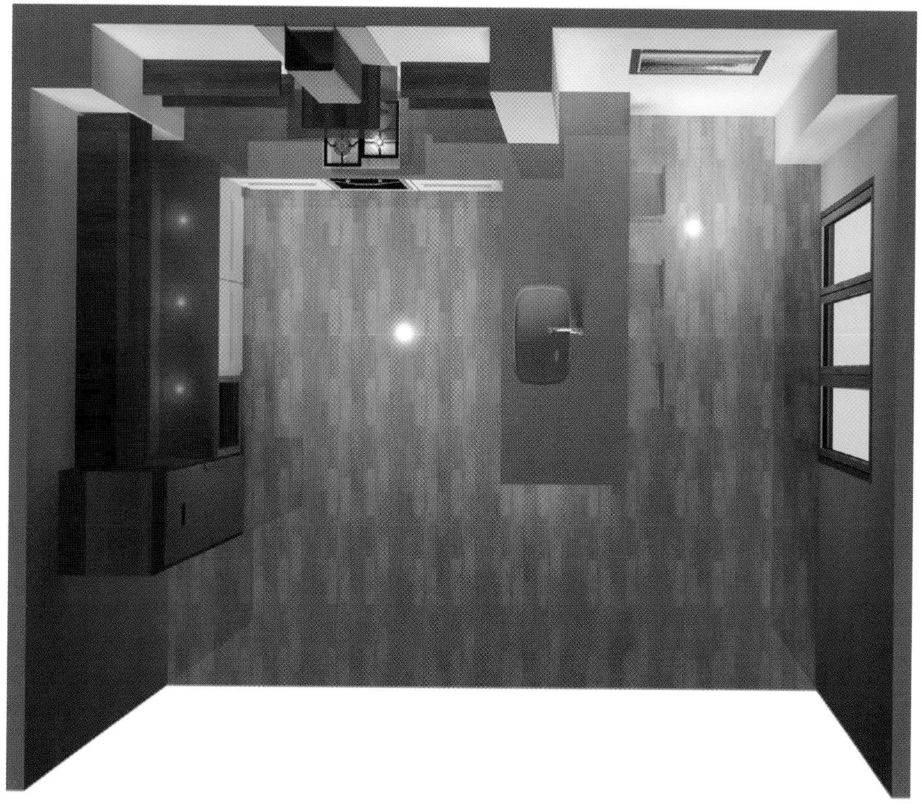

FIGURE 6.19 Bird's-eye view of space.
Courtesy of AutoKitchen

Shading conveys even more information by defining dimension and direction. Adding shadows makes an otherwise flat object three-dimensional. You can shade mechanically or freehand using lines, dots, and tones. Because there are several light sources in an interior, it is difficult to calculate exact shadow delineation. Therefore, the standard practice is to consider two light sources: from the upper left and the upper right. As you draw, think of the light shining over each shoulder and onto your drawing. The top and front surfaces of objects are in the most light and receive little or no shading. The sides of objects not in direct view, such as cabinet sides and the ceiling, are in a light shade. The darkest shades are reserved for areas below overhangs. The principles behind these types of shadows are:

- Parallel surfaces create parallel shadow edges.
- Perpendicular surfaces create sloping shadow edges.

Enhance depth perception by varying tonal values of shades. Two objects that appear equal in tone appear to be in the same spatial plane. Varying the shading tones of each object emphasizes its depth.

There are several principles that may be applied to produce this effect. In black line artwork, shading can show depth, texture, and material. Color can help your client understand the design and show the texture of surfaces as in Figure 6.22. Blue rather than black or gray can be used to shade areas that will be naturally dark when the design is installed. When shading with pencil, the background can be blended by smudging the graphite and lightening it at the same time. These shading techniques can be done with a pencil, pen, or marker. Each medium has its own special look. The final presentation will vary depending on your choice of medium and personal style. By thickening edges, a drawing becomes easier to interpret and more realistic (see Figures 6.20, 6.21, 6.22 and 6.23).

People and accessories also add realism to drawings. There are several books available with line art that can be traced by placing the art under the drawing. Other good sources are your local newspaper advertisement section and department store catalogs. If the size is not exactly right, reduce or enlarge it on a copy machine, then trace it into your drawing. Remember that when you add people and accessories, they typically block a piece

FIGURE 6.20 Perspective illustrating light sources casting shadows.
Courtesy of ProKitchen

FIGURE 6.21 Perspective illustrating light sources casting shadows.
Courtesy of 20-20 Technologies

FIGURE 6.22 Shading a drawing using gray tones.
Courtesy of Tony Hunt, CKD, CBD

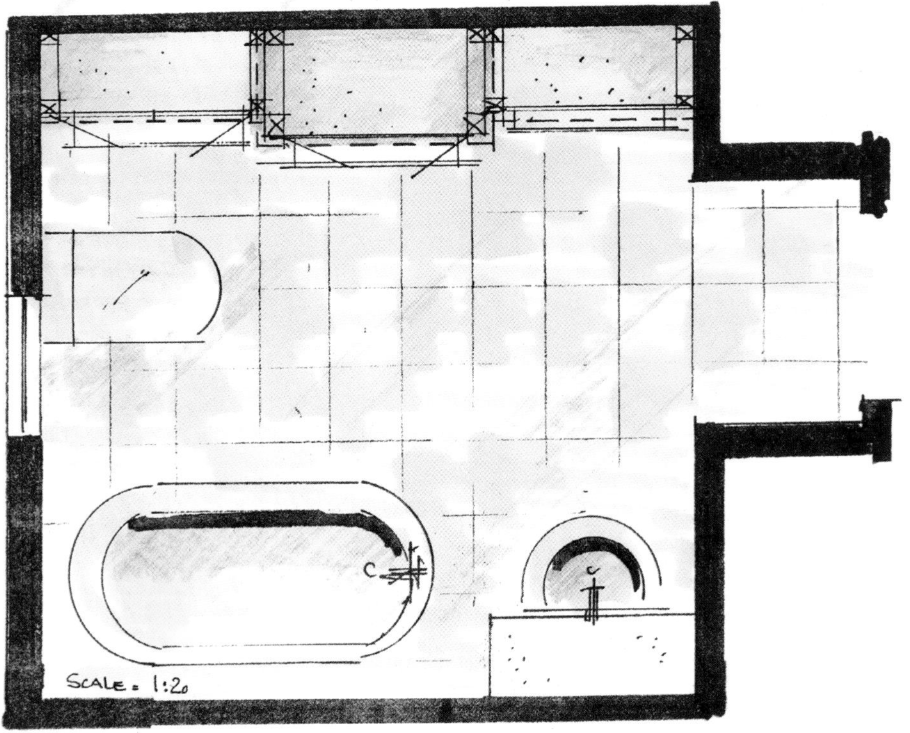

FIGURE 6.23 Shading a drawing using color.
Courtesy of Ines Hanl

of your drawing, such as cabinets or an appliance. Position these extras carefully so as not to distract from your design. Never block something that you especially want to show. Scanned art can be added to your computer-generated drawings and saved, making it available when you need it again. You may even want to consider using digital photographs of your clients, their own accessories and personal items, and the views they will see from their new windows. These will make your design real to your clients (see Figure 6.24).

Color is the ultimate enhancement. Using the colors that will be in clients' space can help them visualize the final design. Watercolor markers are commonly used for color enhancement and are available in many colors popular in the design industry. When selecting a coloring medium, be sure to also purchase black and several shades of cool gray. Begin your color collection with subtle, muted tones and neutral tones rather than bright primary colors. They may look nice, but as with people and accessory enhancements, they can overwhelm the drawing. You also want to be sure that the colors you choose will be a close match to the actual colors used in the design. Color on a perspective can be very helpful but can be a disappointment if the finished space is not what clients saw on your drawing. Less is more when applying color: hint at it in different areas, use markers and pencils together to complement each other. Using colored pencils alone will add texture and highlights, or go over the marker base with them to soften the effect. Outlining the drawing with a black pen and then using colored markers is a very popular technique.

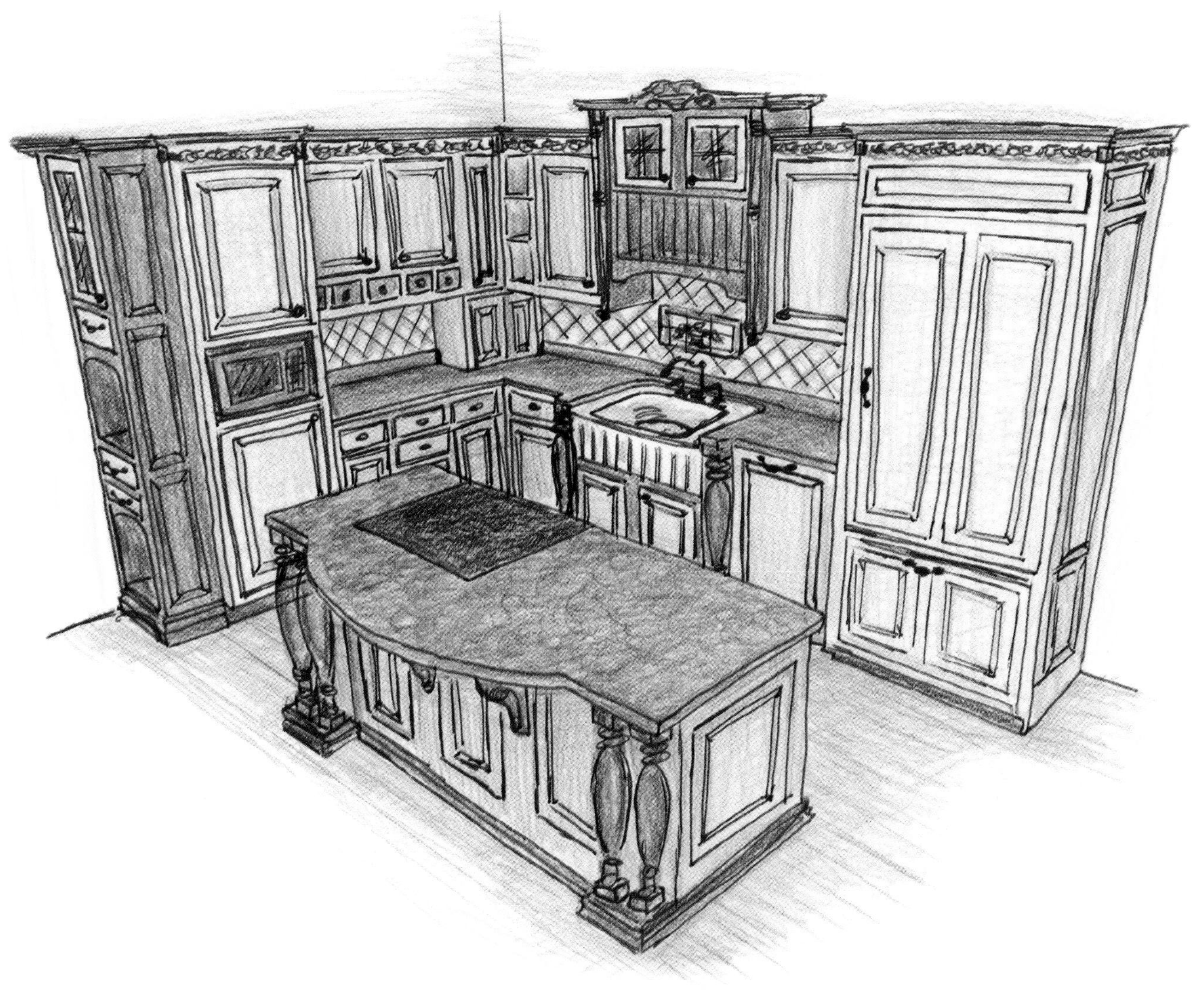

FIGURE 6.24 An example of a perspective enhanced with colored pencils add a realistic touch. Note the details.

Courtesy of Beth Kemmer, CKD

SUMMARY

For the design project, you must complete all of the required drawings discussed in this chapter. Each drawing provides its own important information. As a designer, you will need to understand all components on each drawing. You also must understand the language of the trades and allied professionals.

This chapter covers all important pieces of information that you must include on the drawings. Elevations and perspectives give clients a visual representation of what the space will look like. Your skill as a designer allows you to visualize the space; clients often do not have this ability. Your drawings will help ensure that you and your client are visualizing the same outcome and design intent.

REVIEW QUESTIONS

1. How are new windows indicated on the construction plan? (See "Drafting the Mechanical Plan"page 99)
2. How many switches are there for the S3 symbol? (See "Drafting the Mechanical Plan—Step 4"page 100)
3. Why must we dimension the vertical heights of items on the interior elevation? (See "Drawing an Interior Elevation"pages 106–107)
4. When would it be necessary to draft a detailed drawing? (See "Section Drawings and Detail Drawings"page 110)
5. How is a perspective drawing helpful for presenting your ideas to your client? (See "Perspective Drawings"pages 112–113)

Using the Computer to Design Kitchens and Baths

In the field of design today, computer usage for design is increasing and has changed the way businesses are run. Technology changes continuously. Software companies create new versions of their software, which include enhancements and changes to their programs. CAD stands for computer-aided drafting. Today we can do tasks on the computer that were not possible even a short time ago. Computers allow designers to make quick changes to a drawing, produce a drawing with speed, and create a realistic image of a space. Computers are used for business management as well. Even though computer drafting is commonly used, you still must understand hand drafting to better understand the process of design. Many companies use the computer and also hand draft some design components. Several kitchen and bath design programs are available for creating kitchen and bath drawings using the computer. CAD enables the creation of both two-dimensional and three-dimensional drawings. In this chapter, we identify important computer terminology, discuss computer basics, and look at the kitchen and bath design software programs approved for the NKBA certification exams.

Learning Objective 1: Understand computer terminology.

Learning Objective 2: Understand importance of computer components for CAD.

Learning Objective 3: Identify tasks completed with a computer.

COMPUTER TERMINOLOGY

Before moving on to a discussion of computer-aided drafting (CAD) software in general and NKBA certification exam software in particular, we present a basic overview of computer terminology. These topics will help you to understand how the computer works with the CAD software and the importance of meeting the specifications required for the software program. It is recommended that the computer used always meet or exceed the requirements of the software program. Such a computer may cost more initially, but it is worth the investment.

Hardware—Hardware is the physical equipment, the actual computer.

CPU—Central processing unit. This is the hardware device considered the "brain" of the computer; it processes information so the computer can perform and run applications and operations. The speed at which your system runs a program, downloads files, and loads images depends on the CPU. The number of cores in the processor helps determine how well it performs. The higher the number of cores, the higher the performance. This processor has a great effect on the speed and quality of your renderings in the CAD programs.

Hard drive—The hard drive is the internal storage device. This is where the operating system, files, data, and software applications are stored. You must determine how much storage will be needed for your specific needs and to meet or exceed those required of the software. Also decide on other programs that you would like to have loaded on your computer.

RAM—Random access memory. This is the temporary storehouse for data. If your computer doesn't have sufficient RAM, its operations can slow down as the computer starts using space on the hard drive to handle the data. Having sufficient RAM impacts how quickly and efficiently your CAD software will run. You need to consider how you will be using the computer. For CAD work, you want to be sure it has sufficient memory.

Video card—The video card determines image clarity, color brilliance, and accuracy of motion that you experience on screen. A premium video card is recommended for CAD work.

Monitor—The user should determine what size screen is best for his or her needs. Larger screens are recommended for working with CAD programs as you can see the items more easily on larger screens, and you won't strain your eyes as much as you might with a smaller screen. Another option is to have two monitors. This allows you to work on a floor plan on one monitor and view the elevation or perspective on the other monitor. When using a laptop, a large screen is preferable. Recommended monitor resolution should be 1024 × 768. This allows you to see the icons clearly when working with CAD programs.

Pixel—A pixel is the smallest component of a picture or image on the computer screen. The pixel often looks like a small, single-colored square or dot. Just as with a camera, the higher the number of pixels, the better the quality of picture you will have.

Software—Software is any set of machine-readable instructions that directs a computer's processor to perform specific operations. It includes application software or any other programs run on the computer. To ensure that the programs work properly, you must make sure the computer used meets or exceeds the program's specification requirements. You also must keep up-to-date with newer versions of the software and upgrades that are available. Companies are continuously improving their software and adding new features.

BIM—Building Information Modeling is software that links to a database of project information. This technology allows you to create a virtual three-dimensional model of the structure with all the components. This model replicates how the physical structure would be. All components are tied in together. The software is dynamic; one command affects another and makes changes on corresponding pages. Information on all of the parts and pieces of a project is entered, and changes can be made and shared with others so that several people can be involved and updated.

Operating system—This system performs tasks and runs other programs. The current version of Windows, for example, is an operating system.

Plug-in—A plug-in is a program that works with a host program to provide a specific, on-demand function. There are many different plug-ins available, and typically they are developed by third parties. A plug-in can be designed to work with audio, graphics software, email, and Web browsers.

Images

Categories of electronic art images fall into two categories: raster images and vector images.

Raster image—This is referred to as a bitmap. A raster image is created by drawing with software. Most CAD programs allow you to save drawings in different formats. Raster images include .jpeg or .jpg (Joint Photographic Experts Group), .bmp (Windows bitmap), .tiff (Tagged

Image File Format), .gif (Graphics Interchange Format), .png (Portable Network Graphic), PCX (Personal Computer Exchange/Paintbrush), and PCS (Picture Storage File/Microsoft).

Vector image—Vector images are developed so that they can be scaled up or down without losing quality. Most of the CAD programs for kitchen and bath use the .dxf (Drawing Exchange Format) or .dwg (drawing) format. You can import vector images into the CAD program.

Resolution—*Resolution* refers to the amount of detail a raster image holds. This is the number of pixels per unit of printed length. It is stated as dots per inch (dpi). High-resolution images may be made larger on a computer and produce a smooth result. High resolution is anything over 300 dpi. When a low-resolution image is enlarged, it becomes jagged looking.

Printer or scanner resolution—As with image *resolution*, when the term is applied to a mechanical device, *resolution* refers to the dpi (dots per inch) that the device is capable of producing. The resolution of printers and scanners varies and affects how drawings will print out. In general, the higher the number of dots, the better the quality of the print. A lower-quality resolution will print a drawing that looks as if it is composed of lots of little dots, which is known as pixelation.

File size—The digital size of an image is measured in kilobytes (KB), megabytes (MB), or gigabytes (GB). The file size is in proportion to the image's pixel dimensions. A high-resolution colored image takes up more file space than a low-resolution black-and-white image. Vector files take up less space than raster images, as they are not read as pixels.

File size has several implications. Larger files require more disk space and will slow down your computer. These larger files are also difficult to send over the Internet. To exchange larger files, often we need to use an Internet service, such as a File Transfer Protocol (FTP) site, or to copy them to a CD or flash drive. There are many Internet file sharing sites that designers can use to send larger files of drawings or pictures to clients or others.

Photorealism—Photorealism is a style of computer rendering that looks like a photograph. Items in the rendering look like the actual items, depicting spaces, materials, and textures.

New Trends in Technology

New applications constantly are being developed for use on tablets and smartphones. Some examples include taking a picture and changing it into a three-dimensional model. In some applications, you can take a picture and place measurements on it immediately.

CAD has become mobile. Many software companies have applications to be used on tablets and smartphones. Today it is easy to show your client design ideas on your mobile devices. Taking your mobile device, with all of the project documents loaded on it to meetings, can be especially useful for conducting a presentation

With some software programs, you can take pictures of a product, import it into the software program , and use it as a texture in your design. Data can be shared easily with the today's technology.

Cloud computing is a newer technology that lets you use files and applications over the Internet. With cloud computing, you should not have to manage the hardware or software. Many companies have moved their applications to the cloud. This continues to grow in popularity. Keep in mind that technology is always changing, and more new items are in the works every day.

CAD: A GENERAL OVERVIEW

Drafting using the computer has greatly impacted today's design process. Computers allow users to make quick changes, update drawings, change views, and much more. The ease of sending an email with attached drawings has helped companies run more efficiently. Software programs also are available for accounting, inventory, and management of clients' projects.

CAD allows you to create an accurate drawing in a short amount of time. You can complete the drawings in inches, feet/inches, or metrics. CAD programs are used around the world, and most have units such as currency and dimensions set for users in all locations. Some programs allow you to type in feet/inches and will convert all measures to inches or to metrics.

As previously mentioned, CAD programs enable you to complete a set of drawings in less time than when hand drafting. You can download manufacturers' catalogs of materials, cabinets, fixtures, and appliances into the program and use them on your drawings. You can complete interior elevations and perspective views of the space instantly. As the designer, you can make changes to the floor plan and view those changes immediately, making control of editing efficient. Another added feature of CAD is that you can see a two-dimensional or three-dimensional view while designing the space. This helps you visualize your design intent. An advantage to seeing a dimensional view immediately is that you can see how your design ideas come together in the space and how all of the elements fit together.

The basic commands used in the various CAD software programs are similar, yet each program has its individual strengths and focus. Some CAD programs enable users to design the entire home, from the interior to the exterior. Commands for executing and completing tasks vary among the software programs. The set of drawings may be completed in accordance with the NKBA's Graphics and Presentation Standards. The software for most programs allows you to select the units used on the drawings, imperial (inches) or metric.

Tools for Basic Design

Each CAD program offers a set of design tools that designers use to complete various tasks. Commands for drawing the floor plan include drawing the walls; placing all doors, windows, and openings; and placing all of the cabinetry, appliances, and fixtures into the space. Items may be edited easily as needed.

For the cabinetry, appliances, fixtures, and accessories, some software programs have extensive generic kitchen and bath design products that may be used for placing items on the floor plan in addition to manufacturers' catalogs downloaded into the program.

Manufacturers' catalogs contain actual images of the products that can be downloaded into the library within the software program. This means that you can create a great visual for your client showing the specific materials proposed, such as the counter material or appliance finish they would like for their design project. You can finish off the floor plan with window treatments, accessories, and images of people placed in the space, creating realistic images of the design space.

You can complete the construction plan drawing with the wall symbols since CAD programs contain the various wall types to be used for completing a construction plan. Some programs allow you to produce construction drawings for framing for the entire construction of the home. The drawings may show the footings and foundation. You can note the interior and exterior walls as well as any other architectural feature incorporated into the design.

You also can complete the mechanical plans using CAD. Each software program has features for ease of item placement and a library of mechanical and lighting symbols available for completing the drawings. Tools are available to draw the switch lines and place symbols in accordance with local building codes. Some programs include features to automatically place the electrical symbols to code. Each program has different capabilities for working on drawings. Since design software programs can be costly, it is important to consider which features are important to you and which program will best fit your needs.

You can complete interior elevations with the necessary dimensions, labels, and in accordance with the NKBA Graphics and Presentation Standards. Correct dimensioning is an important factor, as NKBA dimensioning differs slightly from the American Institute of Architects (AIA) standards. For NKBA, we dimension to the finished surface of the interior wall and the outside casing on doors and windows whereas the AIA standards centerlines the windows and doors while dimensioning to the center points of interior walls. As kitchen and bath designers, we always must adhere to the NKBA standards. Some programs may take a few more steps than others to achieve this when drawing. Most programs allow you to dimension either way; all you have to do is choose the method to use. Some software programs have NKBA requirements programmed in for dimensioning automatically.

For elevations, you can add more details as needed. For example, you can label the cabinets with the nomenclature or not. The drawings provide enough information that a cabinet maker can build the cabinets as needed for the space.

Tools for Three-Dimensional Views and Modeling

Using CAD, you can complete perspective drawings quickly. Different views of the space may be completed so that you can see the space in its entirety. The final rendered perspective can be photorealistic, and look like an actual photo of the space.

The technology of today's renderings is advanced and is always changing. Some programs can fine-tune the details of materials and products so that they look true to form and even show reflections. You can adjust the lighting to create different appearances for the space (see Figure 7.1, 7.2, 7.3, and 7.4).

You also can make video clips that will walk you through the space. Some start at one level and walk up the stairs to another level to show the entire completed space. These videos can be exported to others for viewing.

CAD programs allow users to complete detail drawings and section views. Each program has unique command capabilities. The ability to see a cross-section of an object, room, or entire structure allows for better understanding of how the components are put together. Some programs allow you to draw the entire structure so you can see all building components that interact with each other. For example, if you make a change on one floor, related items, such as materials and construction, will be updated on another corresponding floor. The drawings will be related correctly and updated with changes made. Most software companies offer free trial versions for download from the Internet so designers can see how the program works and view its specific features to help determine which program best meets their individual needs.

FIGURE 7.1 Perspective drawing of a kitchen.

Courtesy of Miguel Merida, AutoKitchen

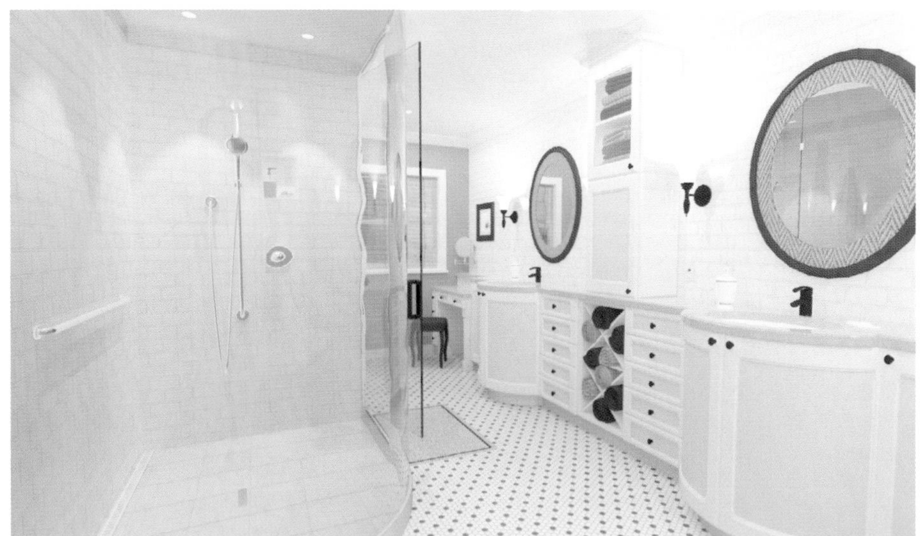

FIGURE 7.2 Perspective of bath using Ray Tracing.
Courtesy of Adrean Stephenson, Chief Architect

Linked Data

Each program has special features relating to the linked data within and outside the program. Some programs are linked with an ordering system enabling you to place an order directly with the cabinet manufacturer that you listed on the drawings. Others create a materials list with all products needed to install and construct the entire project. Many programs download product information in Excel.

You can cut or copy and paste items from the plans into other drawings.You also can import images and actual pictures into the programs to use for materials, textures, or pictures on the wall.

FIGURE 7.3 Perspective drawing of kitchen. Note the lighting effects.
Courtesy of Chris Midgley, ProKitchen

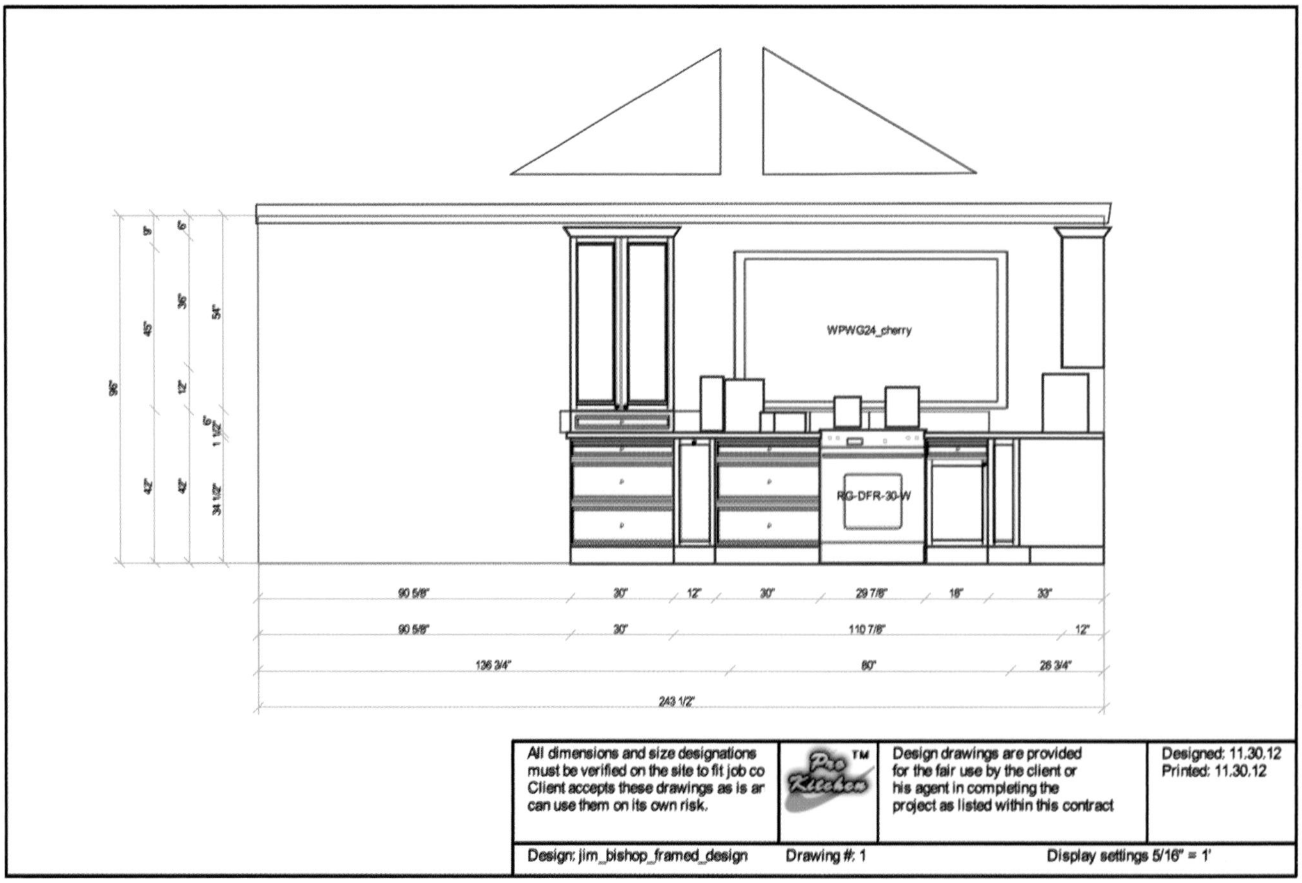
WPWG24_cherry
RG-DFR-30-W
243 1/2"
All dimensions and size designations must be verified on the site to fit job co Client accepts these drawings as is ar can use them on its own risk.
Pro Kitchen TM
Design drawings are provided for the fair use by the client or his agent in completing the project as listed within this contract
Designed: 11.30.12
Printed: 11.30.12
Design: jim_bishop_framed_design
Drawing #: 1
Display settings 5/16" = 1'

FIGURE 7.4 Perspective of a bathroom.
Courtesy of 20-20 Technologies

With most programs, you can place drawings on different layers. This allows features to be turned on or off for viewing desired components on a particular plan. You can place the different drawings on their own title block page and number them just as you can do with a hand-drafted set of plans. You also can place multiple items on one page. For instance, you can place a picture of the floor plan with perspective drawings so individuals can better interpret the design of the space. If you so choose, you can place all the elevations on one drawing along with other views. It is a quick task to change out which drawing you would like displayed.

It is important to examine the programs to see the features they have in order to select the program that best meets your design needs. CAD programs vary in how the tasks are completed and how you can customize and design your project.

NKBA CERTIFICATION SOFTWARE

The four software programs we look at next are approved by the NKBA for the CKD (Certified Kitchen Designer) and CBD (Certified Bath Designer) certification exams. The versions used for the exam are scaled-back ones without the automatic commands; the tasks must be completed manually so as not to give an advantage over those taking the exam using hand drafting. If you are taking the exam using CAD, you will need to see how the program is set up. Trial versions of the modified exam software are made available to candidates approved to sit for the exams. The NKBA does not promote one type of software over another for use in the field; the focus is on acceptable software programs to be used specifically for NKBA certification exams. Many other CAD programs are available that are designed specifically for the kitchen and bath industry. As mentioned earlier, you need to determine which program will best fit your individual design needs.

Autokitchen

Autokitchen® was developed in 1998 when Microcad Software became the first European company to sign an Original Equipment Manufacturer (OEM) with Autodesk® for the development of a kitchen and bath program. This program became Autokitchen. The software is built on the AutoCAD® engine (see Figures 7.5 and 7.6).

Some of the features of the AutoKitchen program are listed next.

- Includes native .dwg files that can be shared with architects and builders.
- Can be downloaded into AutoCAD program.
- Allows placing of three-dimensional (3D) objects instead of drawing line by line.
- Works in imperial or metric systems, or both.
- Perspectives generate quickly and have a photorealistic quality.
- Creates perspectives with different artistic renderings.

FIGURE 7. 5 Example of perspective rendering.
Courtesy of AutoKitchen.

- Generates a quote for project with catalogs and pricing uploaded into the system. Can generate a project list and export it to Excel to personalize and submit your cabinetry order.
- Can customize one cabinet or entire cabinetry in the universal catalogs. Can create a part list per cabinet.
- Video clip feature allows you to walk through the presentation.
- Can create hand-drawn colored images with the Fast Shade Function.
- Can design space or use a Kitchen Design Wizard.
- Automatic or manual insertion of mechanical plan symbols.
- Can customize the exterior of home.
- Extensive library catalog and manufacturers' catalogs.
- Photorealistic perspectives of space using ray tracing technology.
- Estimate 5 is the pricing and ordering software application.

Chief Architect

Chief Architect was created in 1992 for the professional home design software market and was the first object-based 3D CAD system with Smart Object design principles, known as BIM.

Chief Architect has several versions available. Some features of Chief Architect are listed next.

- Has NKBA standards for auto elevation and plan view dimension tools. Can use a Bluetooth or wireless-compatible device to measure a space automatically, then input the distances directly into dimension strings.

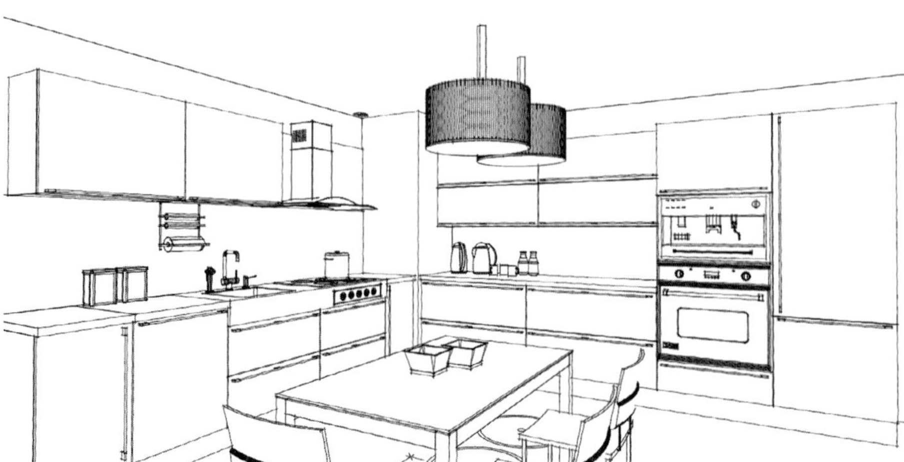

FIGURE 7. 6 Example of perspective drawing.
Courtesy of AutoKitchen.

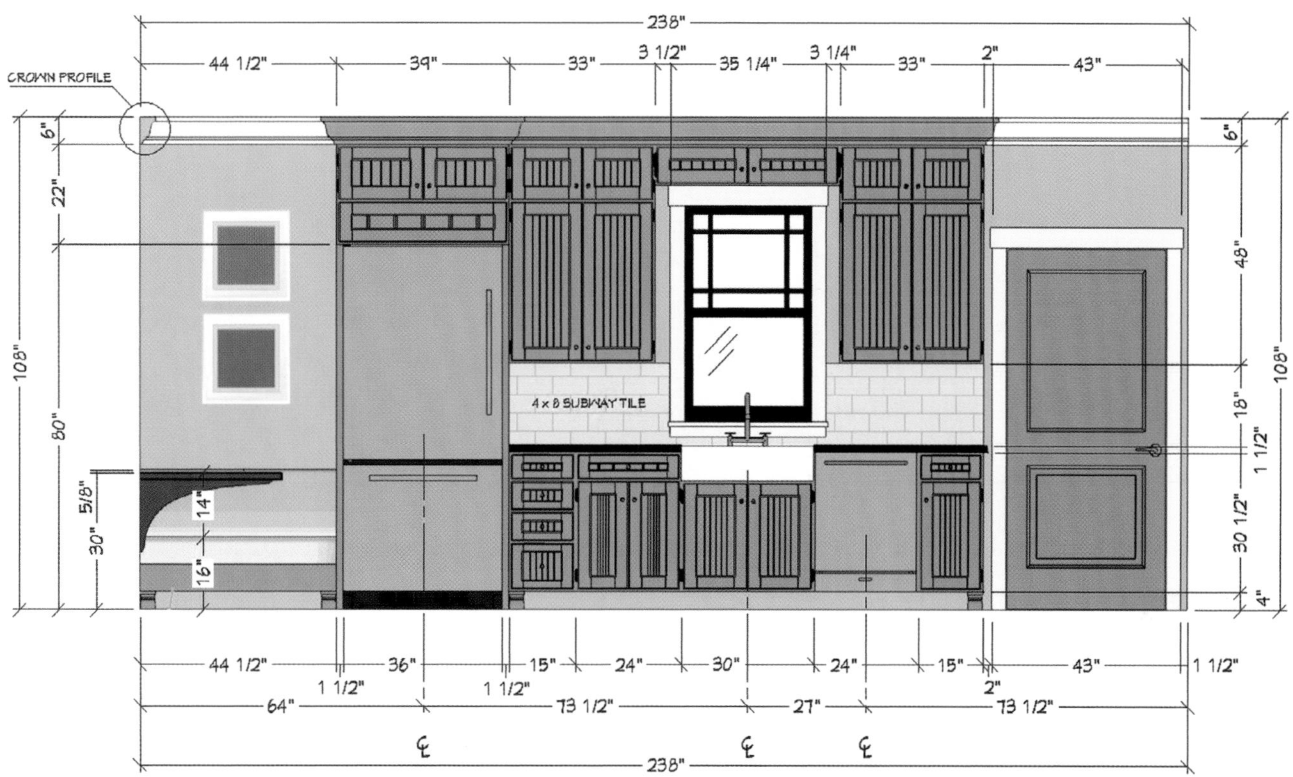

FIGURE 7. 7 Chief Architect elevation.
Courtesy of Chief Architect

- Uses ray trace: can define the time of day for shadows with skylight, windows, and artificial lighting. The Ray Trace Wizard helps generate realistic 3D views that look like realistic photos.
- Artistic rendering: Watercolor, Squiggle line, Painting, Line drawing, Technical illustration, Vector, Glass House, and Duotone.
- Material Painter™: Apply colors, materials, and textures from any image or Web site. Can import specific materials for use.
- Color Chooser™: Choose manufacturer colors, materials, or textures from the library or pull from a digital photo.
- Record three-dimensional views for virtual tours.
- Create any style of custom cabinet with the Smart Cabinet Designer™ tools.
- Extensive catalogs of products and manufacturers' catalogs to download. Schedules can be generated for products on plans.
- Group cabinets, fixtures, appliances, and accessories to create architectural blocks for items such as kitchen islands or entire kitchens. Save to the library for future use.
- CAD tools: Can convert CAD objects to architectural objects.
- Dimensions for One-Click Auto Dimensioning™, Advanced stair and ramp tools for curved, flared, split, and straight.
- Smart Objects (BIM) windows, cabinets, doors, rooms have properties and behave intelligently in the design.
- Materials lists for cost estimating and bidding
- CAD-to-Walls tool imports an AutoCAD file and provides a mapping for layers—a great tool to interchange files with AutoCAD® users. Imports images from SketchUp.
- Time Tracker™ monitors time spent on specific projects.

Figures 7.7 and 7.8 show drawings created with Chief Architect.

FIGURE 7.8 Chief Architect rendering technique.
Courtesy of Chief Architect

ProKitchen

Real View, LLC was founded in 1999 with the goal of providing state-of-the-art Java 3D visualization capabilities to designers, retailers, and manufacturers seeking premium service and increased customer satisfaction. The main 3D library used today by the ProKitchen suite of products was originally developed by the two founders, Leo Perlov and Boris Zeldin. In 2003 Real View entered the kitchen and bath market with the ProQuote pricing system first developed for Craft-Maid, PA, and Adelphi Cabinets, PA. Beginning with the most complex custom lines enabled Real View with experience and knowledge of the industry and products. Real View started developing ProKitchen in 2004; it was released two years later at the Craft-Maid User Group Meeting. ProKitchen brought to the market the new 3D, stable noncrashing program based on Java technology, with new ways of using the exact manufacturer door styles and finishes instead of drawing each one manually and a simplified graphical user interface with only four panels that can split interchangeably.

The following list includes some features of the ProKitchen program.

- Includes over 300 cabinet manufacturer catalogs with over 1,000 fixtures. Can customize cabinets.
- iPad/iPhone/Android integration.
- Java technology makes this program stable with no lockups.
- Countertop module, closet tool allows for custom design.
- Design and edit tools.
- Allows for direct-to-manufacturer ordering. Items placed in drawing will be uploaded to order form for direct ordering to designated manufacturers.
- Create two-dimensional and three-dimensional views.
- Fully rotated 3D quality renderings. Colors, patterns, and finishes appear true to life.

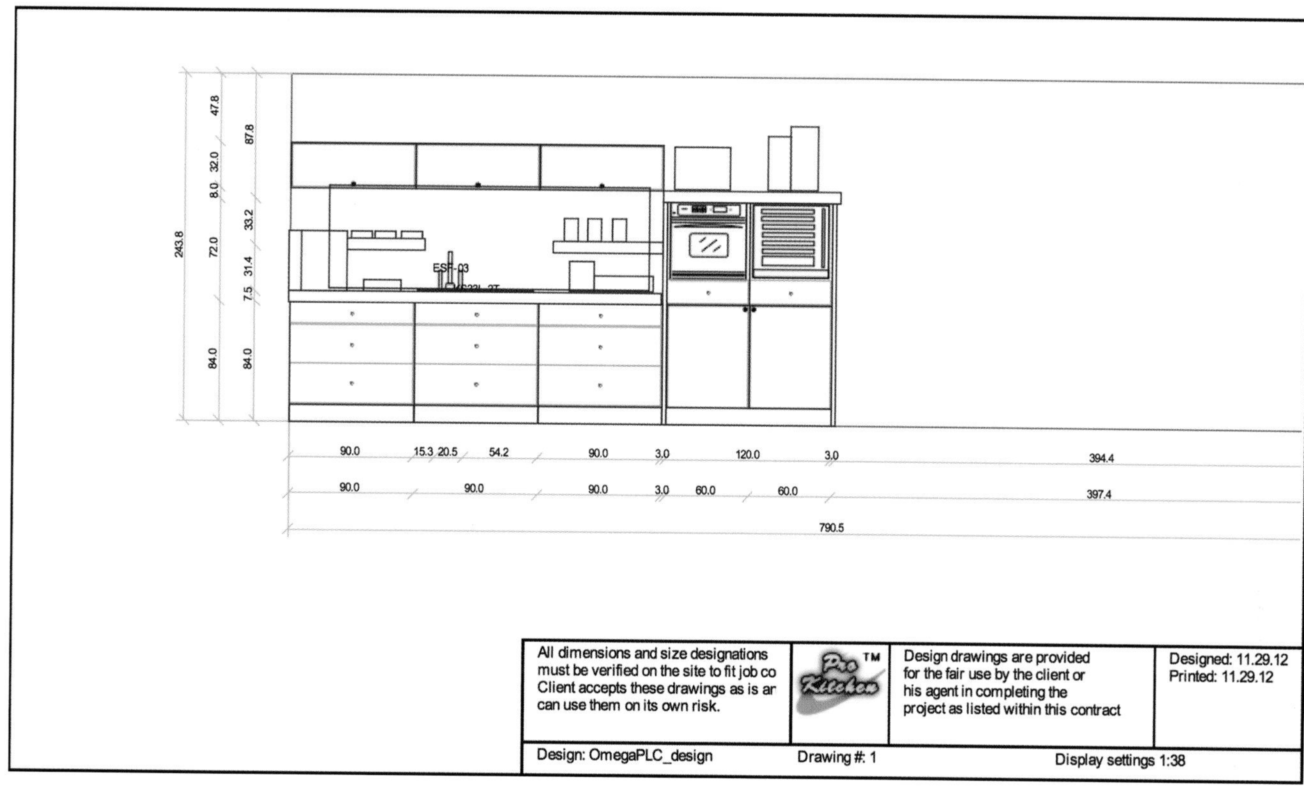

FIGURE 7.9 ProKitchen elevation.

- Subtle textures, highlights, and distressing are clearly replicated.
- Tools to create plans found in a set of drawings.
- Can import items from AutoCAD and SketchUp into the program.

Figure 7.9 is an example of a drawing created with ProKitchen.

20-20 Technologies

20-20 Technologies was founded in 1987. The company operates in eleven countries and is headquartered in Canada

The following list includes some of the features of the 20-20 program.

- Design and editing tools.
- Creates photorealistic images with control of lighting.
- Can import items from SketchUp and AutoCAD.
- NKBA guidelines can be referenced while designing.
- Ability to complete drawings in imperial (inches) or metric.
- Customize cabinets or use manufacture's catalogs for design of space. Linked with manufacturers so order can be placed from drawing information.
- Import images into the design library to use on drawings.
- Download textures to be applied to surfaces in drawings.
- Extensive library of products and manufacturers' catalogs.
- Create elevations and perspectives.
- Create a virtual walk through of the space. Can place different images on one sheet. For example, floor plans can be placed on the same page as perspective drawings or elevations.
- Print to different sizes of paper.
- Additional space planning programs are available.

Figures 7.10 and 7.11 are drawings created with 20-20.

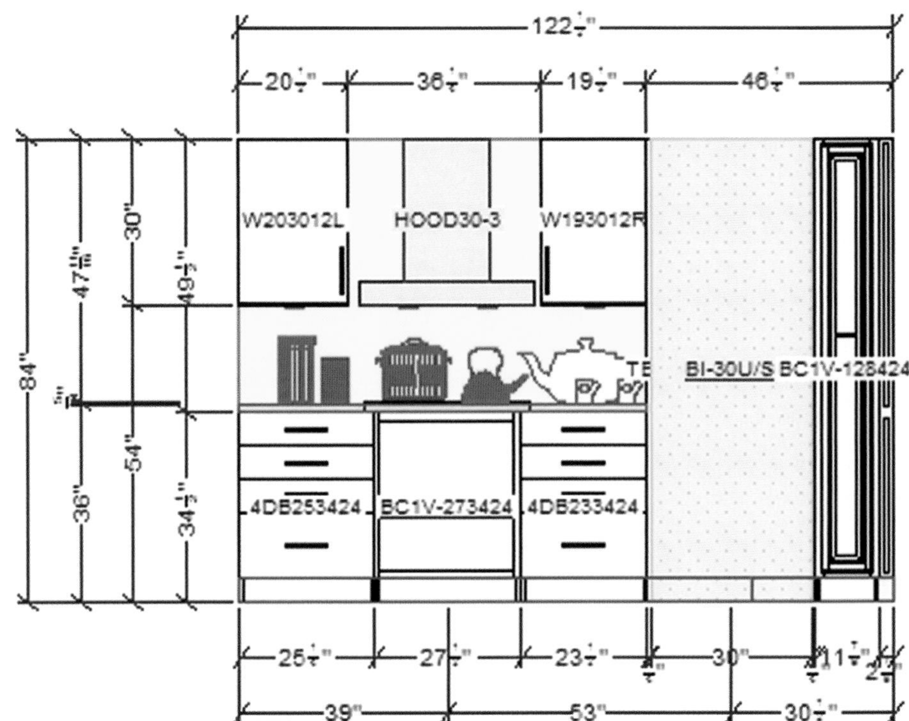

FIGURE 7.10 20-20 Design example of elevation.
Courtesy of 20-20 Technologies

FIGURE 7.11 20-20 Design example of perspective.
Courtesy of 20-20 Technologies

As a designer, you need to research each software product to see which would be the best fit for your design needs. Make sure that each company you consider provides the design software support services you may need. Make sure that the drawings are in accordance with the NKBA Graphics and Presentation Standards. Every software program has its own unique features which are constantly changing to meet the demands of the industry.

SUMMARY

Technology is always changing. Each new version of CAD programs introduces new features. You must keep up with what is available. Today you can do that simply by looking on the Internet to see what is available and new in design. CAD also is becoming more mobile with tablet and smartphone applications. The technology is linked with many products and applications. Cloud computing has opened new doors for companies and how they operate.

You must be proficient with CAD programs when taking the NKBA certification exams. Remember that the automatic commands are disabled so you are drafting manually with the computer.

Make sure that your computer meets or exceeds the recommended requirements in order to run the software program properly. Verify the computer specs to make sure you are getting the correct product. CAD is an efficient and quick way to draft and design a space. Seeing the space visually in a two-dimensional or three-dimensional view while designing is a nice feature of CAD.

REVIEW QUESTIONS

1. Define *photorealism*. (See "Computer Terminology—Images—Photorealism" page 123)
2. How does BIM work in a software program? (See "Computer Terminology" page 122)
3. What is the difference between a raster image and a vector image? (See "Computer Terminology—Images" pages 122–123)
4. Can catalogs from industry manufacturers be downloaded into a CAD program? (See "Tools for Basic Design" page 124)
5. What are video clips used for? (See "Tools for Three-Dimensional Views and Modeling" page 125)

NKBA's Graphics and Presentation Standards

NKBA's Graphics and Presentation Standards for Kitchen and Bathroom Design are included in this book so that you might gain a clearer insight into the concepts for good presentation techniques. The use of these standards is strongly recommended. They contain a specific set of criteria that, when applied by the kitchen and bathroom specialist, produce professional project documents that include the following:

- Floor plan
- Construction plan
- Mechanical plan
- Interpretive drawings (elevations, perspective drawings, oblique, dimetric, isometric, and trimetric drawings and sketches)
- Specifications
- Design statement

Learning Objective 1: Understand the scope of NKBA Graphics and Presentation Standards.

Learning Objective 2: Know what must be included on all drawings, the design statement, and specifications.

Learning Objective 3: Use the NKBA Graphics and Presentation Standards as your reference for NKBA drawings.

PURPOSE OF GRAPHICS AND PRESENTATION STANDARDS

By standardizing floor plans and presentation drawings, kitchen and bathroom designers will:

- Limit errors caused by misinterpreting the floor plan.
- Avoid misreading dimensions, which can result in costly errors.
- Prevent cluttering floor plans and drawings with secondary information, which often makes the documents difficult to interpret.
- Create a clear understanding of the scope of the project for everyone involved in the job.
- Present a professional image to the client.
- Permit faster processing of orders.
- Simplify estimating and specification preparation.
- Maintain the standardization of uniform nomenclature and symbols.

For reference, appendix A presents two sample sets of project documents, one of a kitchen and one of a bathroom.

KITCHEN OR BATH FLOOR PLAN

The floor plan should depict the entire room, when possible. When the entire room cannot be depicted, the floor plan must show the area where cabinetry and appliances are permanently installed. Walls continuing from the kitchen must have a break line so the reader knows the wall is continuous. Walls must show all major structural elements with adjoining areas indicated and labeled (see Figure 8.1). The floor plan must show all major structural elements such as walls, door swings, door openings, partitions, windows, archways, and equipment.

- Kitchen and bath floor plans should be drawn to a scale of ½″ equals 1′ (½″ = 1′-0″) or the metric equivalent (1:20) 1 mm = 1:20 For metric drawings, mm (millimeters) are used.
- Base cabinetry should be depicted using a dashed line. Use a solid line for wall and tall cabinets, countertops, flooring material, furniture, appliances, and fixtures not hidden by another object.
- A separate plan for the soffit is required when it is a different depth than the wall or tall cabinet below it. A separate soffit plan is also recommended when the soffit is to be installed prior to the wall or tall cabinet installation.

The acceptable paper for the original drawings of the floor plan, construction plan, mechanical plan, and interpretive drawings is set at a minimum of 11″ × 17″. Translucent vellum tracing paper, imprinted with a black border and appropriate space for the insertion of pertinent information, is strongly recommended. Copies of original drawings should be presented in blue or black ink only on white paper. Photocopy prints are acceptable. The use of lined yellow note paper, typing paper, scored graph paper, or scored quadrille paper is not acceptable.

Dimensions

- All drawing dimensions on kitchen and bathroom floor plans must be given in inches and fractions of inches only (i.e., 124¼″). Combining dimensions listed in feet and inches or the exclusive use of dimensions listed in feet and inches (10′-4¼″) is not acceptable and should not be used under any circumstances. This also applies to metric equivalent.
- Each set of dimensions should be at least 3⁄16″ apart on separate dimension lines, which are to intersect with witness lines. Dimension lines are preferred ½″ (13 mm) apart. Use slashes to indicate intersecting points. (Slashes are the industry standard but arrows or dots are acceptable. See chapter 5 for a description of dimension lines.)

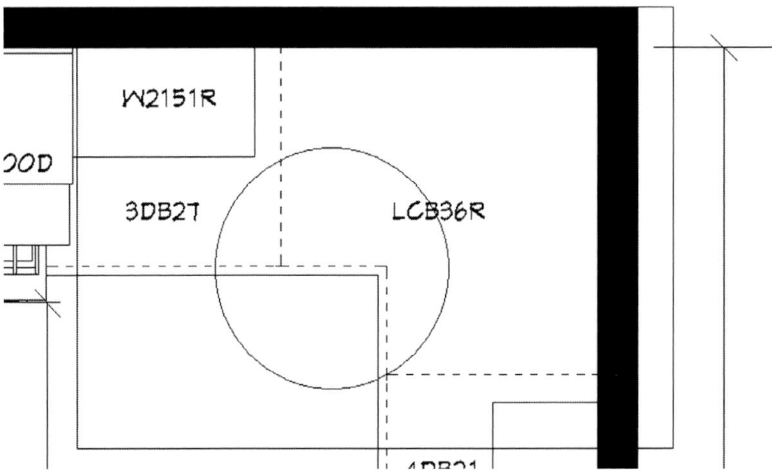

FIGURE 8.1 Base cabinetry should be drawn with dashed line, wall cabinets with solid line, and a solid counter line should represent the counter with correct overhangs.

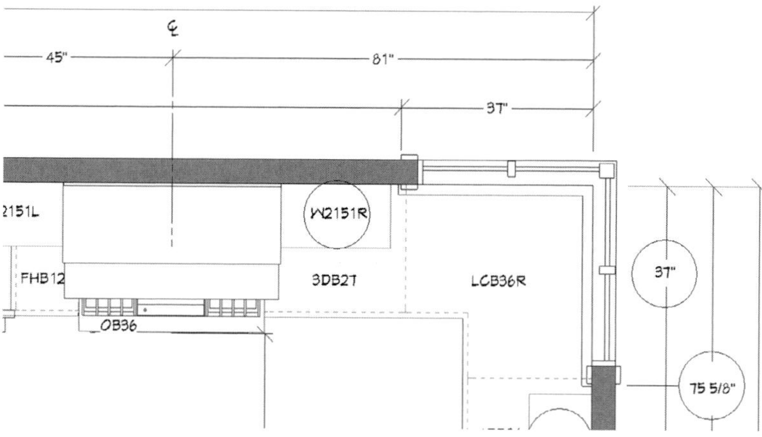

FIGURE 8.2 Dimensions are horizontal and read from the bottom of the plan.

- Dimensions should be shown outside the wall lines whenever possible.
- There are two acceptable dimensioning standards.
  - **a.** One standard lists all dimensions parallel to the title block at the bottom of the vellum paper. Break the dimension line near its midpoint. This mechanical drafting technique eliminates errors in reading dimensions (see Figure 8.2).
  - **b.** The other standard shows all horizontal dimensions and lettering so they are read from the bottom edge and all vertical dimensions so they are read from the right side of plans (see Figure 8.3).
- Use finished interior dimensions on all project documents to denote available space for cabinetry and/or other types of equipment. If you are responsible for specifying the exact method of wall construction, finish, and/or partition placement, include partition center lines as well as the finished interior dimensions on the construction plan.

Minimum Dimensions to Include on Every Floor Plan

- Overall length of wall areas to receive cabinets, countertops, fixtures, or any equipment occupying floor and/or wall space must be shown (see Figure 8.4). This overall dimension always should be the outside line.
- Individually dimension each wall opening (windows, arches, and doors), major appliances, and fixed structures (chimneys, protrusions, and partitions). Show dimensions from the outside trim. Note the trim size in the specification list.

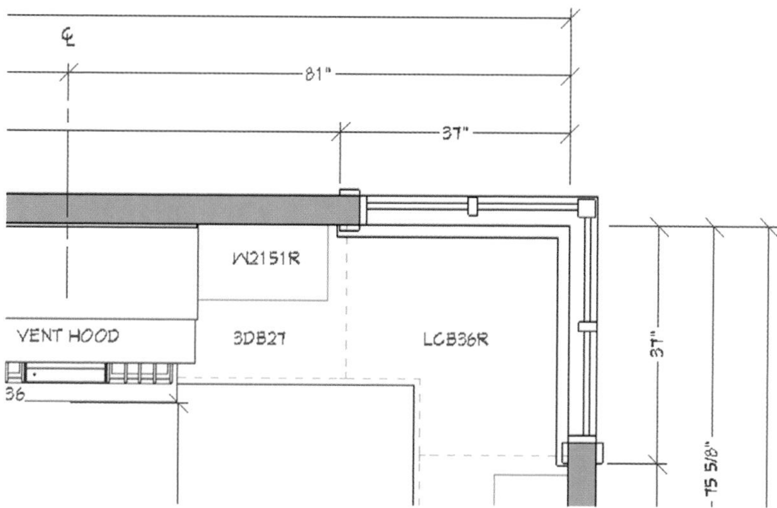

FIGURE 8.3 Dimensions may be read from the bottom (horizontal dimensions) and the right side (vertical dimensions).

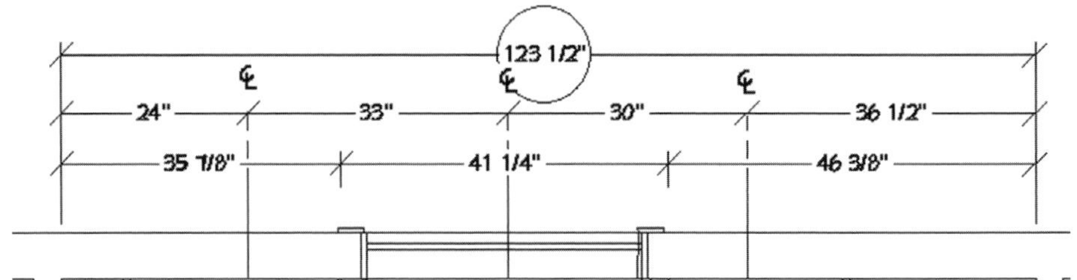

FIGURE 8.4 Overall length must be shown for all walls.

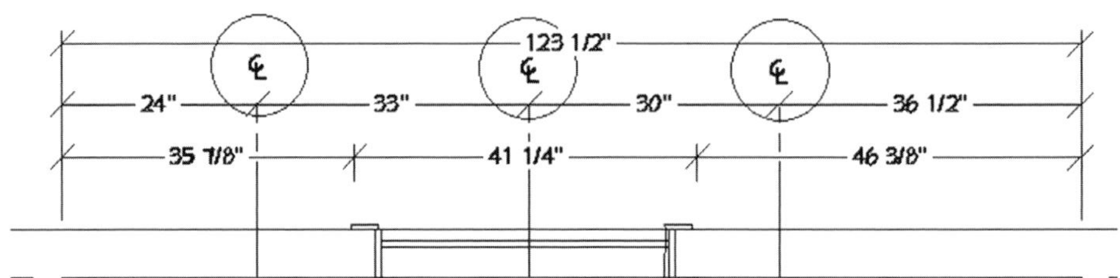

FIGURE 8.5 Note dimension lines closest to walls and centerline dimensions. Include ceiling heights on the floor plan.

- Fixtures remaining in place, such as radiators, must be outlined on the floor plan. These critical dimensions should be the first dimension line. See chapter 5 for a detailed description of the dimensioning process (see Figure 8.5).
- Include additional notes for any deviation from standard height, width, and depth (cabinets, countertops, etc.) (see Figure 8.6).
- Indicate the exact opening for height, width, and depth for areas to be left open to receive equipment, cabinets, appliances, and fixtures at a future date. Refer to chapter 5 for a more in-depth description of the floor plan specifications (see Figure 8.7).
- Items such as island and peninsula cabinets must be shown with the overall dimensions given from countertop edge to the opposite countertop edge, tall cabinet, or wall. Identify the exact location of the structure by dimensions that position it from two directions: from return walls or from the face of cabinets/equipment opposite the structure (see Figure 8.8).

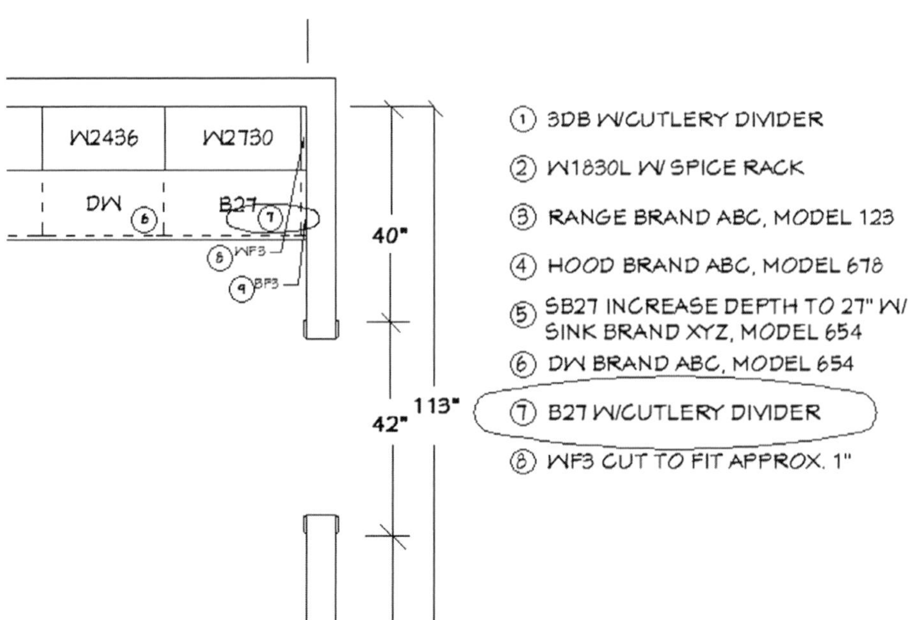

FIGURE 8.6 Floor plan specifications. Show any deviation from standard height, nomenclature descriptions as needed, appliances, fixtures, and so on.

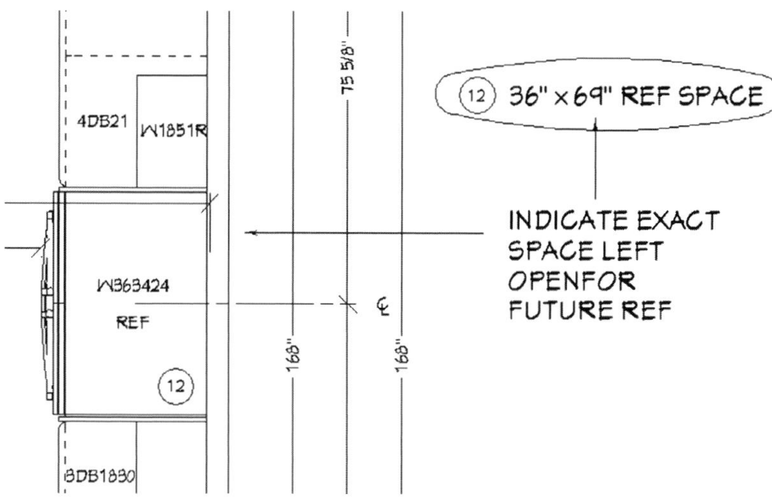

FIGURE 8.7 List the exact openings that need to be included on the floor plan for future installation of equipment, cabinets, appliances, and fixtures.

Centerline Dimensions

- Centerline dimensions must be given for equipment in two directions when possible to indicate the exact location of the equipment for plumbing and wiring purposes (see Figure 8.9).
- Items requiring a centerline include: all appliances, sinks, tubs/showers, toilets, bidets, fan units, light fixtures, heating and air-conditioning ducts, and radiators.
- Centerline dimensions should be pulled from return walls or from the front of cabinets/ equipment opposite the mechanical element (see Figure 8.10).
- Centerlines on the mechanical plan will be indicated by the symbol (CL) followed by a long-short-long broken line that extends into the floor area. When the centerline dimension line is outside the floor area, it is typically shown as the second (and, if required, the third) line following the dimension line that identifies the individual wall segments (see Figure 8.11).

Cabinets, Appliances, and Equipment Nomenclature and Designation

- Cabinets should be designated and identified by manufacturer nomenclature inside the area to indicate their position (see Figure 8.12).
- Cabinet system trim and finish items are designated outside their area, with an arrow clarifying exactly where the trim piece is located (see Figure 8.13).

To ensure clarity, some design firms prefer to number each cabinet on the floor plan and call out all the cabinet nomenclature in the floor plan specification listing. Equally acceptable is the use of circled reference numbers to designate each cabinet on the floor plan, and elevations with the cabinet code listed within the individual unit width on the elevations or placed in a separate cross-referenced list on the elevation page (see Figure 8.14).

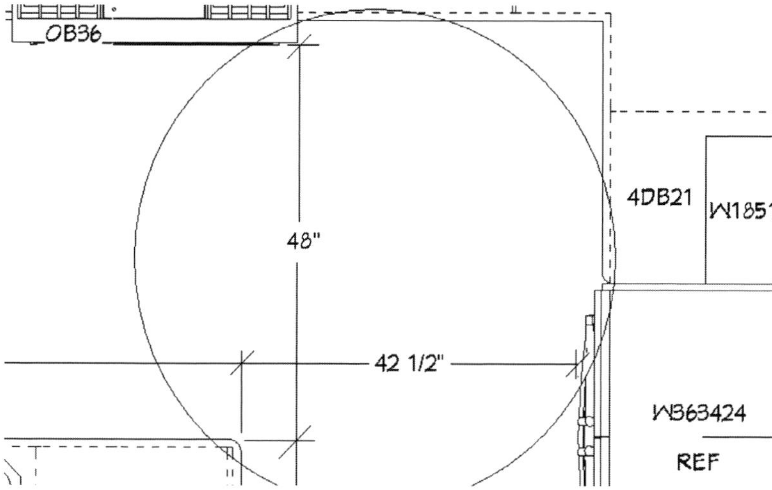

FIGURE 8.8 Clearance dimensions.

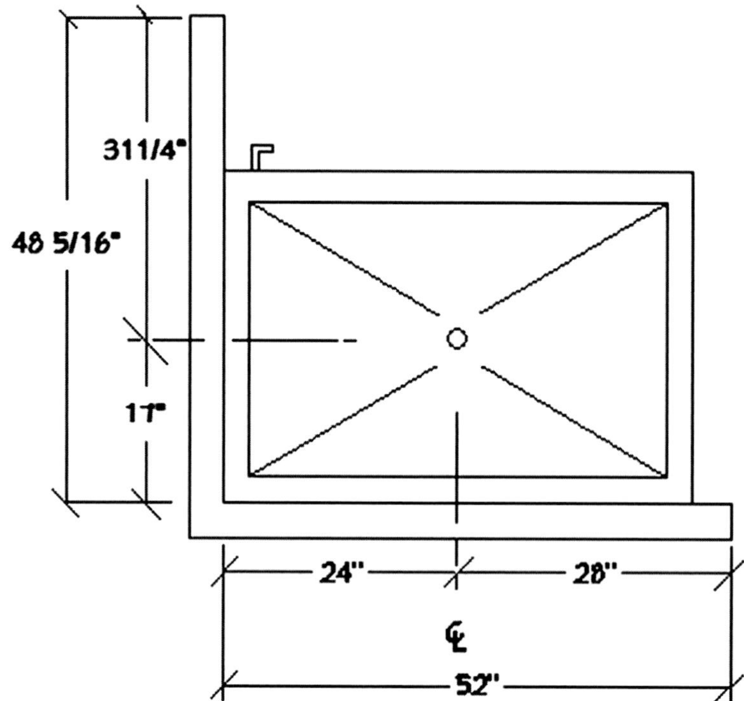

FIGURE 8.9 Centerline dimensions for fixtures and appliances in two directions for exact location. This applies especially to diagonal installations, peninsulas, islands, showers, and tubs.

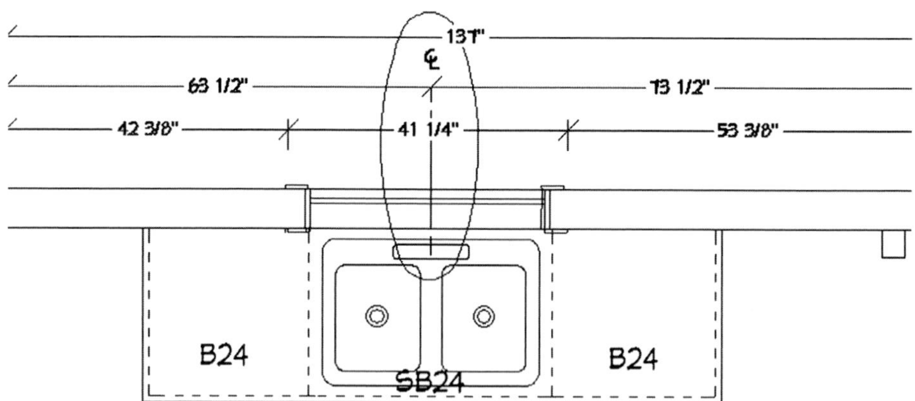

FIGURE 8.10 Centerline dimensions.

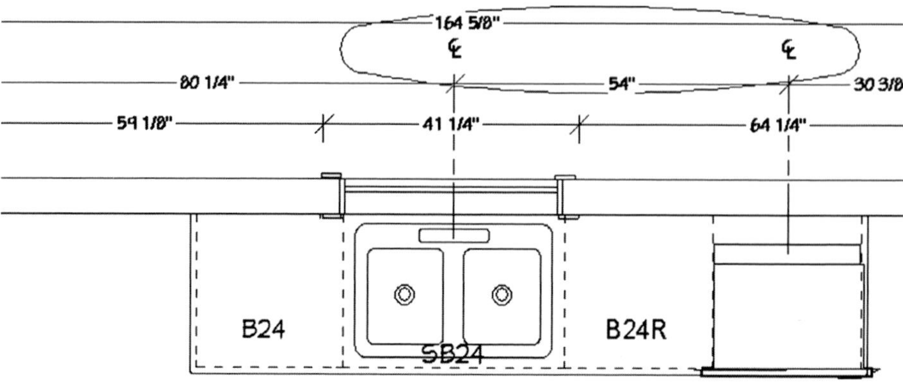

FIGURE 8.11 The centerline dimension is the line just before the overall dimension line. It could be line closest to wall if there are no openings.

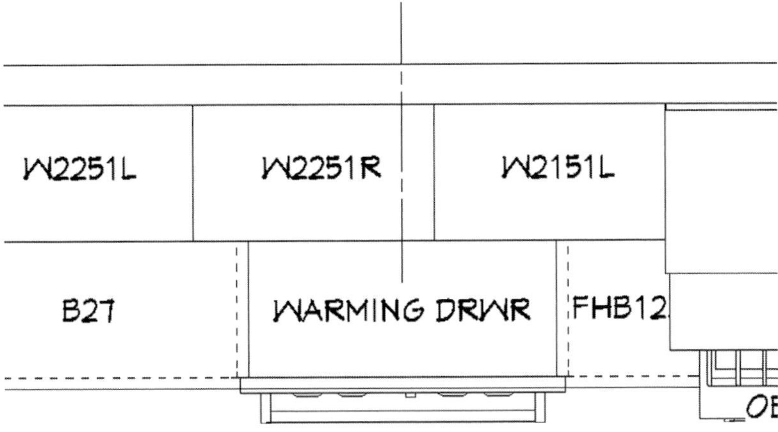

FIGURE 8.12 Center nomenclature on cabinetry.

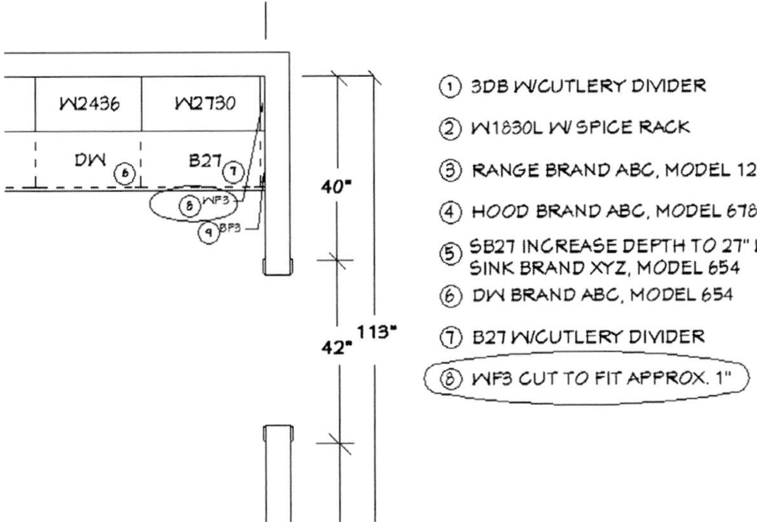

FIGURE 8.13 Leader lines can be used for nomenclature in small areas.

Regardless of the cabinet designation system selected, additional information for supplementary fixtures, appliances, equipment, accessories, and special provisions pertaining to the cabinets must be indicated within the cabinet or equipment area by a circled reference number (see Figure 8.15). This additional information should be listed in the specifications on the floor plan drawing or on a separate sheet of paper.

- Special-order materials or custom design features, angled cabinets, unusual tops, molding, trim details, and the like, should be shown in a section view (or cut view), a plan view in a scale larger than (½″ = 1.0″), or in elevation view. Refer to appendix A for sample kitchen plans and bath plans.

For more information on cabinet nomenclature, see the appendix.

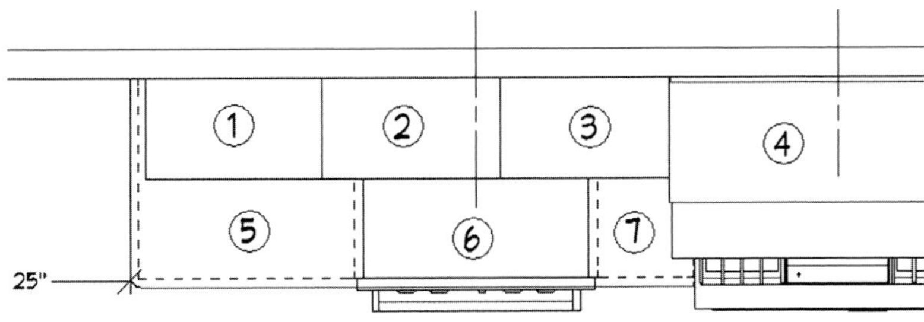

FIGURE 8.14 Optional method for designating nomenclature.

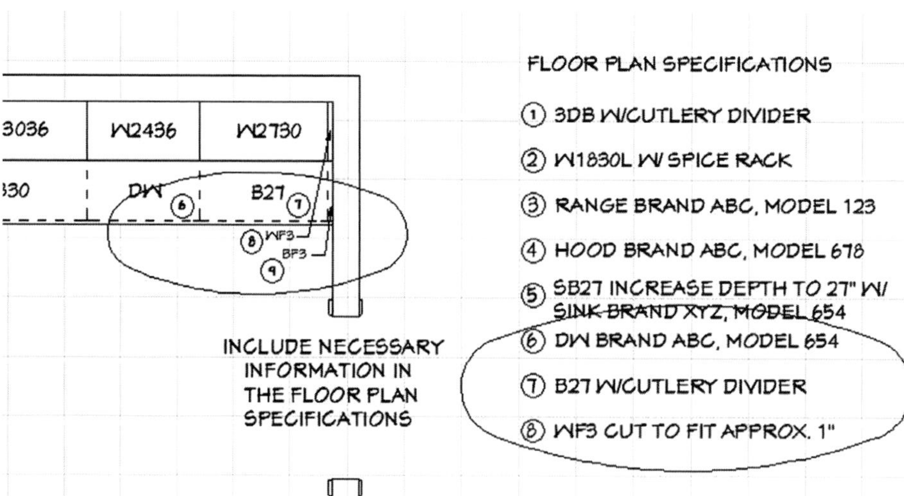

FIGURE 8.15 Space for future appliances is indicated in floor plan specifications.

CONSTRUCTION PLAN

The purpose of the construction plan is to show the relationship of the existing space with that of the new design. Because of the detail involved, construction information is detailed separately so that it does not clutter the floor plan. However, if construction changes are minimal, it is acceptable to combine the construction plan with either the floor plan or the mechanical plan. Refer to appendix A for examples of construction plans.

Construction Plan Symbols

- Existing walls are shown as darkened spaces or hollow outlines.
- Wall sections to be removed are shown with an outline of broken lines.
- For new walls, show the material symbols applicable to the type of construction or use a symbol that is identified in the legend in order to distinguish them from existing partitions (see Figure 8.16)

MECHANICAL PLAN AND SYMBOLS

A separate plan for the mechanical systems will help to clearly identify such work without cluttering the floor plan. Refer to appendix A for examples of plans.

- The mechanical plan should show an outline of the cabinets, countertops and fixtures without nomenclature.
- Appliances should be labeled.
- The mechanicals should be placed in the proper location with the correct symbols.

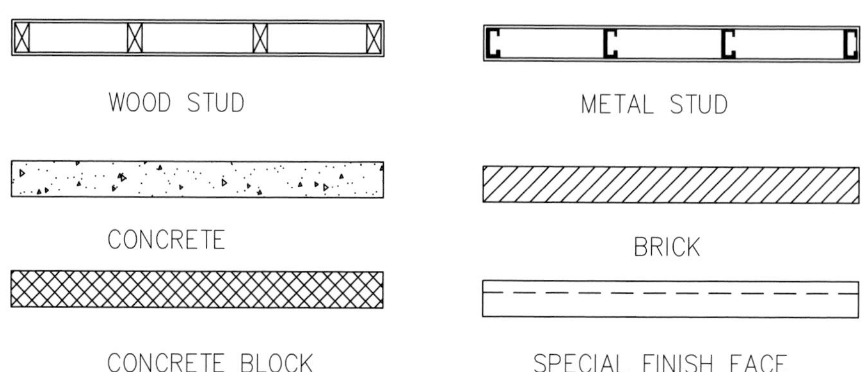

FIGURE 8.16 Construction plan wall symbols.

- All overall room dimensions should be indicated on the plan.
- The mechanical plan consists of the electrical/lighting, plumbing, heating, air conditioning, and ventilation (HVAC) systems. Any minor wall or door construction changes should be detailed on the mechanical plan or on a separate plan.
- A mechanical legend should be included on the plan. This legend will be used to describe the symbols for all switches, outlets, communication items, special-purpose outlets, fixtures, or equipment. Every symbol on the mechanical plan must be cross-referenced and placed in the mechanical legend. The legend should be placed on right side of drawing. The legend may be placed at bottom of drawing if there is not room on right side.
- Centerline dimensions must be indicated for all equipment and should be indicated in two directions when possible. To ensure accuracy, the dimensions should begin at the wall and show centerpoints of objects. Mechanicals requiring centerlines include all appliances, sinks, tubs/showers, toilets, bidets, fan units, light fixtures, heating, air conditioning, ducts, and radiators. Centerline dimensions should be pulled from return walls or from the face of the item being centerlined to a position opposite it. Pulling dimensions from the wall ensures accuracy of placement. On the mechanical plan, centerlines are to be indicated by the CL symbol followed by a long-short-long broken line that extends into the floor area, indicating the centerpoints of the given item (see Figure 8.17).

FIGURE 8.17 The centerline symbol used to show center points of all appliances, fixtures, etc.

INTERPRETIVE DRAWINGS

Interpretive drawings are used as a means of understanding the floor plans. These drawings give a visualization of how the space will look upon completion. Under no circumstances should interpretive drawings be used as substitutes for floor plans. In case of a dispute, the floor plans are the legally binding documents. Interpretive drawings include elevations, perspectives, oblique, dimetric, isometric, and trimetric drawings, and sketches. (See chapter 6 for more details.) Because perspective drawings are not dimensioned to scale, include a disclaimer on all such drawings, such as:

> THIS DRAWING IS AN ARTISTIC INTERPRETATION OF THE GENERAL APPEARANCE OF THE FLOOR PLAN. IT IS NOT MEANT TO BE AN EXACT RENDITION.

Elevations

Elevations must show a full front view of all wall areas and islands receiving cabinets and equipment as shown on the floor plan. A portion of the cabinet doors and drawer front should indicate the style and, when applicable, placement of handles/pulls. Dimension all cabinets, appliances, countertops, fixtures, and equipment in the elevation as follows:

- Widths and heights of all cabinets, appliances, countertops, fixtures, spaces, and equipment must be dimensioned on the elevations.
- Cabinets with toekick and finished height.
- Countertop thickness and backsplash height.
- Doors, windows, and other openings in walls that will receive equipment. List the window/door casing or trim within the overall opening dimensions.
- Permanent fixtures.
- Main structural elements and protrusions, such as chimneys, partitions, and so on.
- Centerlines for all mechanical elements and plumbing.

Perspective Drawings

Perspectives are not drawn to scale. Grids can be used under vellum paper to portray a perspective rendering accurately. Designers have the option of preparing a one-point or two-point perspective with or without the use of a grid.

- Perspectives should be reasonably correct representations of the longest cabinet or fixture run or the most important area in terms of usage.
- Perspectives do not need to show the complete kitchen or bathroom.
- Separate sectional views of significant areas or features are acceptable.

FIGURE 8.18 A quick sketch can serve as a guide for drawing an exact plan of the space.

Oblique, dimetric, isometric, and trimetric are several types of interpretive drawings that can be used to illustrate special cabinets and features, such as countertops or special-order cabinets, where mechanical representation and dimensions are important.

Sketches are a quick way to achieve a total picture of the kitchen or bathroom without exact details in scaled dimensions (see Figure 8.18). A sketch can be studied, adjusted, and sketched over, as the designer and client are discussing the most satisfactory layout for the space.

SPECIFICATIONS

Depending on the complexity of the job, specifications may appear on the plan, they may be listed on a separate form, or a combination of both methods may be used. Either way, specifications are part of the project documents. The NKBA makes its standard specification forms for kitchen and bathroom design and installation available to its members.

The purpose of project specifications is to clearly define the details of the products listed and the scope and limits of the job. They should:

- Define the area of responsibility between the kitchen/bathroom specialist and the purchaser.
- Clearly define all material and work affected by the job, either directly or indirectly.
- Clearly indicate which individual has the ultimate responsibility for all or part of the above.
- Contain descriptive references to all areas of work.

All specification categories must be completed. If the job does not cover any given area, you should write *Not Applicable*, *N/A*, or *None* on the form. Each area must indicate who is responsible for the product and/or task: either the kitchen/bathroom specialist, the owner, or the owner's agent. In all cases, the owner or the owner's agent must receive a completed copy of the project documents prior to the commencement of any work.

All responsibilities for a design project must be clearly defined. Most design projects involve work completed by contractors and subcontractors. The responsibility for follow-through and the completion of a project must be clearly defined so there is no chance any task will be overlooked.

Project Responsibilities

- Kitchen/bathroom designers are responsible for the accuracy of the dimensioned floor plans and the selections and designations of all cabinets, appliances, and equipment, if made or approved by them.
- Any equipment directly purchased by the kitchen/bathroom specialist for resale should be the responsibility of the kitchen/bathroom designer. Further, the specialist must be responsible for supplying product installation instructions to the owner or the owner's agent.
- Any labor furnished by the kitchen/bathroom designer, whether by his or her own employees or through subcontractors paid directly by the designer and working under his or her direction, should be the kitchen/bathroom designer's responsibility. Total responsibility should not be delegated to the subcontractor.
- Any equipment purchased directly by the owner or owner's agent from an outside source should be the responsibility of the owner or owner's agent. The same applies to any subcontractor, building contractor, or other labor directly hired and/or paid by the owner or owner's agent.

DESIGN STATEMENT

The purpose of the design statement is to interpret the design problem and solution in order to substantiate the project to the client. Design statements may be verbal or written. It is important that a design statement be clear, concise, and interesting to the reader. Written statements may be in either paragraph or bulleted/outline format. A design statement should be between 250 and 500 words. It may be a separate document, part of the working drawings, or a combination of both. (Refer to appendix A for examples.) Design statements should clearly outline:

- Design considerations and challenges of the project, including but not limited to: construction budget requirements, client needs and wants, special requests, and lifestyle factors.
- The wants and needs client stated in the Client Survey Form.
- Form, function, economy, and time requirements. (These are typical organizational means to state design problems.)
- How the designer arrived at the solutions and addressed the design considerations and challenges for the project. Use strong verbs before the solution to make an impact. For example, to provide more storage, or to ensure adequate traffic flow, then write your solution. Include aesthetic considerations, such as use of the elements and principles of design (i.e., pattern preferences, finish, color, surface selections, and other details).

TITLING PROJECT DOCUMENTS

When you design a project for a client, you must protect yourself from liability relating to the drawings, and you must protect the drawings themselves from being copied by your competitors. The entire set of paperwork, which includes your design plans, specifications, and contract, are referred to as the project documents.

When presenting the drawings for a kitchen or bathroom, the NKBA recommends that you refer to the drawings as kitchen design plans or bathroom design plans. The design plans should include the following statement in a prominent location in large or block letters:

> DESIGN PLANS ARE NOT PROVIDED FOR ARCHITECTURAL OR ENGINEERING USE. IT IS THE RESPECTIVE TRADES' RESPONSIBILITY TO VERIFY THAT ALL INFORMATION LISTED IS IN ACCORDANCE WITH EQUIPMENT USE, APPLICABLE CODES, AND ACTUAL JOB-SITE DIMENSIONS.

The individual drawings incorporated in the overall kitchen or bathroom design presentation must also be carefully labeled. It is suggested that you refer to these other drawings as floor plans, elevations, mechanical plans, and artist renderings. The NKBA suggests that you include a notation on the artist rendering drawings that reads:

> THIS RENDERING IS AN ARTIST'S INTERPRETATION OF THE GENERAL APPEARANCE OF THE ROOM. IT IS NOT INTENDED TO BE A PRECISE DEPICTION.

Never refer to a design plan as an architectural drawing or even as an architectural-type drawing. Do not include the words *architecture*, *architectural*, *architectural design*, *architectural phase*, or *architectural background* in any project documents that you prepare or on any of your business stationery, promotional information, or presentation materials. Using such terminology in reference to the work that you do or documents that you prepare may result in a violation of various state laws. A court may determine that your use of the word *architecture* or *architectural* could reasonably lead a client to believe that you possess a level of expertise that you do not. Worse yet, a court may find you liable for fraud and/or misrepresentation.

Laws do vary per state; therefore, it is important that you consult with your own legal counsel to be sure that you are acting within the applicable statutes in your area. You must clearly understand what drawings you are legally allowed to prepare and what drawings must be prepared under the auspices of a licensed architect or engineer.

COPYRIGHT AND OWNERSHIP

After drafting the design plans for your client, you should ensure that they will not be copied or used by a competitor. You can do this by copyrighting your design plans. Copyrighting is an international form of protection and exclusivity provided by law to authors of original works, despite whether the work is published or not. Original works of authorship include any literary, pictorial, graphic or sculptured works, such as your design plans, provided they are original works done by you. Copyright protection exists from the moment the work is created in its final form and will endure 70 years after your death.

If two or more persons are authors of an original work, they will be deemed co-owners of its copyright. For example, if you collaborate with an interior designer, you will both be co-owners of the design copyright. An original work generated by two or more authors is referred to as a joint work. Generally, a joint work results if the authors collaborated on the work or if each prepared a segment of it with the knowledge and intent that it would be incorporated with the contributions submitted by other authors. Accordingly, a joint work will be found only when each coauthor intended his or her respective contribution to be combined into a larger, integrated piece. There is no requirement that each of the coauthors work together or even be acquainted with one another.

A work created by an employee within the scope of employment is regarded as work made for hire and normally is owned by the employer, unless the parties explicitly stipulate in a written agreement, signed by both, that the copyright will be owned by the employee. If you are an independent contractor, the work-made-for-hire statute does not include drawings or other design plans. Therefore, the copyright in any kitchen or bath design created by you will remain vested with you until you contractually agree to relinquish ownership.

To secure copyright protection for your plans, you are required to give notice of copyright on all publicly distributed copies. The use of the copyright notice is your responsibility as the copyright owner and does not require advance permission from, or registration with, the Copyright Office in Washington, DC.

A proper copyright notice must include three items:

1. The symbol © or the word *Copyright* or the abbreviation *Copy.* (The © is accepted as the international symbol.)
2. The year of the first publication of the work.
3. The name of the owner of the copyright in the work, or an abbreviation by which the name can be recognized, or a generally known alternative designation of the owner.

The notice should be affixed to all copies of your design plans in such a manner and location as to give reasonable notice of the claim of copyright. An example of a proper copyright notice would be:

COPYRIGHT © 2014 JOE SMITH

As mentioned previously, you or your firm continue to retain copyright protection of your design plan even if the plan is given to the client after he has paid for it. Although the copyright ownership may be transferred, such transfer must be in writing and signed by you as the owner of the copyright conveyed. Normally, the transfer of a copyright is made by contract. In order to protect your exclusive rights, however, you should include a clause in your contract that reads:

> DESIGN PLANS ARE PROVIDED FOR THE FAIR USE BY THE CLIENT OR HIS AGENT IN COMPLETING THE PROJECT AS LISTED WITHIN THIS CONTRACT. DESIGN PLANS REMAIN THE PROPERTY OF (YOUR NAME) AND CANNOT BE USED OR REUSED WITHOUT PERMISSION.

This clause should also be in any agreement between you and a client who requests that you prepare a design plan for his or her review. Such a design plan usually serves as the basis for a subsequent contract between you and the client for the actual installation of the kitchen or bathroom. This type of agreement will prevent the client from obtaining a design plan from you and then taking that plan to a competitor who may simply copy it. As long as you retain the copyright in the design plan, you will be able to sue for infringement any party who has copied your design.

SUMMARY

It is strongly recommended that designers use the NKBA Graphics and Presentation Standards. These standards contain a specific set of criteria that, when applied by kitchen and bathroom specialists, produce professional project documents. By standardizing floor plans and presentation drawings, kitchen and bathroom designers will:

- Limit errors caused by misinterpreting the floor plan.
- Avoid misreading dimensions, which can result in costly errors.
- Prevent cluttering floor plans and drawings with secondary information, which often makes the documents difficult to interpret.
- Create a clear understanding of the scope of the project for everyone involved in the job.
- Present a professional image to the client.
- Permit faster processing of orders.
- Simplify estimating and specification preparation.
- Help in the standardization of uniform nomenclature and symbols.

REVIEW QUESTIONS

1. What is the importance of having graphic presentation standards? (See "Purpose of Graphics and Presentation Standards" page 135)
2. What should the specifications clearly define? (See "Specifications" page 144)
3. List three pieces of information the design statement should include. (See under "Design Statement" page 145)
4. In regard to titling a drawing, what type of drawing must we never call our drawings? (See "Titling Project Documents" page 146)
5. If you work for an employer and your drawings are copyrighted during that period of employment, who owns those drawings? (See "Copyright and Ownership" page 146)

APPENDIX

Sample Kitchen and Bathroom Project Documents

Two sets of sample project documents have been prepared according to the NKBA Graphics and Presentation Standards, one for a kitchen and one for a bathroom. These examples are to be used as references for kitchen and bath design projects.

They include:

- Title page: (Figure 9.1) page 149
- Floor plan: Kitchen (Figure 9.2) page 150; Bath (Figure 9.13) page 170
- Construction plan: Kitchen (Figure 9.3) page 151; Bath (Figure 9.14) page 171
- Mechanical plan: Kitchen (Figure 9.4) page 152; Bath (Figure 9.15) page 172
- Countertop plan: Kitchen (Figure 9.5) page 153; Bath (Figure 9.16) page 173
- Soffit plan: Kitchen (Figure 9.6) page 154; Bath (Figure 9.17) page 174
- Elevations: Kitchen (Figure 9.7, Figure 9.8, Figure 9.9, Figure 9.10) page 155–158; Bath (Figure 9.18, Figure 9.19, Figure 9.20, Figure 9.21) pages 175–178
- Perspectives: Kitchen (Figure 9.11) page 159; Bath (Figure 9.22, Figure 9.23) pages 179–180
- Design statement: Kitchen, page 160; Bath, page 181
- Specifications: Kitchen (Figure 9.12) pages 161–169; Bath (Figure 9.24) pages 182–191

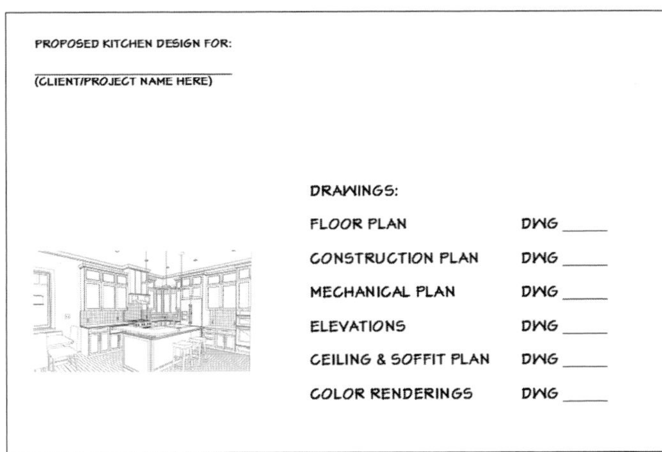

FIGURE A.1 Example of title page in a set of drawings.

SAMPLE KITCHEN PLANS

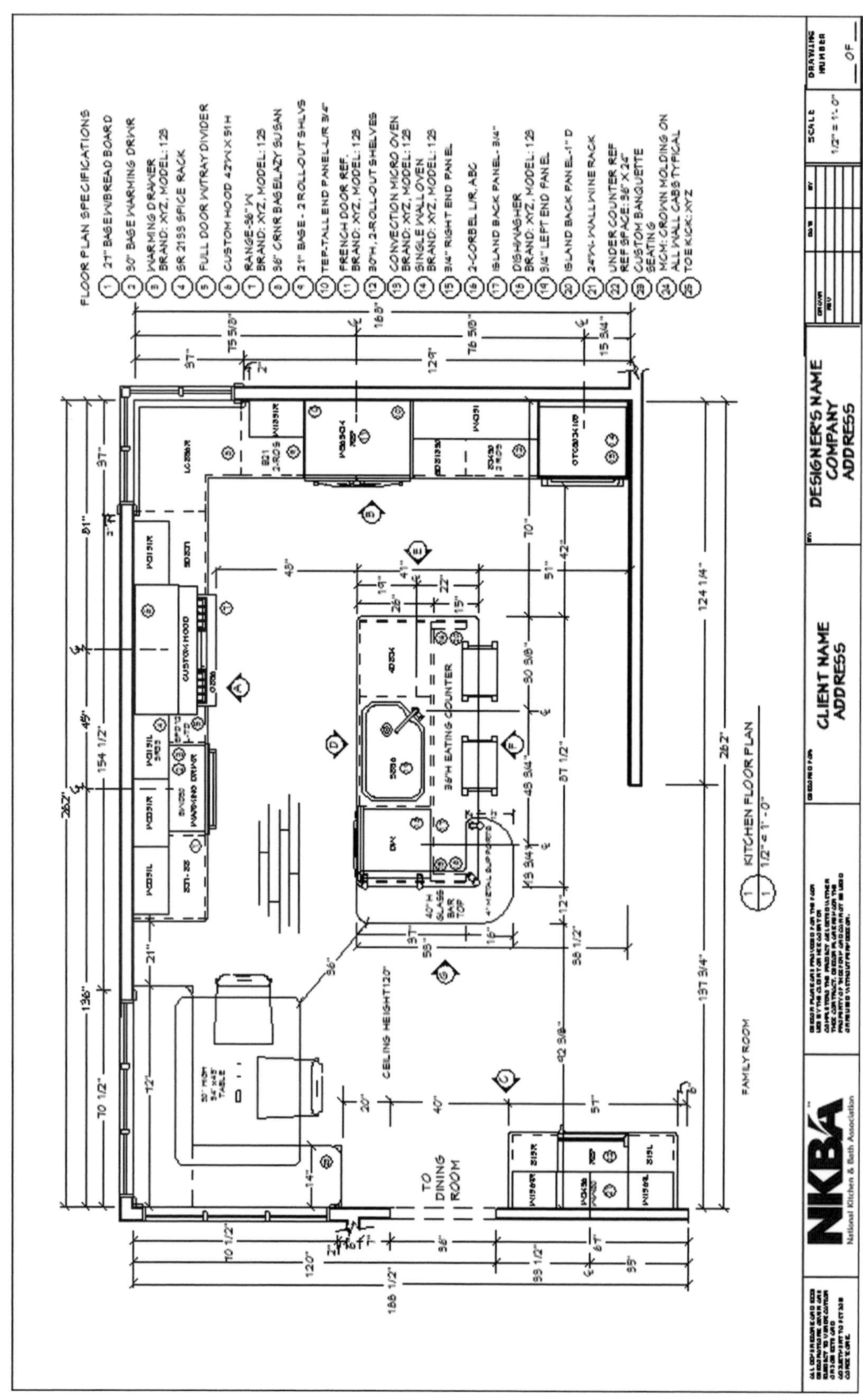

FIGURE A.2 Kitchen floor plan.

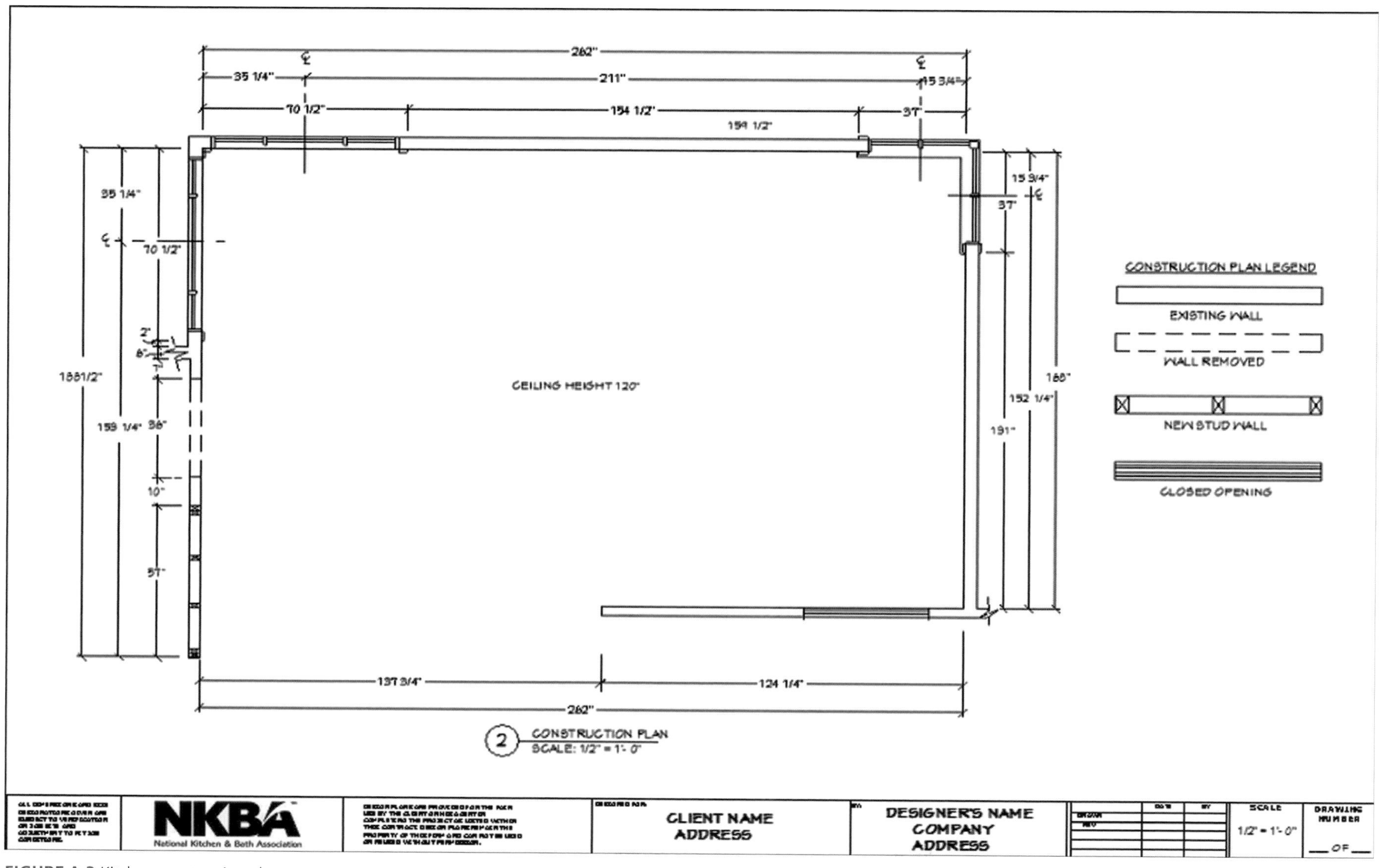

FIGURE A.3 Kitchen construction plan.

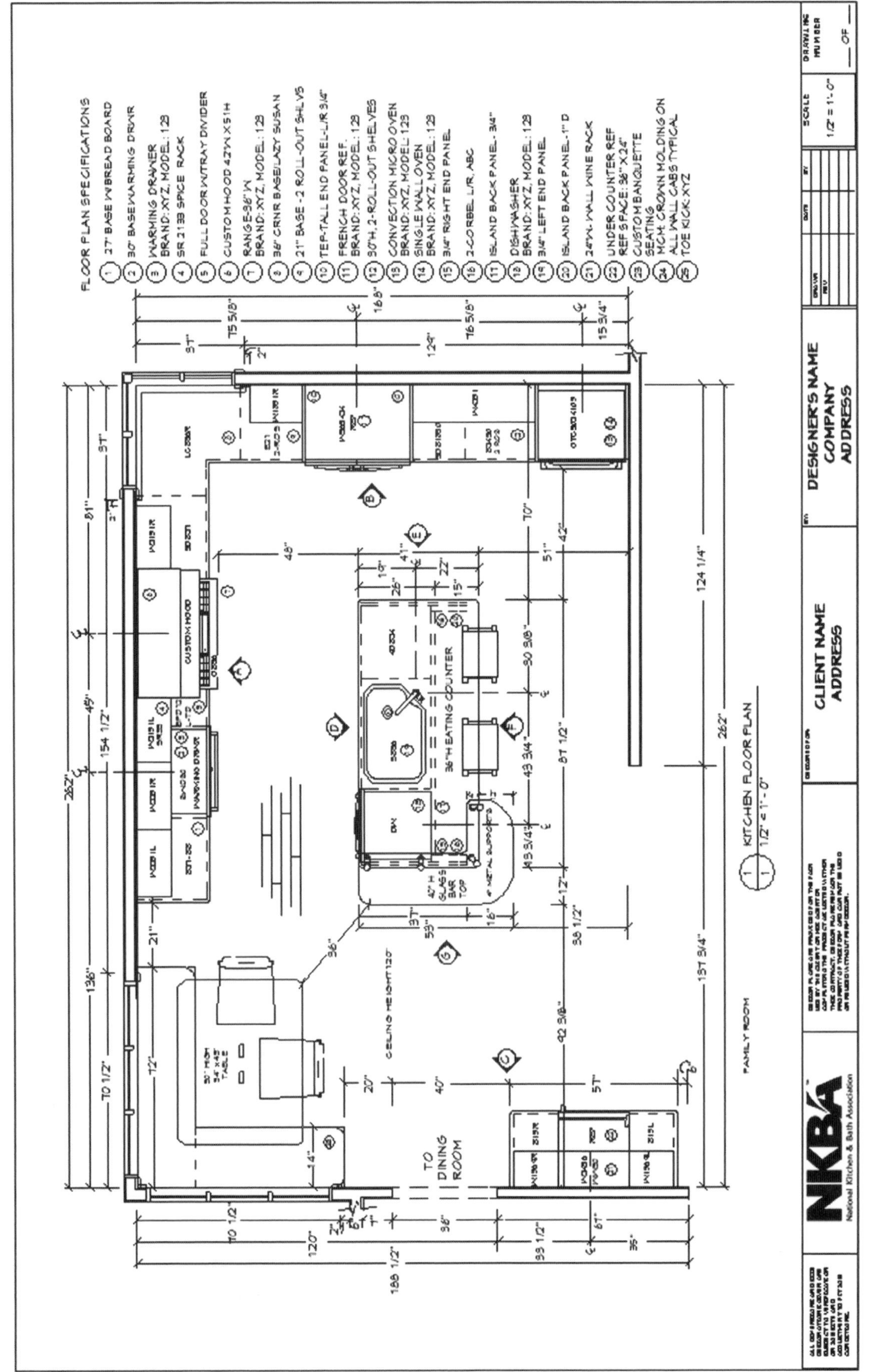

FIGURE A.4 Kitchen mechanical plan.

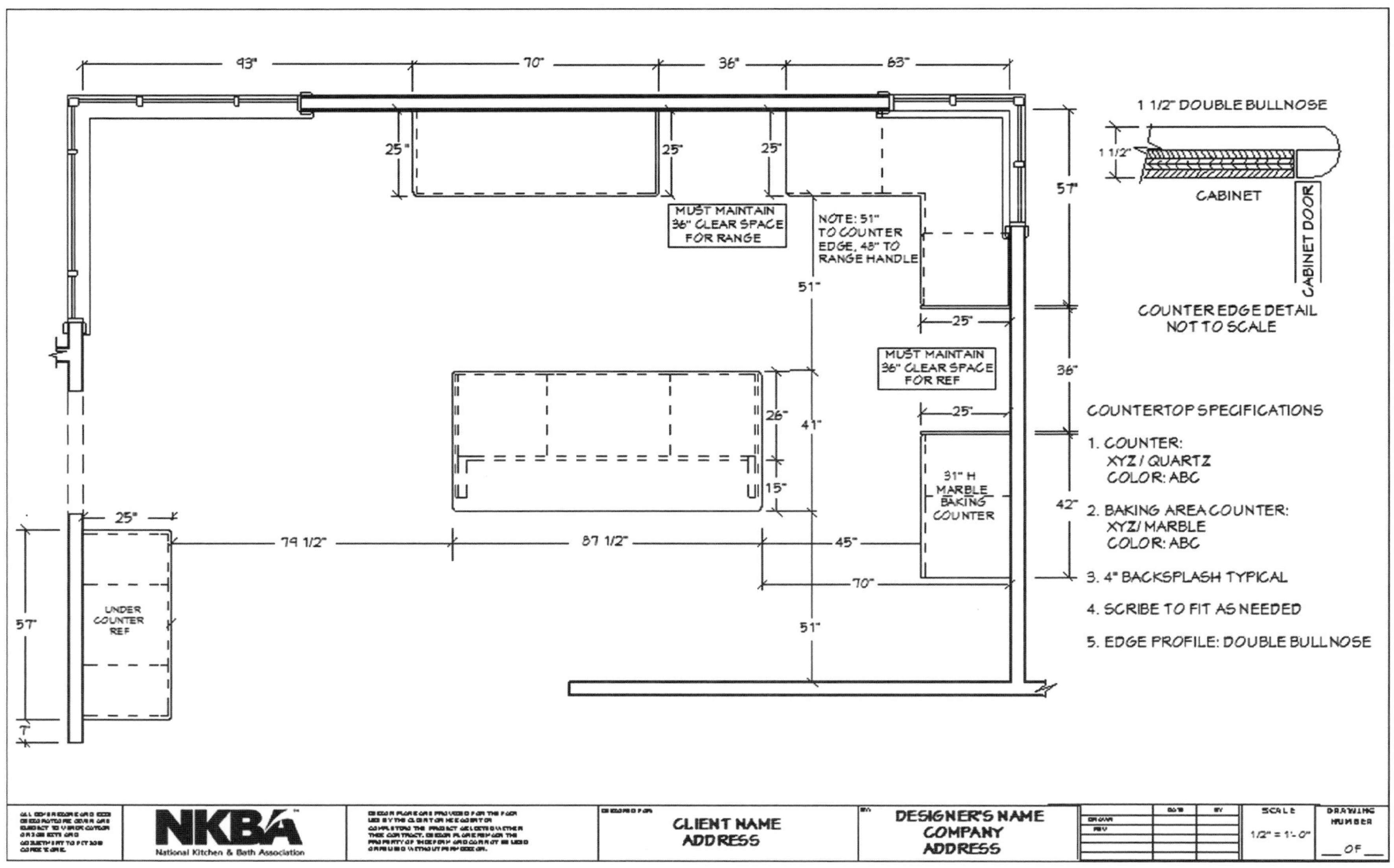

FIGURE A.5 Kitchen countertop plan.

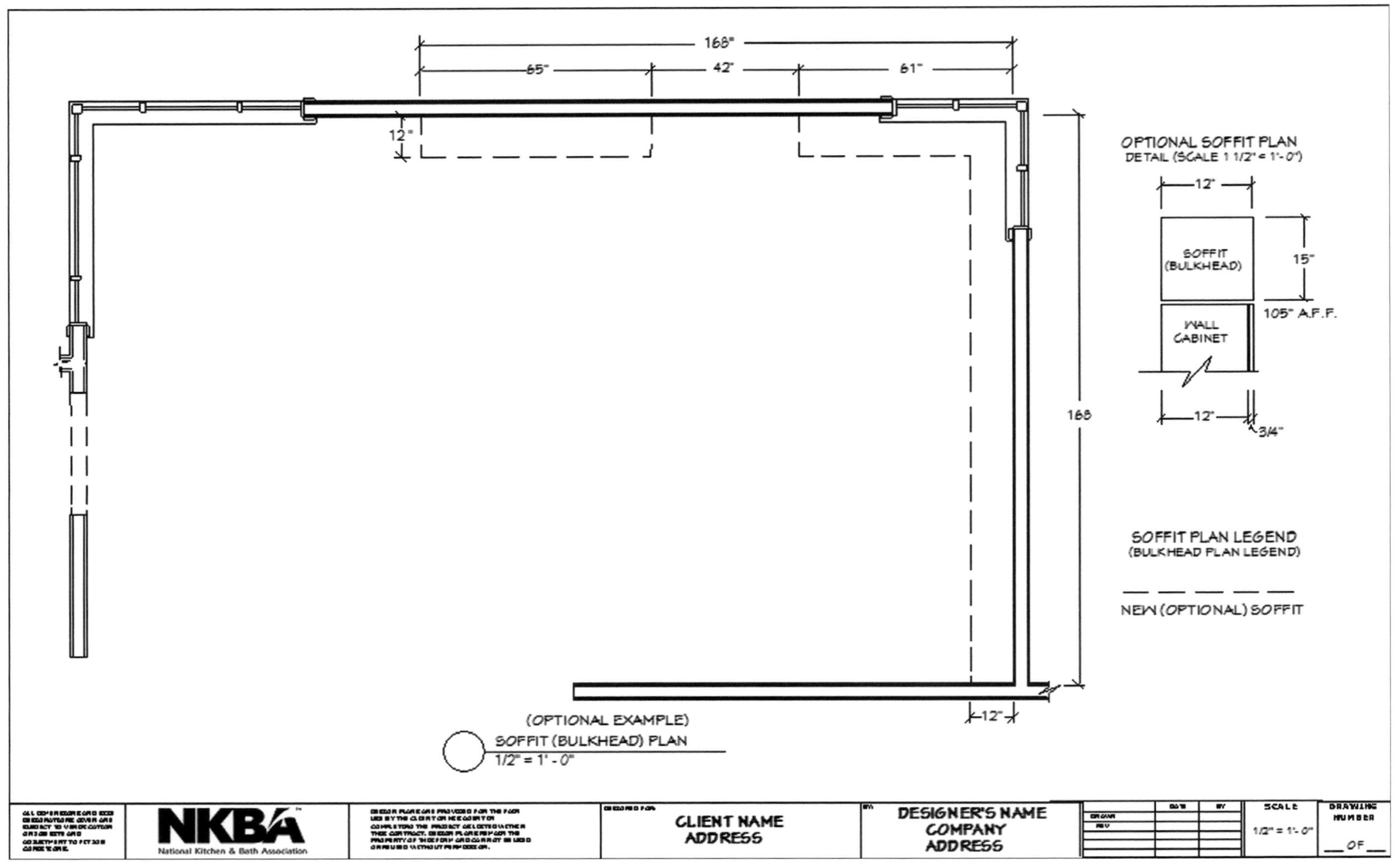

FIGURE A.6 An example of an optional kitchen soffit/bulkhead plan.

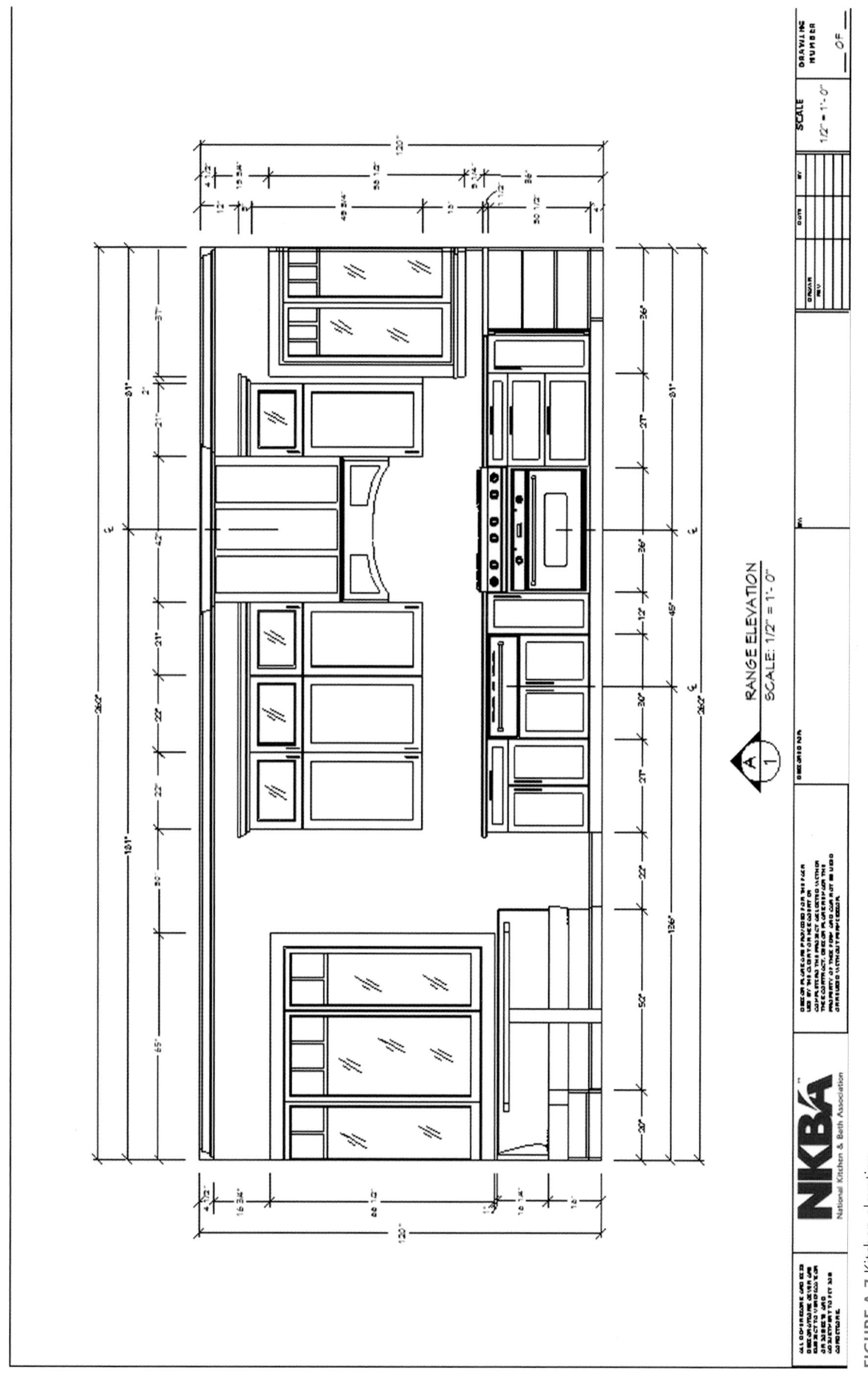

FIGURE A.7 Kitchen elevation.

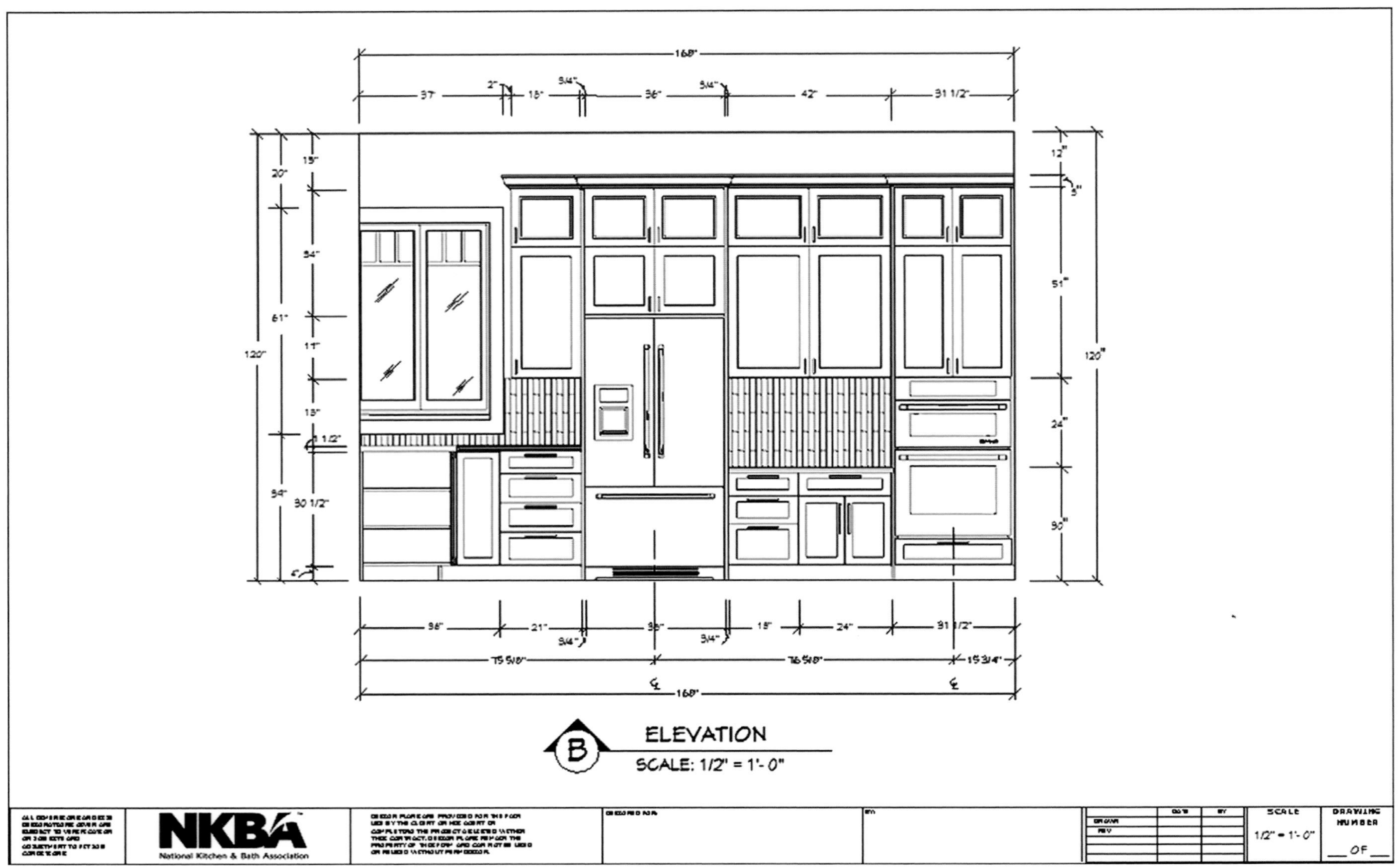

FIGURE A.8 Kitchen elevation.

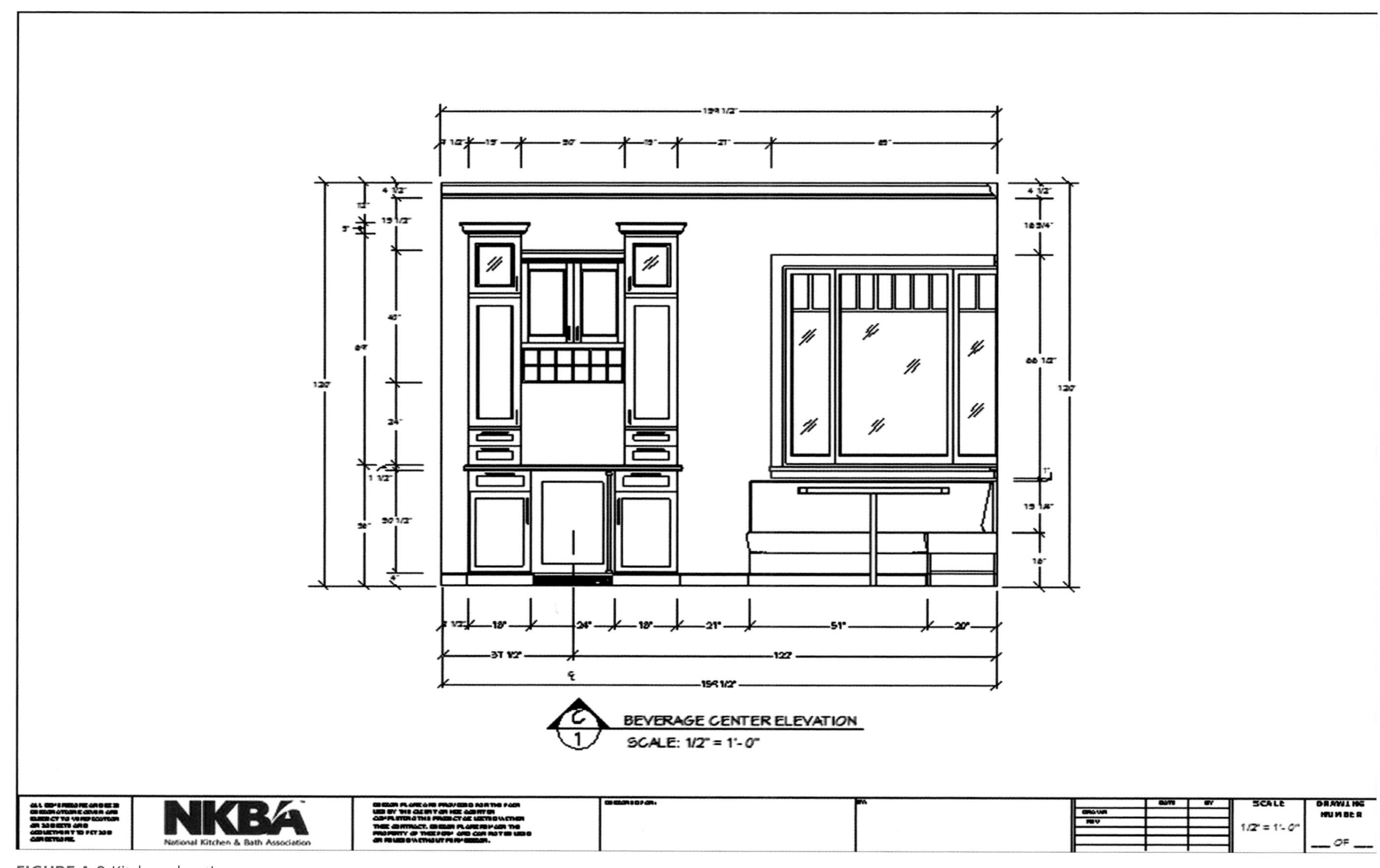

FIGURE A.9 Kitchen elevation.

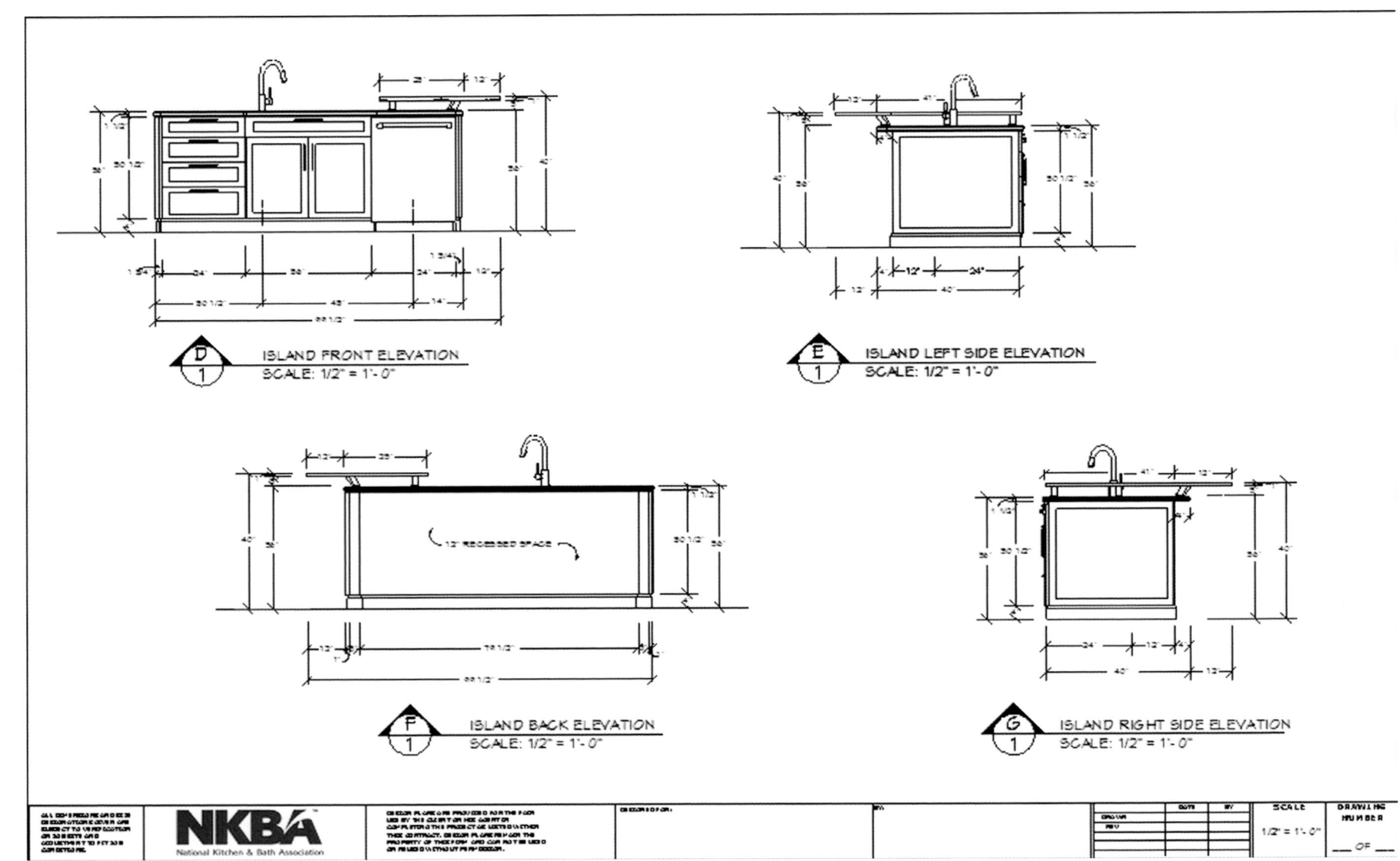

FIGURE A.10 Island elevations.

FIGURE A.11 Perspective drawing.
Courtesy of Adrean Stephenson, Chief Architect

Sample Design Statement for Kitchen Project

The primary challenge was to create a functional space that incorporates additional work areas to meet the wants and growing needs of the family. The client also wants to incorporate more windows to have a better view of the lake. A request was made to provide separate areas that allow for entertaining and baking.

The existing space was insufficient to meet the needs of the family for entertaining and cooking. The current kitchen did not allow for several individuals to cook and bake at the same time and did not have a separate beverage area for entertaining nor easy access to sodas or other drinks. The kitchen space lacked a serving counter. Currently no seating is by the window. The client wanted to incorporate banquette seating by the window to have a better view of the lake and to provide ample space for eating and homework.

The design solution was to design the kitchen with a functional layout providing dedicated work areas. To provide a separate area for baking, a bake center was included with a marble top for rolling out dough and other baking needs. This bake center is located next to the wall oven. The work area between the range and refrigerator has ample counter space by the corner window for natural lighting. To ensure adequate seating and view of the lake, the banquette was located by the window. This will also serve as an area for doing homework. The beverage center was incorporated at the side wall near the family room to provide easy access for entertaining and secondary refrigeration for beverages. To ensure adequate task lighting, undercabinet lighting was provided in all work areas.

An accent serving counter made of tempered glass was mounted on metal posts on the island. Tile on the wall enhances the light cabinetry. The flooring selected was a darker wood for contrast with the light cabinetry. All cabinetry, moldings, appliances, and hardware create a finished look for this space.

Standard Specifications for Kitchen Design and Installation Projects

H.H.I.C

687 Willow Grove Street
Hackettstown, NJ 07840

Standard Specifications for Kitchen Design and Installation

Name: Dr Sara and Jack Blackburn

Home Address: 4540 Mt Vista Lane

City: Hackettstown State: NJ

Phone (Home): 908-555-0021

Phone (Office): His: 908-555-4012

Phone (Office): Her: 908-555-7090 Ext 222

Phone (Office): His Pager 908-555-4312

Phone (Jobsite): Same as home

Jobsite Address: Same as above

City: ______ State: ______

By: H.H.I.C.
Hereafter called "Kitchen Specialist"

Kitchen Specialist will supply and deliver only such equipment and material as described in these specifications. Labor connected with this kitchen installation will be supplied by the Kitchen Specialist only as herein specified.

Any equipment, material and labor designated here as "Owner's responsibility" must be furnished and completed by the Owner, or the Owner's Agent in accordance with the work schedule established by the Kitchen Specialist.

Equipment, material and labor not included in these specifications can be supplied by the Kitchen Specialist at an additional cost for which authorization must be given in writing by the Owner, or the Owner's Agent.

All dimension and cabinet designations shown on the floor plan and elevations / interpretive drawings, which are part of these specifications, are subject to adjustments dictated by job conditions.

All surfaces of walls, ceilings, windows and woodwork, except those of factory-made equipment, will be left unpainted or unfinished unless otherwise specified.

If specifications call for re-use of existing equipment, no responsibility on the part of the Kitchen Specialist for appearance, functioning or service shall be implied.

For factory-made equipment, the manufacturer's specifications for quality, design, dimensions, function and installation shall in all cases take precedence over any others.

FIGURE A.12 Standard Specifications for Kitchen Design and Installation Projects

Cabinetry	Source				
Key: KS= Kitchen Specialist	Use Existing	Furnished by		Installed by	
O= Owner OA= Owners Agent	☐Yes ☒No	KS ☒	O/OA ☐	KS ☒	O/OA ☐

Cabinet 1

Manufacturer: Cookville Cabinets		
Construction: ☒Frame ☐Frameless		
Cabinet Exterior: ☒Wood-Species: Maple	☐Metal ☐Decorative Laminate	☐Other:
Cabinet Exterior Finish: Cinnamon	**Cabinet Interior Material:** Melamine	**Finish:** White
Door Style: Charleston	**Hardware:** YN-7037901	
Special Cabinet Notes: Modification to SB27		

Cabinet 2 ☒ N/A

Manufacturer:		
Construction: ☐Frame ☐Frameless		
Cabinet Exterior: ☐Wood-Species:	☐Metal ☐Decorative Laminate	☐Other:
Cabinet Exterior Finish:	**Cabinet Interior Material:**	**Finish:**
Door Style:	**Hardware:**	
Special Cabinet Notes:		

Fascia & Soffit	Source				
Key: KS= Kitchen Specialist	Use Existing	Furnished by		Installed by	
O= Owner OA= Owners Agent	☐Yes ☐No	KS ☐	O/OA ☐	KS ☐	O/OA ☐

Fascia & Soffit 1

Construction: ☐Flush ☐Extended ☐Recessed ☒Open ☐Remove ☐Other, as per plan:
Finish Material:
Special Fascia / Soffit Notes:

Fascia & Soffit 2 ☒ N/A

Construction: ☐Flush ☐Extended ☐Recessed ☐Open ☐Remove ☐Other, as per plan:
Finish Material:
Special Fascia / Soffit Notes:

FIGURE A.12 (Continued)

Countertops	Source				
Key: KS= Kitchen Specialist	Use Existing	Furnished by		Installed by	
O= Owner OA= Owners Agent	☐Yes ☒No	KS ☒	O/OA ☐	KS ☒	O/OA ☐

Countertop 1

Manufacturer: GHI

Material: Laminate | Color: #7665

Design Details: Deck Thickness 3/4" Material Wood Edge Thickness 1/ 1/2" Edge Detail/Shape: Bevel 45 Degree Color Cinnamon

Backsplash: Thickness 3/4" Height: 4" Color: Cinnamon

End Splash: Thickness 3/4" Height: 4" Color: Cinnamon

Insert: N/A

Special Countertop Notes: Front edge and backsplash to be supplied by Cookville Cabinets. See Countertop Plan for detail. Backsplash and end splashes to be installed after wall covering is installed by owner.

Countertop 2 ☒ N/A

Manufacturer:

Material: | Color:

Design Details: Deck Thickness___ Material___ Edge Thickness___ Edge Detail/Shape:___ Color___

Backsplash: Thickness___ Height:___ Color:___

End Splash: Thickness___ Height:___ Color:___

Insert:

Special Countertop Notes:

Countertop 3 ☒ N/A

Manufacturer:

Material: | Color:

Design Details: Deck Thickness___ Material___ Edge Thickness___ Edge Detail/Shape:___ Color___

Backsplash: Thickness___ Height:___ Color:___

End Splash: Thickness___ Height:___ Color:___

Insert:

Special Countertop Notes:

FIGURE A.12 (Continued)

Fixtures and Fittings

Item	Sink #	Brand Name	Model	Finish	Material	Furnished By		Installed By		Hooked up By	
						K.S.	O/OA	K.S.	O/OA	K.S.	O/OA
Kitchen Sink #1	1	XYZ	654	Satin	Stainless	☒	☐	☒	☐	☒	☐
No. of Holes	1					☐	☐	☐	☐	☐	☐
Faucet #1	1	XYZ	J4110	Brushed	Chrome	☒	☐	☒	☐	☒	☐
Kitchen Sink #2	N/A					☐	☐	☐	☐	☐	☐
No. of Holes						☐	☐	☐	☐	☐	☐
Faucet #2						☐	☐	☐	☐	☐	☐
Kitchen Sink #3	N/A					☐	☐	☐	☐	☐	☐
No. of Holes						☐	☐	☐	☐	☐	☐
Faucet #3						☐	☐	☐	☐	☐	☐
Additional Items											
Strainer	1	XYZ	ST-67	Bright	Chrome	☒	☐	☒	☐	☒	☐
Hot Water Dispenser	N/A					☐	☐	☐	☐	☐	☐
Chilled Water Dispenser	N/A					☐	☐	☐	☐	☐	☐
Lotion Dispenser	N/A					☐	☐	☐	☐	☐	☐
Water Purifier	1	TUA	FW42 US	N/A	N/A	☒	☐	☒	☐	☒	☐
Filtered Water Tap	Above					☐	☐	☐	☐	☐	☐
Accessories											
						☐	☐	☐	☐	☐	☐
						☐	☐	☐	☐	☐	☐
						☐	☐	☐	☐	☐	☐
						☐	☐	☐	☐	☐	☐

Lighting System

Description	Qty	Location	Model #	Transformer	Finish	Lamp Req.	Furnished By		Installed By	
							K.S.	O/OA	K.S.	O/OA
QRS 18" Under Cabinet Fluo	5	Per Plan	FL1833	N/A	White	F15	☒	☐	☒	☐
QRS Recessed Ceiling Fixture	7	Per Plan	UG78C	N/A	Bright	60 watt	☒	☐	☒	☐
							☐	☐	☐	☐
							☐	☐	☐	☐
							☐	☐	☐	☐
							☐	☐	☐	☐

Special Lighting Notes:

FIGURE A.12 (Continued)

Appliances

Item	Brand Name	Width	Model	Finish	Fuel	Furnished By		Installed By		Hooked up By	
						K.S.	O/OA	K.S.	O/OA	K.S.	O/OA
Range	ABC	30	123	White	Electric	☒	☐	☒	☐	☒	☐
Cooktop / Rangetop	N/A					☐	☐	☐	☐	☐	☐
Oven	N/A					☐	☐	☐	☐	☐	☐
Exhaust System A	ABC	36	678	White	Electric	☒	☐	☒	☐	☒	☐
Exhaust System B	N/A					☐	☐	☐	☐	☐	☐
Warming Drawer	N/A					☐	☐	☐	☐	☐	☐
Indoor Grill	N/A					☐	☐	☐	☐	☐	☐
Steam Oven	N/A					☐	☐	☐	☐	☐	☐
Specialty Cooking ____________	N/A					☐	☐	☐	☐	☐	☐
Specialty Cooking ____________	N/A					☐	☐	☐	☐	☐	☐
Specialty Cooking ____________	N/A					☐	☐	☐	☐	☐	☐
Microwave	ABC	17	567	White	Electric	☒	☐	☒	☐	☐	☐
Trim Kit	N/A					☐	☐	☐	☐	☐	☐
Refrigerator #1	Existing	34		White	Electric	☐	☒	☒	☐	☒	☐
Trim Kit	N/A					☐	☐	☐	☐	☐	☐
Refrigerator #2	N/A					☐	☐	☐	☐	☐	☐
Trim Kit	N/A					☐	☐	☐	☐	☐	☐
Wine / Refrigerator Storage Appliance	N/A					☐	☐	☐	☐	☐	☐
Trim Kit	N/A					☐	☐	☐	☐	☐	☐
Freezer	N/A					☐	☐	☐	☐	☐	☐
Trim Kit	N/A					☐	☐	☐	☐	☐	☐
Ice Maker	Included in Ref.		N/A	N/A	Electric	☐	☒	☒	☐	☒	☐
Trim Kit	N/A					☐	☐	☐	☐	☐	☐
Dishwasher #1	ABC	24	953	White	Electric	☒	☐	☒	☐	☒	☐
Trim Kit	N/A					☐	☐	☐	☐	☐	☐
Dishwasher #2	N/A					☐	☐	☐	☐	☐	☐
Trim Kit	N/A					☐	☐	☐	☐	☐	☐
Food Waste Disp.#1	N/A					☐	☐	☐	☐	☐	☐
Food Waste Disp. #2	N/A					☐	☐	☐	☐	☐	☐
Compactor	N/A					☐	☐	☐	☐	☐	☐
Trim Kit	N/A					☐	☐	☐	☐	☐	☐
Computer	N/A					☐	☐	☐	☐	☐	☐
Coffee System	N/A					☐	☐	☐	☐	☐	☐
Telephone / Internet	Existing*		TBD	TBD		☐	☒	☐	☒	☐	☒
Television	N/A					☐	☐	☐	☐	☐	☐
Radio / CD	N/A					☐	☐	☐	☐	☐	☐
VCR / DVD	N/A					☐	☐	☐	☐	☐	☐
Washer	N/A					☐	☐	☐	☐	☐	☐
Dryer	N/A					☐	☐	☐	☐	☐	☐
* KS to locate only						☐	☐	☐	☐	☐	☐

FIGURE A.12 (Continued)

Flooring

Description		Furnished By		Installed By	
		K.S.	O/OA	K.S.	O/OA
Removal of Existing Floor Covering Remove existing vinyl		☒	☐	☒	☐
Remove and Repair Water Damaged Area None observed		☐	☐	☐	☐
Preparation of Floor / Subfloor Prepare for new laminate floor		☒	☐	☒	☐
Installation of Subfloor Underlayment Pad as per laminate manufacturer		☒	☐	☒	☐
New Floor Covering Material Description:		☒	☐	☒	☐
Manufacturer: JRT	Size: 24" X 48"	☒	☐	☒	☐
Pattern Number: TS89003	Pattern Name / Repeat: N/A	☒	☐	☒	☐
Tile Pattern: 12" Square	Grout: N/A	☒	☐	☒	☐
Describe Tile Details:					
Transition / Threshold Treatment At all entrances. Transition appropriate for flooring in other rooms.		☒	☐	☒	☐
Special Flooring Notes:					

Windows and Doors

Item	Brand Name	Model	Finish	Hardware	Furnished By		Installed By	
					K.S.	O/OA	K.S.	O/OA
30" Bi-Fold Door	Pisk Millwork	BF2668	Cinnamon	Use Existing	☒	☐	☒	☐
36" Pocket Door	Pisk Millwork	PD3068	Cinnamon	BHT-690	☒	☐	☒	☐
					☐	☐	☐	☐
					☐	☐	☐	☐
					☐	☐	☐	☐
					☐	☐	☐	☐
Special Window and Door Notes: Stain new doors to match cabinet finish (Cinnamon)								

Decorative Surfaces (Wall, Ceiling, Window Materials)

Description	Material	Color	Finish	Quantity	Furnished By		Installed By	
					K.S.	O/OA	K.S.	O/OA

FIGURE A.12 (Continued)

All walls to be patched and primed	Drywall	N/A	N/A	N/A	☒	☐	☒	☐
Ceiling to be repaired and primed	Drywall	N/A	N/A	N/A	☒	☐	☒	☐
Ceiling to be painted	Texture	Cool White	#12	As needed	☒	☐	☒	☐
Wall covering by owner TBD*	TBD	TBD	TBD	TBD	☐	☒	☐	☒
* Material to be determined later.					☐	☐	☐	☐
					☐	☐	☐	☐
					☐	☐	☐	☐

Special Decorative Surface Notes: Wall and ceiling patched, filled, repaired and primed at new wall and old opening. Owner to finish all walls.

FIGURE A.12 (Continued)

HVAC

Description No changes to HVAC System.	Furnished By		Installed By	
	K.S.	O/OA	K.S.	O/OA
Ventilation ABC Hood, Mdl # 678 with 210 cfm	☒	☐	☒	☐
Rough-In Requirements Through wall into attic.	☒	☐	☒	☐
Run New Duct Work for Ventilation System Duct to outside with roof cap	☒	☐	☒	☐
Heating N/A	☐	☐	☐	☐
Air Conditioning Supply N/A	☐	☐	☐	☐
Details:				

Electrical Work (except as described above in specific equipment sections)

Description	Furnished By		Installed By	
	K.S.	O/OA	K.S.	O/OA
New Service Panel Upgrade 150 amp panel to 200 amp	☒	☐	☒	☐
Code Update As required	☒	☐	☒	☐

Details: Locate new 120v and 240v dedicated circuits per Mechanical Plan. Locate new switches and GFCI receptacles per Mechanical Plan. Locate undercabinet fluorescent lighting and recessed lighting as per Mechanical Plan. Note: Shallow receptacle must be mounted 32" AFF in base cabinet adjacent to refrigerator.

Plumbing (except as described above in specific equipment sections)

Description	Furnished By		Installed By	
	K.S.	O/OA	K.S.	O/OA
New Rough In Requirements: Relocate water line for refrigerator.	☒	☐	☒	☐
	☐	☐	☐	☐
	☐	☐	☐	☐
New Drainage Requirements: N/A	☐	☐	☐	☐
	☐	☐	☐	☐
	☐	☐	☐	☐
New Vent Stack Requirements: N/A	☐	☐	☐	☐
	☐	☐	☐	☐
	☐	☐	☐	☐
Modifications to Existing Lines: Plumb sink and dishwasher with new traps, supply lines and shut-offs.	☒	☐	☒	☐
	☐	☐	☐	☐
	☐	☐	☐	☐
Details:				

FIGURE A.12 (Continued)

General Carpentry (except as described above in specific equipment sections)				
Description	Furnished By		Installed By	
	K.S.	O/OA	K.S.	O/OA
Demolition Work: Relocate opening in bottom wall.				
Walls-Exterior N/A	☐	☐	☐	☐
Walls-Interior Open wall at new doorway location and fill wall at old location.	☒	☐	☒	☐
Windows N/A	☐	☐	☐	☐
Ceiling N/A	☐	☐	☐	☐
Soffit N/A	☐	☐	☐	☐
Existing Fixture and Equipment Removal By KS	☒	☐	☐	☐
Trash Removal Arrange for Dumpster in driveway	☒	☐	☒	☐
Reconstruction / Preparation Work (Except as previously stated)				
Windows N/A	☐	☐	☐	☐
Doors Locate Pocket Door in right wall	☒	☐	☒	☐
Interior Walls Build new wall between dining room and kitchen. Place header over pocket door location.	☒	☐	☒	☐
Exterior Wall N/A	☐	☐	☐	☐
Soffit / Fascia N/A	☐	☐	☐	☐
HVAC Work: N/A				
Replace Vents	☐	☐	☐	☐
Replace Vent Covers Size:___	☐	☐	☐	☐
Millwork: (Note Cabinetry Installation listed under cabinets)				
Crown Molding Stain crown molding to match cabinets (Cinnamon)	☒	☐	☒	☐
Ceiling Details N/A	☐	☐	☐	☐
Window / Door Casing Stain all to match cabinets (Cinnamon)	☒	☐	☐	☐
Baseboard Stain all to match cabinets (Cinnamon)	☒	☐	☒	☐
Wainscoting / Chair Rail N/A	☐	☐	☐	☐
Details:				

Miscellaneous Work		
Description	Responsibility	
	K.S.	O/OA
Material Storage Location Basement	☒	☐
Trash Collection Area Dumpster in driveway	☒	☐
Trash Removal	☒	☐
Jobsite / Room Cleanup Broom clean daily	☒	☐
Building Permit (s) As required	☒	☐
Structural Engineering / Architectural Fees Required for new wall	☒	☐
Inspection Fees As required	☒	☐
Jobsite Delivery To basement	☒	☐
	☐	☐
	☐	☐
	☐	☐

FIGURE A.12 (Continued)

SAMPLE BATHROOM PLANS

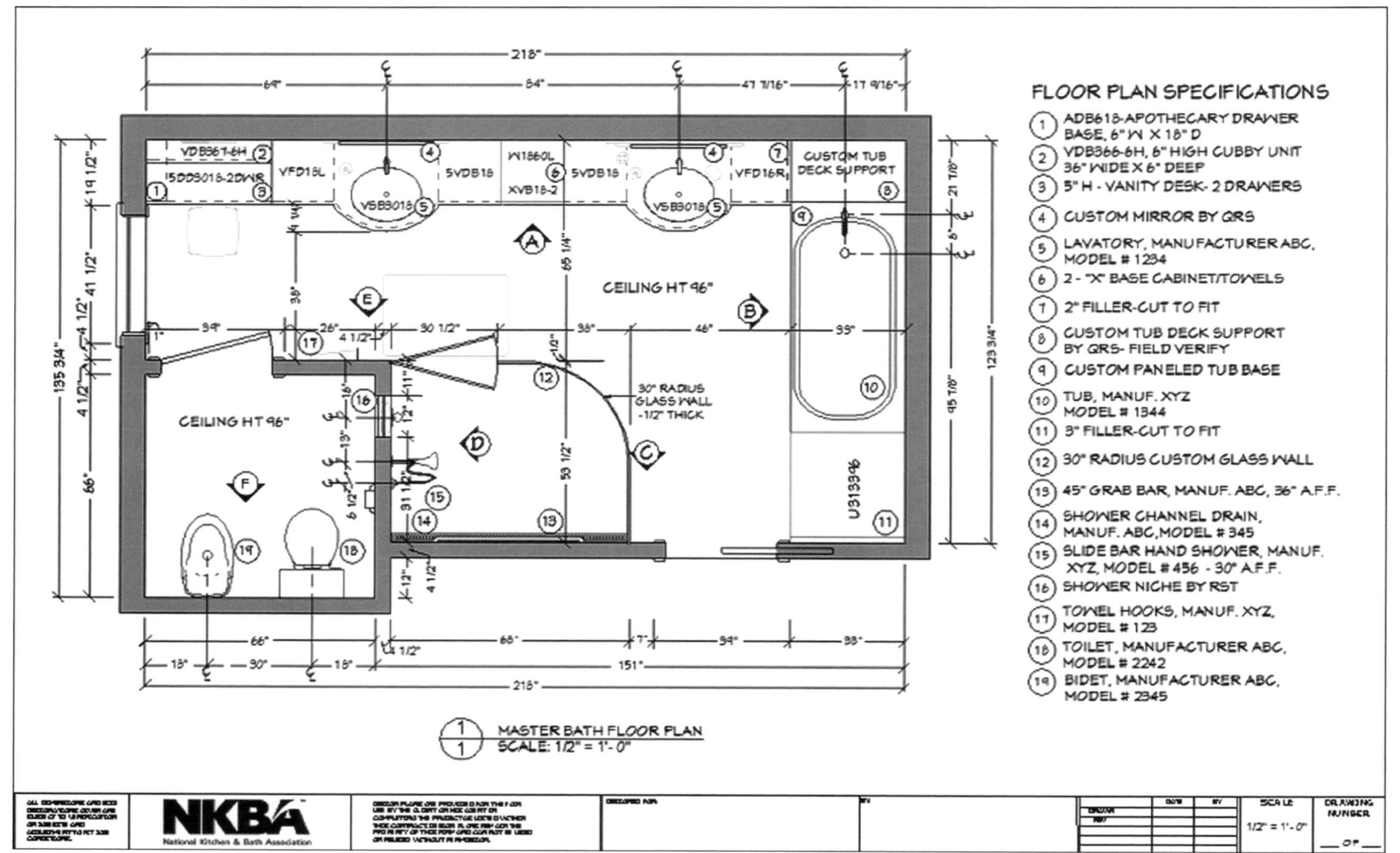

FIGURE A.13 Bathroom floor plan.

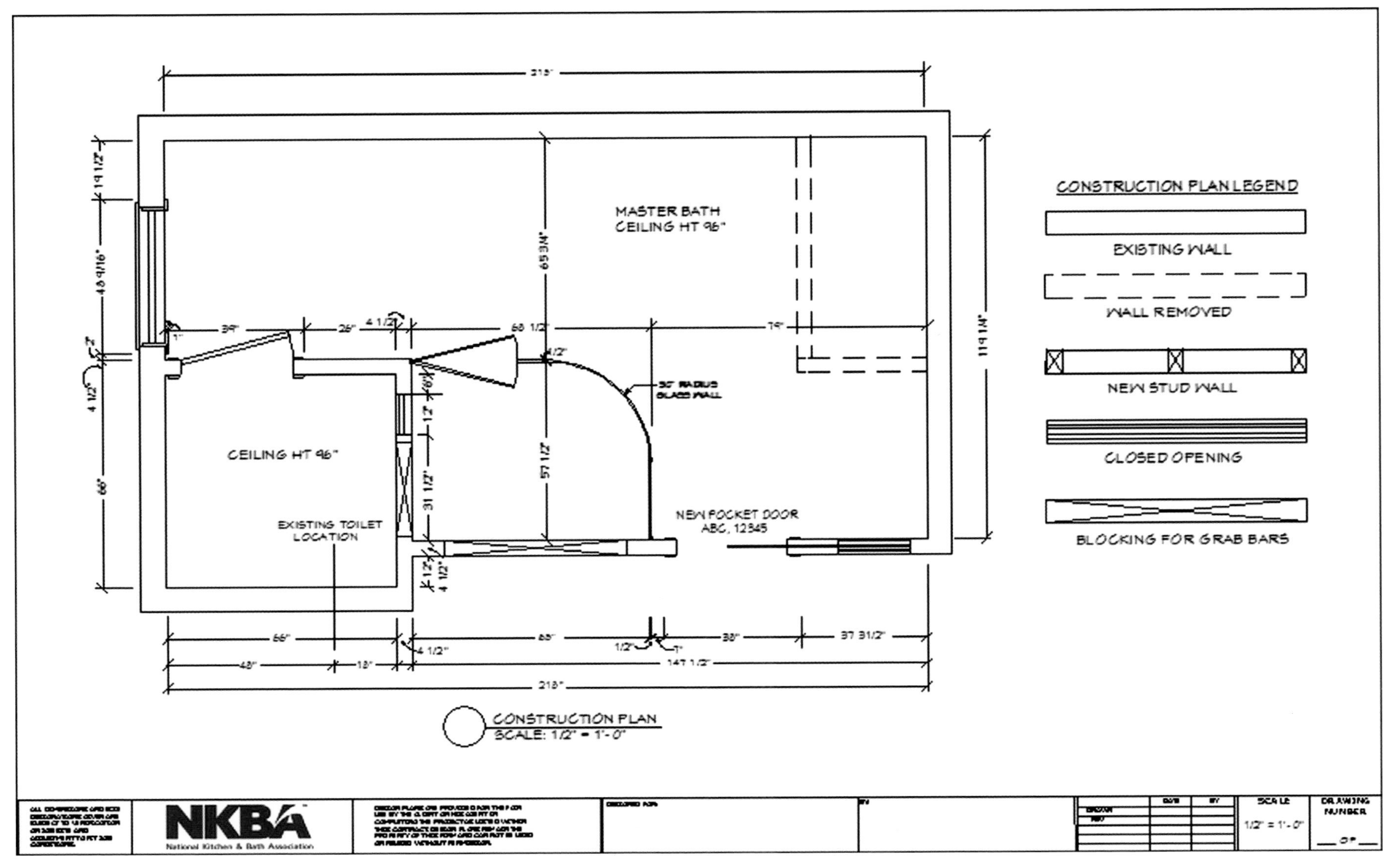

FIGURE A.14 Bathroom construction plan.

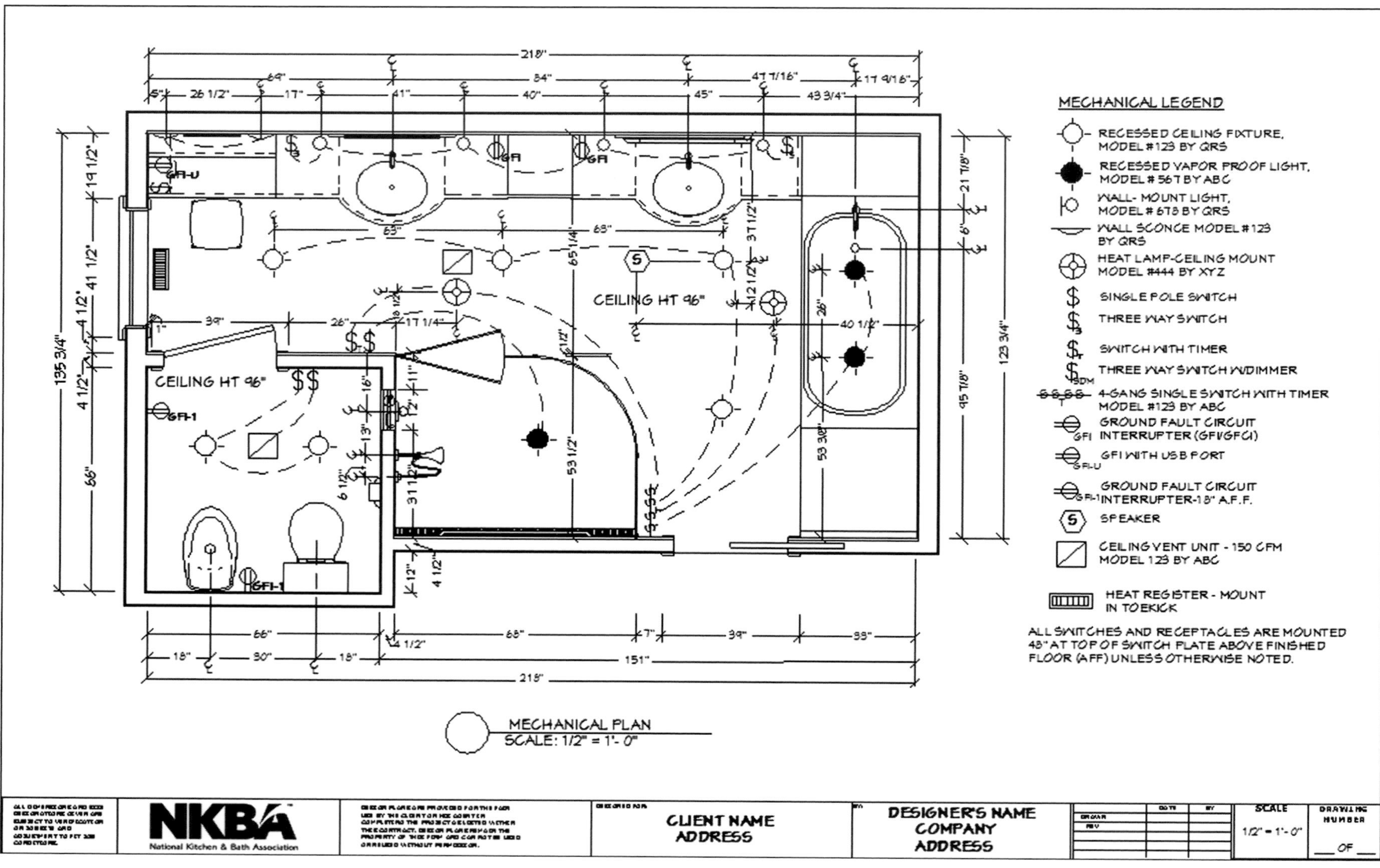

FIGURE A.15 Bathroom mechanical plan.

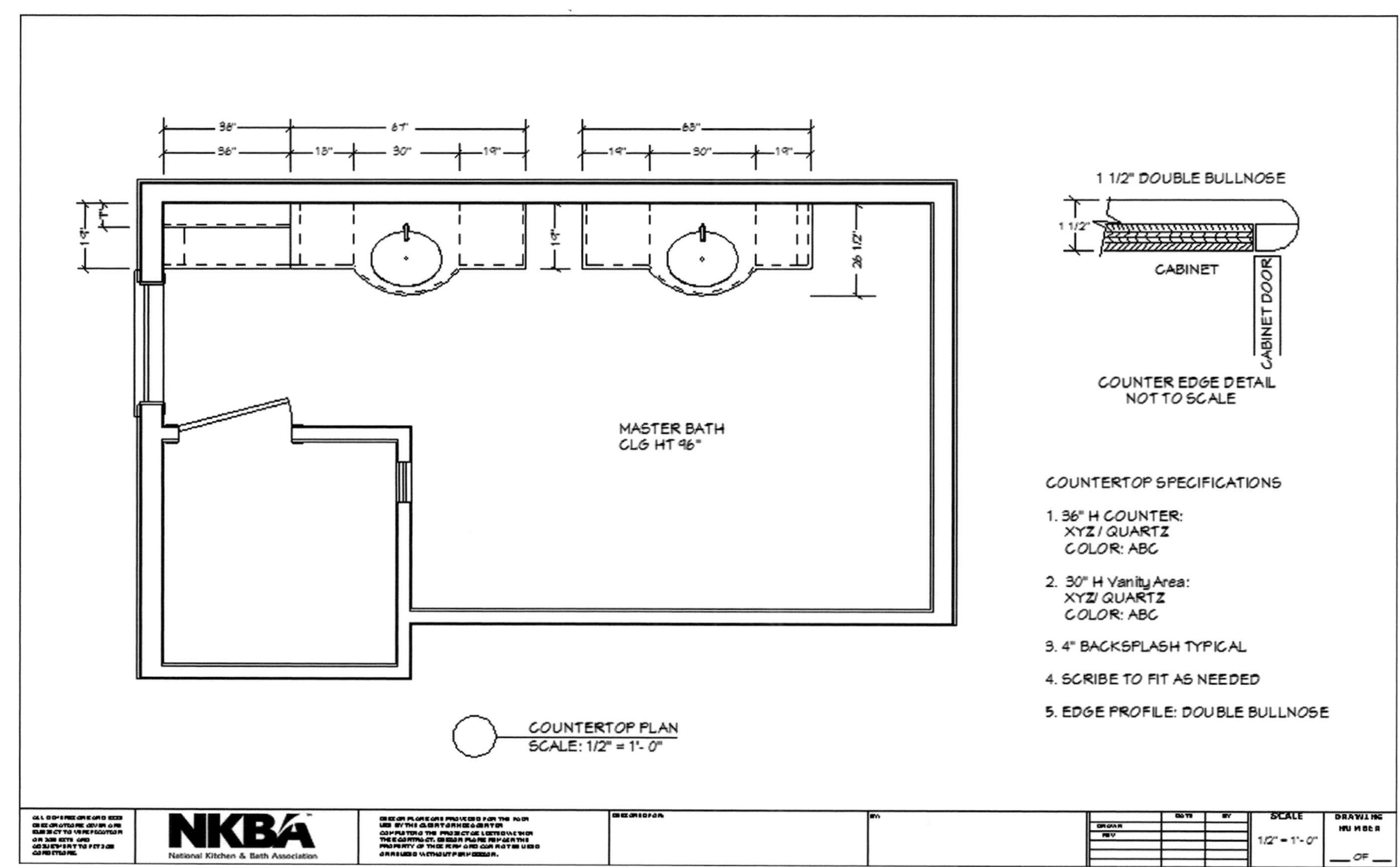

FIGURE A.16 Bathroom countertop plan.

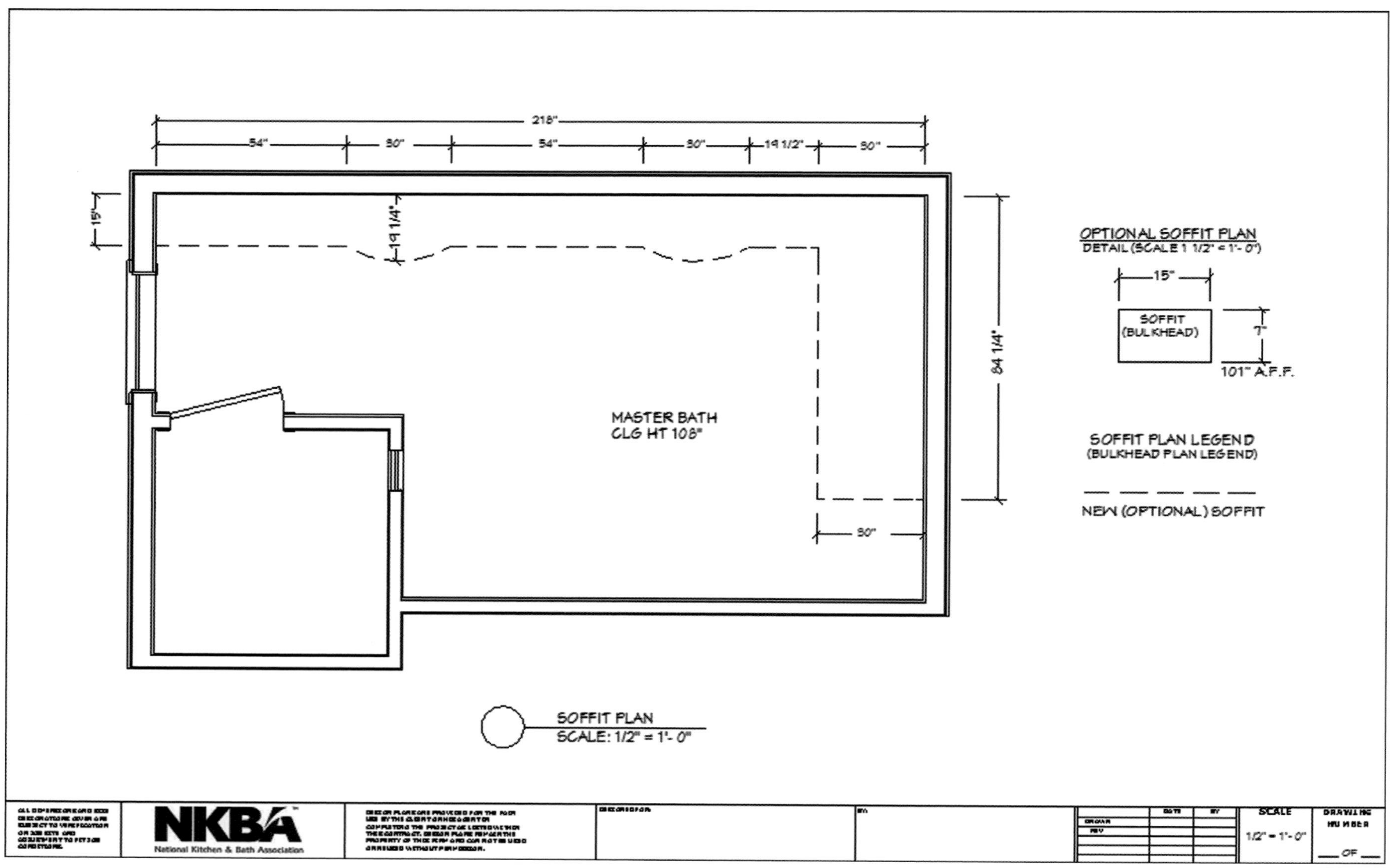

FIGURE A.17 Bathroom soffit/bulkhead plan.

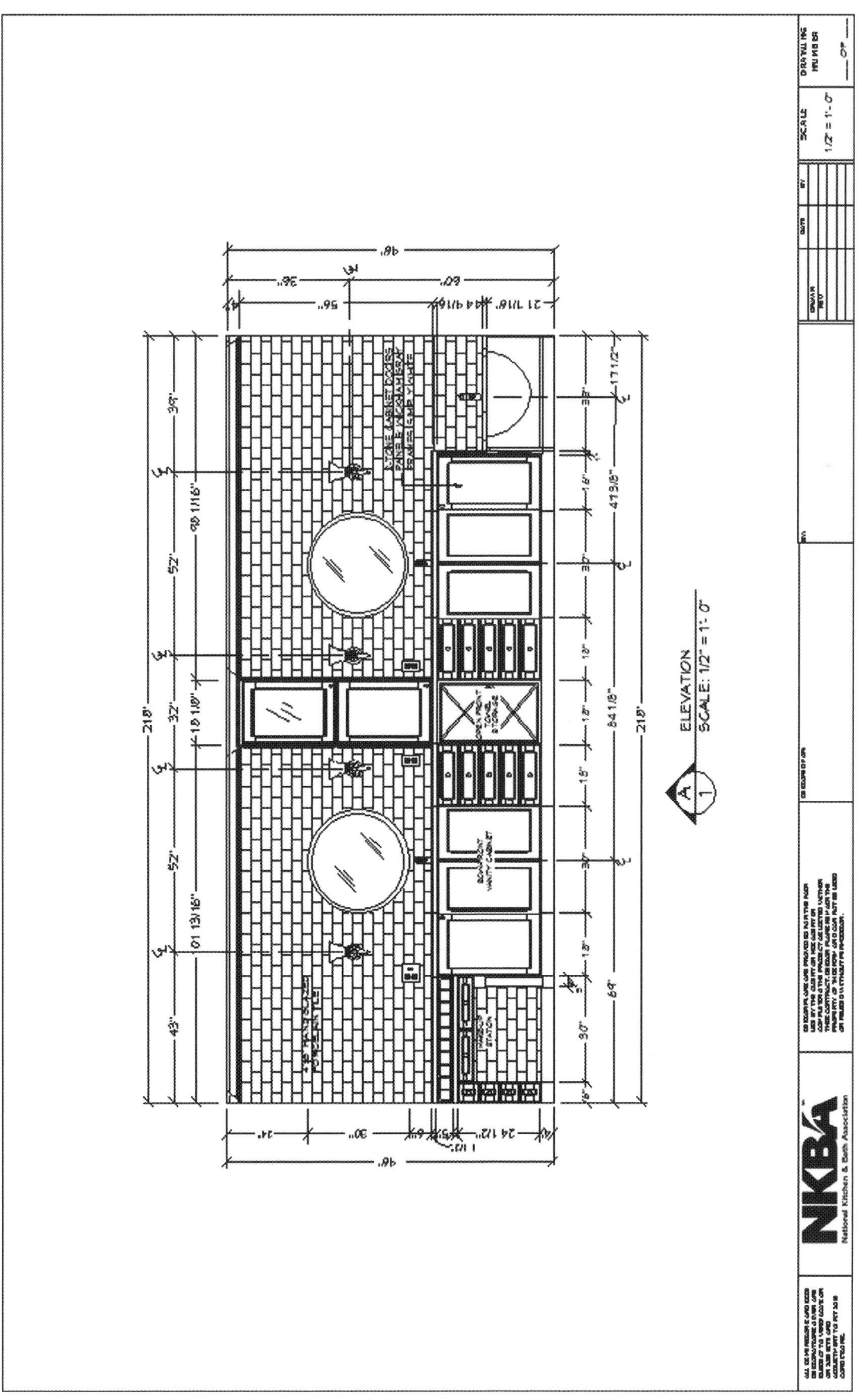

FIGURE A.18 Bathroom elevation.

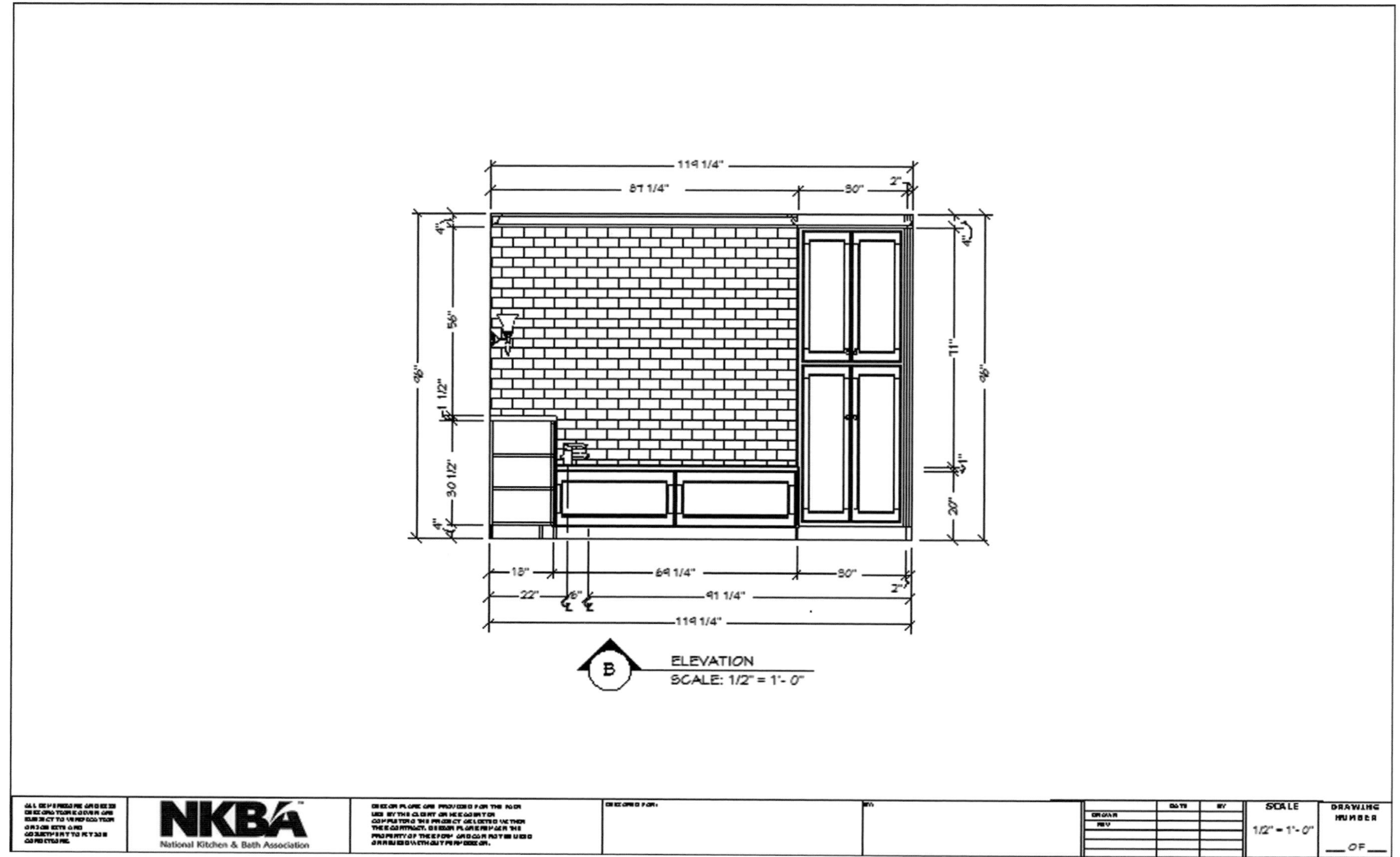

FIGURE A.19 Bathroom elevation.

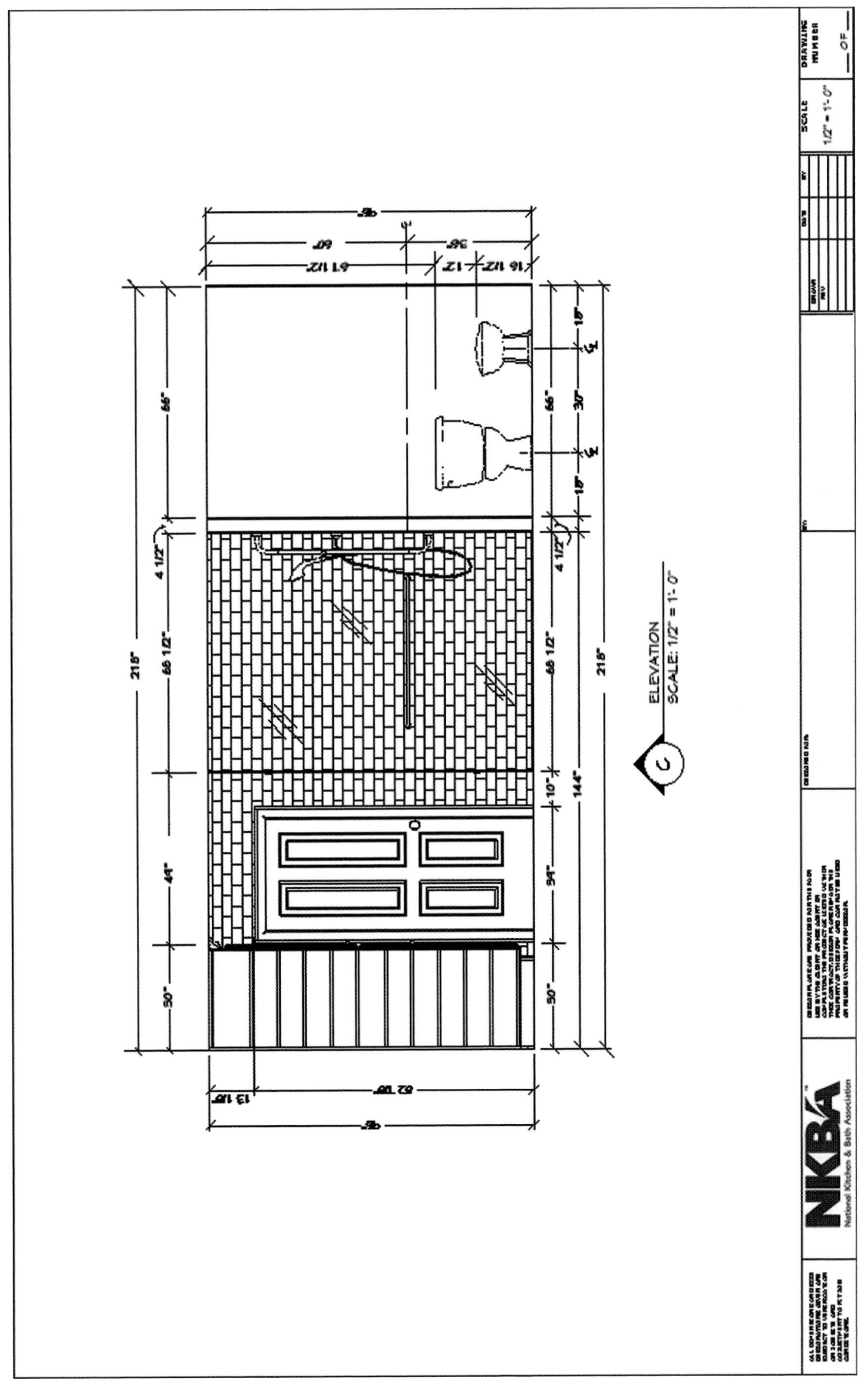

FIGURE A.20 Bathroom elevation.

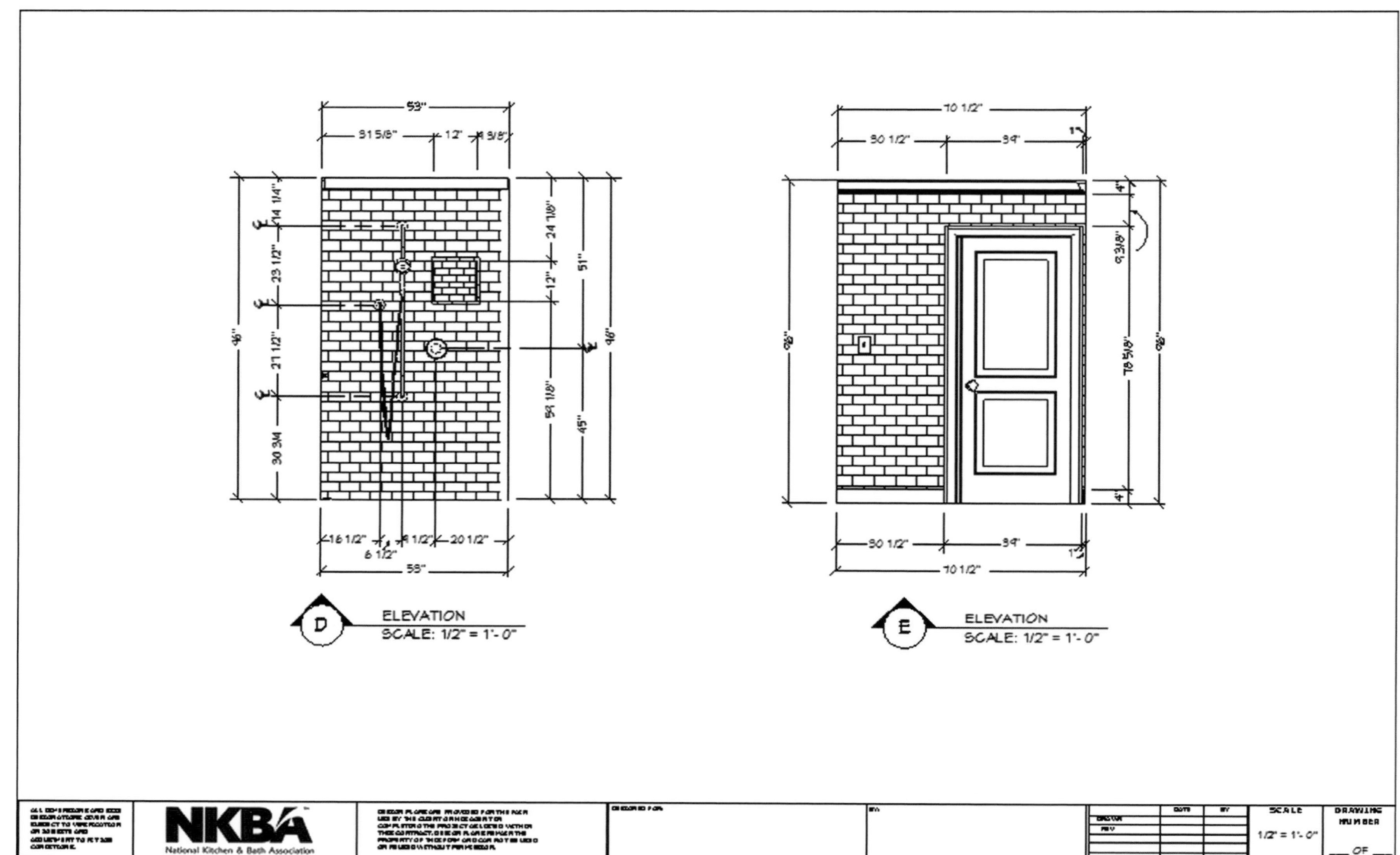

FIGURE A.21 Bathroom elevation.

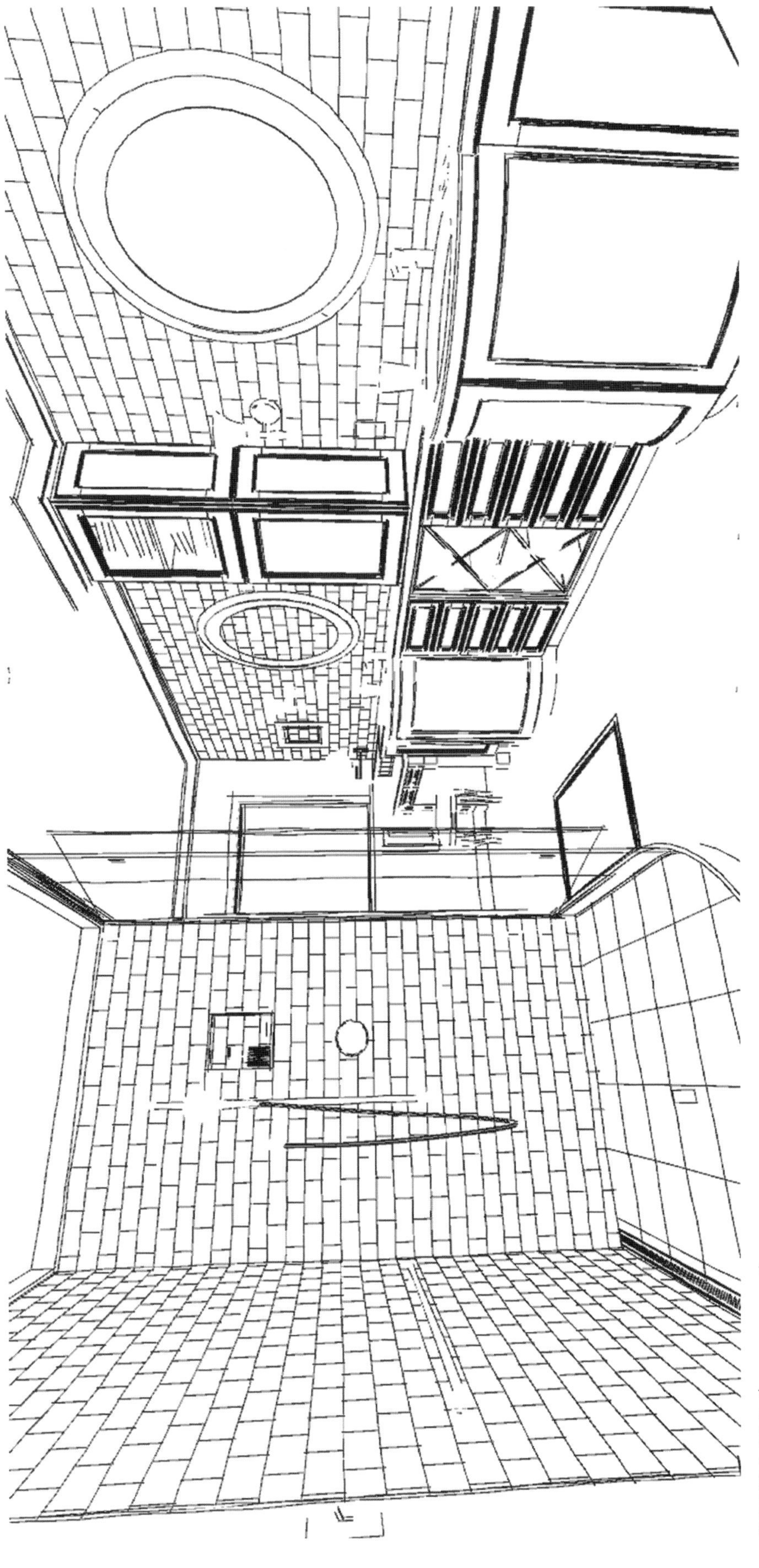

FIGURE A.22 Bathroom perspective.

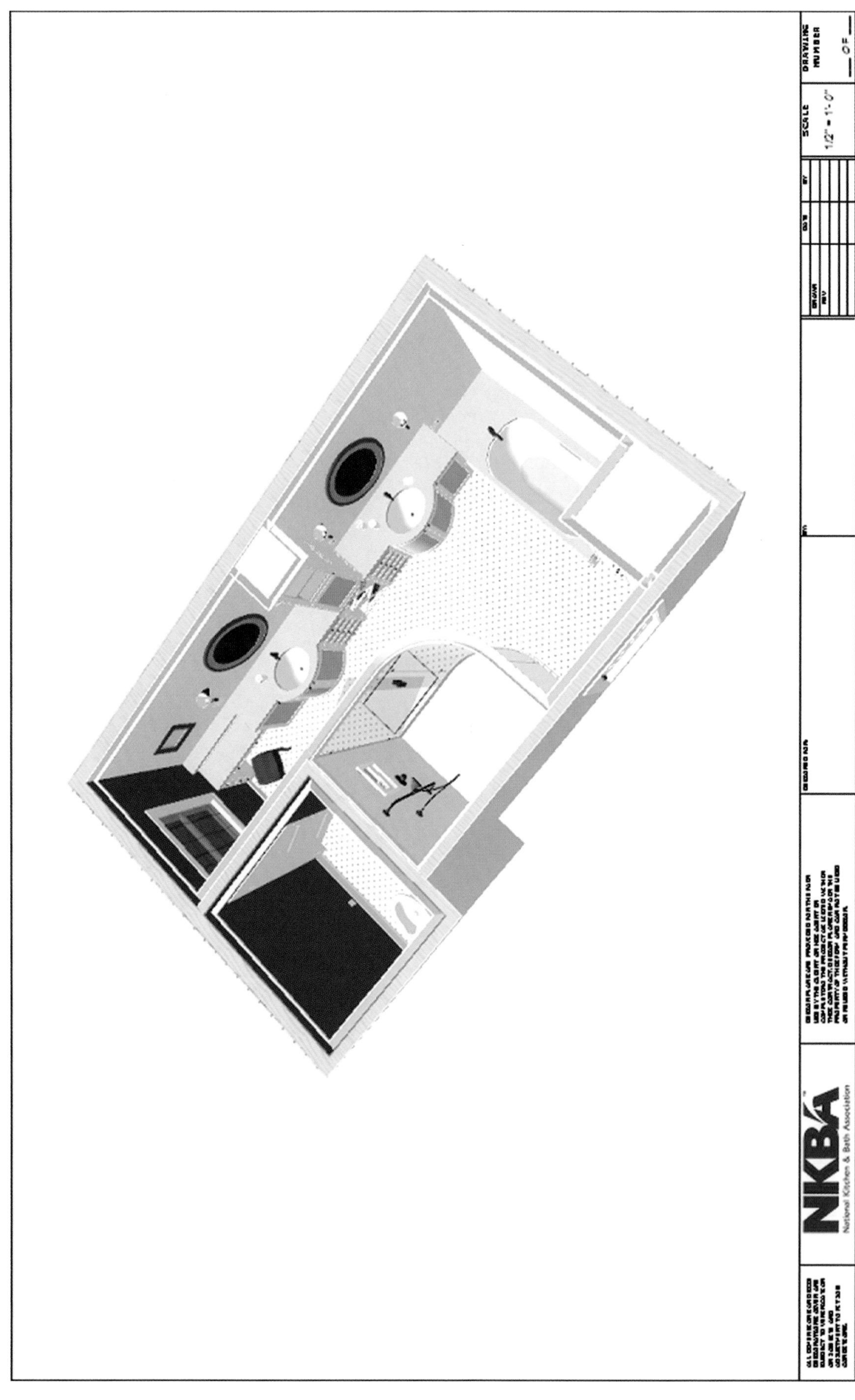

FIGURE A.23 Bird's-eye view of bathroom.

Sample Design Statement for the Bathroom Project

The primary design challenge was to create a master bath for two people with various needs:

- Separate shower and bath area.
- Separate toilet area. Would like a bidet.
- More storage space.
- Barbara Smith: 5′1″, enjoys soaking in the bathtub without disruption and likes to sit while grooming.
- Robert Smith: 6′4″, enjoys long hot showers.
- Existing space was large but not functional:
  - One wall-hung sink for two people of different heights
  - Small linen closet
- Toilet must remain in current location and a bidet to be added.

The design solution:

- To ensure adequate floor space, a pocket door was added.
- Vanities were placed at 36 inches (914 mm) high for a comfortable ergonomic height.
- Make up area was placed at 30 inches (762 mm) with knee space beneath.
- Separate shower and tub meets needs of both clients.
- Storage in the vanity cabinets and the tall cabinet for adequate storage of all personal and shared items.
- Separate bidet and toilet area was provided for privacy.
- Provided sufficient lighting for all tasks completed in bathroom.

Standard Specifications for Bathroom Design and Installation Project

H.H.I.C

687 Willow Grove Street
Hackettstown, NJ 07840

Standard Specifications for Bathroom Design and Installation

Name: Robert and Barbara Smith

Home Address: 7650 Gatewood Lane

City: Hackettstown State: NJ Phone (Home): 908-555-3421

Phone (Office): Her: 908-555-6111

Phone (Office): His cell: 908-555-7792

Phone (Office): N/A

Phone (Jobsite): Same as Home

Jobsite Address: Same as Above

City: ______ State: ______

By: H.H.I.C.

Hereafter called "Bathroom Specialist"

Bathroom Specialist will supply and deliver only such equipment and material as described in these specifications. Labor connected with this Bathroom installation will be supplied by the Bathroom Specialist only as herein specified.

Any equipment, material and labor designated here as "Owner's responsibility" must be furnished and completed by the Owner, or the Owner's Agent in accordance with the work schedule established by the Bathroom Specialist.

Equipment, material and labor not included in these specifications can be supplied by the Bathroom Specialist at an additional cost for which authorization must be given in writing by the Owner, or the Owner's Agent.

All dimension and cabinet designations shown on the floor plan and elevations / interpretive drawings, which are part of these specifications, are subject to adjustments dictated by job conditions.

All surfaces of walls, ceilings, windows and woodwork, except those of factory-made equipment, will be left unpainted or unfinished unless otherwise specified.

If specifications call for re-use of existing equipment, no responsibility on the part of the Bathroom Specialist for appearance, functioning or service shall be implied.

For factory-made equipment, the manufacturer's specifications for quality, design, dimensions, function and installation shall in all cases take precedence over any others.

FIGURE A.24 Standard Specifications for Bathroom Design and Installation Project

Cabinetry	Source				
Key: BS= Bathroom Specialist	Use Existing	Furnished by		Installed by	
O= Owner OA= Owners Agent	☐Yes ☒No	BS ☒	O/OA ☐	BS ☒	O/OA ☐

Cabinet 1 ☐ N/A

Manufacturer: Cookville Cabinets		
Construction: ☒Frame ☐Frameless		
Cabinet Exterior: ☒Wood-Species: Maple ☐Metal ☐Decorative Laminate ☐Other:		
Cabinet Exterior Finish: Nutmeg	**Cabinet Interior Material:** Birch	**Finish:** Natural
Door Style: Lexington	**Hardware:** K-456	
Special Cabinet Notes: Modification to height of VSDB36-35L (34 1/2")		

Cabinet 2 ☒ N/A

Manufacturer:		
Construction: ☐Frame ☐Frameless		
Cabinet Exterior: ☐Wood-Species: ☐Metal ☐Decorative Laminate ☐Other:		
Cabinet Exterior Finish:	**Cabinet Interior Material:**	**Finish:**
Door Style:	**Hardware:**	
Special Cabinet Notes:		

Fascia & Soffit	Source				
Key: BS= Bathroom Specialist	Use Existing	Furnished by		Installed by	
O= Owner OA= Owners Agent	☐Yes ☐No	BS ☐	O/OA ☐	BS ☐	O/OA ☐

Fascia & Soffit 1

Construction: ☐Flush ☐Extended ☐Recessed ☒Open ☐Remove ☐Other, as per plan:
Finish Material: N/A
Special Fascia / Soffit Notes: N/A
OPPTIONAL SOFFIT PLAN AVAILABLE FOR AREA OVER VANITIES ONLY (Note: Not included in estimate.)

Fascia & Soffit 2 ☒ N/A

Construction: ☐Flush ☐Extended ☐Recessed ☐Open ☐Remove ☐Other, as per plan:
Finish Material:
Special Fascia / Soffit Notes:

FIGURE A.24 (Continued)

Surfaces	Source				
Key: BS= Bathroom Specialist	Use Existing	Furnished by		Installed by	
O= Owner OA= Owners Agent	☐Yes ☒No	BS ☒	O/OA ☐	BS ☒	O/OA ☐

Surface 1- Vanity (s)

Manufacturer: GHI	
Material: Solid Surface	**Color:** Artic Sand (#432) and Mid-Night Black (#190)
Design Details: Deck Thickness 1/2 " Material S/S Edge Thickness 1 1/2" Edge Detail Shape Beveled Color See Below	
Backsplash: Thickness_N/A Height:___ Color:___	
End Splash: Thickness_N/A Height:___ Color:___	
Insert: N/A	
Special Notes: Top and bottom layer of front edge is to be Artic Sand. Middle layer to be Mid-Night Black. 1/4 " bevel edge top and bottom. Drop-in lavs by ABC Model #14237	

Surface 2- Tub / Deck / Surround

Manufacturer: RST	
Material: Solid Surface	
Design Details: Deck Thickness 1/2" Material S/S Edge Thickness 1/2". Edge Detail Shape Square Color Artic Sand (#432)	
Wall Backsplash: Thickness_N/A Height:___ Color:___	
End Splash: Thickness_N/A Height:___ Color:___	
Insert: N/A	
Special Notes: RST is to build custom Bath Deck using Solid Surface Material Provided by GHI. Deck designed to contain undermount tub by ABC Model #38771	

Surface 3- Shower Surround

Manufacturer: NOP	
Material: Solid Surface	
Design Details: Deck Thickness 1/2" Material S/S Edge Thickness 1/2" Edge Detail Shape Square Color Artic Sand (#432)	
Backsplash: Thickness_N/A Height:___ Color:___	
End Splash: Thickness_N/A Height:___ Color:___	
Insert: Shower bench to be inlay strips of Mid-Night Black (#190)	
Special Notes: NOP to supply drawing for shower area. Final drawing to be approved by B.S and Owner. Tempered Glass Enclosure by QRS Glass Company.	

Surface 4 - Other ☒ N/A

Manufacturer:	
Material:	
Design Details: Deck Thickness Material Edge Thickness Edge Detail Shape Color	
Backsplash: Thickness___ Height:___ Color:___	
End Splash: Thickness___ Height:___ Color:___	
Insert:	

FIGURE A.24 (Continued)

Special Notes:

Bath Fixtures & Fittings - Water Closet

Use Existing	Furnished by		Installed by	
☐Yes ☒No	BS ☒	O/OA ☐	BS ☒	O/OA ☐

	Brand Name	Model	Configuration	Color / Finish
☒ Round	ABC	77041	C/C	Sand
☐ Elongated				
☐ Soft				
☐ Low Profile				
Trip Lever	ABC	71342C	Std	Chrome
Stop and Supply	ABC	71551C & 71820C	Std	Chrome
Height	Existing	N/A	N/A	N/A

Bath Fixtures & Fittings - Bidet / Bidet Seat

Use Existing	Furnished by		Installed by	
☐Yes ☐No ☒N/A	BS ☐	O/OA ☐	BS ☐	O/OA ☐

	Brand Name	Model	Configuration	Color / Finish
Fittings				
Vacuum Breaker				
Miscellaneous				

Bath Fixtures & Fittings - Bathtub

Use Existing	Furnished by		Installed by	
☐Yes ☒No	BS ☒	O/OA ☐	BS ☒	O/OA ☐

	Brand Name	Model	Configuration	Color / Finish
Bathtub	ABC Undermount Tub	38771	Oval	Sand
Fitting #1	ABC	72310C	8" Spread	Chrome
Fitting #2	N/A			
Fitting #3	N/A			
Waste and Overflow	ABC	74571C		Chrome
Stop and Supply	TRS	P4355		N/A
Miscellaneous				
Size				

Bath Fixtures & Fittings – Jetted Bathtub System

Use Existing	Furnished by		Installed by	
☐Yes ☒No	BS ☒	O/OA ☐	BS ☒	O/OA ☐

	Brand Name	Model	Configuration	Color / Finish
☒Air Jets	ABC	Included with tub	Standard	Sand
☐Adjustable Whirlpool Jets				
☐Massage Whirlpool Jets				
Chromatherapy System				
Fittings				
Miscellaneous	Access: Left Front Bottom			

FIGURE A.24 (Continued)

Bath Fixtures & Fittings - Shower

Use Existing	Furnished by		Installed by	
☐Yes ☒No	BS ☒	O/OA ☐	BS ☒	O/OA ☐

	Brand Name	Model	Configuration	Color / Finish
Pan	NOP	Custom	Rectangular	Artic Sand
Curb	"	"	N/A	Artic Sand
Seat / Bench	"	"	Box	Artic Sand/Mid-Night Black Strips
Shelf / Recess	N/A			
Drain	TRS	C4100	N/A	Chrome
Fittings	ABC	#52355	N/A	Chrome
Shower #1	ABC	#64700C	N/A	Chrome
Shower #2	N/A			
Shower #3-Body Spray	N/A			
Shower #4- Hand-Held	N/A			
Stop & Supply	TRS	P4571C	N/A	N/A
Shower Floor	NOP	Custom	Slope to drain	Artic Sand
Drapery Rod	N/A			
Shower Drapery	N/A			

Bath Fixtures & Fittings – Lavatory 1

Use Existing	Furnished by		Installed by	
☐Yes ☒No	BS ☒	O/OA ☐	BS ☒	O/OA ☐

	Brand Name	Model	Configuration	Color / Finish
Type:				
☐ Under-mount				
☒ Top Mount	ABC	#14237	Rectangular w/ Oval Bowl	Sand
☐ Vessel				
☐ Pedestal				
☐ Integral				
Fittings	ABC	#56302C	Std.	Chrome
Drilling Spread	N/A	N/A	4" Spread	N/A
Stop & Supply	TRS	P4571C	N/A	Chrome
Pedestal Trap Cover				
Miscellaneous				

FIGURE A.24 (Continued)

Bath Fixtures & Fittings – Lavatory 2

Use Existing	Furnished by		Installed by	
☐Yes ☒No ☐N/A	BS ☒	O/OA ☐	BS ☒	O/OA ☐

	Brand Name	Model	Configuration	Color / Finish
❐ Under-mount				
❐ Top Mount	Same as Above			
❐ Vessel				
❐ Pedestal				
❐ Integral				
Fittings	Same as Above			
Drilling Spread	Same as Above			
Stop & Supply	Same as Above			
Pedestal Trap Cover				
Miscellaneous				

Bath Fixtures & Fittings – Steam Bath

Use Existing	Furnished by		Installed by	
☐Yes ☐No ☒N/A	BS ☐	O/OA ☐	BS ☐	O/OA ☐

	Brand Name	Model	Configuration	Color / Finish
Steam Enclosure Materials				
Steam Generator				
Steam Outlet Control				
Miscellaneous				

Bath Fixtures & Fittings – Sauna

Use Existing	Furnished by		Installed by	
☐Yes ☐No ☒N/A	BS ☐	O/OA ☐	BS ☐	O/OA ☐

	Brand Name	Model	Configuration	Color / Finish
Interior Materials				
Heater				
Control				
Miscellaneous				

Bath Fixtures & Fittings – Exercise Equipment

Use Existing	Furnished by		Installed by	
☐Yes ☐No ☒N/A	BS ☐	O/OA ☐	BS ☐	O/OA ☐

	Brand Name	Model	Configuration	Color / Finish
N/A				

FIGURE A.24 (Continued)

Bath Fixtures & Fittings – Miscellaneous

Use Existing	Furnished by		Installed by	
☐Yes ☐No	BS ☐	O/OA ☐	BS ☐	O/OA ☐

	Brand Name	Model	Configuration	Color / Finish

Accessories (as per approved drawing)

Use Existing	Furnished by		Installed by	
☐Yes ☒No	BS ☒	O/OA ☒	BS ☒	O/OA ☐

Item	Qty	Brand Name	Model	Size	Color / Finish
Mirror #1	2	Custom by BS	Custom	28" x 42" High	Frame to match cabinetry
Mirror #2	1	Custom by BS	Custom	26" x 42" High	Frame to match cabinetry
Medicine Cabinet	N/A				
Glass Shelves	N/A				
Towel Bar	TBD*	Owner will supply			
Hydronic / Electric	N/A				
Towel Ring	TBD*	Owner will supply			
Robe Hook	TBD*	Owner will supply			
Tub Soap Dish	TBD*	Owner will Supply			
Shower Soap Dish	TBD*	Owner will supply			
Bidet Soap Dish	N/A				
Lavatory Soap Dish	N/A				
Grab Bar	2	UHM	#C84-30	30"	Sand
Paper Holder	1	Free Standing/Owner will supply			
Magazine Rack	N/A				
Soap / Lotion Dispenser	N/A				
Tumbler Holder	N/A				
Tissue Holder	N/A				
Scale	N/A				
Toothbrush Holder	N/A				
Hamper	N/A				
Toilet Tank Cabinet	1	Cookville Cabinets	VTTW2436	24" x 36"	Maple (Nutmeg)
*TBD (To Be Determined)		Owner will Select and Supply			

FIGURE A.24 (Continued)

Closet Specifications

Use Existing	Furnished by		Installed by	
☐Yes ☐No ☒N/A	BS ☐	O/OA ☐	BS ☐	O/OA ☐

Item	Brand Name	Model	Size	Color / Finish
Poles	N/A			
Shelves				
Drawers				
Shoe Racks				
Belt / Tie /Scarf Racks				
Safe				
Ironing Board				
Pull Down Units				

Lighting System

Description	Qty	Location	Model #	Transformer	Finish	Lamp Req.	Furnished		Installed By	
							B.S.	O/OA	B.S.	O/OA
Keys, Moisture Proof Recessed	1	Shower	K435	N/A	Chrome	60 watt	☒	☐	☒	☐
Keys, Moisture Proof Recessed	2	Tub	K435	N/A	Chrome	60 watt	☒	☐	☒	☐
Spartin *	4	Lav Wall	U7P36	N/A	Chrome	60 watt	☒	☐	☒	☐
Keys, Recessed	1	Toilet	K706	N/A	Chrome	60 watt	☒	☐	☒	☐
ABC (Heat/Light/Vent)	1	Per Plan	#567	N/A	Chrome	60 watt	☒	☐	☒	☐

Special Lighting Notes: The Spartin Fixtures listed are for outdoor use and are sealed fixtures. Suggested because of proximity to bathtub.

Flooring

Description		Furnished By		Installed By	
		B.S.	O/OA	B.S.	O/OA
Hazardous Waste Removal (Asbestos) None Observed To Be Determined (TBD)		☐	☐	☐	☐
Removal of Existing Floor Covering		☒	☐	☒	☐
Remove and Repair Water Damaged Area None Observed TBD		☒	☐	☒	☐
Preparation of Floor / Subfloor See Below		☒	☐	☒	☐
Installation of Subfloor Underlayment Backer Board TM Installed Over Subfloor		☒	☐	☒	☐
New Floor Covering Material Description:		☒	☐	☐	☐
Manufacturer: KLM TILE CO.	Size: 9"	☒	☐	☒	☐
Pattern Number: 56300	Pattern Name / Repeat: N/A	☒	☐	☒	☐
Tile Pattern: COSTAL	Grout: G14-2	☒	☐	☒	☐
Describe Tile Details: PLACE DIAGONAL					
Transition / Threshold Treatment		☒	☐	☒	☐

Special Flooring Notes: FILL AND LEVEL AT OLD CLOSET LOCATION. CHECK FOR WATER DAMAGE AFTER TEAROUT. REPAIR AS NEEDED. NO INDICATION OF ASBESTOS FLOORING. TO BE DETERMINED DURING EXISTING FLOOR REMOVAL.

FIGURE A.24 (Continued)

Windows and Doors

Item	Brand Name	Model	Finish	Hardware	Furnished By		Installed By	
					B.S.	O/OA	B.S.	O/OA
BATH ENTRY DOOR	PISK MILLWORK	30RH-74	MATCH TRIM	KUT #35001	☒	☐	☒	☐
					☐	☐	☐	☐
					☐	☐	☐	☐
					☐	☐	☐	☐
					☐	☐	☐	☐
					☐	☐	☐	☐

Casing **Size:** 2 1/4 **Style:** #1004

Special Window and Door Notes: REMOVE AND CLOSE OPENING AT DOOR TO BEDROOM #3. DESIGNER TO VERIFY TEMPERED GLASS WINDOW.

Decorative Surfaces (Wall, Ceiling, Window Materials)

Description	Material	Color	Finish	Quantity	Furnished By		Installed By	
					B.S.	O/OA	B.S.	O/OA
PATCH AND PRIME ALL WALLS	DRYWALL	N/A	PAINT READY	N/A	☒	☐	☒	☐
PATCH AND PRIME CEILING AS NEEDED	DRYWALL	N/A	LIGHT BEAD	N/A	☒	☐	☒	☐
PAINT WALLS AND CEILING	TBD	TBD	TBD	TBD	☐	☒	☐	☒
WINDOW TREATMENTS	TBD	TBD	TBD	TBD	☐	☒	☐	☒
					☐	☐	☐	☐

Special Decorative Surface Notes: FILL AND PATCH AT WALL AND CEILING OF OLD CLOSET. FILL AND PATCH WALL ON BOTH SIDES AT OLD DOOR OPENING TO BEDROOM #3. DRYWALL, TAPE AND FINISH NEW WALL AT SHOWER. BS TO PRIME WALLS ONLY. OWNER TO PAINT.

HVAC

Description	Furnished By		Installed By	
	B.S.	O/OA	B.S.	O/OA
Ventilation No Changes Required For HVAC System	☐	☐	☐	☐
Rough-In Requirements	☐	☐	☐	☐
Run New Duct Work for Ventilation System New Duct Work For Heat/Light/Vent System	☒	☐	☒	☐
Heating	☐	☐	☐	☐
Air Conditioning Supply	☐	☐	☐	☐

Details: NO CHANGES TO CEILING MOUNTED DUCTS. TIMED SWITCH FOR VENT FAN.

Electrical Work (except as described above in specific equipment sections)

Description	Furnished By		Installed By	
	B.S.	O/OA	B.S.	O/OA
New Service Panel No Changes Required For Existing 200amp Panel	☐	☐	☐	☐
Code Update As Required	☒	☐	☒	☐
Wiring for Heated Tile Floor N/A	☐	☐	☐	☐

Details: ADD NEW CIRCUIT FOR WHIRLPOOL AND HEAT/VENT/LIGHT. VERIFY ALL BATH RECEPTACLES ARE GFCI PROTECTED. ADD LIGHTING, SWITCHES AND RECEPTACLES AS PER MECHANICAL PLAN.

FIGURE A.24 (Continued)

Plumbing (except as described above in specific equipment sections)				
Description	Furnished By		Installed By	
	B.S.	O/OA	B.S.	O/OA
New Rough In Requirements: RELOCATE LAVATORIES TO TOP WALL. RELOCATE TUB SUPPLY LINES. NEW SUPPLY LINES FOR SHOWER.	☒	☐	☒	☐
	☐	☐	☐	☐
	☐	☐	☐	☐
New Drainage Requirements NEW DRAINS FOR LAVATORIES AND SHOWER. REWORK EXISTING TUB DRAIN.	☒	☐	☒	☐
	☐	☐	☐	☐
	☐	☐	☐	☐
New Vent Stack Requirements: NEW VENT STACK REQUIRED FOR LAVATORIES AND SHOWER LOCATIONS.	☒	☐	☒	☐
	☐	☐	☐	☐
	☐	☐	☐	☐
Modifications to Existing Lines: AS REQUIRED PER PLAN.	☒	☐	☒	☐
	☐	☐	☐	☐
	☐	☐	☐	☐
Details: ANY OPENINGS IN WALL FOR PLUMBING MODIFICATIONS WILL BE FINISHED AND PRIMED BY BS WITH PAINT BY OWNER.				

General Carpentry (except as described above in specific equipment sections)				
Description	Furnished By		Installed By	
	B.S.	O/OA	B.S.	O/OA
Demolition Work:				
Walls-Exterior N/A	☐	☐	☐	☐
Walls-Interior Remove Old Closet	☒	☐	☒	☐
Windows/Doors Remove Door to Bedroom #3	☒	☐	☒	☐
Ceiling N/A	☐	☐	☐	☐
Soffit N/A	☐	☐	☐	☐
Existing Fixture and Equipment Removal	☒	☐	☒	☐
Trash Removal To Container in Driveway	☒	☐	☒	☐
Reconstruction / Preparation Work (Except as Previously Stated) N/A				
Windows	☐	☐	☐	☐
Doors	☐	☐	☐	☐
Interior Walls	☐	☐	☐	☐
Exterior Wall	☐	☐	☐	☐
Soffit / Fascia	☐	☐	☐	☐
HVAC Work: N/A				
Replace Vents	☐	☐	☐	☐
Replace Vent Covers Size:_______________	☐	☐	☐	☐
Millwork: (Note Cabinetry Installation listed under cabinets)				
Crown Molding N/A	☐	☐	☐	☐
Ceiling Details N/A	☐	☐	☐	☐
Window / Door Casing All Trim Stained To Match Cabinetry	☒	☐	☒	☐
Baseboard Stained To Match Cabinetry	☒	☐	☒	☐
Wainscotting / Chair Rail N/A	☐	☐	☐	☐
Details:				

FIGURE A.24 (Continued)

Miscellaneous Work

Description	Responsibility	
	B.S.	O/OA
Material Storage Location Cabinetry in Garage, Right Side	☒	☐
Trash Collection Area BS To Arrange for Container in Driveway, Right Side.	☒	☐
Trash Removal Daily to Container	☒	☐
Jobsite / Room Cleanup Broom Clean Daily	☒	☐
Building Permit (s) As Required	☒	☐
Structural Engineering / Architectural Fees N/A	☐	☐
Inspection Fees As Required	☒	☐
Jobsite Delivery To Garage and Storage Container*	☒	☐
*On Site Storage Container for items that will not fit in garage. Between garage and trash container.	☒	☐
	☐	☐
	☐	☐

FIGURE A.24 (Continued)

SUMMARY

This appendix with sample drawings is intended to give you a reference point for drafting the NKBA drawings. It is important to include all items in order to provide enough information for the design project completion. Always remember that you must adhere to the NKBA standards when drawing plans. The dimensions are always in inches (mm), placed at the outside of window and door, and terminate at the interior finished surface of the walls. Any island or peninsula must be dimensioned. These dimensions can be located in the interior of the floor plan, close to the actual object. Be concerned with the usable wall space that you have to work with. The standardization of the drawings helps to keep the drawings consistent, which will ensure good communication with all individuals involved with the project.

APPENDIX

Generic Cabinet Nomenclature

FRAMED CABINETS—IMPERIAL MEASUREMENTS

(Courtesy of David Newton Associates)

Base Cabinet Nomenclature

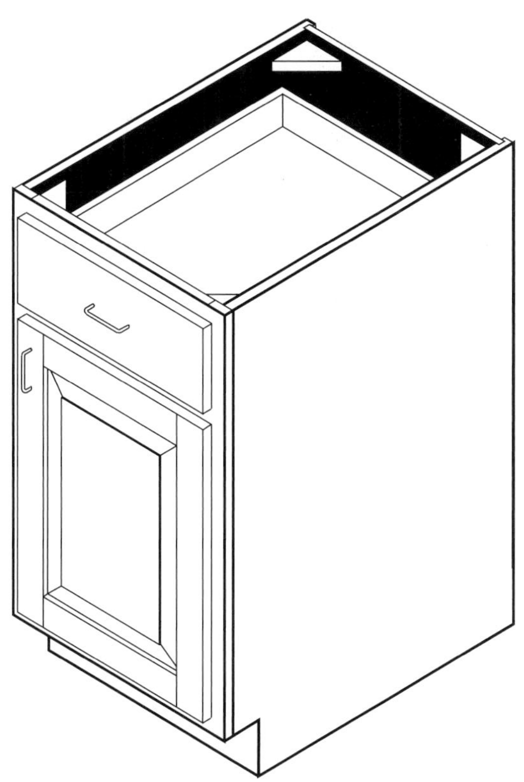

FIGURE B.1 9 3 BASE CABINET (B12R • B15R • B18R • B21R • B24R) Base cabinet with one door and one drawer. Specify hinging L or R. Right shown.

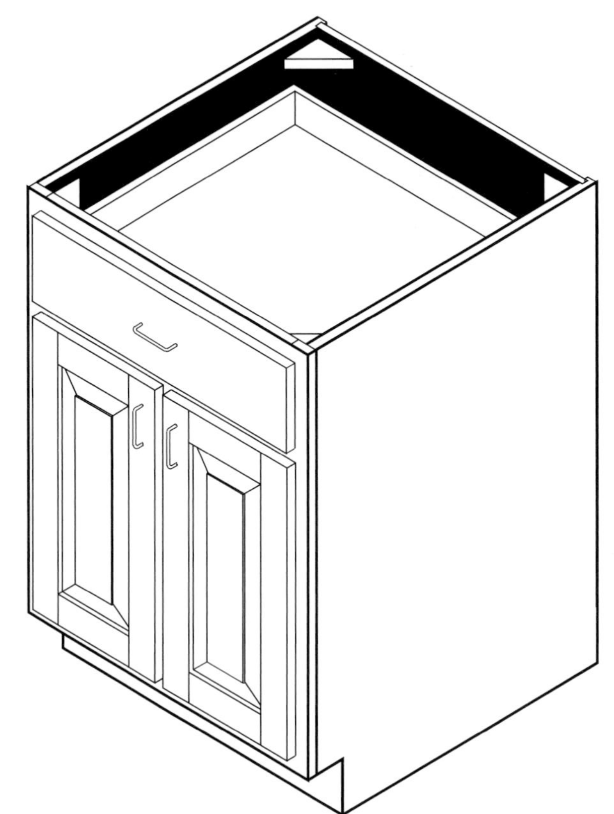

FIGURE B.2 BASE CABINET (BUTT DOORS) (B24) Base cabinet with two doors and one drawer. Doors butt together at center of cabinet opening. No center stile.

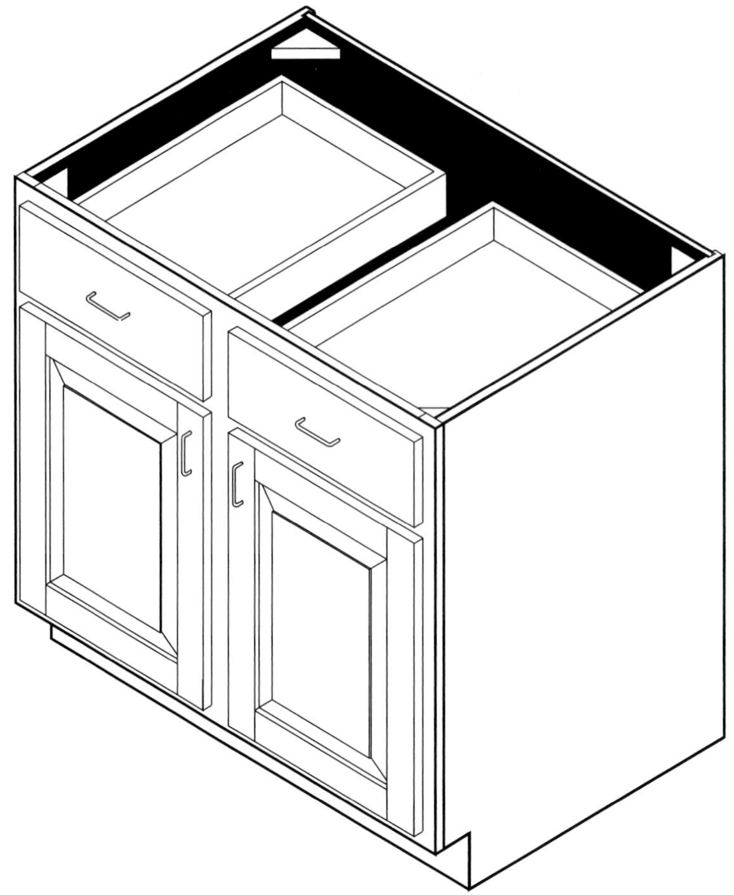

FIGURE B.3 BASE CABINET (B27 • B30 • B33 • B36 • B39 • B42 • B45 • B48) Base cabinet with two doors and two drawers.

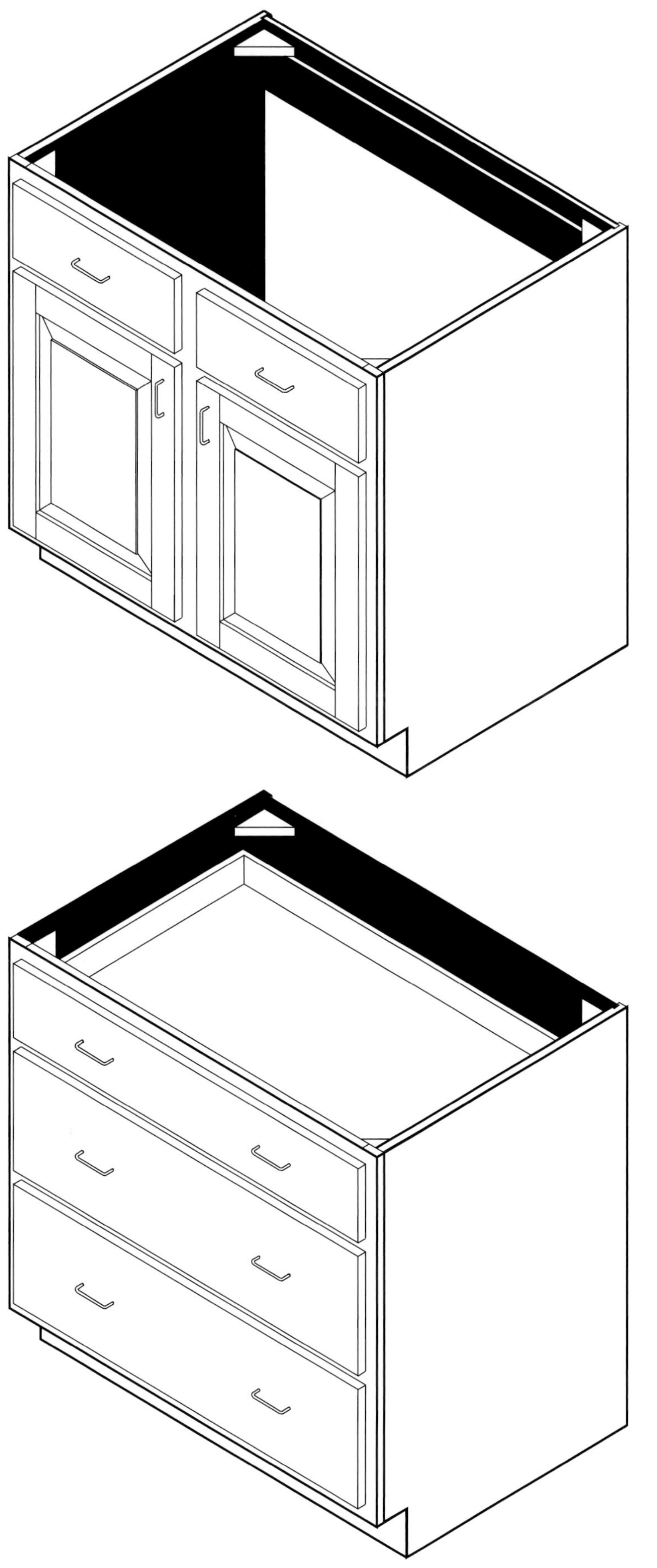

FIGURE B.4 SINK BASE CABINET 9SB24 • SB27 • SB30 • SB33 • SB36 • SB39 • SB42 • SB45 • SB48) Base cabinet with a shelf but without drawers.

FIGURE B.5 9 5 THREE DRAWER BASE CABINET (3DB12 • 3DB15 • 3DB18 • 3DB21 • 3DB24 • 3DB30 • 3DB36. Base cabinet with three drawers. 3DB36 shown.

FIGURE B.6 FOUR DRAWER BASE CABINET (4DB12 • 4DB15 • 4DB18 • 4DB21) Base cabinet with four drawers.

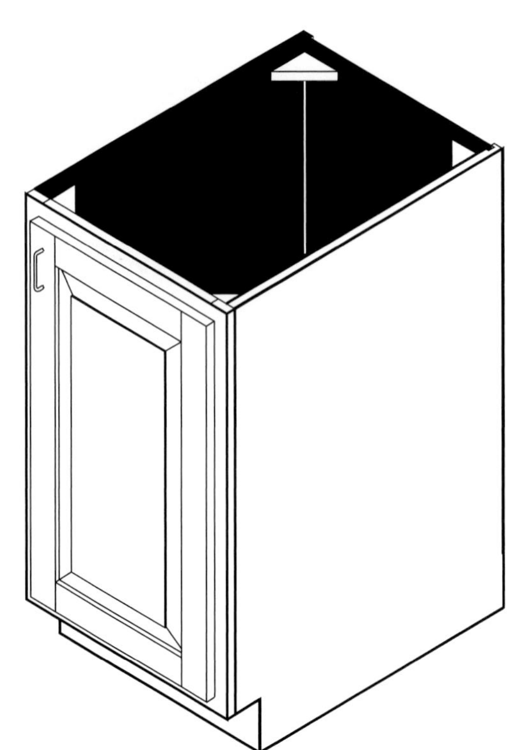

FIGURE B.7 FULL-HEIGHT BASE CABINET (FHB9R • FHB12R • FHB15R • FHB18R • FHB21R • FHB24R) Base cabinet with full-height door, no drawer. Specify hinging L or R. Right shown.

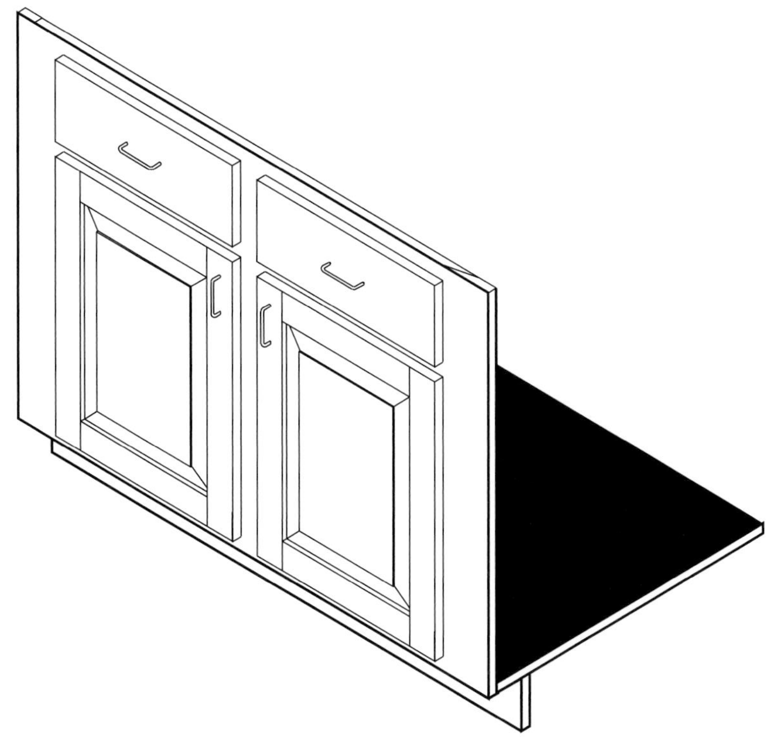

FIGURE B.8 SINK OR RANGE FRONT (FRAME ONLY) (SF24 • SF30 • SF36 • SF42 • SF48) Front of cabinet only, with floor. Wide stiles allow 6″ adjustment in width.

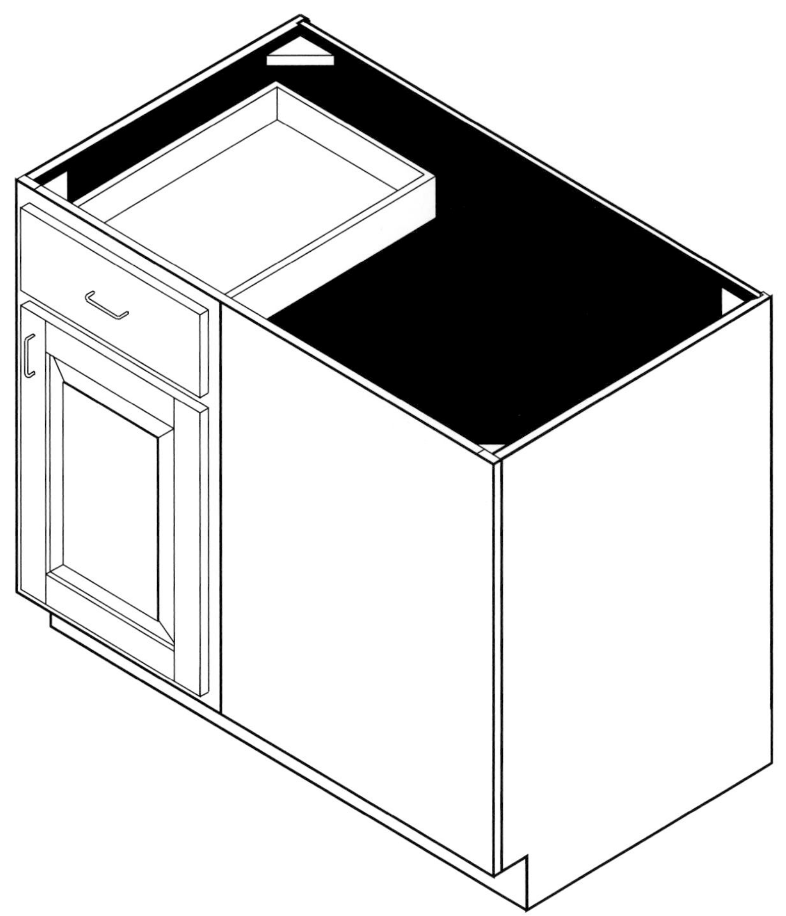

FIGURE B.9 BLIND BASE CORNER CABINET (BBC36 • BBC39 • BBC42 • BBC45 • BBC48) Reversible blind base corner cabinet. Can be pulled up to 5½″. A BF3 filler must be ordered for proper installation. Door and drawer may be moved to opposite side to reverse blind. Blind right shown.

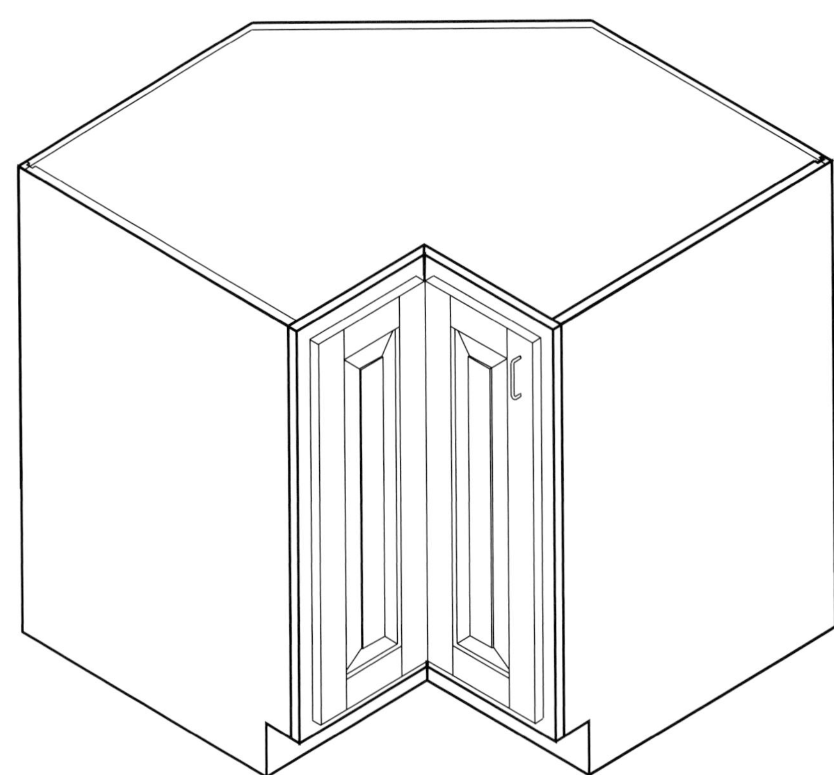

FIGURE B.10 L-CORNER BASE CABINET (LCB36L) "L" shaped base corner cabinet. Specify hinging L or R. Left shown.

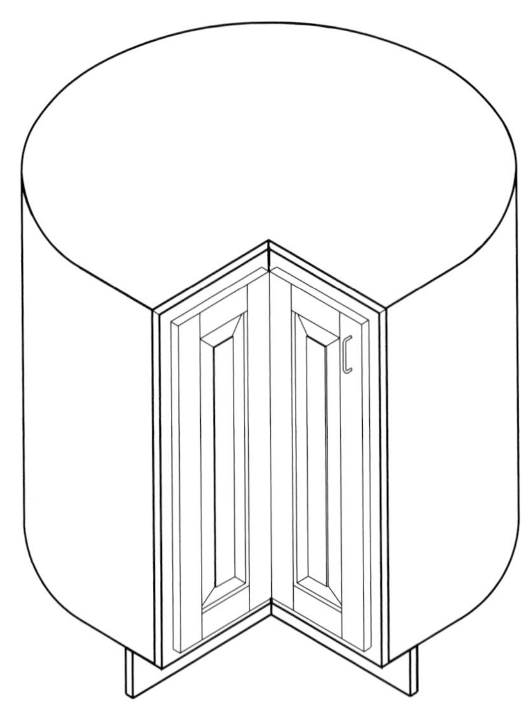

FIGURE B.11 LAZY SUSAN BASE CORNER CABINET (LSB33L • LSB36L) Revolving shelf lazy Susan corner base cabinet. Specify hinging L or R. Left shown.

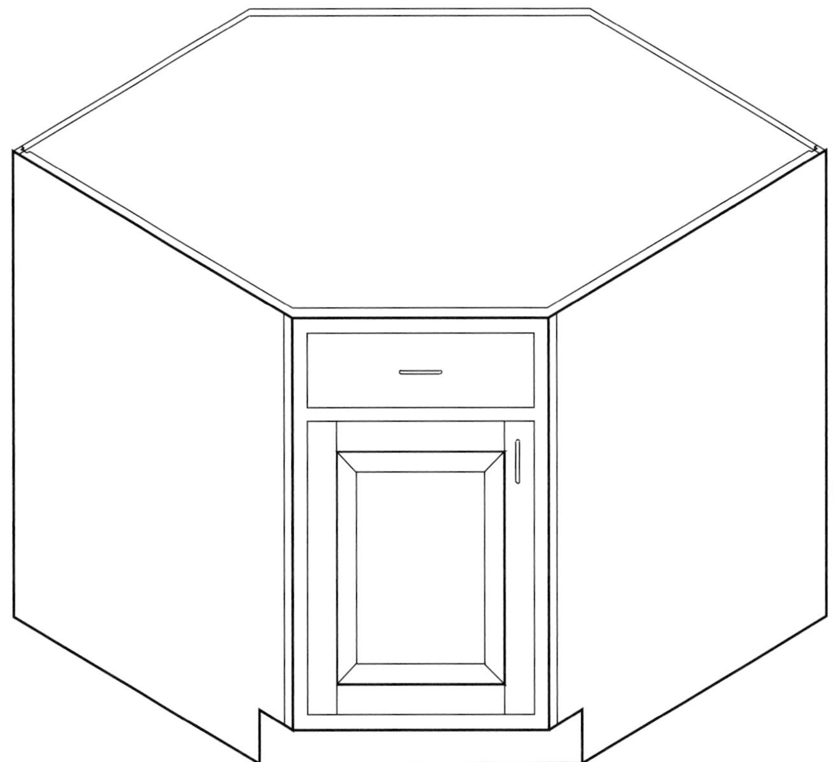

FIGURE B.12 DIAGONAL CORNER BASE CABINET (DCB36L) Diagonal base cabinet for corner application. Specify hinging L or R. Left shown.

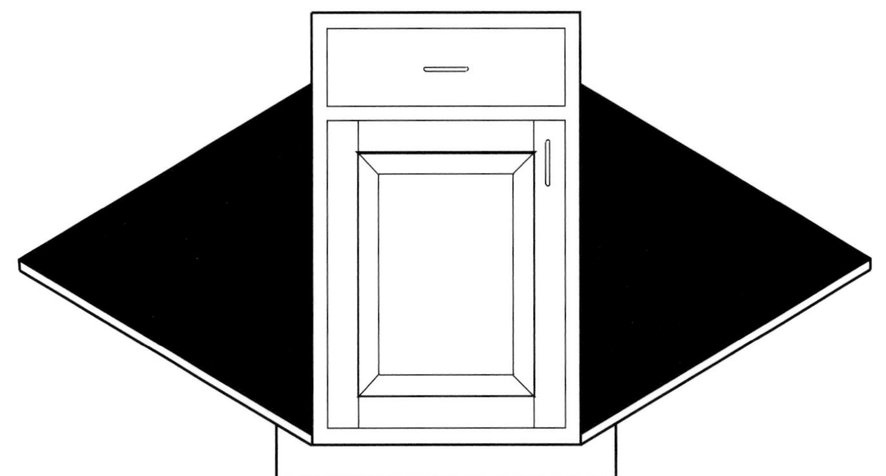

FIGURE B.13 DIAGONAL CORNER FRONT (DCF36L • DCF39L • DCF42L) Diagonal base front with floor, for corner application. Specify hinging L or R. Left shown.

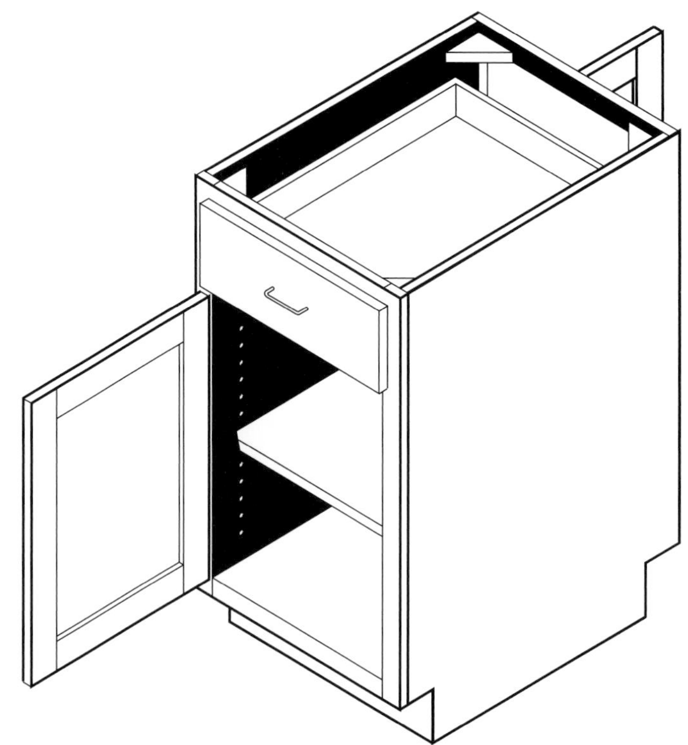

FIGURE B.14 BASE PENINSULA CABINET (BP12L • BP18L • BP24L) Base cabinet with two doors and one drawer. Specify hinging L or R. Left shown.

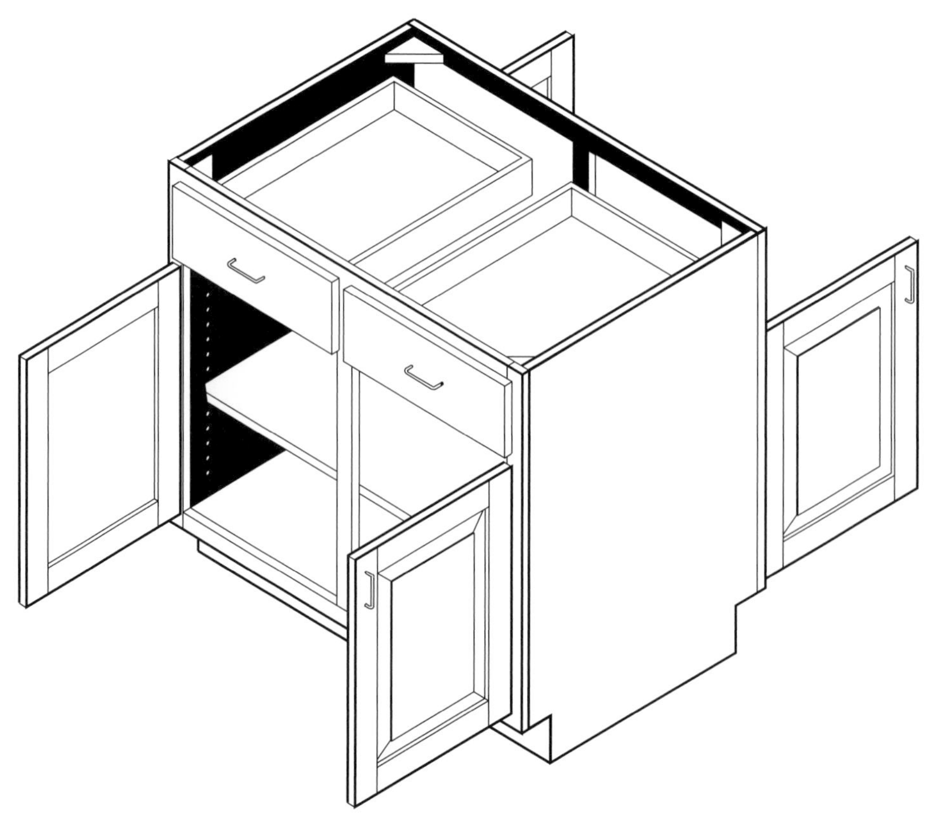

FIGURE B.15 BASE PENINSULA CABINET (BP24 • BP30 • BP36 • BP42 • BP48) Base cabinet with four doors and two drawers.

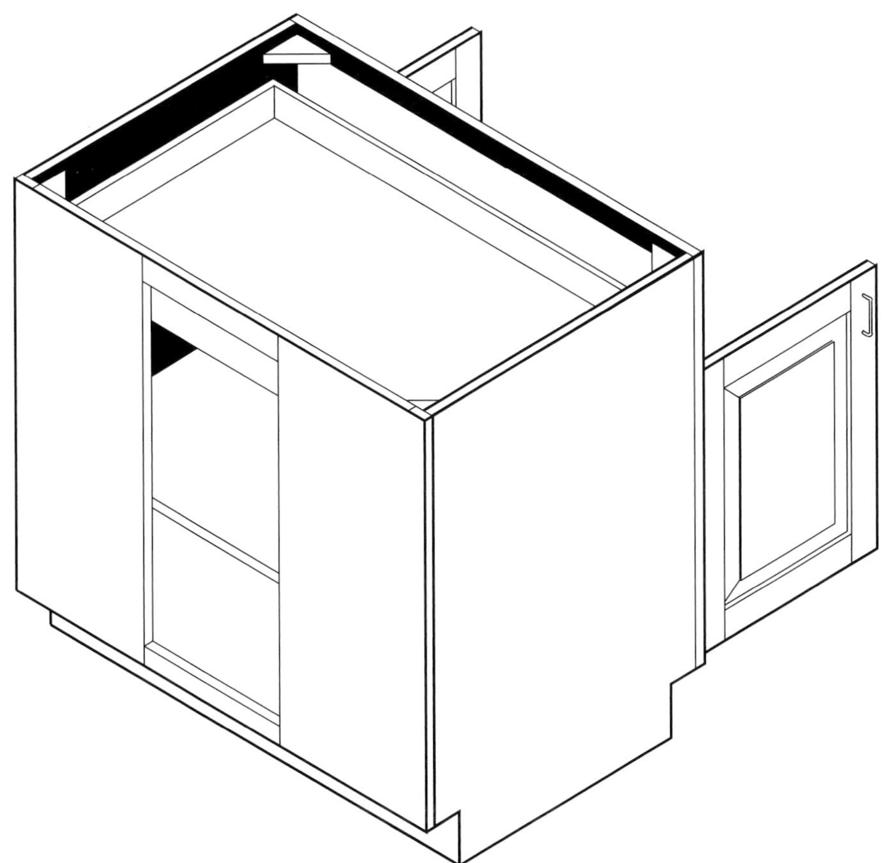

FIGURE B.16 BASE CORNER PENINSULA CABINET (BCP27) Base corner cabinet with two doors and one drawer. Used as a blind corner base cabinet when planning peninsula cabinets. This 27″ wide cabinet eliminates the need for a filler on the inside corner of the kitchen layout. A filler must be planned for any item placed at 90° to the BCP27. Blinded view shown.

Wall Cabinet Nomenclature

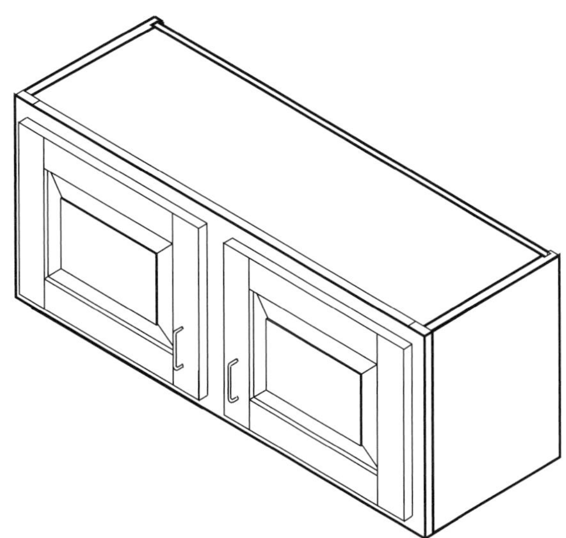

FIGURE B.17 12″ AND 15″ HIGH WALL CABINETS (W3012 • W3312 • W3612 • W3912 • W4212) 12″ high wall cabinets.
W3015 • W3315 • W3615 • W3915 • W4215
15″ high wall cabinets.

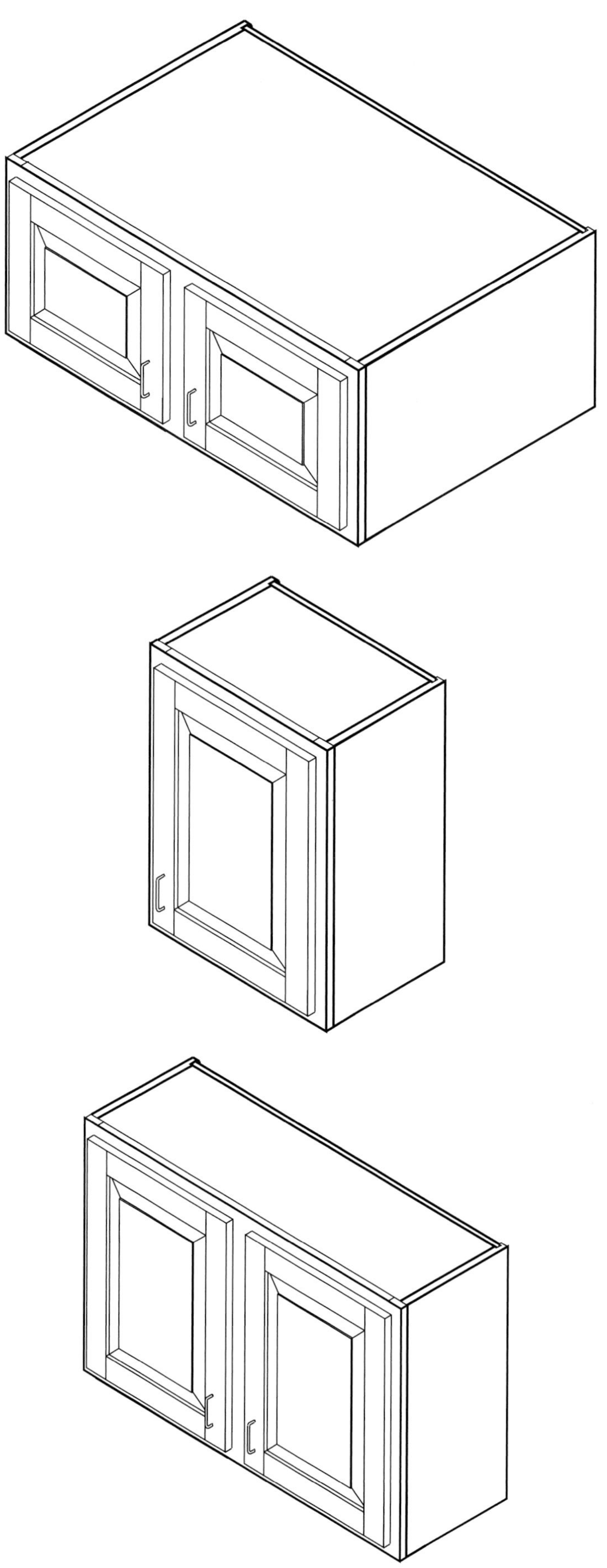

FIGURE B.18 12″ AND 15″ HIGH WALL CABINETS 24″ DEEP
W301224 • W331224 • W361224 • W391224 • W421224 • W481224
12″ high wall cabinets, 24″ deep.
W301524 • W331524 • W361524 • W391524 • W421524 • W481524
15″ high wall cabinets, 24″ deep.

FIGURE B.19 18″ AND 24″ HIGH WALL CABINETS
W1818R • W2118R • W2418R
18″ high wall cabinet, single door. Specify hinging L or R. Right shown.
W1824R • W2124R • W2424R
24″ high wall cabinet, single door. Specify hinging L or R. Right shown.

FIGURE B.20 18″ AND 24″ HIGH WALL CABINETS
W2718 • W3018 • W3318 • W3618 • W3918 • W4218
18″ high wall cabinets.
W2724 • W3024 • W3324 • W3624 • W3924 • W4224
24″ high wall cabinets.

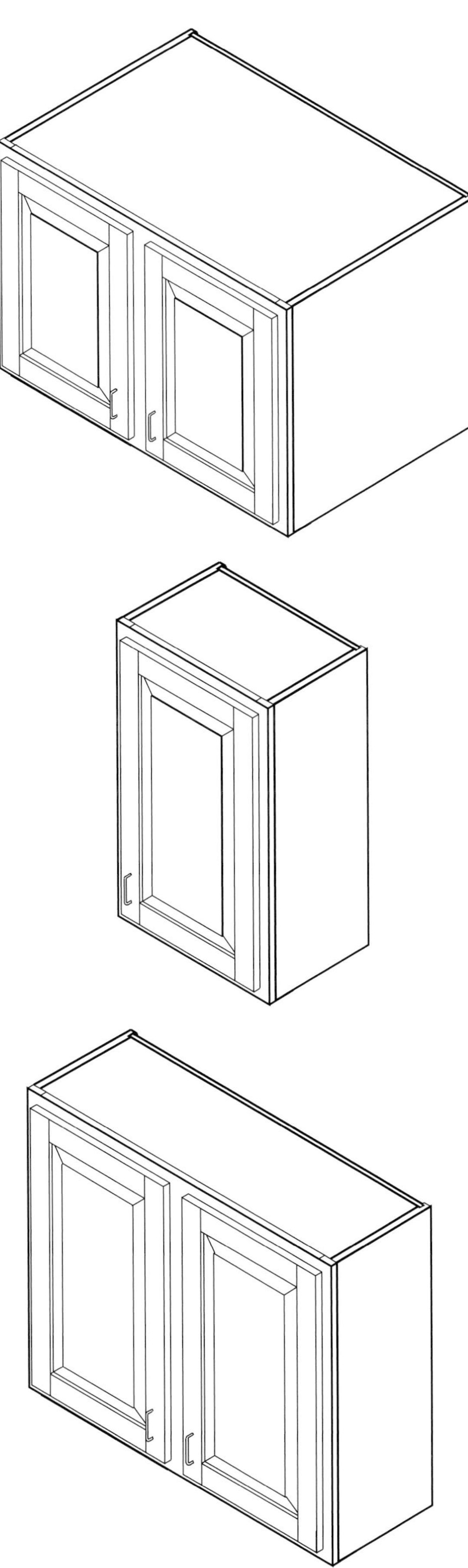

FIGURE B.21 18″ AND 24″ HIGH WALL CABINETS 24″ DEEP
W301824 • W331824 • W361824 • W391824 • W421824
18″ high wall cabinets, 24″ deep.
W302424 • W332424 • W362424 • W392424 • W422424
24″ high wall cabinets, 24″ deep.

FIGURE B.22 30″ HIGH WALL CABINETS
W930R • W1230R • W1530R • W1830R • W2130R • W2430R
30″ high wall cabinets, single door. Specify hinging L or R. Right shown.

FIGURE B.23 30″ HIGH WALL CABINETS
W2430 • W2730 • W3030 • W3330 W3630 • W3930 • W4230 • W4530 • W4830
30″ high wall cabinets.

FIGURE B.24 36″ AND 42″ HIGH WALL CABINETS
W936R • W1236R • W1536R • W1836R • W2136R • W2436R
36″ high wall cabinets, single door. Specify hinging L or R. Right shown.
W942R • W1242R • W1542R • W1842R • W2142R • W2442R
42″ high wall cabinets, single door. Specify hinging L or R. Right shown.

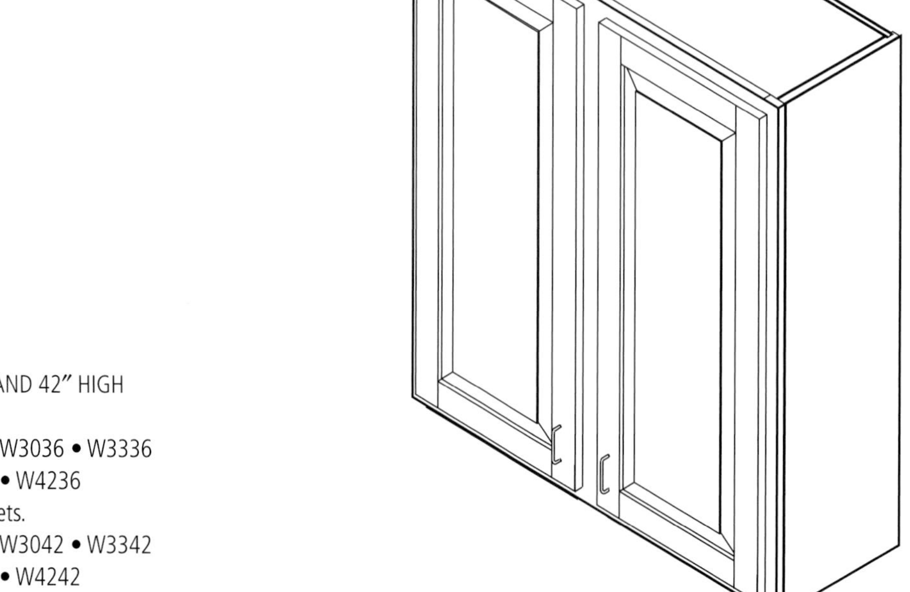

FIGURE B.25 36″ AND 42″ HIGH WALL CABINETS
W2436 • W2736 • W3036 • W3336 • W3636 • W3936 • W4236
36″ high wall cabinets.
W2442 • W2742 • W3042 • W3342 • W3642 • W3942 • W4242
42″ high wall cabinets.

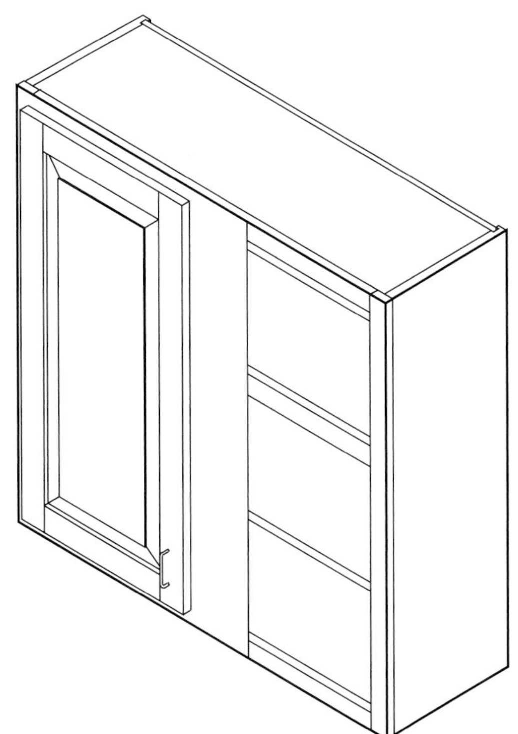

FIGURE B.26 BLIND CORNER WALL CABINET
Must order a WF3 filler for proper installation.
BCW2430R • BCW3030R • BCW3630R • BCW4230R • BCW4830R
30″ high wall corner cabinet for corner application. Specify blind L or R. Right shown.
BCW2436R • BCW3036R • BCW3636R • BCW4236R • BCW4836R
36″ high wall corner cabinet for corner application. Specify blind L or R. Right shown.
BCW2442R • BCW3042R • BCW3642R
42″ high wall corner cabinet for corner application. Specify blind L or R. Right shown.

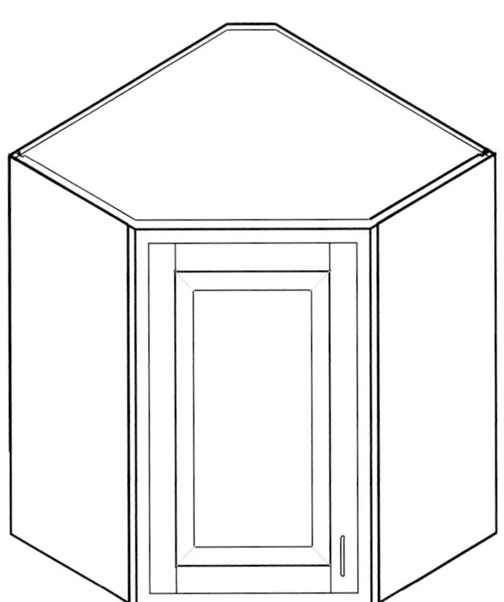

FIGURE B.27 DIAGONAL CORNER WALL CABINET
DCW2430L • DCW2436L • DWC2442L
Diagonal corner wall cabinet for corner applications. Specify hinging L or R. Left shown. Three heights: 30″, 36″, 42″.

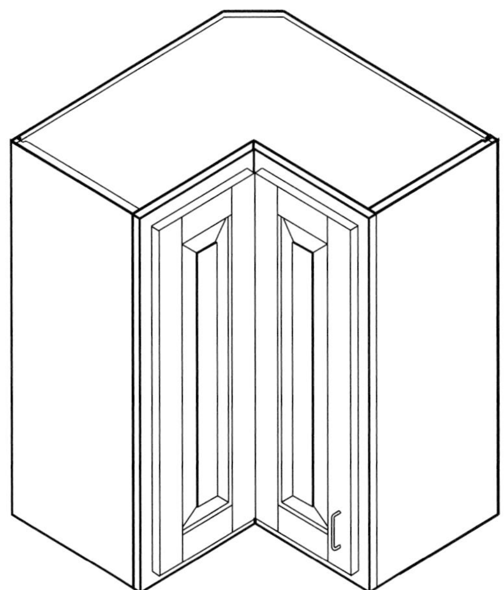

FIGURE B.28 "L" CORNER WALL CABINET
LCW2430L • LCW2436L • LCW2442L
"L" corner wall cabinet for corner applications. Specify hinging L or R. Left shown. Three heights: 30″, 36″, 42″.

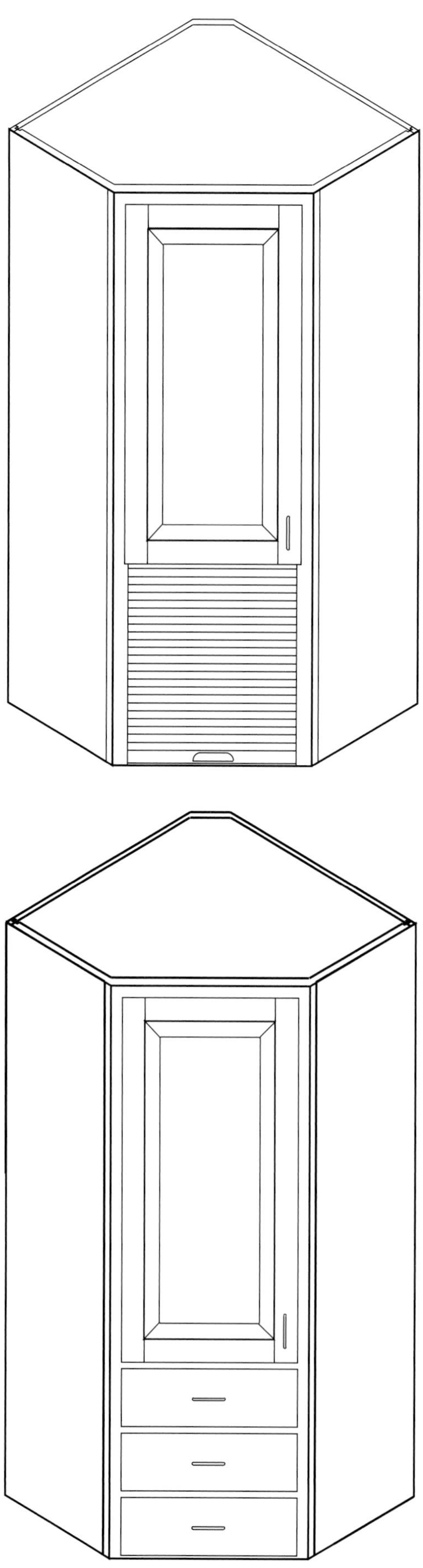

FIGURE B.29 DIAGONAL CORNER WALL CABINET WITH APPLIANCE PANTRY
DCWAP2430L • DCWAP2436L • DCWAP2442L
Diagonal corner wall cabinet with appliance storage for open corner applications.
Specify hinging L or R. Left shown.
Three heights: 30″, 36″, 42″.

FIGURE B.30 DIAGONAL CORNER WALL CABINET WITH THREE DRAWERS
DCW3D2430L • DCW3D2436L • DCW3D2442L

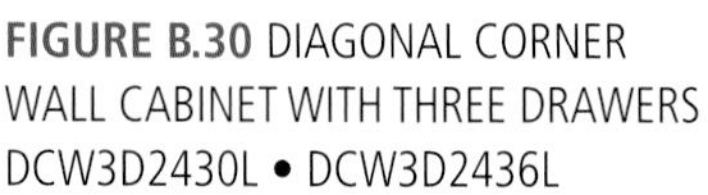

Diagonal corner wall cabinet with drawer storage for corner applications.
Specify hinging L or R. Left shown.
Three heights: 30″, 36″, 42″.

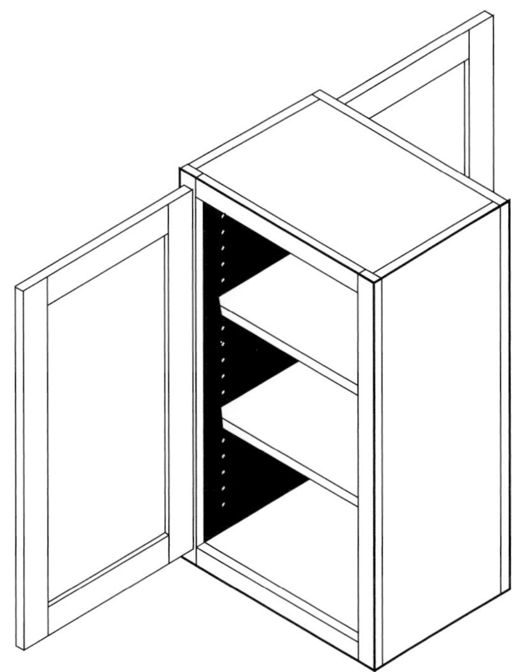

FIGURE B.31 WALL PENINSULA CABINETS
WP1224L • WP1524L • WP1824L • WP2124L • WP2424L
24″ high wall cabinets, two doors. Specify hinging L or R. Left shown.
WP1230L • WP1530L • WP1830L • WP2130L • WP2430L
30″ high wall cabinets, two doors. Specify hinging L or R. Left shown.

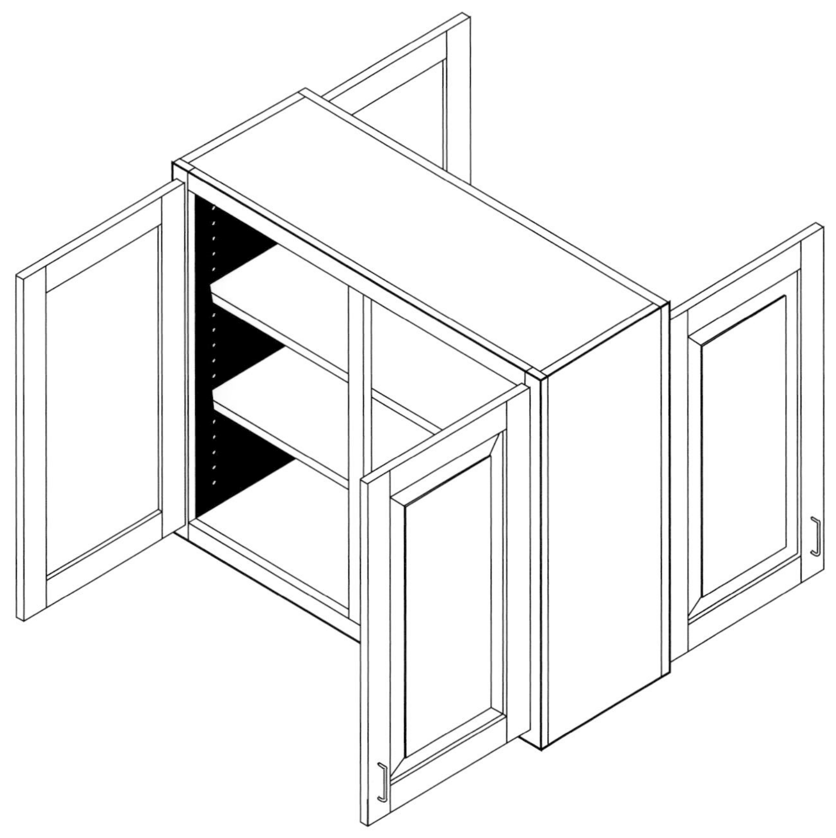

FIGURE B.32 WALL PENINSULA CABINETS
WP2424 • WP3024 • WP3624 • WP4224 • WP4824
24″ high wall cabinets, four doors.
WP2430 • WP3030 • WP3630 • WP4230 • WP4830
30″ high wall cabinets, four doors.

Tall Cabinet Nomenclature

FIGURE B.33 12″ DEEP UTILITY CABINETS
U151284L • U181284L • U241284L
Single door, 12″ deep, 84″ high utility cabinets. Specify hinging L or R. Left shown.
U151290L • U181290L • U241290L
Single door, 12″ deep, 90″ high utility cabinets. Specify hinging L or R. Left shown.
U151296L • U181296L • U241296L
Single door, 12″ deep, 96″ high utility cabinets. Specify hinging L or R. Left shown.
24″ DEEP UTILITY CABINETS
U152484L • U182484L • U242484L
Single door, 24″ deep, 84″ high utility cabinets. Specify hinging L or R. Left shown.
U152490L • U182490L • U242490L
Single door, 24″ deep, 90″ high utility cabinets. Specify hinging L or R. Left shown.
U152496L • U182496L • U242496L
Single door, 24″ deep, 96″ high utility cabinets. Specify hinging L or R. Left shown.

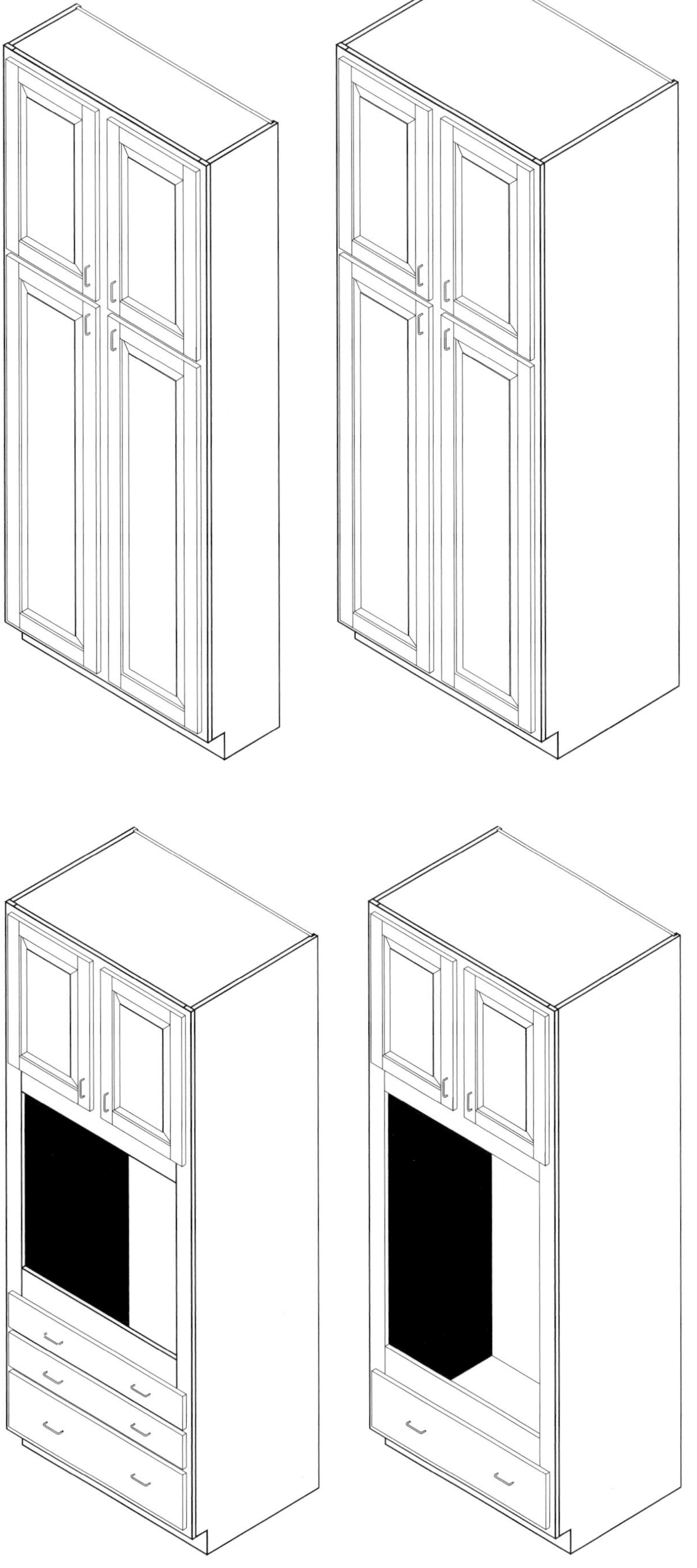

FIGURE B.34 12″ DEEP UTILITY CABINETS
U241284 • U301284 • U361284
Double door, 12″ deep, 84″ high utility cabinets.
U241290 • U301290 • U361290
Double door, 12″ deep, 90″ high utility cabinets.
U241296 • U301296 • U361296
Double door, 12″ deep, 96″ high utility cabinets.
24″ DEEP UTILITY CABINETS
U242484 • U302484 • U362484
Double door, 24″ deep, 84″ high utility cabinets.
U242490 • U302490 • U362490
Double door, 24″ deep, 90″ high utility cabinets.
U242496 • U302496 • U362496
Double door, 24″ deep, 96″ high utility cabinets.

FIGURE B.35 SINGLE OVEN CABINET
SO2784 • SO3084 • SO3384 • SO3684
Universal single oven cabinet, 84″ high.
SO2790 • SO3090 • SO3390 • SO3690
Universal single oven cabinet, 90″ high.
SO2796 • SO3096 • SO3396 • SO3696
Universal single oven cabinet, 96″ high.
DOUBLE OVEN CABINET
DO2784 • DO3084 • DO3384 • DO3684
Universal double oven cabinet, 84″ high.
DO2790 • DO3090 • DO3390 • DO3690
Universal double oven cabinet, 90″ high.
DO2796 • DO3096 • DO3396 • DO3696
Universal double oven cabinet, 96″ high.

Filler Nomenclature

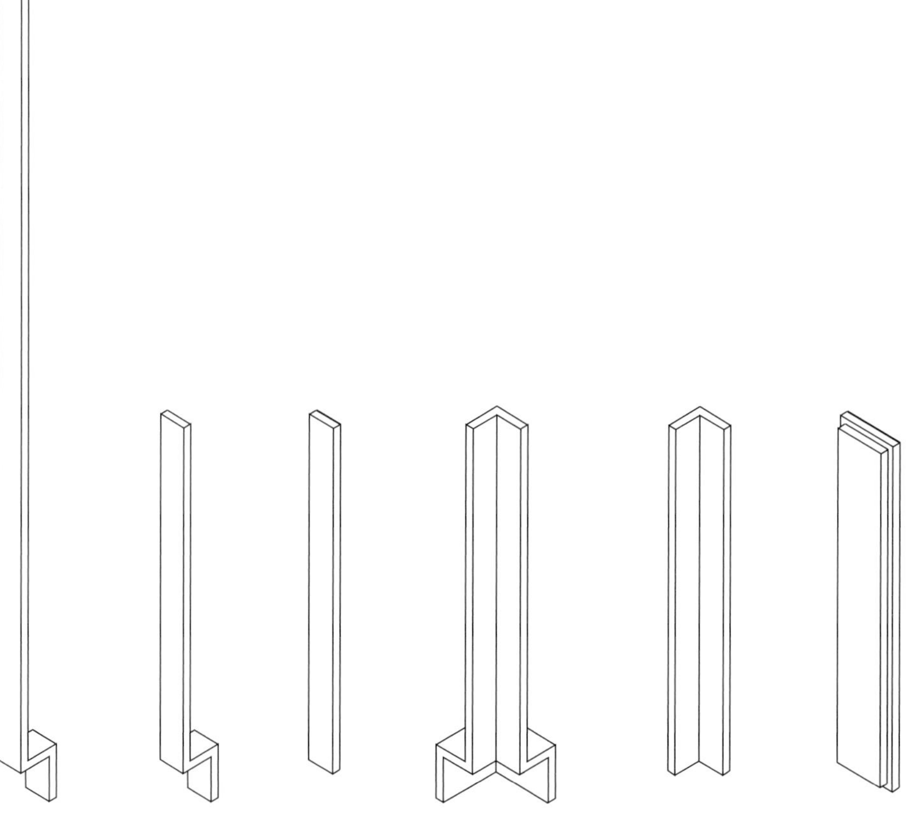

FIGURE B.36 TALL FILLERS (TF3 • TF6) 96″ high in two widths (3″ and 6″) Fillers can be cut in height and width for correct fit.
BASE FILLERS (BF3 • BF6) 34½″ high in two widths (3″ and 6″) Fillers can be cut in height and width for correct fit.
WALL FILLERS (WF3 • WF6) 30″ high in two widths (3″ and 6″) Fillers can be cut in height and width for correct fit. For taller wall fillers, order TF3 or TF6.
CORNER FILLERS (CBF3 • CWF3) Corner wall fillers can be cut in height. Both base and wall fillers can be cut in width.
FULL OVERLAYS (TF03 • TF06 • BF03 • BF06 • WF03 • WF06) Overlays are available for all standard fillers. Designed for use with full-overlay door styles. Specify door style to match door material, finish and edging profile.

Specialty Base Cabinet Nomenclature

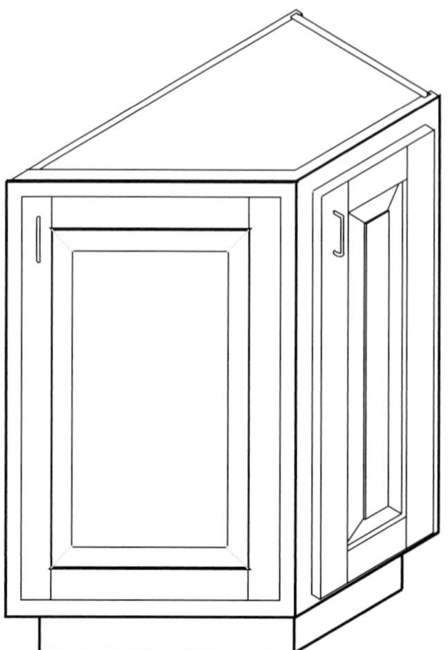

FIGURE B.37 12″ BASE END CABINETS (BEC12R) 12″ wide base end cabinet. Specify L or R. Right shown.

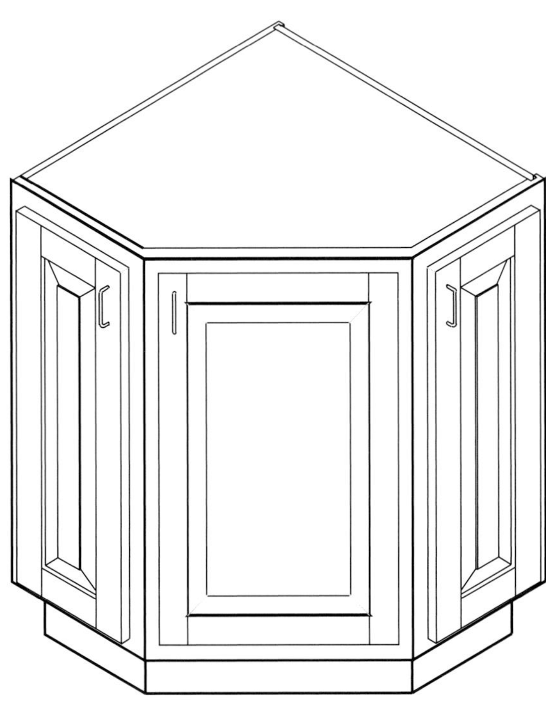

FIGURE B.38 24″ BASE END CABINETS (BEC24R) 24″ wide base end cabinet. Specify L or R. Right shown.

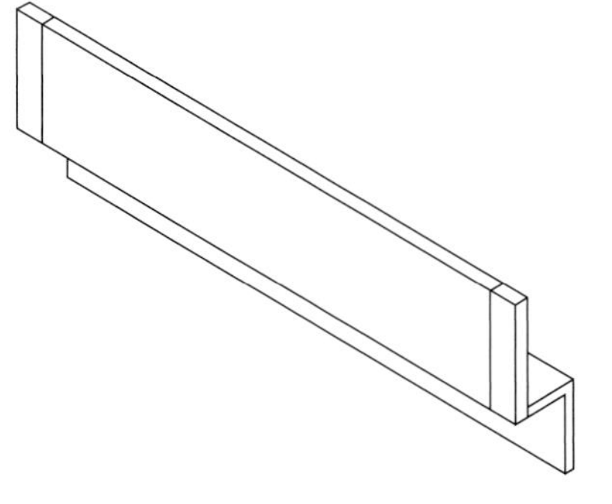

FIGURE B.39 30″ DROP-IN RANGE PANEL (RP30) A 30″ wide panel placed below a drop-in range. Height is adjusted to fit a drop-in range. Toekick is attached.

FIGURE B.40 END PANEL (BEP-3R SHOWN) (WEP • WEP1 1/2 • WEP 3) Wall end panels 12″ deep and 30″ high without toekick notch shown above. Reverse for R or L. (BEP • BEP1½ • BEP 3) A base panel usually placed beside a dishwasher at the end of a base cabinet run. Stile widths of ¾″, 1½″ and 3″. Larger sizes can be reduced in width. Specify L or R. Right shown. (TEP • TEP1½ • TEP 3) A tall panel usually placed beside a refrigerator. Widths of ¾″, 1½″ and 3″. The two larger sizes can be trimmed to a smaller dimension. No toekick. Reverse R or L.

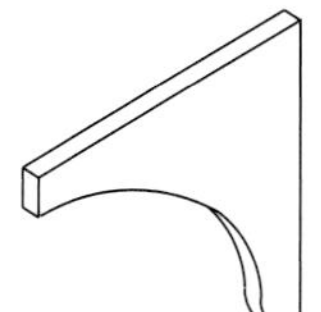

FIGURE B.41 COUNTERTOP BRACKET (CORBEL) (CB) 12″ ´ 12" bracket to support countertop.

Specialty Wall Cabinet Nomenclature

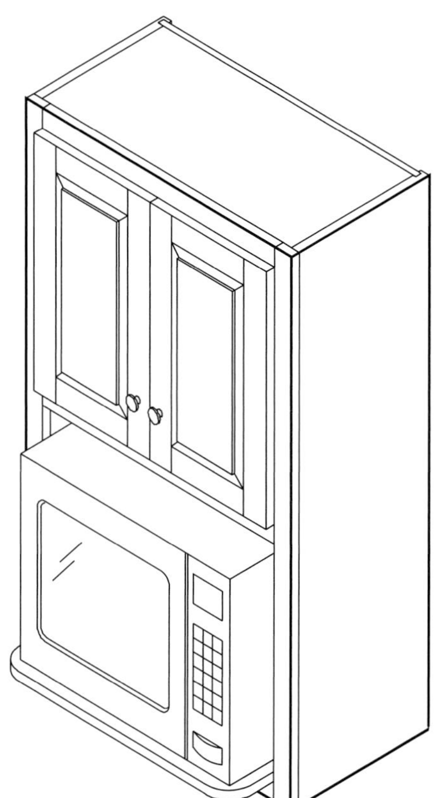

FIGURE B.42 MICROWAVE WALL CABINET (MWC2434 • MWC2734 • MWC3034) Microwave shelf with storage above. Use with 30″ high wall cabinets. (MWC2440 • MWC2740 • MWC3040) Microwave shelf with storage above. Use with 36″ high wall cabinets. (MWC2446 • MWC2746 • MWC3046) Microwave shelf with storage above. Use with 42″ high wall cabinets.

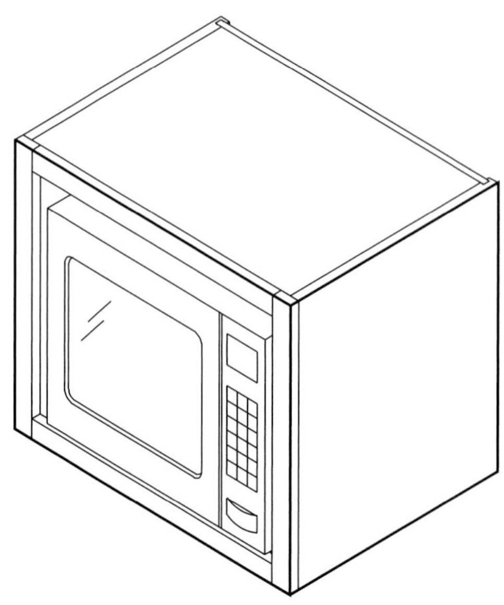

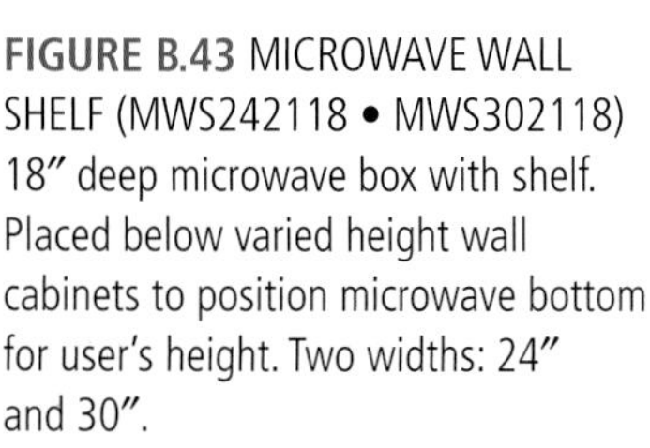

FIGURE B.43 MICROWAVE WALL SHELF (MWS242118 • MWS302118) 18″ deep microwave box with shelf. Placed below varied height wall cabinets to position microwave bottom for user's height. Two widths: 24″ and 30″.

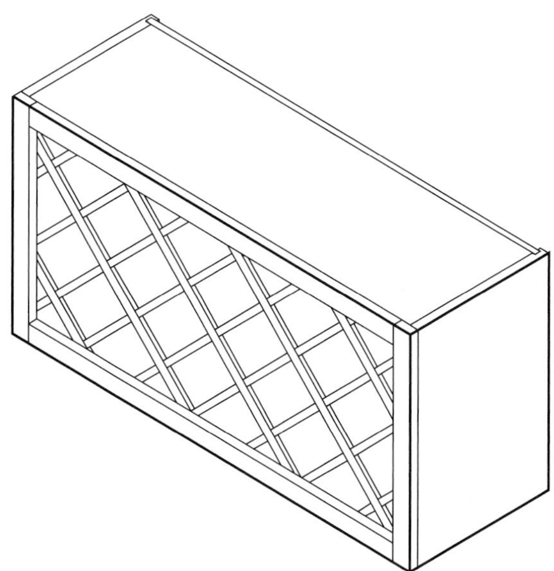

FIGURE B.44 WINE RACK WALL CABINET (WR3018 • WR3618) 18″ high wall cabinet for bottle storage. Can be mounted vertically. (WR3024 • WR3624) 24″ high wall cabinet for bottle storage. Can be mounted vertically. (WR3030 • WR3630) 30″ high wall cabinet for bottle storage.

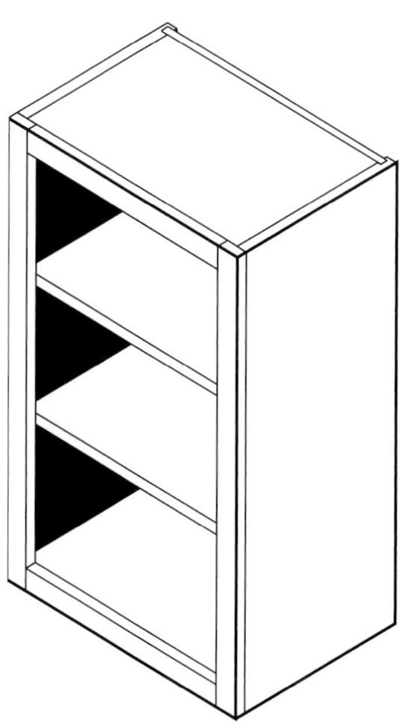

FIGURE B.45 30″ HIGH WALL OPEN CABINET (WO930 • WO1230 • WO1530 • WO1830 • WO2130 • WO2430) 30″ high wall cabinets without a door.

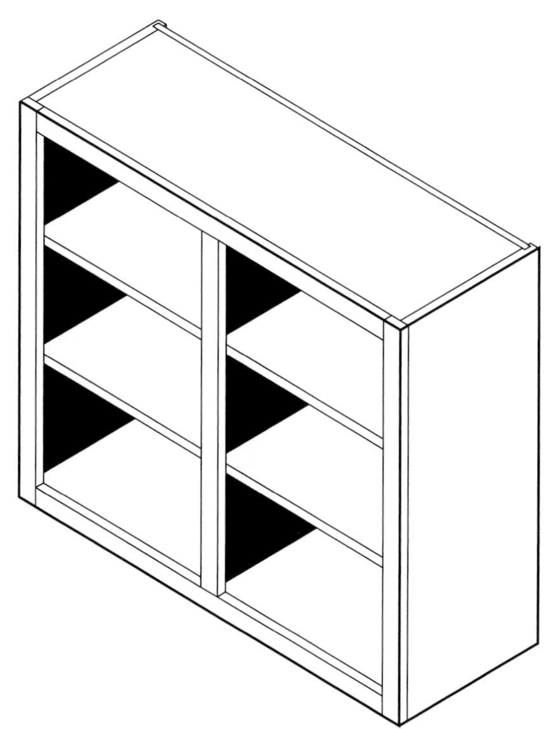

FIGURE B.46 30″ HIGH WALL OPEN CABINET (WO2430 • WO2730 • WO3030 • WO3330 • WO3630 WO3930 • WO4230 • WO4530 • WO4830) 30″ high wall cabinets without doors.

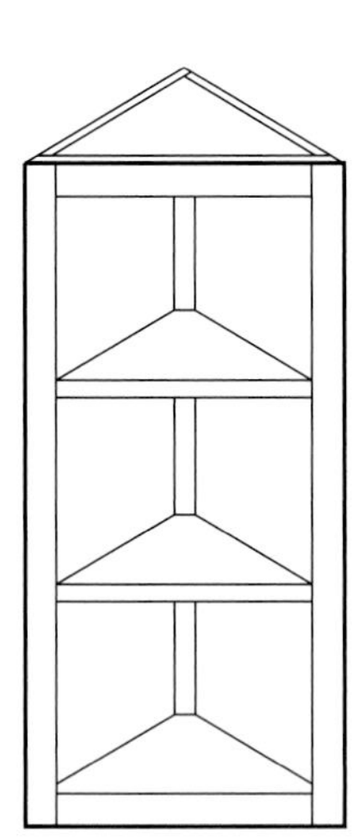

FIGURE B.47 WALL END CABINETS (WEC1230R) 30″ high wall end cabinets. Order with or without door. Specify L or R. (WEC1236R) 36″ high wall end cabinets. Order with or without door. Specify L or R. (WEC1242R) 42″ high wall end cabinets. Order with or without door. Specify L or R.

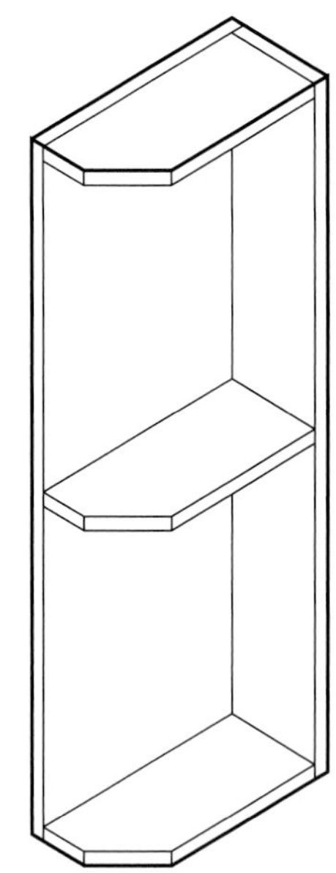

FIGURE B.48 6″ WIDE WALL "WHATNOT" SHELF (WNS630R) 30″ high, 6″ wide whatnot shelf. Specify L or R. Right shown. (WNS636R) 36″ high, 6″ wide whatnot shelf. Specify L or R. Right shown. (WNS642R) 42″ high, 6″ wide whatnot shelf. Specify L or R. Right shown.

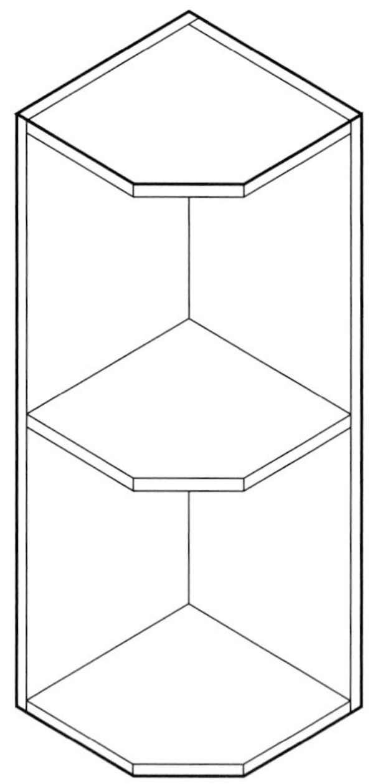

FIGURE B.49 12″ WIDE WALL "WHATNOT" SHELF (WNS1230R) 30″ high, 12″ wide whatnot shelf. Specify L or R. Right shown. (WNS1236R) 36″ high, 12″ wide whatnot shelf. Specify L or R. Right shown. (WNS1242R) 42″ high, 12″ wide whatnot shelf. Specify L or R. Right shown.

FIGURE B.50 APPLIANCE GARAGE (CAP24) 18″ high appliance storage cabinet placed below diagonal corner wall cabinets. (AP24 • AP30 • AP36) 18″ high appliance storage cabinet placed below standard wall cabinets.

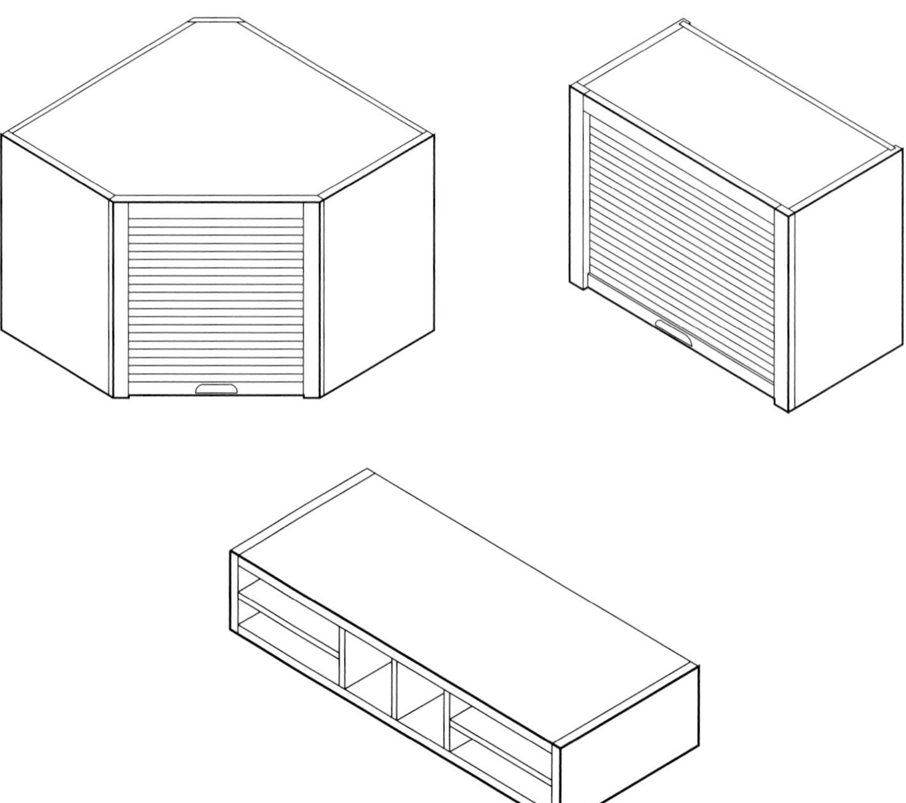

FIGURE B.51 PIGEONHOLE STORAGE (PH30 • PH36 • PH42) 6″ high miscellaneous storage accessory suspended below wall cabinets.

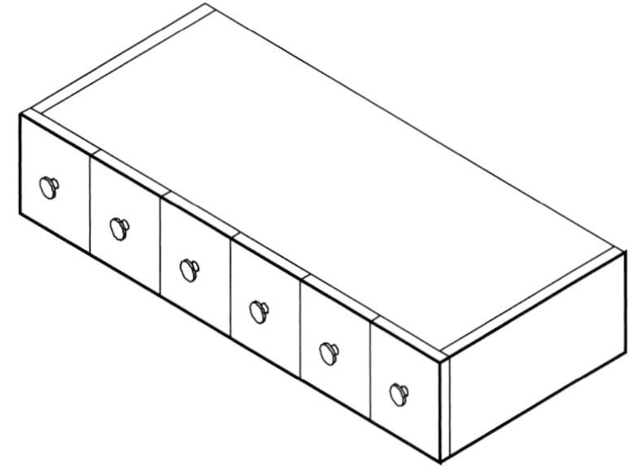

FIGURE B.52 SPICE DRAWERS (SD18 • SD24 • SD30 • SD36 • SD42) 6″ high drawer storage accessory suspended below wall cabinets. Can be mounted vertically.

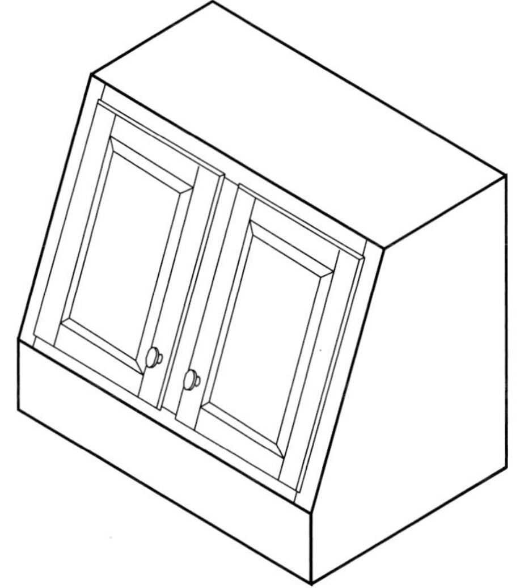

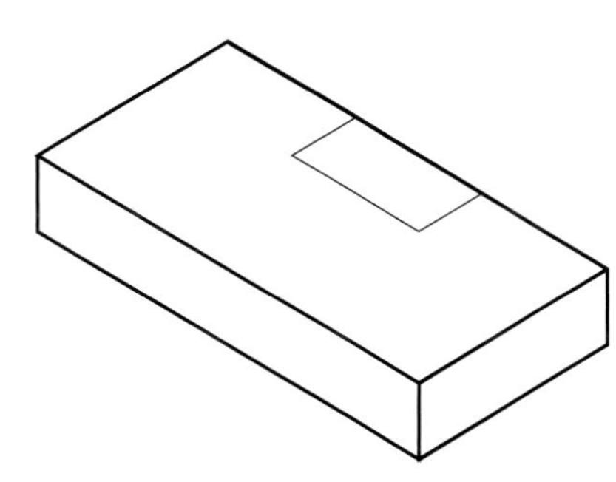

FIGURE B.53 RANGE HOOD (RH30 • RH36) 24″ high wood cover for metal liner and hood assembly. Can also be combined with a light kit for a decorative, non-venting installation over a downdraft-cooking surface. Metal liner included. Order duct or ductless vent kits or light unit separately.

VALANCE BOARDS

Valance boards are placed between or under cabinets to hide light fixtures. These 4½″ high boards are available in 6″ increments from 24″ to 96″ and can be reduced in width for exact fit as needed.

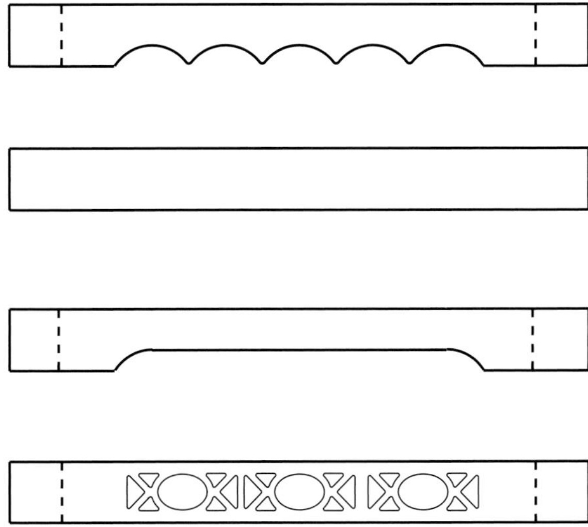

FIGURE B.54 VAL-T. Traditional style shown. Reduce width at both ends equally.

FIGURE B.55 VAL-C. Contemporary style shown.

FIGURE B.56 VAL-A. Arched style shown. Reduce width at both ends equally.

FIGURE B.57 VAL-EC. English Country style shown. Reduce width at both ends equally.

GENERIC BATHROOM NOMENCLATURE

Vanity Base Cabinet Nomenclature

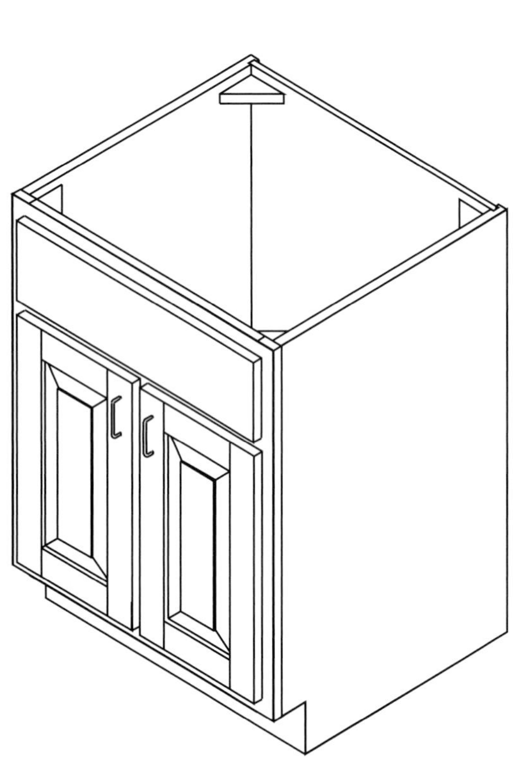

FIGURE B.58 VANITY SINK BASE (VSB24 • VSB27 • VSB30) 21″ deep, 32½″ high. Vanity sink base cabinet with butt-doors and 1/2 shelf.

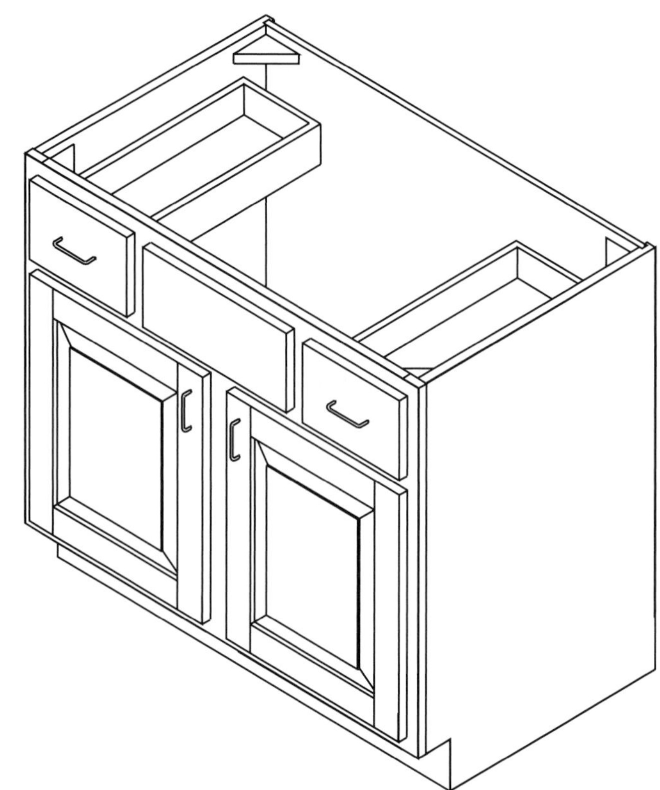

FIGURE B.59 VANITY SINK BASE (VSB36 • VSB39 • VSB42 • VSB45 • VSB48) 21″ deep, 32½″ high. Vanity sink base cabinet with two drawers and ½ shelf.

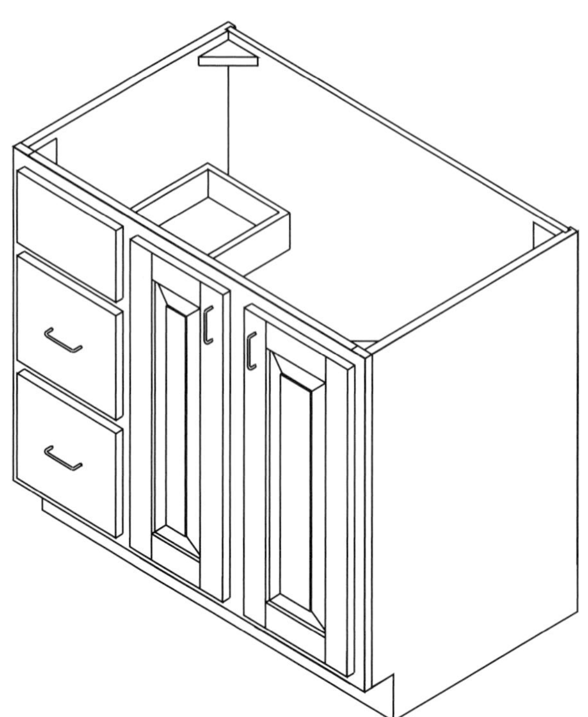

FIGURE B.60 VANITY SINK DRAWER BASE (VSDB24* • VSDB30 • VSDB36 • VSDB42 • VSDB48) 21″ deep, 32½″ high. Vanity sink drawer base cabinet with two drawers on one side only. Specify drawer location right or left (left shown). Full height doors.

*Butt doors.

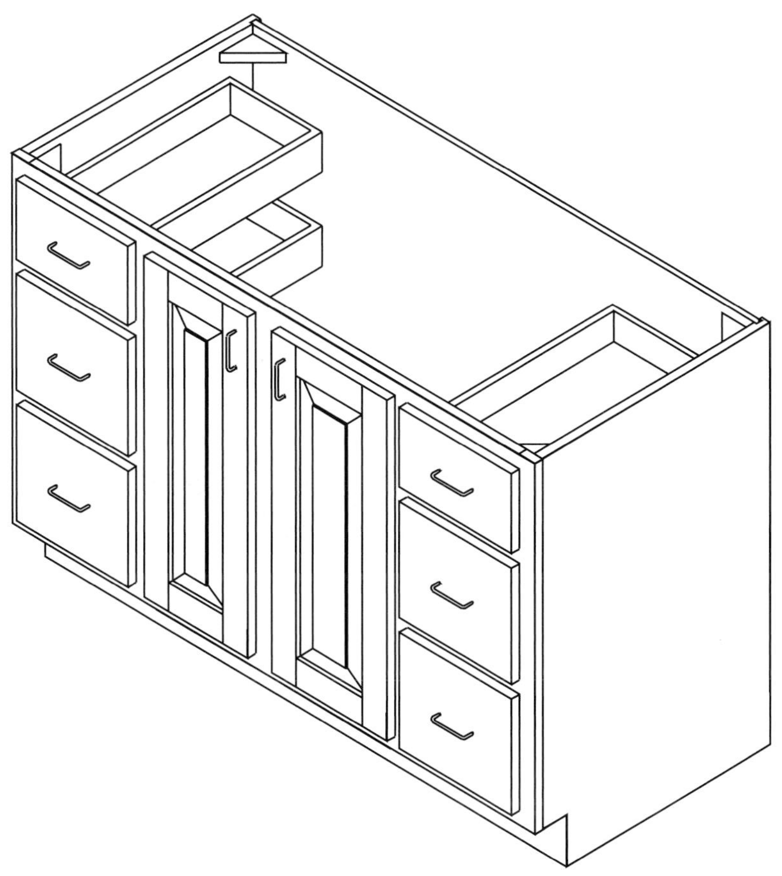

FIGURE B.61 VANITY SINK DOUBLE DRAWER BASE (VSDDB48 • VSDDB54 • VSDDB60*) 21″ deep, 32½″ high. Vanity sink double drawer base cabinet with three drawers on each side.
*VSDDB60 is trimmable to 59″ wide.

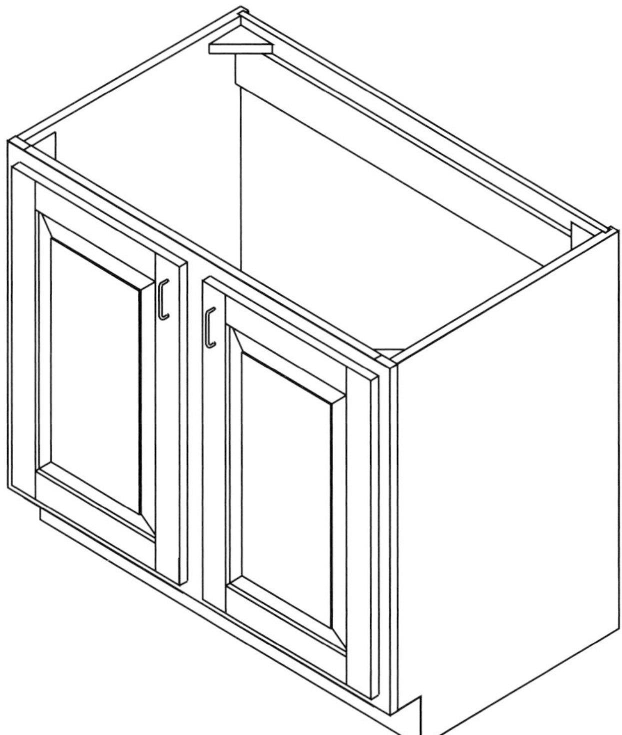

FIGURE B.62 VANITY FULL HEIGHT SINK BASE (VFHSB24* • VFHSB30* • VFHSB36 • VFHS42 • VFHS48) 21″ deep, 32½″ high. Vanity sink base cabinet with full height doors and ½ shelf.
*Butt doors.

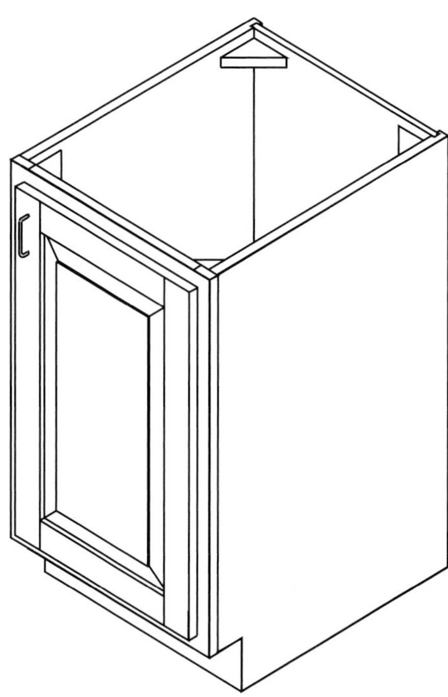

FIGURE B.63 VANITY MINI-SINK BASE (VMSB1618R) 16″ deep, 32½″ high. Vanity sink base cabinet with full height door. Minimal use for tight spaces. Specify hinging R or L (right shown).

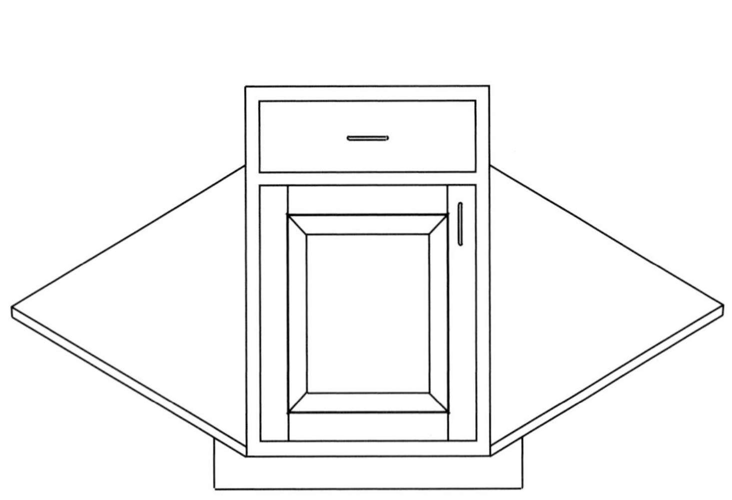

FIGURE B.64 VANITY CORNER SINK FRONT (VCSF33L) 21″ deep, 32½″ high. Requires 33″ of wall space in each direction. Vanity Sink Front with floor. Specify hinging R or L (left shown).

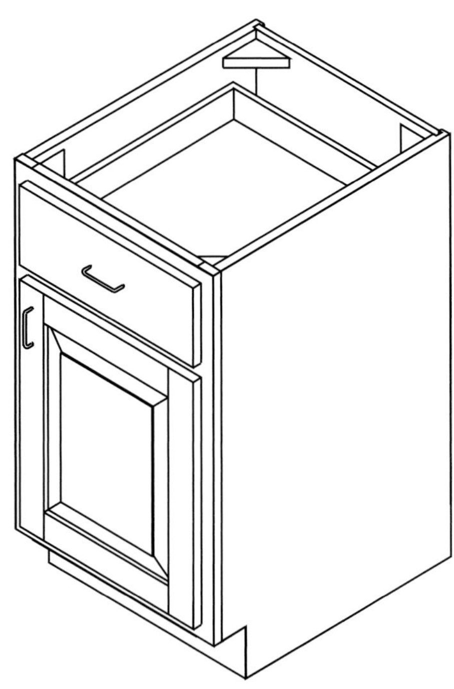

FIGURE B.65 VANITY BASE (VB12R • VB15R • VB18R • VB21R • VB24R) 21″ deep, 32½″ high. Base cabinet with drawer and ½ shelf. Specify hinging R or L (right shown).

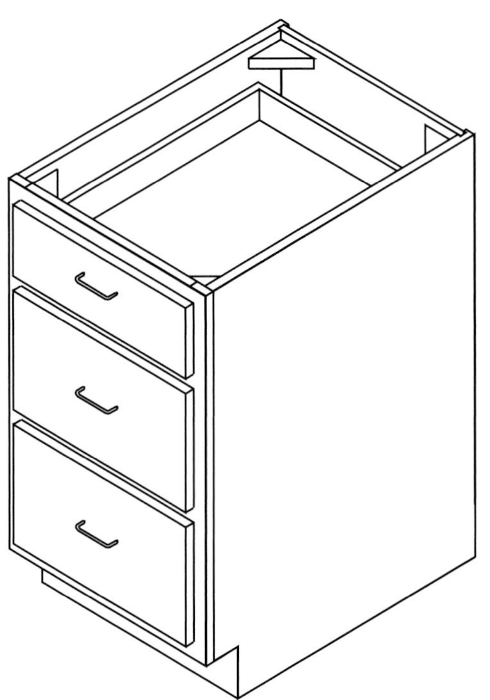

FIGURE B.66 VANITY DRAWER BASE (VDB12 • VDB15 • VDB18 • VDB21 • VDB24) 21″ deep, 32½″ high. Base cabinet with three drawers.

Vanity Tall Cabinet Nomenclature

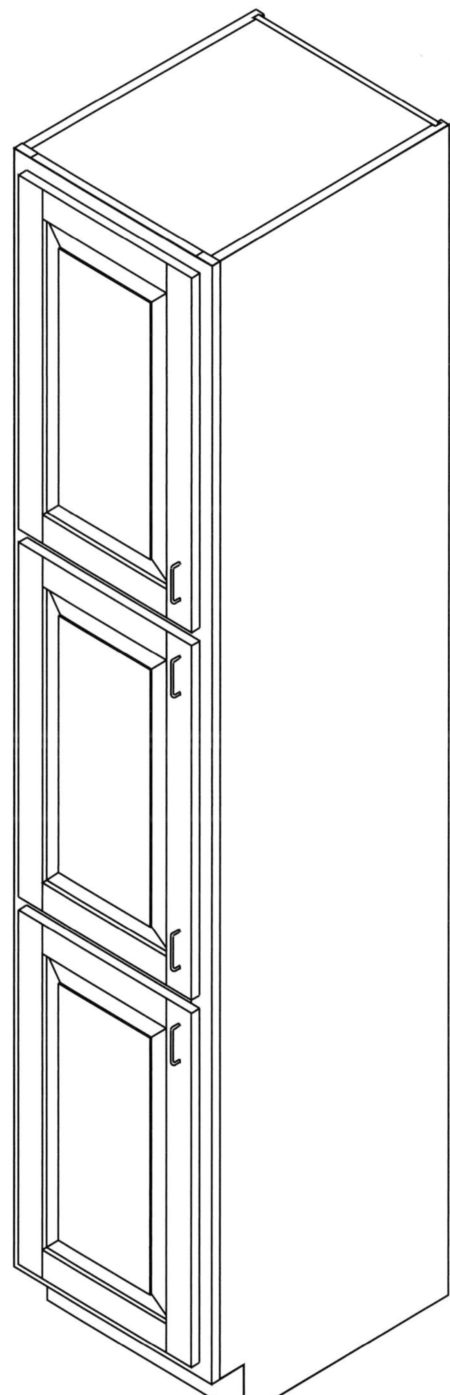

FIGURE B.67 VANITY LINEN CABINET (VLC182184L • VLC182190L • VLC182196L) 21″ deep, 84″, 90″ and 96″ high. Tall cabinet with three doors. Specify hinging R or L (left shown).

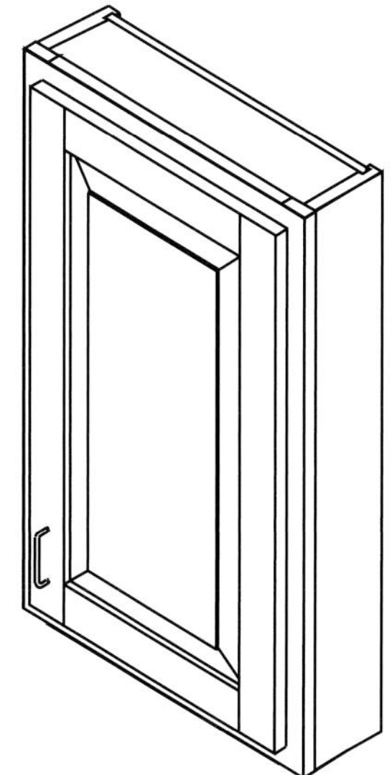

FIGURE B.68 VANITY WALL CABINET (VWC12R • VWC15R • VWC18R • VWC21R • VWC24R) 5″ deep, 30″ high. Specify hinging R or L (right shown).

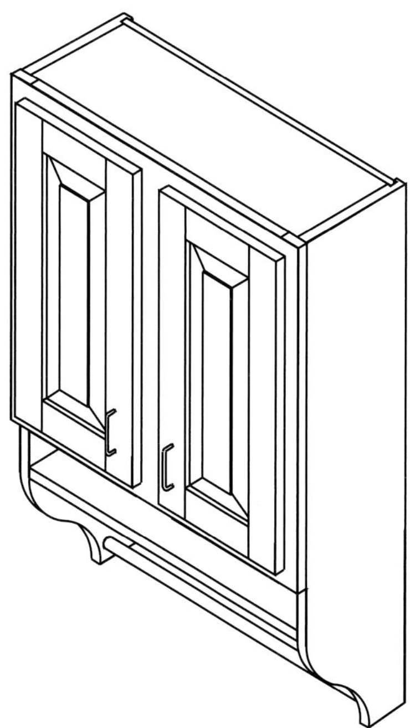

FIGURE B.69 VANITY TOILET WALL CABINET (VTWC24) 9″ deep, 30″ high.

Miscellaneous Vanity Cabinet Nomenclature

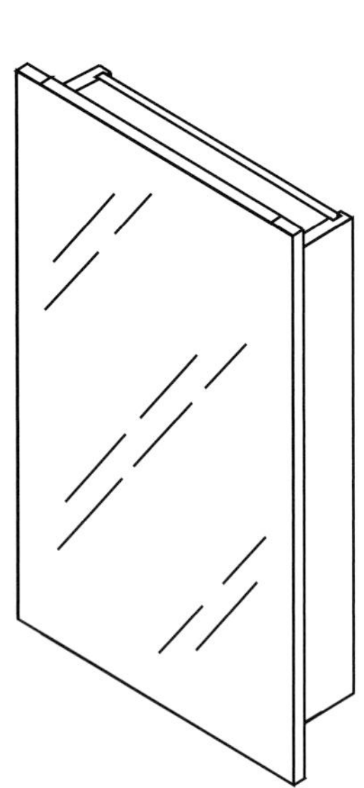

FIGURE B.70 VANITY MEDICINE CABINET (VMC16) Reversible. Can be flush mounted or installed between studs 16″ on center.

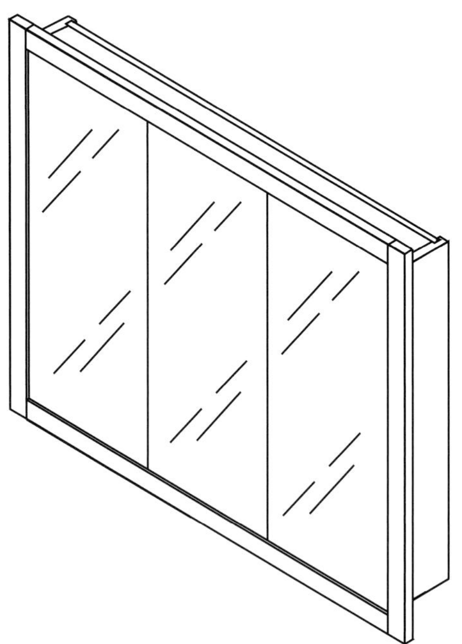

FIGURE B.71 VANITY TRI-VIEW MIRROR (VTVM24 • VTVM30 • VTVM36 • VTVM42 • VTVM48) 4″ deep, 30″ high. Can be flush mounted or recessed.

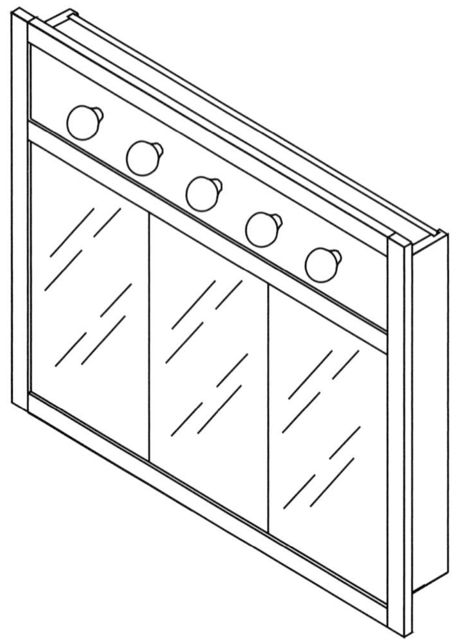

FIGURE B.72 VANITY TRI-VIEW MIRROR/LIGHT BAR (VTVMLBC24 • VTVMLBC30 • VTVMLBC36 • VTVMLBC42 • VTVMLBC48). Contemporary lighting (shown). Can be flush mounted or recessed. 4″ deep, 30″ high. (VTVMLBT24 • VTVMLBT30 • VTVMLBT36 • VTVMLBT42 • VTVMLBT48). Traditional lighting. Can be flush mounted or recessed. 4″ deep, 30″ high.

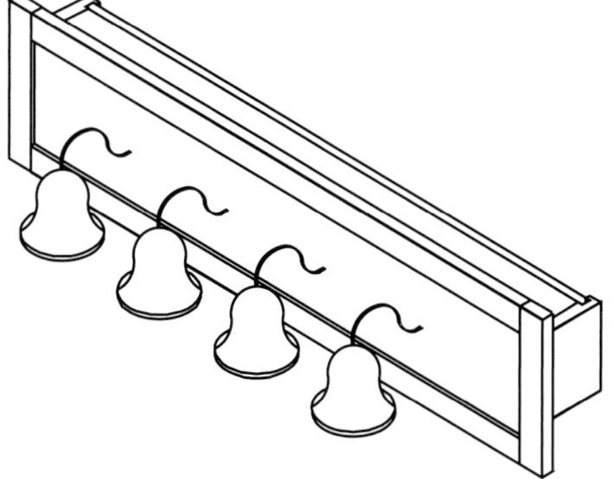

FIGURE B.73 VANITY TRADITIONAL LIGHT BAR (VLBT24 • VLBT30 • VLBT36 • VLBT42 • VLBT48). Traditional lighting. Can be flush mounted or recessed. 4″ deep, 7¾″ high.

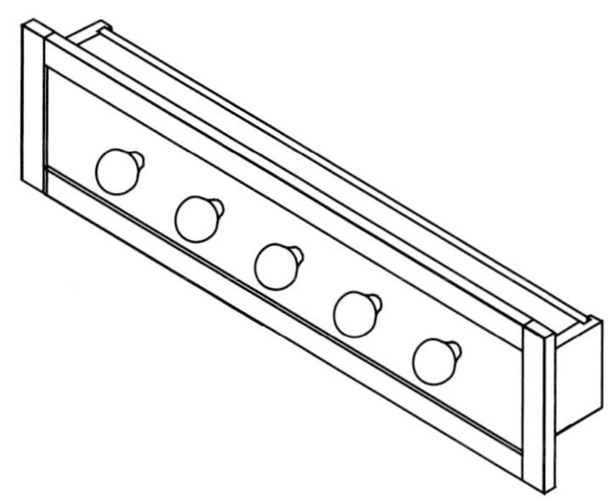

FIGURE B.74 VANITY CONTEMPORARY LIGHT BAR (VLBC24 • VLBC30 • VLBC36 • VLBC42 • VLBC48). Contemporary lighting. Can be flush mounted or recessed. 4″ deep, 7¾″ high.

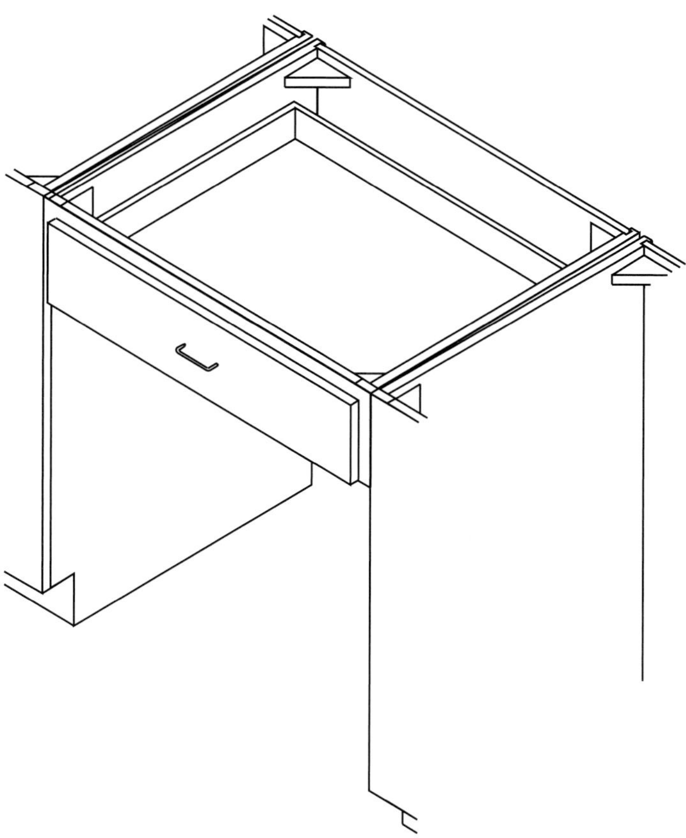

FIGURE B.75 VANITY KNEE DRAWER (VKD27 • VKD30 • VKD33) 21″ deep, 6″ high. All drawers are 3″ trimmable in width.

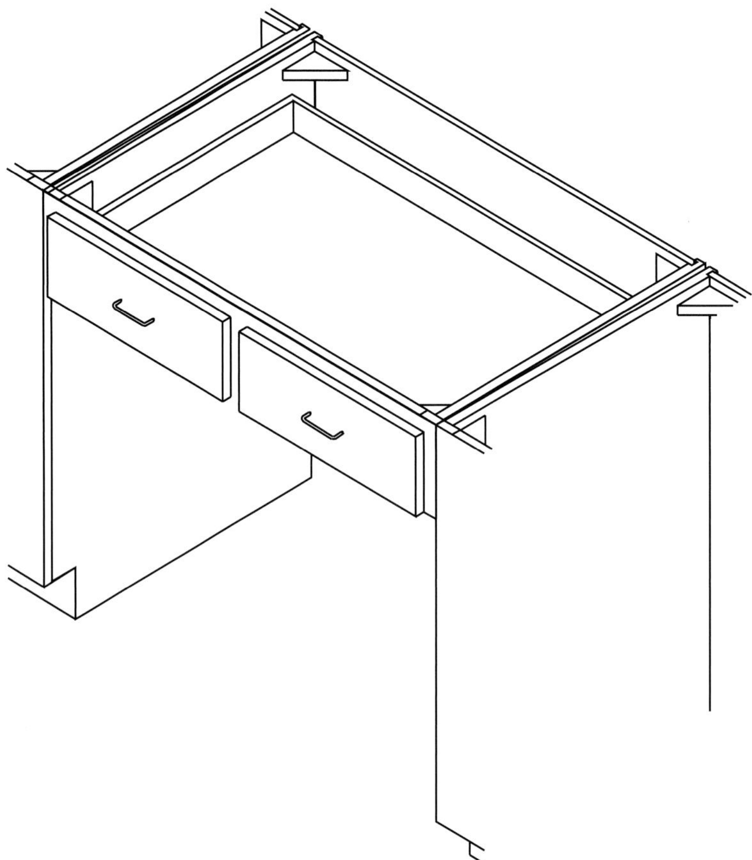

FIGURE B.76 VANITY KNEE DRAWER (VKD36) 21″ deep, 6″ high • Two drawers. 3″ trimmable in width.

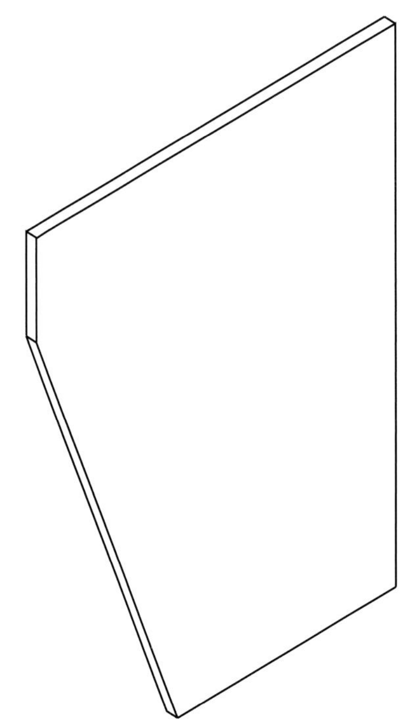

FIGURE B.77 VANITY TAPERED END PANEL (VTEP) 21″ deep, (13½″ at base), 32½″ high.

Filler Nomenclature

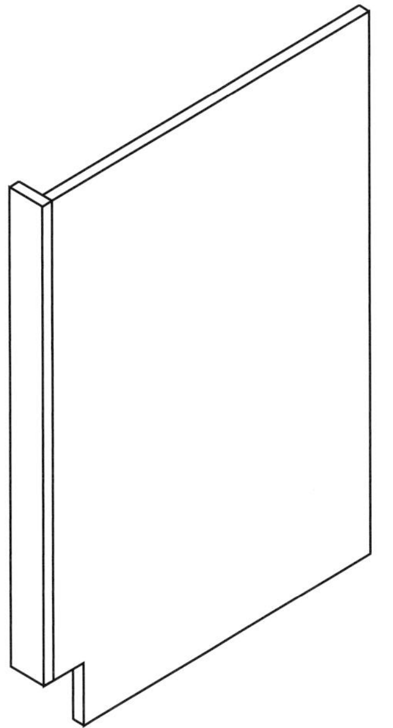

FIGURE B.78 VANITY END PANEL (VEP • VEP1½ • VEP3) 21″ deep, 32½″ high. Cut toekick on site as required.

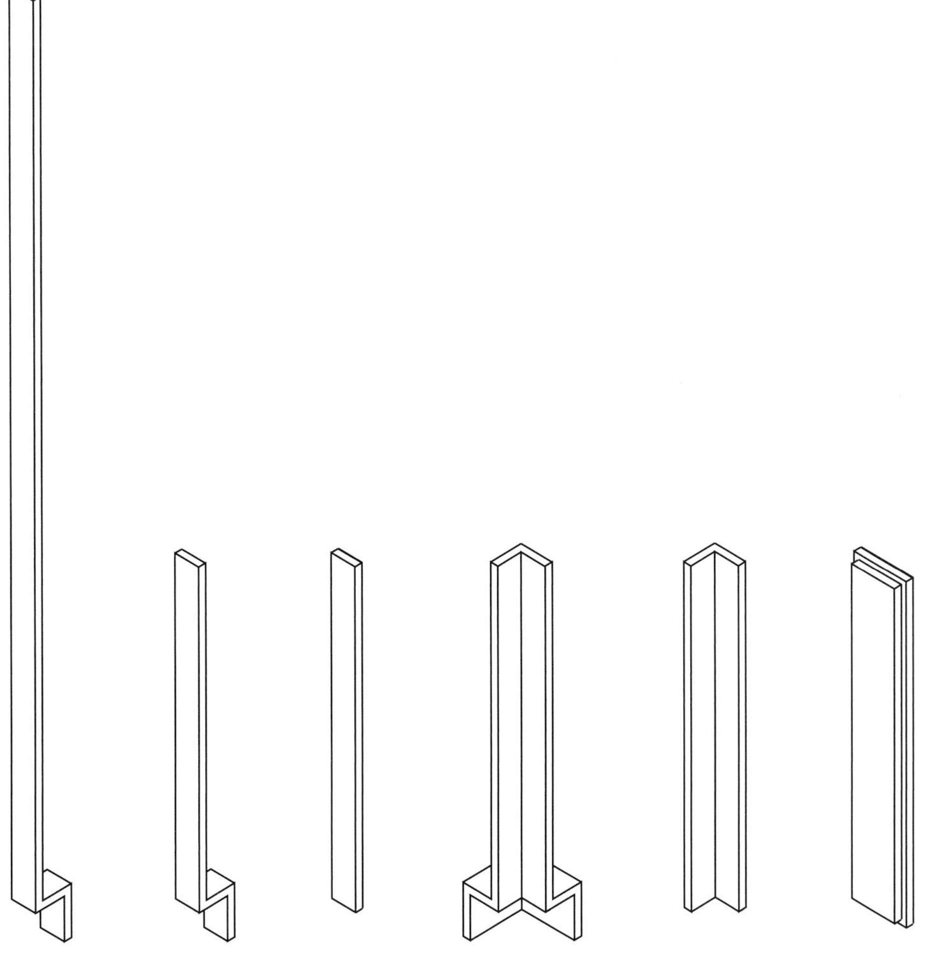

FIGURE B.79 TALL FILLERS (TF3 • TF6) 96″ high in two widths (3″ and 6″). Fillers can be cut in height and width for correct fit.
VANITY BASE FILLERS (VBF3 • VBF6) 32½″ high in two widths (3″ and 6″). Fillers can be cut in height and width for correct fit.
WALL FILLERS (WF3 • WF6) 30″ high in two widths (3″ and 6″). Fillers can be cut in height and width for correct fit. For taller wall fillers order TF3 or TF6.
CORNER FILLERS (CBF3 • CWF3) Corner wall fillers can be cut in height. Both base and wall fillers can be cut in width.

FILLER OVERLAYS (TFO3 • TFO6 • FO3 • BFO6 • WFO3 • WFO3) Overlays are available for all standard fillers. Designed for use with full-overlay door styles. Specify door style to match door material, finish and edging profile.

FRAMELESS CABINET NOMENCLATURE—METRIC

(Courtesy of Poggenpohl)

FIGURE B.80 1 DRAWER 1 FRONT PULL-OUT WITH 1 INTERNAL DEEP DRAWER (U35 • U45 • U50 • U60 • U90)

FIGURE B.81 FRONT PULL-OUT WITH 1 INTERNAL SHALLOW DRAWER AND 1 INTERNAL DEEP DRAWER (U35 • U45 • U50 • U60 • U90)

FIGURE B.82 3 DRAWER UNIT WITH FRONT HEIGHTS: 13 cm + 26 cm + 39 cm (U35 • U45 • U50 • U60 • U80 • U90 • U100 • U120)

FIGURE B.83 4 DRAWER UNIT WITH FRONT HEIGHTS: 13 cm + 13 cm + 26 cm + 26 cm (U35 • U45 • U50 • U60 • U80 • U90 • U100 • U120)

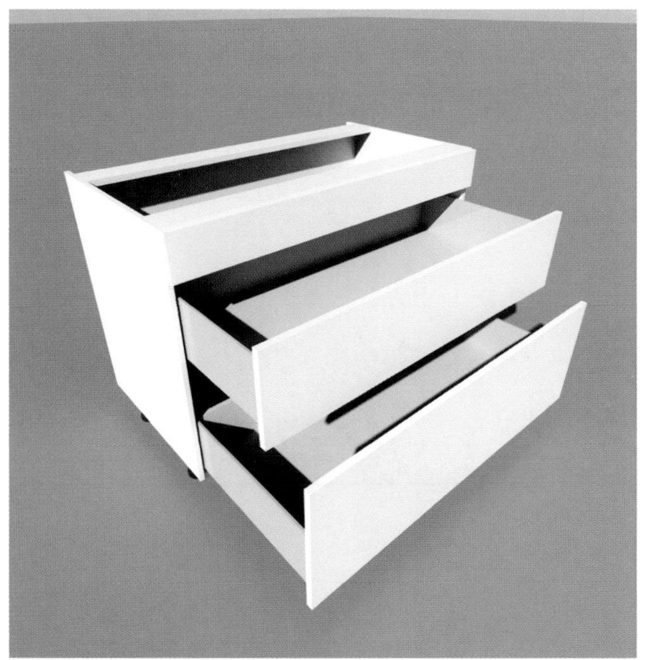

FIGURE B.84 BASE UNIT FOR COOKTOP (UK60 • UK90 • UK100 • UK120)

FIGURE B.85 SINK BASE UNIT WITH 2 DOORS (US70 • US80 • US90 • US100 • US120)

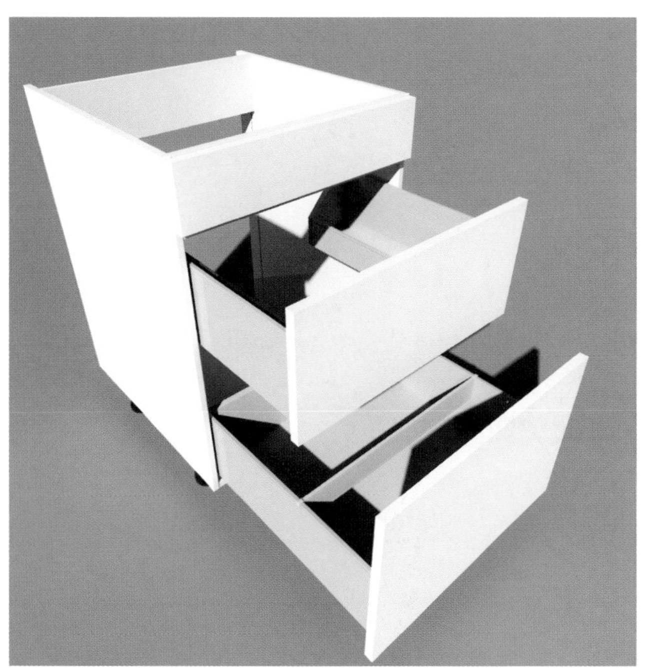

FIGURE B.86 SINK BASE UNIT WITH 1 DEEP DRAWER AND 1 "U" SHAPE DRAWER (US60 • US90 • US100 • US120)

FIGURE B.87 WASTE UNIT WITH DRAWER ON TOP (U45 • U60)

Additional Frameless Cabinets

FIGURE B.88 FOLDING FLAP

FIGURE B.89 FULLY LOADED PANTRY

FIGURE B.90 HINGED 1 DOOR

FIGURE B.91 HINGED 2 DOOR

FIGURE B.92 L SHAPE CORNER

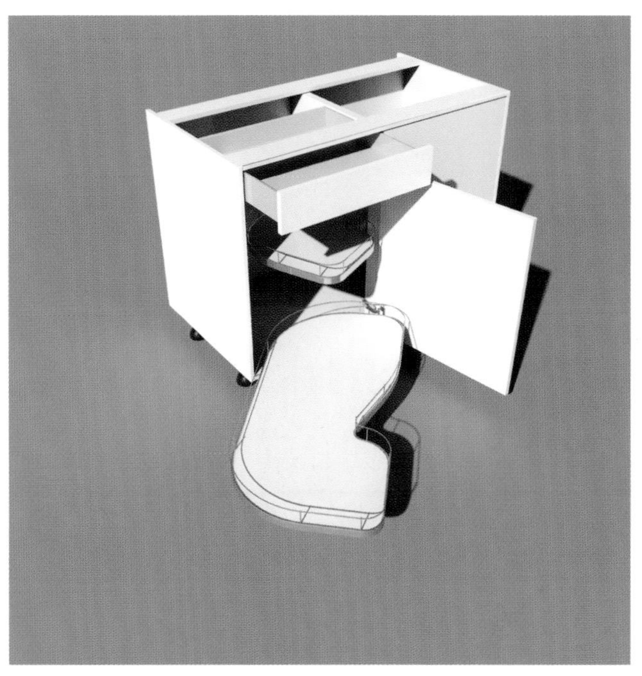

FIGURE B.93 LE MANS CORNER

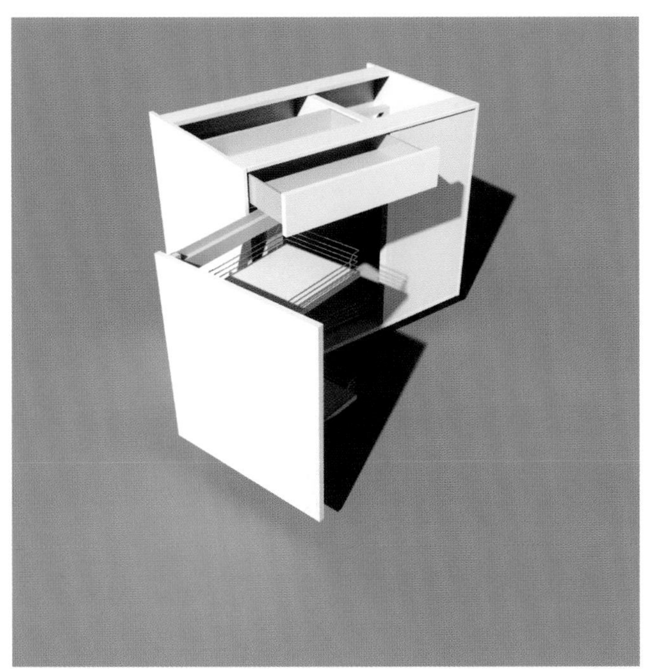

FIGURE B.94 MAGIC CORNER

FIGURE B.95 PULL OUT PANTRY

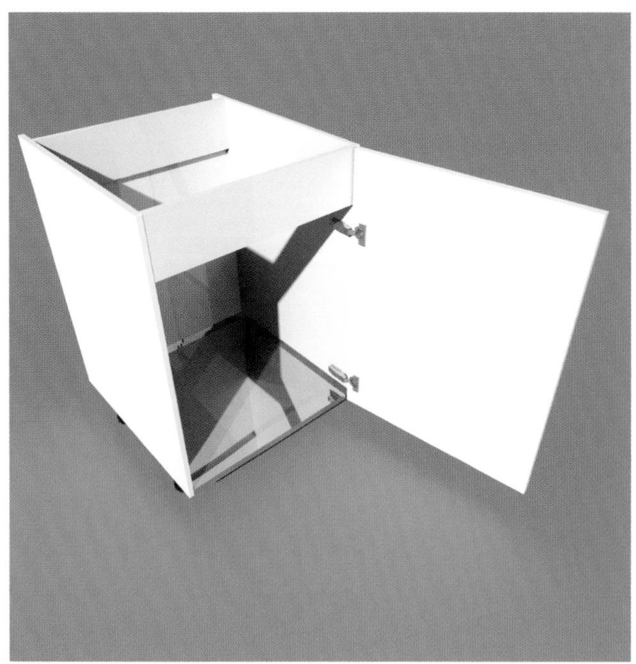

FIGURE B.96 SINK 1 HINGED DOOR

FIGURE B.97 TALL APPLIANCE HOUSING

APPENDIX

Metric Conversions

The standard NKBA kitchen and bathroom drawings in the United States should be drawn at a scale of ½ inch equals 1 foot (½″ = 1′–0″). However, in many parts of the world, the metric system has replaced the imperial (inches) system of measuring. When using the metric system to draft kitchen and bathroom drawings, plans are drafted in mm. The plans show the scale as 1:20.

Converting inches to metrics can be a challenge because the grids of materials do not convert simply or rationally. It is important to note that an exact conversion can result in incorrect measurements. There are two methods for converting inches to metric: the soft conversion (actual metric) and the hard conversion (rounded metric).

Hard metric is the use of "normalized" metric values, and soft metric is the literal mathematical conversion of imperial to metric. For example, 36 inches = 914 mm is soft metric; 36 inches = 900 mm is hard metric. The building industry uses hard conversions from imperial to metric to make the metric units more rational and easier to work with.

METRIC KITCHEN AND BATH DRAWINGS

Metric drawings for kitchen and bath design should be drawn in millimeters (mm). This means that 1″ = 25.4 mm. Figure B.1 can be used as a reference when converting imperial (standard) measures to metric ones (mm).

To calculate inches to millimeters, simply multiply inches by 25.4. To calculate millimeters to inches, divide mm by 25.4.

According to Public Works and Government Services Canada (www.tpsgc-pwgsc.gc.ca):

> The International System of Units (S.I.) must be used to prepare all drawings. The unit for linear dimensioning is the millimetre, except where the scope of the drawing requires the use of the metre, such as in site plans. Integers shall indicate millimetres, e.g. 435, 4300. Decimal numbers with three decimal places shall indicate metres, e.g., 5.435, 4.300. All other dimensions and notations should be followed by the unit symbol.

MEASUREMENT UNITS: FOR NKBA DRAWINGS

METRIC CONVERSION: Inches to mm   1 INCH = 25.4 mm

IMPERIAL (Inches)	ACTUAL METRIC (mm)	ROUNDED METRIC (mm)
1/16"	2 mm	2 mm
1/8"	3 mm	3 mm
3/16"	5 mm	5 mm
1/4"	6 mm	6 mm
5/16"	8 mm	8 mm
3/8"	10 mm	10 mm
7/16"	11 mm	11 mm
1/2"	13 mm	13 mm
9/16"	14 mm	14 mm
5/8"	16 mm	16 mm
11/16"	18 mm	18 mm
3/4"	19 mm	19 mm
13/16"	21 mm	21 mm
7/8"	22 mm	22 mm
15/16"	24 mm	24 mm
1"	25 mm	25 mm
2"	51 mm	50 mm
3"	76 mm	75 mm
6"	152 mm	150 mm
9"	229 mm	225 mm
12"	305 mm	300 mm
15"	381 mm	375 mm
18"	457 mm	450 mm
21"	533 mm	525 mm
27"	689 mm	675 mm
30"	762 mm	750 mm
33"	838 mm	825 mm
36"	914 mm	900 mm
48"	1219 mm	1200 mm
54"	1371 mm	1375 mm
60"	1524 mm	1525 mm
84"	2133 mm	2100 mm
96"	2438 mm	2400 mm

Courtesy of Corey S. Klassen, CKD

MEASUREMENT UNITS:

METRIC CONVERSION: Inches to mm   1 INCH = 25.4 mm

IMPERIAL (Inches)	ACTUAL METRIC (mm)
3"	76 mm
6"	152 mm
9"	229 mm
12"	305 mm
15"	381 mm
18"	457 mm
21"	533 mm
27"	686 mm
30"	762 mm
33"	838 mm
36"	914 mm
39"	991 mm
42"	1067 mm
45"	1143 mm
48"	1219 mm
51"	1295 mm
54"	1372 mm
57"	1448 mm
60"	1524 mm
63"	1600 mm
66"	1676 mm
69"	1753 mm
72"	1829 mm
75"	1905 mm
78"	1981 mm
81"	2057 mm
84"	2134 mm
87"	2210 mm
90"	2286 mm
93"	2362 mm
96"	2438 mm
99"	2515 mm
102"	2591 mm

Courtesy of Corey S. Klassen, CKD

FIGURE C.1

The chart in Figure C.2 shows the conversion of inches to centimeters (cm). Most of the building products in the kitchen and bath design industry use centimeters. For example, some countertop materials use centimeters for thickness and some cabinet lines will use centimeters. Figure B.3 shows the conversion of cabinet sizes from inches to millimeters. It is good to know how to covert both millimeters and centimeters to inches and vice versa.

METRIC EQUIVALENTS

Length

10 millimeters = 1 centimeter (cm)
10 centimeters = 1 decimeter
10 decimeters = 1 meter (m)
10 meters = 1 decameter
100 meters = 1 hectometer
1000 meters = 1 kilometer (km)

Linear Drawing Measurements

1 millimeter = .03937″
1 centimeter = .3937″
1 meter = 39.37″
1″ = 25.4 mm
1″ = 2.54 cm
1″ = .0254m

MEASUREMENT UNITS: ***Optional centimeters***

METRIC CONVERSION: Inches to cm 1 INCH = 2.54 cm

IMPERIAL (Inches)	ACTUAL METRIC (cm)
3"	7.62 cm
6"	15.24 cm
9"	22.86 cm
12"	30.48 cm
15"	38.10 cm
18"	45.72 cm
21"	53.34 cm
27"	68.58 cm
30"	76.20 cm
33"	83.82 cm
36"	91.44 cm
39"	99.06 cm
42"	106.68 cm
45"	114.30 cm
48"	121.92 cm
51"	129.54 cm
54"	137.16 cm
57"	144.78 cm
60"	152.40 cm
63"	160.02 cm
66"	167.64 cm
69"	175 .26 cm
72"	182.88 cm
75"	190.5 cm
78"	198.12 cm
81"	205.74 cm
84"	213.36 cm
87"	220.98 cm
90"	228.60 cm
93"	236.22 cm
96"	243.84 cm
99"	251.46 cm
102"	259.08 cm

FIGURE C.2 Conversion of inches to centimeters.

12″ = 304.8 mm
12″ = 30.48 cm
12″ = .3048 m

Area

100 sq. millimeters = 1 sq. centimeter
100 sq. centimeters = 1 sq. decimeter
100 sq. decimeters = 1 sq. meter
100 sq. meters = 1 acre
10,000 sq. meters = 1 hectare
100 hectares = 1 sq. kilometer

Square Measure

1 sq. inch = 6.4516 sq. centimeters
1 sq. foot = 9.29034 sq. decimeters
1 sq. yard = .836131 sq. meter
1 acre = .40469 hectare
1 sq. mile = 2.59 sq. kilometers

Cubic Measure

1 cubic inch = 16.3872 cubic centimeters
1 cubic foot = .028318 cubic meters
1 cubic yard = .76456 cubic meters

CASE DIMENIONS:

SIZE CHART FOR STANDARD DIMENI SONS : Inches to mm 1 INCH = 25.4 mm

	CASE	NOMINAL	ACTUAL IMPERIAL	ACTUAL METRIC		NOMINAL	ACTUAL IMPERIAL	ACTUAL METRIC
DEPTHS	Base, Wall	24	24"	610 mm	WIDTHS	6	6"	152 mm
	Vanity, Vanity Full Height	21	21"	533 mm		9	9"	229 mm
	Base, Wall, Tall	15	15"	381 mm		12	12"	305 mm
	Wall, Tall	12	12"	305 mm		15	15"	381 mm
						18	18"	457 mm
HEIGHTS	Wall	6	6"	152 mm		21	21"	533 mm
	Wall	12	12"	305 mm		24	24"	610 mm
	Wall	15	15"	381 mm		27	27"	686 mm
	Wall	18	18"	457 mm		30	30"	762 mm
	Wall	21	21"	533 mm		33	33"	383 mm
	Wall, Vanity	24	24"	610 mm		36	36"	914 mm
	Wall	27	27"	686 mm		39	39"	991 mm
	Wall, Base, Vanity Full Height	30	30"	762 mm		42	42"	1067 mm
	Wall	36	36"	914 mm		45	45"	1143 mm
	Wall	39	39"	991 mm		48	48"	1219 mm
	Wall	42	42"	1067 mm		54	54"	1371 mm
	Wall Counter	48	48"	1219 mm		57	57"	1449 mm
	Wall Counter	54	54"	1371 mm		60	60"	1524 mm
	Wall Counter	60	60"	1524 mm				
	Tall	84	79 ½"	2019 mm				
	Tall	90	85 ½"	2172 mm				
	Tall	96	91 ½"	2324 mm				

All actual dimensions exclude a standard 4 ½" (114 mm) toe -kick. Actual manufacturer dimensions may vary.

FIGURE C.3 Example of cabinet conversions in mm.
Courtesy of Corey S. Klassen, CKD

Long Measure

1 inch = 25.4 millimeters
1 foot = .3 meter
1 yard = .914401 meter
1 mile = 1.609347 kilometers

Commonly Used Measurements for Kitchen Landing Areas, Work Isles, and Preparation Centers

Inches to millimeters using soft metric conversion

9 inches = 229 millimeters
12 inches = 305 millimeters
15 inches = 381 millimeters
18 inches = 457 millimeters
21 inches = 533 millimeters
24 inches = 610 millimeters
36 inches = 900 millimeters
42 inches = 1067 millimeters
48 inches = 1219 millimeters

Inches to millimeters using hard metric conversion

9 inches = 225 millimeters
12 inches = 300 millimeters
15 inches = 375 millimeters
18 inches = 450 millimeters
21 inches = 525 millimeters
24 inches = 600 millimeters
36 inches = 900 millimeters
42 inches = 1100 millimeters
48 inches = 1200 millimeters

NKBA PLANNING GUIDELINES CHECKLISTS

The NKBA Kitchen and Bathroom Planning Guidelines Checklists are a useful reference when planning your design. These checklists, based on the NKBA Kitchen and Bathroom Planning Guidelines with Access Standards, include recommended measurements shown in imperial (inches) and metric equivalents (millimeters) (soft conversion) or meters where applicable. Depending on your client's needs, your design plan may meet or exceed the recommended guidelines.

Kitchen Planning Guidelines Checklist

1. Door entry is 32″ (813 mm) clear opening
2. Door does not interfere with safe operation of appliance
   Appliance doors do not interfere with one another
3. Distance between 3 primary work centers is no more than 26′ (7.9 m)
   No leg less than 4′ (1.2 m) or more than 9′ (2.7 m)
   No leg intersects island/peninsula or other obstacle by no more than 12″ (305 mm)
4. Tall obstacle does not separate two primary work centers
5. No major traffic should cross through the work triangle
6. Work aisle is 42″ (1067 mm) for one cook, 48″ (1219 mm) for two cooks
7. Walkway width is 36″ (914 mm)
8. 32″ (813 mm) behind seated diner if no traffic
   36″ (914 mm) behind seated diner to edge past
   44″ (1118 mm) behind seated diner to walk past

9. 30″ (762 mm) high table/counter: allow 24″ (610 mm) wide × 18″ (457 mm) deep per diner
36″ (914 mm) high counter: allow 24″ (610 mm) wide × 15″(381 mm) deep per diner
42″ (1067 mm) high counter: allow 24″ (610 mm) wide × 12″ (305 mm) deep per diner
10. One sink adjacent to or across from cooking surface and refrigerator
11. Sink landing area if level counter height: 24″ (610 mm) and 18″ (457 mm) Sink landing area if varied counter height: 24″ (610 mm) and 3″ (76 mm)
12. Continuous countertop 36″ (914 mm) wide × 24″(610 mm) deep next to sink for prep area
13. Dishwasher within 36″ (914 mm) of sink edge 21″ (533 mm) standing space to side of dishwasher
14. Two waste receptacles: one at sink; one for recycling
15. Auxiliary Sink countertop frontage: 18″ (457 mm) and 3″ (76 mm)
16. Refrigerator landing area: 15″ (381 mm) on handle side or on either side of a side-by-side, or above, or within 48″ (1219 mm) across from the refrigerator
17. Cooking surface landing area: 12″ (305 mm) and 15″ (381 mm) at height of cooking surface
On island or peninsula include 9″ (229 mm) behind the cooking surface
18. 24″ (610 mm) between cooking surface and protected noncombustible surface
30″ (762 mm) between cooking surface and an unprotected/combustible surface
Follow manufacturer's specifications for a microwave/hood application
19. Correctly sized, ducted ventilation system, at least 150 cfm
Minimum required exhaust rate for ducted hood: 100 cfm
20. Cooking surface not under operable window
No flammable window treatments over cooking surface
Fire extinguisher located near exit of kitchen
21. Microwave bottom 3″ (76 mm) below user's shoulder, between 54″ (1372 mm) and 15″ (381 mm) off the finished floor
22. Microwave landing area: 15″ (381 mm) above, below, or adjacent to handle side
23. Oven landing area: 15″ (381 mm) beside or within 48″ (1219 mm) across from oven
24. Combine landing areas by using longest measure and adding 12″ (305 mm)
25. Total countertop frontage: 158″ long (4013 mm), 24″(610 mm) deep, with 15″ (381 mm) clearance above
26. Counters have clipped or rounded edges
27. Shelf/drawer frontage total: 1400″ (35.5 m) for small kitchen (>150 sq. ft.) 1700″ (43 m) for medium kitchen (151-350 sq. ft.)
2000″ (50 m) for large kitchen (< 351 sq. ft.)
28. Shelf/drawer frontage at sink: 400″ (10 m) for small kitchen (> 150 sq. ft.)
480″ (12 m) for medium kitchen (151-350 sq. ft.)
560″ (14 m) for large kitchen (< 351 sq. ft.)
29. One corner cabinet includes a functional storage device
30. GFCI outlets at countertop receptacles
31. Task lighting at work surfaces
General lighting with at least one switch at entry
Window/skylight area equals 8% of kitchen square footage

Bathroom Planning Guidelines Checklist

1. Door entry is 32″ (813 mm) clear opening
2. Door does not interfere with fixture
Door does not interfere with cabinet
3. Ceiling height over fixtures is 80″ (2032 mm)
4. 30″ (762 mm) clear space at lavatory
21″ (533 mm) clear space at lavatory
30″ (762 mm) clear space at tub
21″ (533 mm) clear space at bathtub
30″ (762 mm) clear space at shower

24″ 610 mm) clear space at shower
30″ (762 mm) clear space at toilet/bidet
21″ (533 mm) clear space at toilet

5. Single lavatory centered at 20″ (508 mm)
Single lavatory centered on 15″ (381 mm) or 4″ (102 mm) from wall
6. Double lavatory centered on 36″ (914 mm)
Double lavatory centered on 30″ (762 mm), or 4″ (102 mm) apart
7. Lavatory between 32″ (813 mm) and 43″ (1092 mm) high
8. Counter edges clipped or rounded
9. Shower size at least 36″ × 36″ (914 × 914 mm)
Shower size is 30″ × 30″ (762 × 762 mm) to 36″ × 36″ (914 × 914 mm)
10. Shower controls 38″–48″ (965 –1219 mm), useable inside and outside the spray
Bathtub controls between tub rim and 33″ (838 mm)
11. Tub/shower controls pressure balanced and/or thermostatic mixing
12. Shower includes seat 17″–19″ (432–483 mm) above shower floor, 15″ (381 mm) deep,
Shower seat does not infringe on shower size
13. Waterproof material in shower 3″ (762 mm) above showerhead rough-in
Waterproof material extends to 72″ (1829 mm) from finished floor
14. Grab bars at tub/shower areas 33″–36″ (813–914 mm) from floor
Walls reinforced for grab bars at tub/shower
15. Tempered glass used at tub/shower door, enclosure less than 60″ (1524 mm) and at window and doors below 18″ (457 mm) from floor
16. Shower door opens out or no shower door
17. No steps at tub
18. Slip resistant flooring
19. Access panels installed per manufacturers' instructions
20. Toilet/bidet placed 18″ (457 mm) on center
Toilet/bidet placed 15″–18″ (381–457 mm) on center
21. Toilet compartment is 36″ × 66″ (914 × 1676 mm)
Toilet compartment is between 30″ × 60″ 762 × 1524 mm) and 36″ × 66″ (914 × 1676 mm)
22. Storage 15″ and 48″ (381 and 1219 mm) above the floor
23. Full height mirrors or placed at user height, maximum 40″ (1016 mm) above the floor
Toilet paper 8 –12″ (203–305 mm) to front of toilet, centered 15″–48″ (381–1219 mm) above the floor
Accessories should be 15″ to 48″ (381 to 1219 mm) above the floor
24. GFCI receptacles located where needed, 15″ to 48″ (381 to 1219 mm) above the floor.
25. General and task lighting provided, at least one switch at entry
Switches 15″–48″ (381–1219 mm) above the floor and operable with minimal effort
Task lighting beside vanity mirror
26. Mechanical exhaust vented to the outside, with control 15″–48″ (381–1219 mm) above the floor, operable with minimal effort, easy to read, and with minimal noise pollution.
27. Supplemental heat source, with thermostats at 15″–48″ (381–1219 mm) above the floor and operable with minimal effort.

Glossary

A

AFF:
Abbreviation for "above finished floor." The finished floor surface is the point of where height measurements are taken.

A size paper:
Standard size of paper 8½″ × 11″ for architectural size. Metric size in mm is A4; 21 × 297.

Acute angle:
Angle less than 90 degrees.

Adjustable triangle:
Adjustable tool used for drawing angles ranging from 0 to 45 degrees.

Aesthetics:
How pleasing the item or design looks.

AIA:
American Institute of Architects (professional organization).

Alphabet of lines:
Refers to the standardized line types developed for the design industry.

Ambient light:
General lighting which is a soft indirect light that fills the entire room with illumination.

Ampere (amp):
The measure of electrical current.

ANSI:
Abbreviation for American National Standards Institute.

Architect's scale:
Triangular drafting tool used to draw lines at a reduced scale. Typical scale for NKBA drawings is 1/2″– 1′– 0″ which translates as ½″ will represent 1′ on a drawing.

Architectural symbol:
Standardized symbols used to represent items such as materials, electrical items, appliances, etc.

Architectural Graphics Standards:
Standards developed for the architecture/design industry.

Ashlar stonework:
This stonework consists of cut or squared stones mostly rectangular in shape of various sizes placed in an exact pattern.

Axonometric:
Drawing which shows three surfaces of an object. Types of axonometric drawings include the isometric, dimetric and the trimetric. The isometric is commonly used in design and all lines are drawn at a 30 degree angle.

B

B size paper:
Standard size of paper 11″ × 17″ for architectural size. Metric in mm is A3; 297 × 420.

Base cabinets:
Base cabinets sit on the floor and come in many different sizes and configurations. Standard depth is 24″ (610 mm) and height is 34½″ (876 mm). The standard countertop height is 1½″ (38 mm). The standard height of base cabinet and countertop is 36″ high (914 mm). Base cabinets have a standard toe kick at bottom which is 4″ to 5″ high (102-127 mm) and 3″ deep (76 mm).

Bill of material:
A component of the design project that lists all the materials needed for the project.

Bird's eye view:
The view while looking down on the floor from a view above around ceiling height.

Blueprint (blue line):
Drawing that is a blue line drawing printed on white paper or white lines on a blue background. This older method used a Diazo machine which used ammonia and special paper to create these prints. Today modern copiers and plotters can print multicolored lines on white paper or any other desired color of paper.

Borderlines:
Very heavy lines used to form a boundary for the drawing. The NKBA vellum comes pre-printed with the borderline on the sheet.

Break line:
Line type used to denote the part of the drawing which was removed or not drawn in its entirety which shows the continuation of the item break line is on.

Bubble diagram:
Part of the programming process which uses bubbles to represent the activities in the space to be designed. The preliminary design stage which helps to develop the floor plan. The circles or "bubbles" show the spatial relationship of proposed areas.

Building code:
Legal requirements designed to protect the public by providing guidelines for structural, electrical, plumbing and mechanical areas of a structure. One must make sure to comply with their local building code.

Building information modeling (BIM):
Software that creates 3D models and is linked to a database of project information. Items are interactive and update in accordance with changes made.

Bulkhead:
Referred to as a soffit, is the space closed off above the wall cabinets to the ceiling. Sizes can vary and project out past the depth of the cabinets. A bulkhead/soffit can also be constructed on the ceiling of kitchen or bathroom as an architectural design feature, often used for special lighting treatments.

Byte:
A basic unit of measurement of information storage in computer science, one single unit of information.

C

C size paper:
Standard size of paper that is 17″ x 22″ for architectural size. Metric size in mm is A2; 420x594.

CAD (Computer aided drafting):
Vector based software that allows drafters to draw two-dimensional and three-dimensional drawings.

Carbon monoxide (CO) detector:
A device that detects dangerous concentrations of carbon monoxide.

Casement window:
Has sashes hinged at the side so the window swings outward.

Casing:
The trim around a window or door that covers the space between the jamb and rough framing.

Catalog:
In regards to a CAD software program, these are images with information of products to be used while using the computer aided program. There are generic and manufacturer's catalogs available.

Ceiling height:
Distance from the finished floor to the finished ceiling.

Centerline (CL):
Type of line that indicates the center point of an item. With NKBA drawings, centerline the appliances and fixtures for accurate placement. This is a line with long and short dashes.

Central processing unit (CPU):
Processor of the computer that processes the information so your computer can perform and run the applications and all operations.

Certified Bath Designer (CBD):
Professional certification through the NKBA. (Refer to NKBA.org)

Certified Kitchen Designer (CKD):
Professional certification through the NKBA. (Refer to NKBA.org)

CGI (computer graphics imagery):
A three-dimensional picture created with three-dimensional computer graphics software.

Circuit:
A path through which electricity flows from a source to one or more devices and then returns to the source.

Circuit breaker:
A safety device designed to open and close a circuit by non-automatic means, and to open the circuit automatically on a predetermined overload of current.

Clearance:
The distance between two objects.

Clerestory window:
A window placed high on a wall.

Client Survey Form:
Form developed by the NKBA used for gathering information about client and project. This form should be thoroughly completed at the start of the design process.

Closed plan:
A floor plan where the rooms have walls with doors or door openings into the other spaces.

Cloud computing:
Technology that allows one to use files and applications over the internet.

Colored pencil:
Used to render a perspective drawing with color.

Compass:
Drafting tool used to draw circles and arcs on a floor plan or other drawing.

Concept:
An idea from which a design develops.

Concrete:
A solid state mixture of cement, gravel, water and sand which is used as a building material.

Concrete block:
This is a unit of concrete formed into a hollow or solid masonry block.

Construction documents:
The part of the design process in which the design is finalized and legally binding drawings and specifications are created.

Construction plan:
In the set of NKBA drawings, the construction plan is a drawing that shows all changes made to the walls of the given space.

Countertop plan:
This drawing shows the countertops for the given space along with dimensions. It can be used to assist with obtaining a bid for the countertop.

Convenience outlet:
An electrical receptacle attached to a circuit to allow electricity to be drawn for appliances or lighting.

Converge:
To come together.

Cove:
Molded trim of a concave shape used about cabinet construction and other built-ins.

Crosshatch lines:
Used to show that the feature has been sectioned, also called section lines.

Crown molding:
A decorative molding used at the top of cabinets and at ceiling corners.

Cutting plane line:
A line used to define the location of the imaginary cut through an item which will cross-reference with a section view.

Cutting plane height (cut height):
Height that the imaginary cut was made for the floor plan view. For NKBA drawings the cutting plane height is at the ceiling height so all details of space can be viewed. For AIA standards, the cutting plane height is between 48″ and 60″.

D

D size paper:
Standard size paper that is 24″ × 36″ for architectural size. Metric size in mm is A1; 594 × 841.

Design development:
The part of the design process in which a solution is taken from schematic diagrams to the actual drawings.

Design statement:
A document created by the designer for the design project stating the design challenges, how and why changes were made in the space and explanation of the design solutions.

Detail:
An enlarged drawing of a specific area of item to show how components are put together for a better understanding.

Digital copy:
A copy in an electronic file format.

Dimension line:
A line type that runs parallel to object lines and indicates the measurement between two points of that given object used to indicate dimensions for lengths and widths of items as well as clearances. NKBA standards place dimensions within the dimension line.

Dimetric:
A paraline drawing that skews its horizontal axes to any angle between 0 degrees and 90 degrees, both angles may be different.

Dimmer switch:
A special switch that allows the light to be adjusted to the desired brightness. Also referred to as a rheostat.

Dividers:
A tool resembling a compass, but with points on both legs. It is used for transferring distances without numerical measurements by the use of points on legs as location markers.

Double hung window:
Has two sashes with one at the top and one at bottom of window. The top and bottom can both be slid open vertically. Some models allow the window to pop out for cleaning.

Download:
To bring in data or a program by way of copying or transferring from another computer or server into one's computer.

Draft:
Technical drawing with hard-line, architectural drafting tools.

Drafting board:
A smooth surface on which paper is placed to create drawings.

Drafting brush:
A tool used to brush off eraser crumbs or lead particles from the paper. This tool has a longer wooden handle and bristles typically made of horsehair.

Drafting tape:
Used to adhere the drawing paper to the drawing surface. It is similar to masking tape but is not as sticky and can be easily removed.

Drafting dots:
Small circular pieces of the drafting tape used to adhere the sheet of paper to the drafting surface.

Draughting pencil:
A wood barrel pencil available in various grades of lead.

Drawn to scale:
A term used to indicate that the drawing's sizes and distances can be accurately measured.

Drywall:
Interior covering material, such as gypsum board or plywood, that is applied in large sheets or panels.

Duplex outlets:
Electrical wall outlet having two plug in receptacles.

E

Ellipse:
A geometric figure resembling an elongated circle, characterized by its degree of flatness and length of its long axis.

Eraser:
Used to erase pencil or pen marks. Comes in stick form and other shapes.

Eraser shield:
A small, thin piece of metal with different sizes and shapes of openings used for erasing lines on a drawing.

Existing walls:
Wall of a given structure that are the original walls.

Export:
To send data from one location to another. For example, data can be copied from a software program and sent to a different type of file such as a picture.

Extension line:
A solid line type that denotes the end point of the dimension line. Also referred to as the witness line.

F

File size:
The size of file measured in bytes: kilobytes (KB), megabytes (MB), or gigabytes (GB)

File transfer protocol:
A means of moving large files between different hard drives by using the Internet server.

Filter:
A special effect applied to a photo or drawing inside digital imaging software.

Fixture:
An item of electric or plumbing equipment.

Fixture line:
Lines used to indicate the shape of a kitchen, laundry, or bathroom fixtures and appliances on a drawing.

Flexible curve:
Also referred to as the irregular curve, is a piece of flexible rubber with a flat bottom, used to create any desired curve. Some flexible curves come with a scale on them for measuring.

Floor plan:
Top view, orthographic drawing that shows the room as looking down at it from above. The viewing height for NKBA plans is at ceiling height.

Floor plan specifications:
Specifications found on the right side of the floor plan with specific information pertaining to the given floor plan drawing.

Fluorescent light:
Light that is produced by an arched electrical current between electrodes at opposite end of a gas filled tube.

Focal point:
A point of interest.

Footprint:
The perimeter outline of the given space.

Folding rule:
A wooden tape measure that can be folded down by sections and opened up to create a rigid measuring device.

French curve:
Drafting tool made of plastic with various curves which comes in different sizes and configurations and is used to draw a curved lines. Used often to draw the switch line on the mechanical plan.

French doors:
A pair of hinged glass doors that meet in the center of the opening and swing into the room.

G

Gas pipes:
Pipe that supplies gas to appliance. A gas range would have a gas pipe.

Gigabyte:
A thousand megabytes.

Glazing:
Glass installed in windows or doors. The glass is set or made to be set in frames

Grade:
The surface of the ground around a structure.

Graphic:
A visual representational or image of an object.

Graphite:
A mineral used as lead in pencils.

Grid:
A pattern of regularly spaced horizontal or vertical lines forming squares.

Grid paper:
Paper with printed squares that can be assigned a numeric value and be represented to a scale such as ¼″ or ½″.

Ground fault circuit interrupter (GFCI or GFI):
A safety outlet unit designed to detect any moisture or change in electrical current and will shut electricity off to that outlet if detected.

Guidelines:
Light lines used for architectural lettering on a drawing and help regulate the height of the letters for consistency.

Gypsum board:
An interior finishing material attached to the studs and is made of gypsum and fiberglass and covered with paper.

H

Hard-wired:
Power that is dedicated to a particular item and is permanently wired into the system. There is no plug in for the electricity.

Hatching:
A series of parallel lines that are straight, diagonal or curved that are evenly spaced apart.

Header:
A structural member in light-frame construction which runs perpendicular to the floor and ceiling joists for support and to create opening.

Height line:
A vertical line in a perspective drawing on which measurements can be made. This is the only true height line

Hidden object line: (hidden line)
A line type that represents edges and surfaces of an item which is underneath or behind a particular element or visible surface and cannot be seen in the given view of the drawing.

High resolution:
A raster image over 300 dots per inch. High resolution images can be made larger without getting pixelated.

Hopper window:
A window that is hinged at the bottom and swings to the inside of the house.

Horizon line:
The horizontal location in a perspective drawing where the sky and ground appear to converge.

Horizontal sliding window:
This window has two sashes and a track attached to the head jamb and sill which provides for the horizontal opening of the window.

House drain:
The drain line into which all stacks empty into.

I

Image file:
A resource of photos, textures.

Imperial units:
Units in inches.

Import:
To bring a file, such as a photo or drawing, into a software program from its storage location.

Incandescent:
Light produced when the current runs through a filament.

Individual appliance circuits:
Circuits that serve a given appliance.

Inkjet printer:
A computer printer that operates by propelling tiny droplets of liquid ink onto paper. These range in various sizes and provide good color.

Interior elevation: (elevation)
A two-dimensional, front-view orthographic drawing. This includes walls, islands and any other built-in items. This drawing shows the width and height of items.

Interior trim:
This general term refers to all finish molding, casing, baseboard, and cornice applied to the space.

International Residential Code (IRC):
Residential building codes developed by the International Code Council for single-family housing.

International System (SI) Metric Units:
The metric system of measure in which the meter is the basic unit of measure. For NKBA drawings, the millimeter is used for the measurement unit.

Isometric:
A paraline drawing that skews two horizontal axes at a 30 degree angle. This drawing is to scale and lines can be accurately drawn to the given scale.

J

Jalousie window:
This window has a series of narrow, horizontal slats of glass fastened to an aluminum frame. They open all at once.

K

Keying:
The process of linking items on the floor plan to a schedule that describes them.

Kilobyte:
A thousand bytes.

L

Label:
A symbol that identifies drawings and references them to other components in a drawing.

Label maker:
A device that prints labels onto adhesive backed plastic tape. Most come in clear, black, white and other colors of tape.

Landing:
The platform floor area of stairs typically found at a point along the stairs, such as an L shape, and at the top or bottom of the run of stairs.

Large-format copy machine:
A machine that digitally scans, and prints, large-size copies.

Laser printer:
The laser printers directly scan the item over the printer's photoreceptor. This results in a fast, high quality copy.

Layout line:
Also referred to as construction lines, are very light lines drawn to assist with drawing and placing object lines.

L stairs:
This set of stairs had a landing where the direction of stairs changes.

Lead pointer:
A sharpener for the 2 mm leads.

Leader line:
A thin, dark line with a note at one end and an arrow at the other, pointing to a specific feature.

Legend:
A list that explains a particular symbol found on a drawing.

Lettering guide:
A plastic tool used that allows the individual to draw light guidelines which regulate letter height on a drawing for consistently sized letters.

Light emitting diode (LED):
An LED is an electronic device that emits light when an electrical current is passed through it. The LED's are energy efficient and have a long lifespan.

Line quality:
How good the specified line looks in accordance to how the standardized line should look.

Line type:
Each standardized line found on a drawing has a specific name, meaning and purpose.

Line weight:
Refers to how thick or thin a line is. Each line type has its own line weight on a drawing.

Load bearing wall:
The support wall that holds the floor or roof loads in addition to its own weight.

Low-voltage:
An electrical system that uses less than a 50-volt current instead of the 110v/120v. A transformer is used to convert the electrical power to the needed voltage.

Lux:
The metric measurement in the International System (SI) for the amount of light that falls on a surface. It is measured as one lux equal to the amount of light that falls on one square meter which is placed one meter from the light source.

M

Material symbols:
Symbols used to represent the materials used on a drawing.

Mechanical pencil:
A multipiece holder for leads used for hand drafting.

Mechanical plan:
In the set of NKBA drawings, the mechanical plan shows plumbing, lighting, electrical, heating and ventilation information. The drawing must have a mechanical legend on right side.

Megabytes:
A thousand kilobytes.

Metric scale:
A measuring tool similar to the architect's scale, but for International System (SI) units. NKBA drawings are typically drawn in millimeters.

Millimeter (mm):
Unit of metric measurement used for NKBA drawings. 25 mm = 1″– 0″.

Millwork:
Woodwork, cabinetry and any building product made in a mill or factory.

Mullions:
The vertical members that are placed between the units of a window or door. These can be wood or material window or door is made of.

Muntins:
The small vertical and horizontal bars that separates the panes of glass of a window.

N

National Electric Code (NEC):
Electrical codes developed which allow for safety and standards for the minimum safe electrical installations adopted by jurisdictions throughout the United States.

NKBA (National Kitchen and Bath Association):
A professional association for kitchen and bath designers and professionals.

NKBA Graphic Presentation Standards:
These are standards set by the NKBA for NKBA drawings.

NKBA template:
Forty five degree triangular sheet of plastic with laser cut-outs for symbols used on drawings and also includes measurement increments on edges of this template.

Nomenclature:
The labeling system used for cabinetry. W is for wall, B for base, etc. Includes sizes.

Nominal:
Refers to the common size terminology for standard items in construction instead of their actual size. For example a 2 × 4 stud is actually 1.5″ × 3.5″.

Nosing:
The rounded projection found on the stair tread that extends past the face of the riser (vertical portion of the stair).

Not to scale (NTS):
A term that tells the viewer that a drawing has not been reduced or enlarged in such a manner that dimensions and distances cannot be accurately measured.

O

Object lines:
The line type that indicates the outline of the main features of the object. These are thick lines and of most importance in the hierarchy of lines.

Oblique:
A measureable drawing technique of a space or object that shows three faces, but is drawn true shape and size. The angles are other than 90 degree for the axes.

Obtuse angle:
An angle larger than 90 degrees.

On center:
A measurement taken from the center of one item to the center of another item. With NKBA drawings, one dimensions the center points of all appliances and fixtures. centerline the NKBA plans to the center points of all appliances and fixtures.

One point perspective:
A three-dimensional drawing showing depth and has one vanishing point.

Optical character recognition (OCR):
Software that scans printed documents and saves them as text files.

Orthographic drawing:
This drawing communicates the size and shape of object through related two-dimensional views.

Orthographic projection:
A drawing technique that deconstructs a three-dimensional object into multiple two dimension views.

Overhead lines:
Series of long dashes to denote an item above the ceiling plane such as a skylight or soffit/bulkhead on a drawing.

P

Paraline:
A pictorial projection technique that produces one view of an object skewed along two axes making it look three-dimensional.

Parallel bar:
A horizontal straightedge located on the drafting board. Some are installed on the drafting board or can be locked in place on a portable drafting board.

Partition:
In the design industry, it is another name for wall or item that separates item from another.

Perspective:
A drawing technique that creates an image in three-dimension including height, width and depth. The perspective drawing has vanishing points that all lines converge to.

Perspective scale:
In a perspective drawing, the image gets larger as it gets closer to the viewer. It is not a true scale, but rather a perspective scale.

Photorealism:
A computer rendering style that looks like an actual photograph.

Pictorial presentation:
A visual representation of how the finished item will appear.

Picture window:
The fixed-glass unit of a window that does not open.

Pixel:
The smallest component of an image or picture on a computer screen or printout.

Pixel dimensions:
The number of pixels along the height and width of a raster image.

Pixelation:
The effect caused by displaying a raster image at such a large size that the individual pixels are visible to the eye, giving the image a jagged appearance.

Plastic lead:
Drawing stick made of plastic that combines the ease of pencil with the dark look of ink.

Plug-in:
A program that interacts with a host program to provide a specific on-demand function.

Poché:
A symbol that represents a texture of a construction material.

Pocket door:
This door slides into the wall allowing a full access without a door swing.

Polyester film:
A transparent plastic sheet used for ink or plastic lead work. A popular film used is Mylar.

Portfolio:
Leather or plastic carrying case designed to hold drawings, documents, and presentation boards of a design project. There are many different styles available. Plastic sleeves allow one to place items within for viewing. Some models have a binder that you can open and change out drawings in the portfolio.

Protractor:
Tool used to draw or measure angled lines.

C Theorem:
Used to check for squareness of a corner. Measure out 36″ from one corner and 48″ from the other corner. Measure the distance between these two points. If the distance is 60″, the corner is square.

Q

Quadrille paper:
A good-quality white ledger paper with light-blue lines that are ruled on it.

R

Rail:
The horizontal member in a cabinet.

Random access memory (RAM):
Temporary storehouse for computer. Having sufficient RAM will impact how quickly and efficiently your CAD software will run.

Raster image:
A collection of pixels created by drawing with a software program or by scanning hand-drawn artworks.

Read from right:
Refers to the text and dimensions for all vertical elements on a drawing to be positioned facing the right side so the items are read from the right hand side of drawing.

Receptacle:
This allows for an item to be plugged in and attached to a circuit to allow the electricity to be used for appliances or lighting. Also referred to as a convenience outlet.

Reflected ceiling plan:
The view of the ceiling as if a mirror was placed below, reflecting the items placed on the ceiling. Items shown include lights, speakers, fans, vents, etc.

Register:
The outlet or grille installed at the termination of the air duct found in a forced air system. Must show on the mechanical plan.

Resolution:
The amount of detail an image holds, expressed as dots per inch (dpi) or pixels per inch (ppi)

Rheostat:
Also referred to as a dimmer, regulates the electric current for a light switch which allows the lights to be dimmed.

Riser:
The vertical component of a step.

Rub-on letters:
Adhesive-backed decals available in different fronts, colors, and sizes.

S

Schematic design:
The part of the design process in which a solution is developed

Scribbling:
A technique that uses random, multidirectional lines to create value and texture.

Section lines:
A line type that represents where the cutting plane occurred and sectioned. Also referred to as crosshatch lines.

Shutoff valve:
The valve used to control turning the water off to a given fixture. They are typically located close to the fixture such as a sink or toilet.

Sketch:
To free hand draw an image or idea. Sketches are typically not to a scale.

Smoke detector:
Device designed to detect smoke in a house and give off a loud warning signal. The installation of smoke detector must be in compliance with local building codes.

Soffit:
Referred to as a bulkhead, is the space closed off above the wall cabinets to the ceiling. Sizes can vary and protrude out past the depth of the cabinets. A soffit/bulkhead can also be constructed on the ceiling of kitchen or bathroom as an architectural design feature, often used for special lighting treatments.

Specifications:
Describe the quality of work and materials.

Specification form:
NKBA Specification Form specifies materials used and who is responsible for the given task or item.

Standard lead holder:
Holds 2 mm lead for drafting.

Stickyback:
Adhesive-backed plastic film that can be put in a printer tray. Used for notes on a drawing, labels, etc.

Stiles:
The vertical piece on a panel door or cabinet. An extended stile is an increased width of the stile on left or right side of cabinet.

Stud:
The vertical wall framing member. A 2 × 4 stud is actually 3½″.

T

Tablet:
In regards to computers, the tablet is a portable device that is combined with the computing power of a laptop or desktop computer and is larger than a smart phone. Like the smart phone, there are useful design related applications that can be downloaded into the tablet.

Task lighting:
Lighting placed at areas where tasks are completed such as by sink, over island/peninsula and under wall cabinets.

Technical inkpen:
Refillable, multi-piece drawing tool used for ink drawings.

Technique:
A method or way of working with materials to create an artwork.

Tempered glass:
Glass that is heat-treated designed to resist breakage.

Template:
A piece of plastic with laser-cut shaped outlines of items such as furniture, plants, fixtures, electrical symbols, and geometric shapes drawn to scale for use on floor plans and some elevations.

Three-dimensional (3-D):
Image or object showing height, width and depth.

Three-way switch:
A switch that allows a light to be turned off at two locations.

Title block:
A graphic containing information about the project such as company name, address, etc. These are place at the bottom or right hand side of a drawing.

Title page:
Front page of the set of drawings that indicates page numbers along with names of all drawings found in this set of drawings.

Tooth:
A paper's surface texture, various from smooth to rough.

Tracing paper:
A thin, less expensive semi-transparent paper available in tablets and rolls

Tread:
The horizontal member of each step in which one steps on when walking up or down the steps.

Trim:
Refers to the finish materials such as moldings, trim applied around doors and windows and at the floor or ceiling of rooms.

Trimetric:
A paraline drawing that skews it horizontal axes to any angle between 0 degree and 90 degree, both angles may be different. Each axis has a different scale and all are foreshortened.

True length:
Actual length.

Two-point perspective:
A drawing with two vanishing points showing the space in three-dimension.

V

Vanishing point:
Location to which a set of parallel lines converges in a perspective drawing.

Vector image:
Graphic images that are electronically coded so that they are represented in lines which allow the image on a computer display screen to be rotated and proportionally scaled

Vellum:
A semi opaque, high quality paper used with lead or ink.

Vents:
The opening in ductwork or pipes that allows air, gas or liquid to flow out of or into the room.

Video clips in CAD:
Images in the design that can be captured in the software program to "walk" you through the space. Each CAD software program has this set up differently and allows one to create a video you can save.

Video card:
Component of a computer that determines the clarity, color brilliance and accuracy of motion that you experience on the screen.

Visible object line:
A line type that defines an object.

Volts (voltage):
The amount of energy per unit. Appliances generating heat require a 240v (220v) and convenience outlets require 120v (110v).

W

Wall cabinets:
The standard wall cabinets are typically 12″ deep (305 mm). Some wall cabinets range up to 18″ deep (457 mm). Wall cabinets are installed 15″ to 18″ (381 mm to 457 mm) above the countertop.

Waste pipes:
Large pipe that carries away the discharge of waste and water from a fixture that uses water.

Water closet:
Common name for the toilet.

Winder:
The triangular tread found on a stairway.

Winder stairs:
The landing is pie-shaped steps for the stairs.

Witness line:
Also referred to as the extension line. This solid line denotes the end point of the dimension line.

Work aisle:
In the kitchen, it is the space required to perform tasks in the kitchen centers. The space is measured from counter edge to counter edge—the clear work space.

Work triangle:
The distance between the three primary work centers which include the refrigerator, cooking surface and the cleanup/prep primary sink.

References

Bassler, Bruce. 2008. *Architectural Graphic Standards*, 11th ed. Hoboken, NJ: John Wiley & Sons.

Bassler, Bruce and John Ray Hoke Jr. 2000. *Architectural Graphic Standards*, 9th ed. Hoboken, NJ: John Wiley & Sons.

Kicklighter, Clois E. 2004. *Architecture Residential Drafting and Design*. Tinley Park, IL: Goodheart-Wilcox.

Kilmer, W. Otie, and Rosemary Kilmer. 2009. *Construction Drawings and Details for Interiors*. Hoboken, NJ: John Wiley & Sons.

Herres, David. 2012. *NEC*. New York, NY: McGraw-Hill.

Cline, Lydia Sloan. 2012. *Drafting and Visual Presentation for Interior Designers*. Upper Saddle River, NJ: Prentice Hall.

Public Works and Government Services Canada. National CADD Standards. www.tpsgc-pwgsc.gc.ca/biens-property/cdao-cadd/index-eng.html

Index